Lecture Notes in Computer Science

Lecture Notes in Artificial Intelligence 16059

Founding Editor

Jörg Siekmann

The series Lecture Notes in Artificial Intelligence (LNAI) was established in 1988 as a topical subseries of LNCS devoted to artificial intelligence.

The series publishes state-of-the-art research results at a high level. As with the LNCS mother series, the mission of the series is to serve the international R & D community by providing an invaluable service, mainly focused on the publication of conference and workshop proceedings and postproceedings.

Wang-Zhou Dai
Editor

Learning and Reasoning

4th International Joint Conference on Learning and Reasoning, IJCLR 2024 and 33rd International Conference on Inductive Logic Programming, ILP 2024 Nanjing, China, September 20–22, 2024 Proceedings

Springer

Editor
Wang-Zhou Dai
School of Intelligence Science and Technology
Nanjing University
Nanjing, China

ISSN 0302-9743 ISSN 1611-3349 (electronic)
Lecture Notes in Artificial Intelligence
ISBN 978-3-032-09086-7 ISBN 978-3-032-09087-4 (eBook)
https://doi.org/10.1007/978-3-032-09087-4

LNCS Sublibrary: SL7 – Artificial Intelligence

This Springer imprint is published by the registered company Springer Nature Switzerland AG
The registered company address is: Gewerbestrasse 11, 6330 Cham, Switzerland

Preface

This volume presents the proceedings of the 4th International Joint Conference on Learning and Reasoning (IJCLR 2024), held at Nanjing University, Nanjing, China, from 19–22 September 2024, in conjunction with the 33rd International Conference on Inductive Logic Programming (ILP 2024). This edition was of particular significance: it marked the first official proceedings of IJCLR, and the first time that IJCLR, ILP, and their affiliated events were hosted in China.

The origins of IJCLR lie in the unification of several long-standing conferences and workshops that had each contributed for decades to the study of learning and reasoning in artificial intelligence: ILP, the International Workshop on Approaches and Applications of Inductive Programming (AAIP), the International Workshop on Neural-Symbolic Learning and Reasoning (NeSy), the International Workshop on Statistical Relational AI (StarAI), and, more recently, the International Workshop on Cognitive AI (CogAI). Since its inception in 2021, IJCLR has served as a common home for these communities. Commencing with this edition, IJCLR matured from an umbrella framework into a consolidated conference with a single archival proceedings. ILP, AAIP, and CogAI were fully integrated into the programme. Concurrently, NeSy and StarAI maintained their distinct conferences/workshops, focusing on their respective specialized topics. This consolidation reflects the broader ambition of IJCLR: to provide a unified venue for advancing the integration of machine learning and formal reasoning.

IJCLR 2024 received over 80 submissions (including the Journal Track), of which 20 papers were accepted for inclusion in this volume. The conference programme was complemented by over 20 recent papers presented at the poster sessions, and by 14 invited talks from world-leading researchers in this field. All accepted papers were spotlighted during the conference, and three poster sessions provided ample opportunity for in-depth discussion for all the participants. A memorable anecdote of this event was the forecast arrival of Tropical Storm Pulasan on 22nd September; fortunately, after making its landfall in Shanghai, it suddenly changed course and dissipated to the northwest, leaving Nanjing with a sunny and pleasant day for the last day of the conference.

The proceedings are organised into three chapters that reflect the breadth of the field: Inductive Logic Programming, Learning and Reasoning with Uncertainty, and Formal Reasoning with Large Language Models. Collectively, they cover foundational advances, novel methods, and applied perspectives on vision, robotics, trustworthy AI, and natural language understanding.

The conference also featured the presentation of awards generously sponsored by Springer. The Best Paper Award was conferred upon *MisCC: Misinformation Detection on Counterfactual Claims* (Li, Belle, & Ross). Two Best Student Paper Awards were presented to *Inventing Recursive Predicates by Sampling and Folding Deduced and Abduced Atoms* (Qiu & Ichise) and *An Inductive Logic Programming Approach for Feature-Range Discovery* (Cyrus, Varghese, & Tamaddoni-Nezhad). These awards underscore the high calibre of contributions across both established and emerging researchers.

We are deeply indebted to the authors for their submissions, to the invited speakers for sharing their insights, to the Programme Committee and reviewers for their diligent work, and to the local organising team at Nanjing University for ensuring the smooth execution of the event. Our gratitude also extends to our sponsors, whose support made this conference possible.

We hope this inaugural IJCLR proceedings volume will serve as a landmark for future work in the integration of learning and reasoning, and as a testament to the strength of a community united in advancing the foundations of artificial intelligence.

January 2025 Wang-Zhou Dai

Organization

General Chair

Zhi-Hua Zhou	Nanjing University, China

Program Chair

Wang-Zhou Dai	Nanjing University, China

Area Chairs

Neil Bramley	University of Edinburgh, UK
Wang-Zhou Dai	Nanjing University, China
Cèsar Ferri	Universitat Politècnica de València, Spain
Alireza Tamaddoni-Nezhad	University of Surrey, UK
Qing Li	Beijing Institute for General Artificial Intelligence, China
Emanuele Sansone	KU Leuven, Belgium
Jiajun Wu	Stanford University, USA

Journal Track Chair

Alireza Tamaddoni-Nezhad	University of Surrey, UK

HLC Plenary Chair

Stephen Muggleton	Imperial College London, UK

Workflow Chair

Yu-Cong He	Nanjing University, China

Program Chair Assistant

Yun-Ze Li	Nanjing University, China

Steering Committee

Neil Bramley	University of Edinburgh, UK
Alan Bundy	University of Edinburgh, UK
Cèsar Ferri	Universitat Politènica de València, Spain
Donato Malerba	Università degli Studi di Bari Aldo Moro, Italy
Stephen Muggleton	Imperial College London, UK
Luc De Raedt	KU Leuven, Belgium
Ute Schmid	University of Bamberg, Germany
Alireza Tamaddoni-Nezhad	University of Surrey, UK

Organization Committee

Tian-Zuo Wang	Nanjing University, China
Zi-Long Wang	Nanjing University, China
Yu-Zhe Zhou	Nanjing University, China
Xin-Shuang Zhang	Nanjing University, China

Program Committee

Alan Bundy	University of Edinburgh, UK
Alireza Nezhad-Tamaddoni	University of Surrey, UK
Armin Mustafa	University of Surrey, UK
Bonan Zhao	Princeton University, USA
Cèsar Ferri	Universitat Politècnica València, Spain
Chiaki Sakama	Wakayama University, Japan
Claude Sammut	University of New South Wales, Australia
Cristina Cornelio	IBM Research, Switzerland
Cunjing Ge	Nanjing University, China
Damiano Azzolini	University of Ferrara, Italy
Dany Varghese	University of Surrey, UK
Eleonora Misino	University of Bologna, Italy
Emanuele Sansone	KU Leuven, Belgium
En-Hao Gao	Nanjing University, China
Fabrizio Riguzzi	University of Ferrara, Italy

Contents

Inductive Logic Programming

Inventing Recursive Predicates by Sampling and Folding Deduced and Abduced Atoms

Taosheng Qiu[1,3,(✉)] and Ryutaro Ichise[1,2]

[1] National Institute of Informatics, Tokyo, Japan
tsq@nii.ac.jp
[2] Tokyo Institute of Technology, Tokyo, Japan
ichise@iee.e.titech.ac.jp
[3] The Graduate University for Advanced Studies, SOKENDAI, Tokyo, Japan

Abstract. Inductive Logic Programming systems that handle recursion and predicate invention (PI) generally have limited scalability. A problem is that they search program spaces syntactically, which cannot be effectively guided by utilizing data relations. We propose to restrict the Datalog language to allow a constructive approach to synthesize programs with recursive PI. The learning procedure consists of incremental generalization steps that monotonically explain more examples with new rules. The generalization consists of four steps: Deduction, Abduction, Sampling, and Triangulation (DAST). The deduction and abduction extend background knowledge and unexplained examples to allow for creating recursive rules with invented predicates. The sampling and triangulation perform random walks on deduced and abduced atoms and fold the sampled long rules into many short rules to invent predicates. We implemented DAST with beam search and tested it on various learning tasks. The proposed method shows scalability advantages, especially on tasks that require PI and recursion. Our method synthesizes list reversal, which we believe was unsolved before without any learning bias.

Keywords: Inductive Logic Programming · Predicate Invention · Chain Datalog Programs

1 Introduction

Inductive logic programming (ILP) is distinguished from other machine learning methods for its expressivity, especially in synthesizing complex recursive programs with predicate invention (PI). Meanwhile, scalability is a critical problem in ILP. Most ILP systems use syntactic search and do not consider data relations, leading to limited scalability due to the vast space of semantically equivalent or invalid programs, which prohibits them from practically learning and inventing more than a few sentences and predicates.

A possible way to utilize data relation is to semantically transform, i.e., generalize or specialize programs instead of simply manipulating symbols in them,

W.-Z. Dai (Ed.): ILP 2024, LNAI 16059, pp. 3–18, 2026.
https://doi.org/10.1007/978-3-032-09087-4_1

so relations can be utilized by explaining some examples for each transformation step, pruning the search space effectively. Learning from data relations is widely applied in other machine learning fields but is used less in ILP due to the high cost of program transformation.

In this work, we consider a program space called UCC program, which is suitable for efficient inductive inference, while still being expressive enough to represent a wide range of complex recursive programs. While inducing UCC rules is efficiently achieved by random walking, walking in background knowledge BK cannot create recursive rules in most cases. To solve this problem, we propose to incrementally generalize UCC programs to cover more positive examples, using predicates invented in previous steps. A generalization step consists of Deduction, Abduction, Sampling and Triangulation (DAST). The deduction and abduction parts use previously invented predicates to extend background knowledge BK and positive examples E^+ to enable recursive rule creation. The sampling and triangulation parts create and fold a UCC rule to invent new predicates. An iterative width-doubling beam search using DAST as search steps is implemented and benchmarked on various learning tasks, showing its scalability advantage.

This paper is structured as follows: Sect. 3 defines the terminology and a `droplast` example for later reference. Section 4 discusses the program space that the proposed method searches in and its expressivity. Section 5 gives details of DAST method and the beam search. Section 6 gives experiment settings and results.

2 Related Work

Many ILP systems make little use of data relation. Instead, they require problem-specific biases like metarules [7] or mode declarations [13] to improve synthesis efficiency with compromised generality. Earlier ILP systems inductively generalize programs like inverse resolution [16] or relative least general generalization [17] are generally computationally expensive. Other systems like FOIL [18] are closer to syntactic search for their symbol-level search on rule creation rather than induction on examples.

Several recent ILP systems start utilizing semantic information in test stage to constrain the generation. The Learning from Failure method [5] considers program subsumption to prevent generating programs failed by similar reason. The Provenance Guided Search [14,19] analyzes the derivation tree to trace the explained or unexplained examples. These methods reduce the search space by creating constraints from test stage, but still limits utilization of relations in generation stage.

On the other hand, the Example-guided Synthesis (EGS) [21] learns queries from enumerating neighbor areas of an example. While EGS does not handle PI or recursion, Mobius [22] uses EGS to generate non-recursive rules and further generalizes them into a recursive program. Generalization from data is also considered in some functional programs synthesis system [10]. Most of these systems first explain all examples, then generalize them into recursive form. For a complex task, a single step of explaining all examples may produce a huge program which is less efficient for further recursion folding.

ILP examples are often given in relational form, which can be represented as a knowledge graph. Extracting symbolic rules from knowledge graph is also an important problem in knowledge engineering. Existing methods include AMIE system [9,11] and path ranking algorithm [12]. Compared with ILP, rule extraction in knowledge engineering focuses more on handling noise and incompleteness but less on recursion and PI.

3 List Transformation

First, we define the list transformation task and provide `droplast` as an example throughout this paper. List transformation tasks find programs that convert example input lists into output lists. Based on Datalog, clauses are written in first-order logic syntax with omitted quantifiers like $path(x,z) \leftarrow edge(x,y) \wedge path(y,z)$. Unless otherwise noted, a clause with more than one term contains no constant and is called a *rule*; a clause with one term is fully grounded and is called an *atom*. We only use dyadic predicates and convert monadic predicates like $f(x) \Rightarrow f(x,x)$. We may abbreviate $f(x,x)$ into $f(x)$.

A list l is a bit sequence like `100` with i-th element mapped to a constant l_i and null-terminated by appending an extra element. Each element c has exactly one value among $\{0, 1, null\}$ represented by atom $\{v_0(c), v_1(c), v_n(c)\}$. Each pair of adjacent elements is connected by the *successor* predicate s like $s(l_1, l_2)$.

The list transformation task consists of example pairs of input and output lists i, o. Head elements of input and output lists representing the whole list are associated by an atom $io(i_1, o_1)$. Output lists are padded to a fixed length to obfuscate length information. Correct and incorrect values of output lists are given in E^+ and E^-. The rest atoms are provided in BK. As an advantage, *all* negative examples can be efficiently covered with no need to permutate lists as in function-based representation. Different examples' lists have distinct element constants and the BK, E^+, E^- from all examples are finally merged.

The `droplast` task is a list transformation task of copying the input list with the last element removed. Figure 1 shows an example of input `100` and output `10`. Each atom $p(c_1, c_2)$ is represented as a directed edge $c_1 \xrightarrow{p} c_2$. A solution program Π is given in the right part. The generated atoms are list below:

$$BK: io(i_1,o_1), s(i_1,i_2), s(i_2,i_3), s(i_3,i_4), v_1(i_1), v_0(i_2), v_0(i_3), v_n(i_4),$$
$$s(o_1,o_2), s(o_2,o_3), s(o_3,o_4)\ldots \text{until pad length},$$
$$E^+: v_1(o_1), v_0(o_2), v_n(o_3), \quad E^-: v_0(o_1), v_n(o_1), v_1(o_2), v_n(o_2), v_0(o_3), v_1(o_3).$$

4 Program Space

In this section, we define the program space of the proposed method. Starting from UCC as generalized chain Datalog rule (Sect. 4.1) which can be triangulated

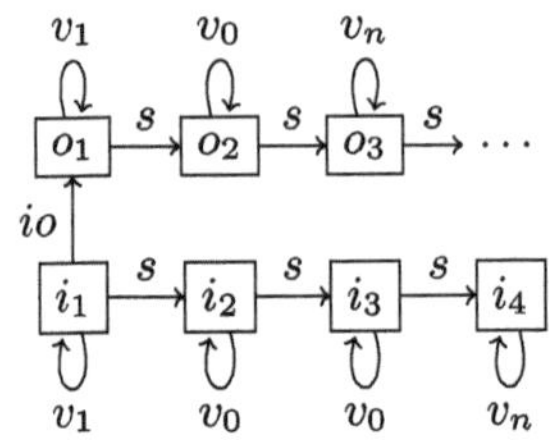

Step (k)	Rules (π_k)
1	$cp2(z,y) \leftarrow s(x,z) \wedge io(x,y)$
	$v_n(y) \leftarrow cp2(x,y) \wedge v_n(x)$
2	$notend(y) \leftarrow cp2(x,y) \wedge v_0(x)$
	$cp(x,y) \leftarrow io(x,y) \wedge notend(y)$
	$v_0(y) \leftarrow cp(x,y) \wedge v_0(x)$
3	$v_1(y) \leftarrow cp(x,y) \wedge v_1(x)$
4	$notend(y) \leftarrow cp2(x,y) \wedge v_1(x)$
5	$io(x,z) \leftarrow cp2(x,y) \wedge s(y,z)$

Fig. 1. example input and output list pair of `droplast` (left) and a solution (right).

by repeated fold transformations (Sect. 4.2), a UCC program is a sequence of triangulated rules $\{\pi_k\}$, where invented predicates may not be used before their invention. (Sect. 4.3).

4.1 Undirected Concatenated Chain (UCC) Rule

Definition 1. *Let $n \geq 1$, x_i be distinct variables, p_i be predicates, X_i, Y_i take variable symbols x_i as values, P_i take predicate symbols p_i as values. A UCC rule has the form:*

$$P_0(X_0, Y_0) \leftarrow \bigwedge_{1 \leq i \leq n} P_i(X_i, Y_i), \tag{1}$$

where for each $i \equiv j+1 \pmod{n+1}$, $0 \leq i \leq n$:

$$P_i(X_i, Y_i) \in \{p_i(X_i, Y_i), p_i(Y_i, X_i)\}, \tag{2}$$

$$X_i \in \begin{cases} \{Y_j\}, & X_j \neq Y_j \\ \{Y_j, x_0\}, & X_j = Y_j \end{cases} \quad Y_i \in \begin{cases} \{x_i\}, & i = 0 \\ \{x_i, X_i\}, & i \neq 0 \end{cases} \tag{3}$$

A UCC is associated with a sampled walk (explained in Sect. 5.2) with starting point related to Y_0 and end point related to X_0. UCC extends chain rule [2] by allowing "reversed" predicate direction $P(x,y) = p(y,x)$ (Eq. 2) and repeated argument $Y_i = X_i$ and in which case resetting next X_i to starting point $X_i = Y_0 = x_0$ (Eq. 3). UCC reduces to chain rule by removing these extensions:

Theorem 1. *Every chain rule is a UCC rule.*

Proof. Let $Y_i = x_i$, $X_i = Y_j = x_j$. $P_0(x_n, x_0) = p_0(x_0, x_n)$, $P_i(x_{i-1}, x_i) = p_i(x_{i-1}, x_i)$ for $i \geq 1$. Equation 1 becomes $p_0(x_0, x_n) = p_1(x_0, x_1) \wedge \cdots \wedge p_n(x_{n-1}, x_n)$, with x_i as distinct variables, which is the definition of chain rule. □

Example 1. A UCC with variable mapping is given below. $\overleftarrow{p}$ denotes reversed predicate. This example corresponds to `droplast` step 2 in Example 2.

$$\begin{aligned} & P_0(X_0, Y_0) \leftarrow \overleftarrow{P_1}(X_1, Y_1) \wedge P_2(X_2, Y_2) \wedge \overleftarrow{P_3}(X_3, Y_3) \wedge P_4(X_4, Y_4) \\ \Rightarrow\ & P_0(x_0, x_0) \leftarrow \overleftarrow{P_1}(x_0, x_1) \wedge P_2(x_1, x_1) \wedge \overleftarrow{P_3}(x_0, x_3) \wedge P_4(x_3, x_3) \\ \Rightarrow\ & v_0(x_0) \leftarrow cp2(x_1, x_0) \wedge v_0(x_1) \wedge io(x_3, x_0) \wedge v_0(x_3) \end{aligned}$$

4.2 Triangulated Rules

We define triangulated rules, a set of rules converted from a UCC rule by repeated folding transformation.

Definition 2. *Let P'_k take predicate symbols as value, given UCC: $P_0(X_0, Y_0) \leftarrow \bigwedge_{1\leq i\leq n} P_i(X_i, X_i)$ with $n \geq 2$, its* triangulation *is defined as rules $\pi = \{r_j\}$ for $2 \leq j \leq n$:*

$$r_j = P'_j(Y_0, X_{j+1}) \leftarrow P_j(X_j, Y_j) \wedge P'_{j-1}(Y_0, X_j), \tag{4}$$

$$\begin{cases} P'_j = P_1, & j = 1 \\ P'_j \neq P'_{j'}, & j' \neq j, 1 < j < n \\ P'_j = P_0, & j = n \end{cases} \tag{5}$$

In Eq. 5, P'_j is defined as the first body predicate for $j = 1$ and the head predicate for $j = n$. For other j, P'_j are invented new predicates. We show that triangulation is a sequence of fold transformations [20], thus gives equivalent program. First, we introduce fold transformation as follows.

Lemma 1. *For rule $C \in \Pi$ with clause $H \leftarrow B_1 \wedge \cdots \wedge B_m \wedge B_{m+1} \wedge \cdots \wedge B_{m+n}$ and rule $F = I \leftarrow B'_1 \wedge \cdots \wedge B'_m$. The rule $C' = H \leftarrow I\theta \wedge B_{m+1} \wedge \cdots \wedge B_{m+n}$ with respect to substitution θ is a fold of C by F: $C \xrightarrow{F} C'$, s.t. Π is equivalent to $(\Pi \setminus \{C\}) \cup \{F, C'\}$, if*

1. *$B_i = B'_i\theta$ for $i \leq m$;*
2. *for variables $\{v\}$ occur in B'_i but not I (namely internal variables), all $v\theta$ are distinct and do not occur in H and B_i for $i > m$;*
3. *Predicate I does not occur in Π.*

Theorem 2. *UCC Triangulation on UCC rule C (Eq. 1) corresponds to a fold sequence $C_1 \xrightarrow{r_2} C_2 \xrightarrow{r_3} \ldots \xrightarrow{r_{n-1}} C_{n-1}$ with r_j defined in Definition 2 and*

$$C_j = \begin{cases} C = P_0(X_0, Y_0) \leftarrow \bigwedge\limits_{1\leq i\leq n} P_i(X_i, Y_i), & j = 1 \\ P_0(X_0, Y_0) \leftarrow P'_j(Y_0, X_{j+1}) \wedge \bigwedge\limits_{j<i\leq n} P_i(X_i, Y_i), & 1 < j < n-1 \\ r_n = P'_n(Y_0, X_{n+1}) \leftarrow P_n(X_n, Y_n) \wedge P'_{n-1}(Y_0, X_n), & j = n-1 \end{cases}$$

Proof. When $n = 2$, there is no folding, and we trivially have $C_1 = r_2$. When $n \geq 3$, for each $2 \leq j \leq n-1$, we check the correctness of fold operation $C_{j-1} \xrightarrow{r_j} C_j$ through the three rules in Lemma 1 with $m = 2$.

For Rule 1, the body of r_j is syntactically equivalent to the first and second body term in C_{j-1}. Therefore, $B_i = B'_i\theta$ for $i \leq 2$ under identity substitution $\theta = \theta_I$. For Rule 2, the possible internal variables in each r_j (Eq. 4) are X_j and Y_j, which take possible values $V_1 = \{x_{j-1}, x_j, x_0\}$. All variables in H, B_i for $i \geq m+1 = 3$ are X_0, Y_0, X_i, Y_i for $i \geq j+2$, which take possible values

$V_2 = \{x_0, x_n\} \cup \{x_l \mid l \geq j+1\}$. $V_1 \cap V_2 = \{x_0\}$ but $x_0 = Y_0$ is not an internal variable. Therefore, all possible internal variables $V_1 \setminus \{x_0\}$ do not occur in V_2. For Rule 3, P'_j for $2 \leq j \leq n-1$ are defined as invented predicates, thus cannot appear in Π. Therefore, the triangulation is the fold sequence $C \xrightarrow{r_2} C_2 \xrightarrow{r_3} \dots \xrightarrow{r_{n-1}} C_{n-1} = r_n$. □

A case of triangulation is given later in Example 2. Similar to Datalog's deductive safety [1, Chapter 5], triangulated rule is guaranteed to be both deductively and abductively safe.

Theorem 3. *The rule $r_j = P'_j(Y_0, X_{j+1}) \leftarrow P_j(X_j, Y_j) \wedge P'_{j-1}(Y_0, X_j)$ is deductively and abductively safe, i.e., for each term in r_j, all its variables occur in other terms as well.*

Proof. If $X_{j+1} = Y_j$, all Y_j, Y_0, X_j appear in two terms. If $X_{j+1} = Y_0$, then $X_j = Y_j$ (from Eq. 3). $r_j = P'_j(Y_0, Y_0) \leftarrow P_j(X_j, X_j) \wedge P'_{j-1}(Y_0, X_j)$, both Y_0, X_j appear in two terms. □

4.3 UCC Program

A sequence of triangulated rules forms a UCC program. Invented predicates are not allowed to be used before or when they are invented.

Definition 3. *UCC program is a sequence of triangulated rules $(\pi_1, \dots, \pi_K)$, that if P_j in UCC rule $C_{k'}$ (Eq. 1) which $\pi_{k'}$ is triangulated from is assigned to a predicate invented in π_k, then $k < k'$.*

Now we consider UCC program's expressivity. Existing works associate chain program with pseudo-regular language [3] or context-free language [23]. These works discuss expressivity with human-written queries. However, in learning tasks, non-terminal symbols corresponding to non-observable invented predicates cannot be used until invented. Under this requirement, we show that UCC program at least recognizes all regular languages. Strings like xyz are encoded by adding anchor constants $c_0 \xrightarrow{x} c_1 \xrightarrow{y} c_2 \xrightarrow{z} c_3$ then converted into atoms $x(c_0, c_1)$, $y(c_1, c_2)$, $z(c_2, c_3)$. First, UCC normal form is defined as follows.

Definition 4. *UCC normal form consists of 3 types of production rules: $S \to a$, $A \to ab$, $A \to aB$.*

UCC normal form can be converted from any right-regular grammar by the following procedure: For each rule $A \to a$, $A \neq S$, find all rules $B \to bA$, add rules $B \to ba$, and remove $A \to a$. This rule form is desired because UCC use length-3 rules.

Theorem 4. *Every right-regular grammar is recognized by some UCC program.*

Proof (sketch). For the three rules in UCC normal form. Each $S \rightarrow a$ can be converted to triangulated rules as follows by inventing a dummy predicate p_a:

$$p_a(x) \leftarrow a(x,y) \wedge a(x,y), \quad S(x,y) \leftarrow p_a(x) \wedge a(x,y).$$

For the rest two rules, they can be converted to

$$A(x,z) \leftarrow a(x,y) \wedge b(y,z), \quad A(x,z) \leftarrow a(x,y) \wedge B(y,z). \tag{6}$$

A, B are arbitrary non-terminal symbols (including S), a is arbitrary terminal symbol. Predicates converted from non-terminal symbols (except for S) are all invented.

Map each rule in Eq. 6 to a rule in the state transition diagram with a as edges and A, B, b as states (b as final states). Starting from marking S and all final states and leave rest non-terminal nodes unmarked. Sample a path starts and ends with marked nodes and all middle points unmarked (we can always cut off the path wherever we meet a marked middle point), so these predicates are yet unused and allowed to be invented. Add corresponding rules in the path to the program, mark nodes in the path, and repeat sampling. If no path can be sampled, rest nodes are either unreachable to any b thus are not terminating, or unreachable from S thus can never be visited. Therefore, the final UCC program contains rules to recognize the regular language. □

While UCC program contains all regular language recognition programs, it is more expressive by containing non-linear programs, reversed predicates and repeated variables. In Sect. 6.2 we use examples constructed by the marking method in this proof to practically verify the learnability of regular languages.

5 Generalization with DAST

The Deduction, Abduction, Sampling and Triangulation (DAST) procedure adds new rules to UCC program to explain a positive example. Deduction and abduction extend BK and E^+ using invented predicates (Sect. 5.1); Sampling and triangulation create new rule and fold it to invent new predicates. (Sect. 5.2). An iterative width-doubling beam search is implemented to use DAST generalization to explore the program space (Sect. 5.3).

5.1 Deduction and Abduction

Simply explaining examples from E^+ using BK can only create a set of independent rules. To relate rules together, we use previously created rules to deduce and abduce new atoms utilizing invented predicates. We give the definition of deduction and abduction below.

$$Cn(\Pi_k, BK) = \{d \mid \Pi_k \cup BK \models d\}, \tag{7}$$

$$E_k^+ = E^+ \setminus Cn(\Pi_k, BK), \tag{8}$$

$$Ab(\Pi_k, E_k^+, BK) = \{a \mid E_k^+ \cap Cn(\Pi_k, BK \cup \{a\}) \neq \emptyset\}. \tag{9}$$

Algorithm 1. WALK(f, F) takes an atom to be explained $f = p_0(c_x, c_y)$ and atoms F to sample from, returns a UCC rule C.

```
Shuffle {c_0, c_{-1}} := {c_x, c_y}
if c_0 = c_y then P_0(x, y) = p_0(x, y) else P_0(x, y) = p_0(y, x)
Initialize the rule C = P_0(X_0, Y_0) ← (empty body)
if c_x = c_y then {X_0, Y_0} := {x_{-1}, x_0} else {X_0, Y_0} := {x_0, x_0}
for l := 1 to ∞ do
    (C, c') := WALKSTEP(F, c_0, C, c, l).
    action := sample({stop, continue})
    if c' = c_{-1} ∧ action = stop then
        Unify Y_l and X_0
        return C
    c := c'
function WALKSTEP(F, c_0, C, c, l)
    if X_{l-1} ≠ Y_{l-1} then action := reuse else action := sample({reuse, reset})
    if action = reuse then X_l := Y_{l-1} else X_l := Y_0, c := c_0
    if sample({normal, reversed}) = normal then
        p_l(c, c') := sample(F), P_l(x, y) := p_l(x, y)
    else
        p_l(c', c) := sample(F), P_l(x, y) := p_l(y, x)
    if c = c' then action := repeat else action := assign
    if action = repeat then Y_l := X_l else c := c', Y_l := new variable
    Append P_l(X_l, Y_l) to the end of C
    return (C, c)
```

In Eq. 7, $Cn(\Pi_k, BK)$ is the consequence given rules Π_k and atoms BK. The consequence is subtracted from E^+ to compute the unexplained positive examples E_k^+ (Eq. 8). Atom a that deduces any unexplained positive example with $BK \cup \{a\}$ defines the abduced atoms $Ab(\Pi_k, E_k^+, BK)$ (Eq. 9). Unexplained examples themselves are also included in abduced atoms $E_k^+ \subset Ab(\Pi_k, E_k^+, BK)$.

Deduction and abduction's implementations are based on seminaive bottom-up evaluation [1, Chapter 13]. Abduction's implementation is similar to deduction by swapping any body term with head term. Due to deductive and abductive safeties (Theorem 3), the output term can always be grounded. Compared with the general NP-hard abduction [8], this one-step abduction can be computed under polynomial time like deduction.

5.2 Sampling and Triangulation

Let X_i, Y_i take variables as values, P_i takes predicates as values, given an atom f to explain and a set of atoms F, the sampling algorithm WALK(f, F) in Algorithm 1 produces a UCC rule which explains f using atoms sampled in F.

Proposition 1. *If* WALK(f, F) *returns* C, $\{C\} \cup F \models f$.

The algorithm has a main part and a function WALKSTEP. The main part initializes the head term of C, then iteratively calls WALKSTEP in a loop. Whenever the visiting constant forms a walk cycle $c = c_{-1}$, there is a chance to stop

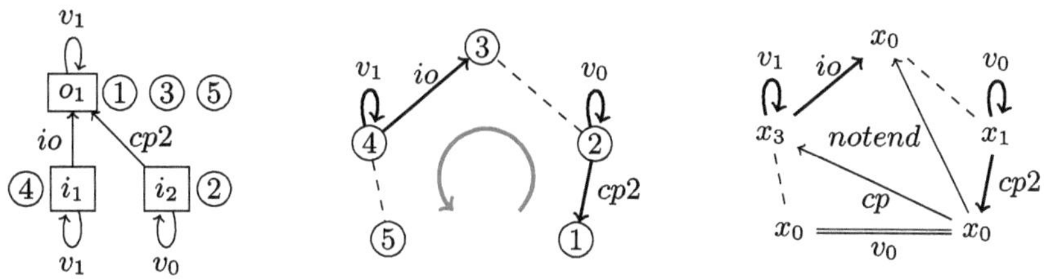

Fig. 2. random walking order marked by circled number (left) and sampled atoms (middle), triangulation of converted UCC (right) of step 2 of `droplast`.

and output the rule. The WALKSTEP function appends one term to the UCC rule with one step of random walk $c \to c'$ on F. The first action selected from *reset* and *reuse* in Line 13 corresponds to X_i value options in Eq. 3. Then, an atom with c as one constant is sampled from F, performing a step of random walking. If c is the second argument, the direction of P is reversed (Eq. 2). If no such atom can be found, the whole sampling fails. The second action *assign* and *repeat* in Line 19 corresponds to Y_i value options in Eq. 3.

Once a UCC rule is sampled, its triangulation is directly given by Eq. 4. Additionally, the last rule r_n has a chance to duplicate with head replaced with an invented predicate without *reset*. For example, if $r_n = v_1(y) \leftarrow io(x, y) \wedge v_1(x)$. A sentence $r'_n = inv(x, y) \leftarrow io(x, y) \wedge v_1(x)$ may be randomly added.

Example 2. Figure 2 visualizes the sampling and triangulation of `droplast` step 2. The left part showing the atoms sampled by random walking is a subgraph of Fig. 1, with $cp2(i_2, o_1)$ added as a deduced fact (Sect. 5.1) from step 1. The middle part shows *repeat* and *reset* actions by loops and dashed edges. The right part shows triangulation corresponding to the fold sequence $C_1 \xrightarrow{r_2} C_2 \xrightarrow{r_3} r_4$:

$$
\begin{aligned}
C_1 : &\quad v_0(x_0) \leftarrow cp2(x_1, x_0) \wedge v_0(x_1) \wedge io(x_3, x_0) \wedge v_0(x_3) \\
r_2 : &\quad inv1(x_0) \leftarrow v_0(x_1) \wedge cp2(x_1, x_0) \\
C_2 : &\quad v_0(x_0) \leftarrow inv1(x_0) \wedge io(x_3, x_0) \wedge v_0(x_3) \\
r_3 : &\quad inv2(x_3, x_0) \leftarrow io(x_3, x_0) \wedge inv1(x_0) \\
C_3 = r_4 : &\quad v_0(x_0) \leftarrow v_0(x_3) \wedge inv2(x_3, x_0)
\end{aligned}
$$

r_2, r_3, r_4 is equivalent to step 2 in Fig. 1 with $inv1 = notend$, $inv2 = cp$.

5.3 Search Algorithm

We integrate DAST into an iterative width-doubling beam search to implement a learning system to find Π given BK, E^+, E^- that $E^+ \subset Cn(\Pi, BK) \wedge E^- \cap Cn(\Pi, BK) = \emptyset$. A single round of BEAM search defined in Algorithm 2 will be called iteratively with $w = 1, 2, 4, 8, \ldots$ until it succeeds.

Inside BEAM, programs in each generation G are uniformly sampled and generalized by EXPLAIN into the next generation G'. A generation is finished

Algorithm 2. BEAM(BK, E^-, E^+, w, R_{max}) performs a round of beam search with width w and max EXPLAIN rounds R_{max} per generation.

1: G:=$\{(\Pi_0 = \emptyset, BK, E^+))\}$, G':=$\{\}$
2: **for** *depth*:=1 **to** ∞ **do**
3:     **for** n:=1 **to** $w \cdot R_{max}$ **do**
4:         (Π_k, Cn, Ab):=EXPLAIN(BK, E^+, E^-, *sample*(G))
5:         **if** EXPLAIN is *success*, Π_k **then return** Π_k
6:         **if** EXPLAIN is *fail* **then continue**
7:         G':=$G' \cup \{(\Pi_k, Cn, Ab)\}$
8:         **if** $|G'| \geq w$ **then break**
9:     G:=G', G':=$\{\}$
10:    **if** $G = \emptyset$ **then return** *fail*
11: **function** EXPLAIN($BK, E^+, E^-, (\Pi_{k-1}, Cn, Ab)$)
12:    C:=WALK(*sample*(Ab), Cn)
13:    $\pi_k = \{r_1, \ldots, r_n\}$:=*triangulate*($C$)
14:    Π_k:=$\Pi_{k-1} \cup \pi_k$
15:    Cn:=*SeminaiveDeduction*(Π_k, BK)
16:    **if** $Cn \cap E^- \neq \emptyset$ **then return** *fail*
17:    E_k^+:=$E^+ \setminus Cn$
18:    **if** $E_k^+ = \emptyset$ **then return** *success*, Π_k
19:    Ab:=*SeminaiveAbduction*(Π_k, E_k^+, Cn)
20:    **return** (Π_k, Cn, Ab)

when G' collects enough w programs or max exploration rounds constant R_{max} is reached. If no program is generated in current generation, the beam search fails. Any successful EXPLAIN stops learning with success.

EXPLAIN function performs DAST generalization, with efficiently cached deduction and abduction step: for each newly triangulated program, its Cn and Ab are immediately computed and cached in search state to be reused in all samplings and triangulations. EXPLAIN *fails* or *succeeds* if the program has any coverage on E^- or complete coverage on E^+. Normally, EXPLAIN returns the new program Π_k with Cn and Ab to cache.

Theorem 5. BEAM *always halts, i.e., the iterative width-doubling beam search generates unbounded amount of programs.*

Proof (sketch). We prove this by showing unexplained positive examples are strictly decreasing: $E_{k+1}^+ \subset E_k^+$. For any Π_{k+1} as Π_k's child node in beam search, $\Pi_k \subset \Pi_{k+1}$ so $E_{k+1}^+ \subseteq E_k^+$. Let $f \in Ab$ to be sampled in Line 12. From Ab's definition, $\exists e^+ \in E_k^+ : \Pi_{k-1} \cup BK \cup \{f\} \models e^+$. Apply Proposition 1 to get $\Pi_{k-1} \cup BK \cup \{C\} \models e^+$, or $\Pi_k \cup BK \models e^+$ (Theorem 2), equivalently $e^+ \in Cn(\Pi_k, BK)$. Therefore, $e^+ \notin E_{k+1}^+$. □

6 Experiments

We explore three important properties of DAST generalization with beam search. In Sect. 6.1, we check the scalability of our implementation compared with existing ILP system. In Sect. 6.2, we check the learnability of DAST on regular languages. In Sect. 6.3, we check the effectiveness of DAST method when examples become more complex.

6.1 Scalability

In this section, we test the scalability of our method on list transformation tasks defined in Sect. 3 and some classical ILP learning tasks. List transformation is probably the most well-known and challenging task in program synthesis. Our task of learning v_0, v_1 and v_n is hard for existing systems: we cannot find any expressive ILP system that learns multiple related predicates, so we simplify the task into learning v_1 only for existing systems. Also, most ILP systems cannot use currently learning predicate in BK, so v_1 is renamed to v_1' in E^+, E^-.

We compare our system with Popper [5], one of the most popular and performant ILP system. According to Popper's homepage, its PI [6] is currently very expensive and we have to limit max variables and body length to 4. We also test Popper optimized for list transformation (named Popper-f), using Prolog list with disabled PI and helper predicates *head*, *tail*, *cons*, *empty*, v_0, v_1, v_0', v_1'. Popper's direction annotation requires *cons* and distinct v', v for input and output values. We terminate Popper when any solution is discovered. All tasks use all sequences $1 \leq |s| \leq 3$ as BK, E^+, E^-. All experiments run single threaded on i7-8650u CPU, 16GB memory, 600 s timeout.

Task descriptions and results are given in Table 1. DAST with its compact search space gives considerably better performance than Popper on our setting. Notably, DAST synthesizes `reverse`, which we believe was not yet solvable without any helper functions or learning biases. The synthesized programs of `reverse` and `aabb` are given in Fig. 3. Meanwhile, Popper set to learn v_1 only may give rules unusable for learning v_0 or v_n later, e.g., with recursion avoided. This is a limitation of common practice of lifelong learning [4] a new predicate only after the previous was fully learned, compared with learning multiple related predicates simultaneously. For Popper-f, the bias specialized for list transformation helps it to reduce program sizes significantly. For example, `dupfirst` can be easily solved as $dupfirst(x, y) \leftarrow head(x, z) \wedge cons(z, x, y)$. Popper-f with PI disabled cannot efficiently encode programs like `not`:

$$not(x, y) \leftarrow h(x, u) \wedge t(x, v) \wedge not(v, z) \wedge enot(u, w) \wedge c(w, z, y)$$
$$enot(x, y) \leftarrow v_1(y) \wedge v_0'(x) \qquad enot(x, y) \leftarrow v_0(y) \wedge v_1'(x)$$

with $h = head$, $t = tail$, $c = cons$, *enot* is invented as elementwise not. Without PI, *enot* needs to be folded, producing rules with more literals.

Note that Popper-f's `droplast` performance is slower than original Popper, which uses different biases for each task and value conditions are excluded from program space for droplast. Popper-f is specialized for list transformation, while we still require a unified bias for all tasks. As a result, Popper-f generated 33 times more programs to find a solution.

Table 1. scalability benchmark result in running seconds. T/O marks timeout. List-specialized Popper-f skips rest tasks

Task	DAST	Popper	Popper-f	Description
`path`	0.06	0.54	–	basic path
`gp`	0.00	0.55	–	grandparent relation
`ancestor`	0.07	2.51	–	ancestor relation
`undir`	0.21	19.39	–	undirected path
`evenpath`	0.00	6.16	–	path of even length
`oddpath`	0.01	0.62	–	path of odd length
`len5p`	0.00	51.88	–	path of 5 or more steps
`first`	0.00	13.72	0.57	1-length list of 1st element
`second`	0.00	45.11	1.33	1-length list of 2nd element
`copy`	0.04	126.54	0.50	copy list
`not`	0.09	127.34	T/O	logical NOT each element
`dropfirst`	0.10	97.69	0.39	skip first element
`setfirst`	0.93	T/O	0.80	set first element to 1
`flipfirst`	0.19	108.23	4.81	flip first element
`last`	23.79	129.95	1.99	1-length list of last element
`droplast`	9.27	81.08	465.49	skip last element
`rm0`	5.76	T/O	T/O	skip element of value 0
`dupfirst`	0.51	T/O	0.43	duplicate first element
`aabb`	71.93	T/O	T/O	repeat each element
`from1`	T/O	T/O	12.30	skip until first 1
`reverse`	195.82	T/O	T/O	reverse the list

6.2 Learnability on Regular Languages

In this section, we check if regular languages with appropriate examples can be learned by DAST. We generate all regular languages (under equivalence of distinct variable substitution) with at most 4 rules in UCC normal form (Def. 4) $A \to ab$ or $A \to aB$ as rules $S \to a$ can be independently learned. Then, we create example strings with sampling and marking technique given in Proof of Theorem 4. For example, regular language $a^*(bca^*)^*bde$ with 4 rules and state transition diagram:

$$S \to bA|aS, A \to de|cS \quad \Leftrightarrow \quad \overset{a}{\circlearrowleft} S \underset{c}{\overset{b}{\rightleftarrows}} A \xrightarrow{d} e$$

generates example set $\{[bde],\, b[c]bde,\, [a]bde\}$. Brackets surround paths or cycles covering new rules. Note that $[abde]$ is not a path or cycle because S is revisited.

Step	Rules
1	$*p1(x,y) \leftarrow io(z,x) \wedge s(z,y)$ $*p2(x,y) \leftarrow v_n(y) \wedge *p1(x,y)$ $*p3(x,y) \leftarrow s(y,z) \wedge *p2(x,z)$ $v_1(x) \leftarrow v_1(y) \wedge *p3(x,y)$
2	$*p1(x,y) \leftarrow s(z,y) \wedge *p1(x,z)$
3	$*p4(x,y) \leftarrow s(z,x) \wedge *p3(z,y)$ $*p3(x,y) \leftarrow s(y,z) \wedge *p4(x,z)$
4	$v_n(x) \leftarrow io(y,z) \wedge *p4(x,y)$
5	$v_0(x) \leftarrow v_0(y) \wedge *p3(x,y)$

Step	Rules
1	$v_0(x) \leftarrow io(y,x) \wedge v_0(y)$
2	$v_1(x) \leftarrow io(y,x) \wedge v_1(y)$
3	$*p1(x,y) \leftarrow io(y,z) \wedge s(z,x)$ $v_1(x) \leftarrow v_1(y) \wedge *p1(x,y)$
4	$*p2(x,y) \leftarrow s(z,x) \wedge *p1(z,y)$ $io(x,y) \leftarrow s(z,x) \wedge *p2(y,z)$
5	$*p3(x,y) \leftarrow v_0(y) \wedge *p1(x,y)$ $v_0(x) \leftarrow *p1(x,y) \wedge *p3(x,y)$
6	$v_n(x) \leftarrow io(y,x) \wedge v_n(y)$

Fig. 3. learned `reverse` and `aabb` programs. Invented predicates are marked by $*$.

These strings are further converted into atoms in BK and E^+ using encoding in Sect. 4.3. Learning is repeated until the correct program is discovered.

For the result, we check all 1.6×10^4 regular languages with at most 4 rules to be correctly learned with generated examples. Therefore, DAST's search algorithm is likely to be weakly complete [15] on regular language recognition. This experiment is given on regular language as a well-known expressivity class, while its approach may be extended to verify the completeness on whole UCC program space.

6.3 Scalability on Example Complexity

One limitation of learning recursion from relation is the requirement on simple examples as "hints". Consider two types of tasks: tasks like `not` are not strongly affected by large examples because the induction can be initiated from any example; tasks like `droplast` have more dependency since a short sentence is needed to quickly traverse to the end of the list to initiate the construction of the recursion. To measure its impact, we test the two tasks repeatedly with incremental example sizes. For each max sentence length $3 \leq l_{max} \leq 9$, we generate 10 random lists with length l uniformly sampled from $1 \leq l \leq l_{max}$, and create BK, E^+ and E^- from the random lists for DAST. Each l_{max} is repeated for 25 times to get the distribution.

The result is given in Fig. 4. For `not`, there is a steady increase of learning time with increased list length in learning data. This is because our method primitively picks random positive examples, thus becomes slower in finding explainable examples in longer lists. For `droplast`, the growth is more significant, giving several timeouts. Therefore, `droplast` task is more susceptible to suboptimal data distribution.

In general, we consider the impact of data distribution on scalability is still in the acceptable range. Furthermore, an unbalanced dataset may indicate some hidden rules. For example, if a graph consists of paths with length ≥ 10, while syntactic search can quickly find the ordinary path definition, it may be a less accurate model to describe that relation.

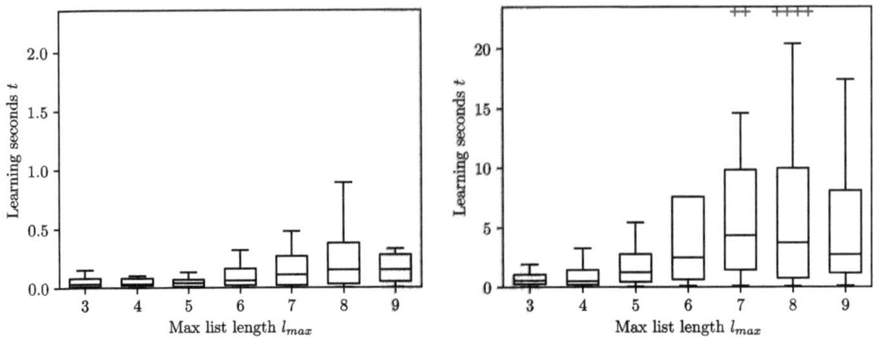

Fig. 4. Data scalability tests of `not` (left) and `droplast` (right). A plus sign marks a timeout $t > 60$ s. The graphs are scaled by proportion to average time at $l_{max} = 3$.

7 Conclusion

In this work, we propose a system to synthesize Datalog programs from iteratively explaining more examples. The search space defined by UCC programs is based on extended chain Datalog programs to overcome its expressivity limitations. We discuss the expressivity of UCC programs and show that it reduces to the expressivity class of regular languages when all rules are linear. Based on the representation, we introduce the DAST generalization, which is responsible for inventing predicates and creating recursions, and implement a search algorithm on top of it. Our experiments demonstrate that the search algorithm allows for learning multiple predicates simultaneously and performs better on various ILP tasks compared to existing systems. We also check the learnability of all regular languages under a fixed length and discuss the algorithm's scalability concerning example complexity.

Expressivity is a main concern in this work. An example that cannot be expressed in UCC is the `scc` task, which asks if two points are reachable to each other: $scc(x, y) \leftarrow path(x, y) \wedge path(y, x)$, where *path* as a recursive definition needs to be invented. Our current random walking method cannot sample $path(x, y)$ and $path(y, x)$ simultaneously. Unrestricted sampling techniques like randomly adding neighbor nodes are likely to compromise scalability. Our future work is to consider the following solution: It is actually too strict that every step must explain no negative example. If we allow rule like $scc(x, y) \leftarrow path(x, y)$ which covers both new positive and negative examples to be temporarily created, then further constrain it by adding more body literals, we might be able to learn these rules with conjunctive conditions.

References

1. Abiteboul, S., Hull, R., Vianu, V.: Foundations of Databases. Addison-Wesley (1995)
2. Afrati, F., Papadimitriou, C.: The parallel complexity of simple chain queries. In: Proceedings of the Sixth ACM Symposium on Principles of Database Systems, pp. 210–213. Association for Computing Machinery (1987)
3. Afrati, F., Gergatsoulis, M., Toni, F.: Linearisability on datalog programs. Theoret. Comput. Sci. **308**(1), 199–226 (2003)
4. Cropper, A., Dumančić, S., Muggleton, S.H.: Turning 30: new ideas in inductive logic programming. In: Proceedings of the 29th International Joint Conference on Artificial Intelligence, pp. 4833–4839 (2020)
5. Cropper, A., Morel, R.: Learning programs by learning from failures. Mach. Learn. **110**(4), 801–856 (2021). https://doi.org/10.1007/s10994-020-05934-z
6. Cropper, A., Morel, R.: Predicate invention by learning from failures. arxiv:2104.14426 (2021)
7. Cropper, A., Morel, R., Muggleton, S.: Learning higher-order logic programs. Mach. Learn. **109**(7), 1289–1322 (2019). https://doi.org/10.1007/s10994-019-05862-7
8. Eiter, T., Gottlob, G.: The complexity of logic-based abduction. J. ACM **42**(1), 3–42 (1995)
9. Galárraga, L.A., Teflioudi, C., Hose, K., Suchanek, F.: Amie: association rule mining under incomplete evidence in ontological knowledge bases. In: Proceedings of the 22nd International Conference on World Wide Web, pp. 413–422 (2013)
10. Kitzelmann, E., Schmid, U.: Inductive synthesis of functional programs: an explanation based generalization approach. J. Mach. Learn. Res. **7**(15), 429–454 (2006)
11. Lajus, J., Galárraga, L., Suchanek, F.: Fast and exact rule mining with amie 3. In: The Semantic Web, pp. 36–52 (2020)
12. Lao, N., Cohen, W.: Relational retrieval using a combination of path-constrained random walks. Mach. Learn. **81**, 53–67 (2010)
13. Law, M., Russo, A., Broda, K.: Iterative learning of answer set programs from context dependent examples. Theory Pract. Logic Program. **16**(5–6), 834–848 (2016)
14. Mendelson, J., Naik, A., Raghothaman, M., Naik, M.: GenSynth: synthesizing datalog programs without language bias. In: Proceedings of the AAAI Conference on Artificial Intelligence, pp. 6444–6453 (2021)
15. Muggleton, S.: Inverse entailment and progol. N. Gener. Comput. **13**(3–4), 245–286 (1995)
16. Muggleton, S., Buntine, W.L.: Machine invention of first order predicates by inverting resolution. In: Proceedings of the 5th International Conference on Machine Learning, pp. 339–352 (1988)
17. Muggleton, S.H., Feng, C.: Efficient induction of logic programs. In: Proceedings of International Conference on Algorithmic Learning Theory, pp. 368–381 (1990)
18. Quinlan, J.R.: Learning logical definitions from relations. Mach. Learn. **5**(3), 239–266 (1990)
19. Raghothaman, M., Mendelson, J., Zhao, D., Naik, M., Scholz, B.: Provenance-guided synthesis of datalog programs. In: Proceedings of the ACM on Programming Languages, pp. 1–27 (2019)
20. Seki, H.: Unfold/fold transformation of general logic programs for the well-founded semantics. J. Log. Program. **16**(1–2), 5–23 (1993)

21. Thakkar, A., Naik, A., Sands, N., Alur, R., Naik, M., Raghothaman, M.: Example-guided synthesis of relational queries. In: Proceedings of the 42nd International Conference on Programming Language Design and Implementation, pp. 1110–1125 (2021)
22. Thakkar, A., Sands, N., Petrou, G., Alur, R., Naik, M., Raghothaman, M.: Mobius: synthesizing relational queries with recursive and invented predicates. In: Proceedings of the ACM on Programming Languages, pp. 1394–1417 (2023)
23. Ullman, J.D., Van Gelder, A.: Parallel complexity of logical query programs. In: 27th Annual Symposium on Foundations of Computer Science, pp. 438–454 (1986)

From Model-Based Learning to Model-Free Behaviour with Meta-Interpretive Learning

Stassa Patsantzis(✉)

University of Surrey, Guildford, UK
s.patsantzis-@surrey.ac.uk

Abstract. A "model" is a theory that describes the state of an environment and the effects of an agent's decisions on the environment. A model-based agent can use its model to predict the effects of its future actions and so plan ahead, but must know the state of the environment. A model-free agent cannot plan, but can act without a model and without completely observing the environment. An autonomous agent capable of acting independently in novel environments must combine both sets of capabilities. We show how to create such an agent with Meta-Interpretive Learning used to learn a model-based Solver used to train a model-free Controller that can solve the same planning problems as the Solver. We demonstrate the equivalence in problem-solving ability of the two agents on grid navigation problems in two kinds of environment: randomly generated mazes, and lake maps with wide open areas. We find that all navigation problems solved by the Solver are also solved by the Controller, indicating the two are equivalent.

Keywords: ILP · Meta-Interpretive Learning · Planning

1 Introduction

A *model* is a theory that describes the possible states of an environment and the way in which the state of the environment changes as a result of an agent's actions. An *environment* may be an abstract domain such as the set of all lists or the Cartesian plane, a virtual environment, such as a computer simulation or game, or a physical environment such as a real-world location. An *action* is a predicate that relates a description of the current state of an environment to a new state; in other words, a transition relation over states. An *agent* is a program that generates a sequence of actions connecting an initial state to a desired goal state; what we call a *plan*. To generate such a sequence of actions is to solve a *planning problem*. A *model-based* agent is an agent that solves planning problems given a model. A *model-free* agent is an agent that selects actions without a model and, therefore, without a plan. We call a model-based agent a "solver for planning problems" or, simply, *solver* and a model-free agent a *controller*.

W.-Z. Dai (Ed.): ILP 2024, LNAI 16059, pp. 19–34, 2026.
https://doi.org/10.1007/978-3-032-09087-4_2

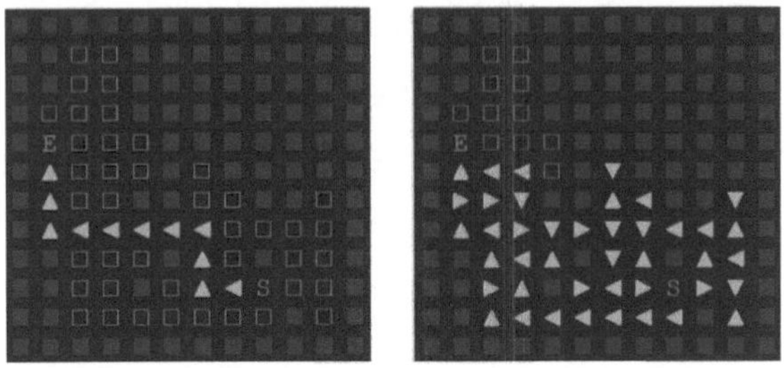

(a) Model-based Solver (b) Model-free Controller

Fig. 1. A model-based Solver can predict the effect of its future actions and plan ahead, but requires knowledge of its environment. A model-free Controller cannot plan and must explore its environment but can act without knowledge of the environment. Green tiles: passable; red tiles: unpassable; S: start; E: goal. (Color figure online)

Figure 1 illustrates the difference between planning by a model-based Solver and acting by a model-free Controller. In the Figure the environment is a map of a lake with islands (alternatively a cave system) where red tiles represent unpassable locations, green tiles passable locations and the letters S and E a starting and goal location respectively. Yellow arrows show agent trajectories.

Planning with a model implies some knowledge of the structure of an environment. The Solver in Fig. 1a is initially given a map of the environment, which it can fully observe, and uses this map to generate the set of all possible moves between adjacent, passable map tiles. The Solver then uses this navigation model to plan a direct path from S to E. The Controller in Fig. 1b is not given the map of the environment, cannot directly observe S or E, and can only observe whether map tiles adjacent to its current location are passable or unpassable. The Controller explores its environment to find a path from S to E.

A model-based solver and a model-free controller have complementary advantages and disadvantages. An autonomous agent capable of acting independently in arbitrary environments must combine the capabilities of both. In this paper we show how the two sets of abilities can be combined by using Meta-Interpretive Learning (MIL) [11] to learn a solver, and use the solver to generate examples to learn a controller that solves the same problems as the solver.

Our ultimate goal is the development of an action-selection component of an Autonomous Agent Architecture that must guide a mobile robot to survery missions in environments with dynamic and unobserved features so that the autonomous agent guiding the robot must combine the capabilities of both solver and controller. Full details are reserved for future work.

Inductive Logic Programming as Model-Based Learning. *Plannning is the model-based approach to autonomous behaviour* [4] in the sense that a planning agent's behaviour is derived from a model and a planning problem by means of an inference procedure (typically a search algorithm such as A^*). Inductive Logic Programming (ILP) [8] can be seen as the model-based approach to *machine learning* where the "model" is a background theory and a new

$S(s_1, s_2) \leftarrow Step\_down(s_1, s_2).$
$S(s_1, s_2) \leftarrow Step\_left(s_1, s_2).$
$S(s_1, s_2) \leftarrow Step\_right(s_1, s_2).$
$S(s_1, s_2) \leftarrow Step\_up(s_1, s_2).$
$S(s_1, s_2) \leftarrow Step\_down(s_1, s_3), S(s_3, s_2).$
$S(s_1, s_2) \leftarrow Step\_left(s_1, s_3), S(s_3, s_2).$
$S(s_1, s_2) \leftarrow Step\_right(s_1, s_3), S(s_3, s_2).$
$S(s_1, s_2) \leftarrow Step\_up(s_1, s_3), S(s_3, s_2).$

(a) Grid navigation solver

$Step\_down([id, x/y, t], [id, x/y^{-1}, t')$
$Step\_left([id, x/y, t], [id, x^{-1}/y, t')$
$Step\_right([id, x/y, t], [id, x^{+1}/y, t'])$
$Step\_up([id, x/y, t], [id, x/y^{+1}, t'])$

(b) Grid navigation solver model

$Step\_right([maze\_a, 0/6, s], [maze\_a, 1/6, f])$
$Step\_down([maze\_a, 2/6, f], [maze\_a, 2/5, f])$
$Step\_left([maze\_a, 2/0, f], [maze\_a, 1/0, f])$
$Step\_left([maze\_a, 1/0, f], [maze\_a, 0/0, e])$
% ... 56 more actions

(c) Solver model instantiated to Maze A

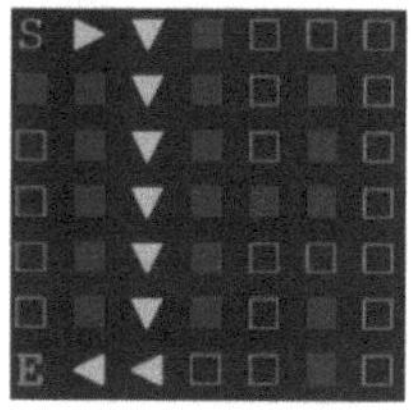

(d) Path in Maze A

$Step\_right([maze\_b, 0/6, s], [maze\_b, 1/6, f])$
$Step\_down([maze\_b, 2/6, f], [maze\_b, 2/5, f])$
$Step\_up([maze\_b, 4/0, f], [maze\_b, 4/1, f])$
$Step\_down([maze\_b, 6/1, f], [maze\_b, 6/0, e])$
% ... 56 more actions

(e) Solver model instantiated to Maze B

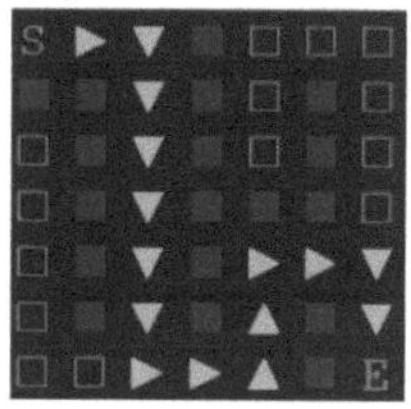

(f) Path in Maze B

Fig. 2. A Solver for grid navigation problems learned with MIL.

hypothesis is derived by an inference procedure given a set of examples. To learn planning programs, i.e. solvers, with ILP, we can structure the background theory as a set of action predicates and give a set of planning problems as examples. For a solver to be general, it must be a recursive program, therefore we use MIL, a form of ILP capable of learning recursion.

Figure 2 lists a grid navigation solver as a set of definite clauses. The solver's body consists of eight clauses of the predicate $S/2$, where each argument s_i is a Prolog list representing an initial or end state of the environment. Each clause of $S/2$ changes the environment state by moving an agent one step to each of the four directions up, right, down or left, recursively. The solver's model consists of the step actions $Step\_up, Step\_right, Step\_down, Step\_left$, implemented as dyadic predicates, listed in un-instantiated form in Fig. 2b. The two arguments of each action, shared with $S/2$, represent the state of the environment before and after the action is taken as a list of first-order terms: id, a map identifier, x/y, the coordinates of an agent on the map, and, t, the type of map *tile* at x/y, one of the constants f, w, e, s for floor, wall, start and end tile, respectively; wall tiles are not passable and so they are not featured in actions' state arguments.

4 Controller state labels: $Q = \{q_0, q_1, q_2, q_3\}$
4 Action labels: $A = \{up, right, down, left\}$
15 Observation labels: $O = \{pppp, pppu, ppup, ppuu, pupp, pupu, puup, puuu, uppp, uppu, upup, upuu, uupp, uupu, uuup\}$
960 4-tuples: $|Q \times O \times A \times Q|$

(a) Finite State Controller labels

$(q_0, upuu, right, q_1)$
$(q_1, upup, right, q_1)$
$(q_1, uupp, down, q_2)$
$(q_2, pupu, down, q_2)$
$(q_2, ppup, left, q_3)$
$(q_3, upup, left, q_3)$

(b) FSC for Maze A

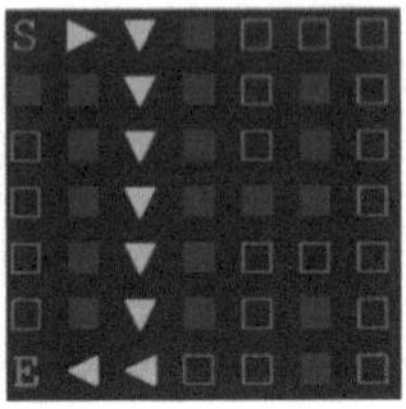

(c) Path in Maze A

$(q_1, upup, right, q_1)$.
$(q_1, pupp, down, q_2)$.
$(q_1, uupp, down, q_2)$.
$(q_2, ppup, right, q_1)$.
$(q_2, pupu, down, q_2)$.
$(q_0, uppu, right, q_1)$.
$(q_0, upuu, right, q_1)$.
$(q_0, pupu, up, q_0)$.
$(q_1, puup, up, q_0)$.

(d) FSC for Maze B

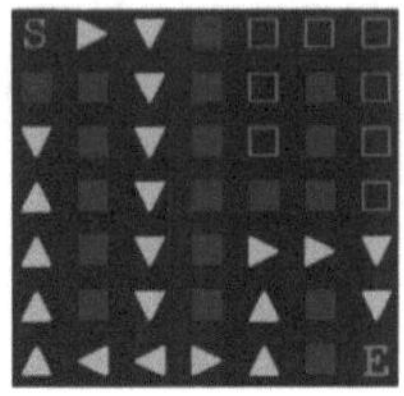

(e) Path in Maze B

Fig. 3. Finite State Controllers for mazes A, B trained with the Solver in Fig. 2a.

The solver's model must be instantiated to the coordinates and tile types of a map before it can be used by the solver to solve that map. Two examples of instantiated models are listed in Figs. 2c, 2e for two mazes, Maze A and B. The two mazes are identical save for the position of the end tile and so their instantiated models are almost identical. Figures 2d, 2f illustrate the solutions of the two mazes by the solver where each yellow arrow corresponds to a step action in the indicated direction.

The solver in Fig. 2 was learned by the MIL system Louise [12] as described in Sect. 5.1.

Finite State Controllers for Model-Free Behaviour. When its model cannot be instantiated a model-based solver cannot plan. An alternative is found in Finite State Controllers (FSCs) [2] a formalisation of the concept of Finite State Machines from video games and robotics. A FSC is a set of 4-tuples (q, o, a, q') mapping pairs (q, o) of current *controller* state[1] and observation labels, to pairs (a, q') of action and next controller state labels. Figure 3 lists two maze-solving FSCs for mazes A and B in Fig. 2, and their sets of labels. Each observation label is a string $\{U, R, D, L\} \in \{u, p\}^2$ denoting whether map tiles in the directions up, right, down or left, respectively, from the agent's current map location, are passable (p) or unpassable (u). For example, the string *upuu* denotes that only the tile to the right of the agent is passable. Action labels denote that the agent must move up, right, down or left. The two FSCs in Fig. 3 were learned by Louise from solutions of mazes A and B generated by the solver in Fig. 2a.

FSCs are model-free in that they have no representation of the environment state, or the way actions modify that state; they are only a mapping between

[1] Controller states are not *environment* states.

pairs of labels. In particular, FSC observation labels represent an agent's *belief* about the state of the environment. Additionally, FSCs are *efficient* in that they do not need to search a large state-space like planners, or, indeed, solvers. Conversely, an FSC is equivalent to a Deterministic Finite State Transducer [6] a.k.a. a Mealy Machine [7], i.e. a Regular Automaton and so can only generate one sequence of actions, e.g. the maze FSC in Fig. 3b can only solve mazes where the exit can be reached by moving right, down, or left, like Maze A in Fig. 2d, whereas the FSC in Fig. 3d can only solve mazes where the exit can be reached by moving right, down or up, like Maze B in Fig. 2f. Finally, the literature on FSCs does not describe a concrete method to *execute* FSCs, only their notation as sets of 4-tuples.

Contributions. We identify FSCs as a promising framework for the development of model-free controllers solving the same problems as model-based solvers in partially observable environments. We make the following contributions.

- We formalise a notation for model-based learning of planning problem solvers as a higher-order background theory for MIL.
- We extend the framework of FSCs to Nondeterministic FSCs.
- We implement a set of FSC *executors*, stack-machines that take as input a set of FSC tuples and execute them in order.
- We implement a novel approach to Simultaneous Localisation and Mapping (SLAM) used by executors to avoid cycles.
- We show that a solver and a controller that solve the same problems can be learned by MIL using our model notation.
- We demonstrate empirically that our learned solver and controller can solve the same planning problems.
- We implement two new libraries in Prolog: *Controller Freak*, to learn controllers from solvers; and *Grid Master* to solve navigation problems on grids.

Implementation code and experiment data are available at the following URL: https://github.com/stassa/ijclr24.

2 Related Work

2.1 Meta-Interpretive Learning

Meta-Interpretive Learning (MIL) [9,11] is a new form of Inductive Logic Programming (ILP) [8,10] where the background theory is a higher-order program that includes both first- and second-order definite clauses. Hypotheses learned by MIL are first-order definite programs, i.e. logic programs in Prolog. Hypotheses are learned by SLD Refutation of training examples, which can be both positive or negative, given as Horn goals to a meta-interpreter capable of second-order SLD Resolution. During Resolution, substitutions of second-order variables in the higher-order background theory are derived which applied to their corresponding second-order clauses yield the first-order clauses of a hypothesis. MIL has been shown capable of learning recursion and of predicate invention without the limitations of earlier ILP systems [13].

2.2 Finite State Controllers

A Finite State Controller (FSC) [2] is a set of 4-tuples (q, o, a, q'), where $q, q' \in Q, o \in O, a \in A$ are constants serving as labels for controller states, observations and actions, respectively. A tuple (q, o, a, q') corresponds to a mapping between pairs (q, o) and (a, q') and the set of all tuples in an FSC to the *transition function* $Q \times \text{O} \rightarrow A \times Q$ that controls the actions of an agent, so that in controller state q, when the observation label o is input, the FSC outputs action label a and transitions to controller state q'. In [2] an approach is described to derive FSCs from contingent planning problems through a series of transformations to classical planning, via conformant planning, problems [4]. The approach is demonstrated in a number of domains including navigation on grids that we also demonstrate here, but transformation betwen planning problems is subject to high computational costs.

Compared to contingent plans and policies derived from Markov Decision Processes (MDPs) and Partially Observable MDPs (POMDPS) [2] claim that FSCs are: a) general, in that they can solve multiple problems in a domain; b) compact, in that they only need comprise a few controller states; and c) robust to uncertainty in initial and goal conditions and the effects of actions. Generality of FSCs is formalised in [1] and their compactness is self-evident. We could not find evidence of FSC robustness to uncertainty in the literature; we leave the matter to future work.

To be used as an action selection mechanism for an autonomous agent, an FSC must be executed in a loop by an external process. Such a process must connect the FSC to an environment by passing observation and action labels between the FSC and the environment. Such a mechanism has not, so far, been described in the literature. In Sect. 4 we implement a set of *executors* that perform this function in conjunction with a virtual environment for grid navigation problems.

FSCs are equivalent to Deterministic Finite State Transducers (FSTs), a.k.a. Mealy machines[2]. In an FSC's tuples, observation and action labels are the inputs and outputs, respectively, of a deterministic FST's transition function, and each pair $Q \times O$ is mapped to exactly one pair $A \times Q$, such that there exists a single tuple (q, o, a, q') for each pair (q, o) in an FSC. Being equivalent to *Deterministic* FSTs, in other words, Regular Automata, FSCs cannot deal with ambiguities in the sense that they can only successfully solve planning problems where the same action must always be taken in the same circumstances. While this may be sufficient, or even desired, that is not always the case.

As an example of the difficulty in dealing with ambiguities, consider the two mazes A and B in Fig. 4, identical in structure, but with an end tile (E) placed in a different location. An FSC solving maze A must turn left at the cell marked with a yellow X in order to reach the exit, therefore the same FSC will not be able to solve maze B where it must turn *right* at the X to reach the exit[3].

[2] This equivalence is not noted in earlier work.

[3] The same limitation obtains when learning optimal policies from (PO)MDPs, as e.g. with Reinforcement Learning where this limitation was recently identified as *implicit*

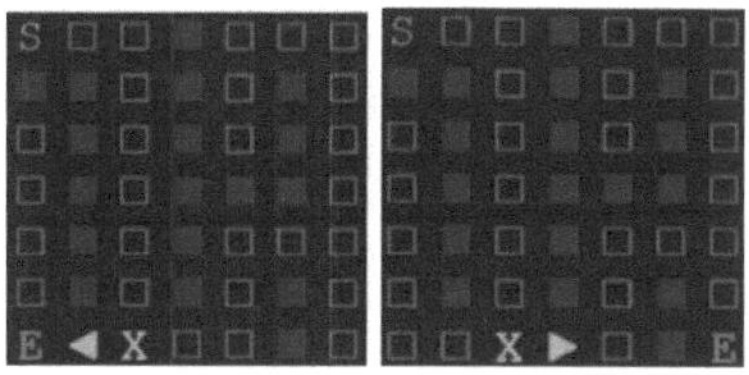

(a) Maze A (b) Maze B

Fig. 4. An example of ambiguity in a maze environment. The two mazes, Maze A and Maze B have identical structure but the end tile E is placed in a different location. In Maze A, an agent must turn left at the yellow X to reach the exit at E, but in Maze B it must turn right instead, as indicated by the yellow arrows. (Color figure online)

In Sect. 3 we extend FSCs to *Nondeterministic* FSCs and in Sect. 4 implement executors with a stack that permit an FSC to backtrack or reverse course to fully explore an environment and solve ambiguous environments.

3 Framework

3.1 MIL Planning Model

To learn a solver for planning problems with MIL we structure the higher-order background theory given to a MIL system as a model of the planning domain and give as an example a planning problem. We call such a background theory and example a *MIL Planning Model.*

Definition 1. *(MIL Planning Model) A MIL Planning Model $\mathcal{T}$ is a 5-tuple $\{\mathcal{F}, \mathcal{S}, \mathcal{A}, \mathcal{M}, e\}$ where:*

- *$\mathcal{F}$ is a set of first-order terms that we call* fluents.
- *$\mathcal{S}$ is a set of states $\{s_1, ..., s_m\}$, where each s_i is a set of* instances *of the fluents in $\mathcal{F}$, given as a Prolog list.*
- *$\mathcal{A}$ is a set of dyadic definite clauses with heads $A_1(s_{11}, s_{12}), ..., A_n(s_{n1}, s_{n2})$, where each $s_{i1}, s_{i2} \in \mathcal{S}$, and $\mathcal{A}$ defines a* transition relation *between states.*
- *$\mathcal{M}$ is the set containing the two second-order definite clauses: $P(x, y) \leftarrow Q(x, y)$ (called "Identity") and $P(x, y) \leftarrow Q(x, z), P(z, y)$ ("Tailrec") with P, Q existentially quantified over the set of predicate symbols in $\mathcal{A}$ and the symbol $S/2$, and x, y, z universally or existentially quantified over $\mathcal{S}$.*
- *e is a Horn goal $\leftarrow S(s_{in}, s_g)$ given as a training example, where $s_{in}, s_g \in \mathcal{S}$ are an initial state and a goal state of a planning problem, respectively.*

We call s_{i1}, s_{i2} in an action A_i the input *and* output *states of A_i, respectively.*

partial observability [5], the characteristic of a domain where an arbitrary instance of a problem does not include every observation possible in all problem instances.

Clauses of action predicates in $\mathcal{A}$ are selected for Resolution by unification so the fluents in actions' state-lists act as both preconditions and effects, unlike in STRIPs-like planning models where there is a clear distinction between the two.

Given a MIL Planning Model, a MIL system must return a *planning hypothesis* H such that $\mathcal{A} \cup H \models e$. We say that H solves the planning problem in e. We call H a *solver* for e. In particular, H is a *model-based* solver and its model is the set of ground instances of clauses in $\mathcal{A}$[4].

Definition 2. *(MIL Planning Hypothesis) A MIL Planning Hypothesis H is a set of first-order definite clause instances of* Identity *and* Tailrec *such that each P in a head literal $P(x,y)$ in* Identity *or* Tailrec *and the last body literal $P(z,y)$ in* Tailrec *is a literal of the predicate $S/2$ as in $e \in \mathcal{T}$, and each body literal $Q(x,y)$ or $Q(x,z)$ in* Identity *and* Tailrec *respectively is a literal of an action predicate $A_i(s_{i1}, s_{i2})$ in $\mathcal{A} \in \mathcal{T}$. If $\mathcal{A} \cup H \models e$, H is a* solver *for e.*

3.2 Nondeterministic Finite State Controllers

We extend the definition of Finite State Controllers, adapted, in Definition 3, from [2], to *Nondeterministic* Finite State Controllers.

Definition 3. *(Finite State Controller) Let Q be a set of controller state labels, O a set of observation labels, A a set of action labels, and let C be a function $Q \times O \rightarrow A \times Q$. C is a Finite State Controller, denoted as the set of 4-tuples (q, o, a, q') where $q, q' \in Q, o \in O, a \in A$ and $(q, o) \rightarrow (a, q') \in C$. Note that all FSC labels are constants, or strings of constants.*

Definition 4. *(Nondeterministic Finite State Controller) Let Q, O, A be as in Definition 3, let $R = Q \times O \times A \times Q$, and let $C \subseteq R$. We call C a Nondeterministic Finite State Controller for R. We denote C as the set of 4-tuples (q, o, a, q') that correspond to the subset of R in C, where $q, q' \in Q, o \in O, a \in A$.*

We will henceforth refer to Nondeterministic FSCs simply as FSCs, only clarifying the determinism property where it is not clear from the context. We call a sequence of FSC tuples the FSC's *behaviour*:

Definition 5. *(FSC Behaviour) Let C be a Nondeterministic FSC and $B = \langle T_1, ..., T_n \rangle$ a sequence of 4-tuples in C, such that for every $t_i, t_{i+1} \in B$ if $t_i = (q, o, a, q')$ then $t_{i+i} = (q', o', a', q'')$. We call B the* behaviour *of (an agent controlled by) C.*

[4] In this case the meaning of "model" converges to that in First Order Logic.

Table 1. Grid navigation solver model with controller labels used to generate FSC behaviours to learn a grid navigation FSC with MIL.

$Step\_down([id, x/y, t, [q\|Qs], [o\|Os], [a\|As], [q'\|Qs']], [id, x/y^{-1}, t', Qs, Os, As, Qs'])$
$Step\_left([id, x/y, t, [q\|Qs], [o\|Os], [a\|As], [q'\|Qs']], [id, x^{-1}/y, t', Qs, Os, As, Qs'])$
$Step\_right([id, x/y, t, [q\|Qs], [o\|Os], [a\|As], [q'\|Qs']], [id, x^{+1}/y, t', Qs, Os, As, Qs'])$
$Step\_up([id, x/y, t, [q\|Qs], [o\|Os], [a\|As], [q'\|Qs']], [id, x/y^{+1}, t', Qs, Os, As, Qs'])$

4 Implementation

4.1 Controller Freak

We implement, in Prolog, a new library called *Controller Freak* that defines Prolog predicates to learn FSCs from solvers, by MIL. Predicates in Controller Freak take as input a set of planning problems E and a solver H where the set of fluents F in actions $\mathcal{A}$ in H's model includes the sets of labels Q, O, A that must be accepted by C, the FSC to be learned. A set of actions $\mathcal{A}$ extending the grid navigation solver model in Fig. 2b with FSC labels is listed in Table 1.

Solving each $e \in E$ with H generates sequences of labels corresponding to example behaviours B of C used to compose the following MIL-learning problem:

- First-order Background theory: $Q \times O \times A \times Q$
- Second-Order Background theory: $\{Identity, Tailrec\}$
- Examples: Set of FSC behaviours B

Solving this MIL-learning problem results in a set of definite clauses, C_p, that represent C in the form of a recursive logic program. Further processing by Controller Freak predicates transforms C_p into the set of 4-tuples of C.

4.2 Grid Master

We implement, in Prolog, a library for grid navigation problems called *Grid Master*, defining predicates in three modules: a) A *Map* module is used to manage grid-style maps in text format, where each "cell" of a map is a string. A generator for maze maps called *MaGe* is included with Grid Master. b) An *Action Generator* module is used to generate actions for a MIL Planning Model given a map. c) A *Map Display* module is used to display maps and the progress of a grid navigation agent through a map, as in the map figures in this paper.

Grid Master allows the definition of game-like virtual environments with which an agent can interact to solve a map. An initial *Basic Environment* is included that manages navigation on mazes, and similar grids with a start and end location. The Basic Environment a) initialises an agent's starting location on a map, b) receives action labels from, and returns observation labels to, a controller (via an executor) as the agent navigates the map, and c)

```
executor_bck(Gs,_Q0,_O,As,Gs,As):- !.
executor_bck(Fs,Q0,O,[A|Acc],Gs,As):-
    controller_tuple(Q0,O,A,Q1)
    ,environment_action(Fs,A,O1,Fs1)
    ,executor_bck(Fs1,Q1,O1,Acc,Gs,As).
```

Fig. 5. Backtracking FSC Executor. *Fs*: initial fluents. *Q*0: current controller state label. *O*: current observation label. *A*: Next action label. *Acc*/*As*: Action label accumulator. *Gs*: Goal fluents. *Q*1, *O*1: next state and observation labels.

determines whether the agent has reached the end location on the map. Additionally, the Basic Environment can receive as input a sequence of action labels from a solver, and "play them back" to determine whether the solver has reached the end location.

4.3 Executors

An *executor* is an interpreter for FSCs implemented as a loop that passes a current pair (q, o) to an FSC, receives a pair (a, q') and passes the action label a of this pair to an environment to obtain a new observation label o, until a goal state is reached. Initial and goal states are represented as fluents not directly observed by the executor, or the FSC it is executing. Instead the environment, e.g. the Basic Environment, or the sensor and actor models on a robot, translate current environment states to observation labels and action labels to new environment states.

We define two kinds of executors: backtracking and reversing; and two variants, with and without SLAM.

Backtracking Executor. We implement a Backtracking Executor that performs the loop described in Sect. 4.3 in the simplest possible way, as a recursive procedure in Prolog, that is allowed to backtrack and obtain further pairs (a, q') while the goal state has not been reached. Thus, the Backtracking Executor implicitly uses Depth First Search with backtracking (DFS) and a stack managed by the Prolog runtime, to "jump back" to locations on a map where alternative actions can be taken. The Backtracking Executor is listed, as Prolog code, in Fig. 5.

Reversing Executor. Backtracking causes an environment to be "reset" to a previous state, e.g. with respect to an agent's coordinates in the environment. That may not be possible in all environments. In particular, simulator-like virtual environments such as the Basic Environment may allow backtracking but real-world environments such as the physical world, do not. Thus the Backtracking Executor cannot be used in the real world.

```
executor_rev(Gs,_T1,_Ss,As,Gs,As):- !.
executor_rev(_Fs,_T1,[],As,_Gs,As):- !.
% T1 is a partially ground 4-tuple (q,o,A,Q')
executor_rev(Fs,T1,Ss,[T0|Acc],Gs,As):-
    % All ground instances of T1 are pushed to the stack.
    push_tuples(T0,T1,Ss,Ss_1)
    % T2 is a ground instance of T1 (q,o,a,q')
    ,pop_tuple(Ss_1,T2,Ss_2)
    % T3 is a new, partially ground 4-tuple (q',o',A',Q'')
    ,environment_state_transition(Fs,T2,Fs1,T3)
    ,push_reverse(T2,Ss_2,Ss_r)
    ,executor_rev(Fs1,T3,Ss_r,[T2,T0|Acc],Gs,As).
```

Fig. 6. Reversing FSC Executor. Fs: initial fluents. $T1$: current FSC 4-tuple, partly ground. Ss: stack of FSC 4-tuples. $T0$: last FSC tuple, fully ground. Acc/As: FSC 4-tuple accumulator. Gs: goal fluents. *In body literals*: $T2$: next fully ground instance of $T1$. $T3$: new, partly ground FSC 4-tuple.

To allow FSCs to be used in real-world environments we implement a Reversing Executor that manages a stack explicitly, pushing on the stack the reverse of each FSC 4-tuple executed. When no more tuples can be pushed on the stack the first 4-tuple popped from the stack is the reverse of the last executed 4-tuple, causing the FSC to explicitly retrace its steps. When the last reverse-tuple is popped from the stack, the next 4-tuple is a not-yet tried alternative and the agent explores a new path, or the stack is empty and execution terminates.

The reverse of a tuple is determined by an FSC. Only the reverse of a pair (a, q') need be defined, rather than the reverse of every tuple[5]. Not all action-state pairs will have a reverse, thus not all decisions can be reversed.

The Reversing Executor is listed, as Prolog code, in Fig. 6.

Grid SLAM. When a map has wide areas of passable tiles an FSC can be stuck going around in loops. To avoid this we implement Simultaneous Localisation and Mapping (SLAM) as a Grid Master predicate used by an executor to update a SLAM-constructed map by placing obsevation labels on a grid that is continuously expanded as the FSC explores an environment. A SLAM executor marks the last location of an FSC on the SLAMming map as visited and an FSC is only allowed to re-visit a location when reversing course, with a Reversing (SLAM) executor, thus avoiding cycles. Details of the SLAM implementation are left for future work for lack of space. Figure 7 illustrates SLAMming maps constructed with our method.

[5] This does not violate the model-free nature of an FSC: the reverse-pair relation is specific to an FSC and does not depend on the environment. The same relation can be used to avoid oscillations, e.g. to avoid following a “down” with an “up” action.

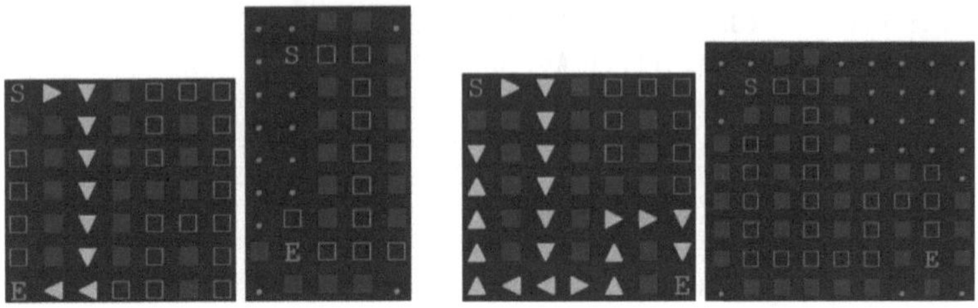

(a) Maze A (b) Maze A SLAM (c) Maze B (d) Maze B SLAM

Fig. 7. Grid SLAM: mapping of an unseen environment during FSC execution with Reversing Executor (yellow arrows). Grey dots: unobservable tiles. (Color figure online)

5 Experiments

We show empirically that a grid navigation solver can be learned by MIL and used to learn an FSC capable of solving the same problems as the solver.

We carry out experiments in two types of environments with grid-based maps. The first type of environment are maps of mazes generated by the Grid Master *MaGe* module. The second type of environment, illustrated in Fig. 1 are maps of open areas with obstacles, modelling lakes with islands, or caves, generated by the dungeon map generator in the R-language package *r.oguelike* [3]. We refer to the latter type of environment as "Lake maps".

Each MaGe map has a start and end tile placed automatically, at random. For Lake Maps we find it difficult to generate new maps programmatically, so we pre-generate 10 maps of dimensions 20×20 and create new planning problems by randomly placing a start and end tile in each map for each new problem.

Both types of environment are accessed via the Grid Master Basic Environment as described in Sect. 4.2. The salient difference between the two types of environment is that MaGe maps have no open areas of passable tiles where an agent can get stuck in a loop ("plazas"), whereas Lake Maps are predominantly made of such plazas. The MaGe maps thus effectively test the ability of an agent to find a path through a fully-connected graph without cycles, wheras the Lake maps test the ability of an agent to find a path through a graph with cycles.

5.1 Learning a Model-Based Solver with MIL

We find that we can learn a general grid navigation solver with MIL from a single example of a simplified grid-based map consisting of only four passable (floor) tiles. We name this map *Zero* and illustrate it in Fig. 8a.

The initial, uninstantiated model for the target solver is listed in Fig. 2b. To instantiate this model we use Grid Master's Action Generator module to generate the set of all 8 possible ground actions in the Zero map. We manually create a *generalised* training example where each fluent is left as a non-ground

(a) Zero map

Second-Order Definite Clauses M:
$(Identity)\ P(x, y) \leftarrow Q(x, y)$
$(Tailrec)\ P(x, y) \leftarrow Q(x, z), P(z, y)$
Actions $\mathcal{A}$:
$Step\_down([zero, 0/1, f], [zero, 0/0, f])$
$Step\_down([zero, 1/1, f], [zero, 1/0, f])$
$Step\_left([zero, 1/0, f], [zero, 0/0, f])$
$Step\_left([zero, 1/1, f], [zero, 0/1, f])$
$Step\_right([zero, 0/0, f], [zero, 1/0, f])$
$Step\_right([zero, 0/1, f], [zero, 1/1, f])$
$Step\_up([zero, 0/0, f], [zero, 0/1, f])$
$Step\_up([zero, 1/0, f], [zero, 1/1, f])$
Example e:
$s([zero, x_s/y_s, t_s], [zero, x_e/y_e, t_e).$

(b) Zero map MIL Planning Problem

Fig. 8. MIL Planning Problem for Map Zero.

term, except for the map identifier. The resulting MIL Planning Model is listed in Fig. 8b.

We train Louise on the MIL Planning Problem listed in Fig. 8b and obtain the solver listed in Fig. 2a. Inspecting the logic program in Fig. 2a should leave no doubt that it is a general procedure for grid map navigation which systematically tries every available direction, recursively, until it reaches a goal state defined by the second argument in each head literal. Nevertheless we test this learned solver on two sets of environments: 100 maze maps with dimensions 100×100; and 10×50 Lake maps (i.e. we generate 50 instances for each of the 10 Lake maps)[6]. Results are listed in the *Experiment 1* rows of Table 2.

5.2 Learning a Model-Free Controller with MIL

The ambiguity illustrated in Fig. 4 suggests a large number of diverse environments would be needed to use our solver to train a controller that can solve the same navigation problems as the solver. We observe that the effect of ambiguity is that not all observation labels will be included in FSC behaviours generated by the solver and so a complete mapping between observation and action labels will not be seen in training. Following from this observation we use the set of observation labels we want the target FSC to recognise, to generate 15 training maps of dimensions 3×3, one for each of the 15 observation labels in the target FSC, excluding the impossible *uuuu* (i.e. all-unpassable) label. We call these training maps, illustrated in Fig. 9, *Observation Matrices.*

Solving each Observation Matrix with our learned solver, given the model in Table 1, we generate one to four FSC behaviours, each mapping an observation

[6] We test fewer Lake map problems because the solver is executed in SWI-Prolog with tabling which avoids looping in plazas but requires a lot of RAM for experiments.

Table 2. Experiment results. Instances: number of environment instances tested. Solved: percentage of instances solved. Steps: mean number of actions taken by an agent navigating between start and end tiles. FSC-BT: Backtracking executor. FSC-RE: Reversing executor. FSC-BT(S) Backtracking SLAM executor. FSC-RE(S) Reversing SLAM executor.

Experiment	Agent	Environment	Dimensions	Instances	Solved	Steps
Experiment 1	Solver	MaGe map	100 × 100	100	100%	816.04
		Lake map	20 × 20	10 × 50	100%	11.23
Experiment 2	FSC-BT	MaGe map	100 × 100	100	100%	816.04
	FSC-RE	MaGe map	100 × 100	100	100%	3942.78
	FSC-BT(S)	Lake map	20 × 20	10 × 50	92%	69.54
	FSC-RE(S)	Lake map	20 × 20	10 × 50	100%	132.98

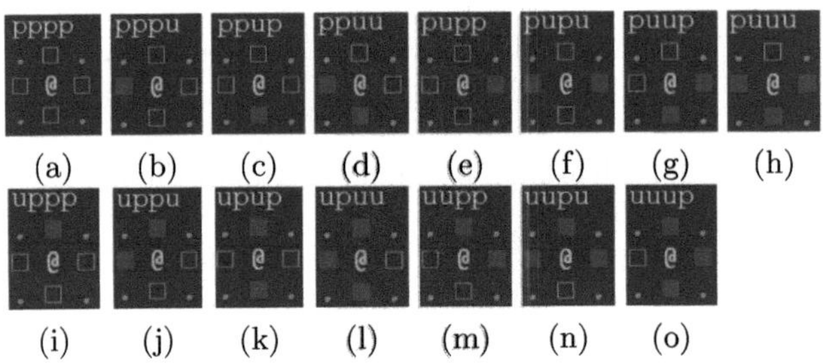

Fig. 9. Observation Matrices for Grid Navigation FSC. Yellow @ sign: agent. (Color figure online)

label to the up to four action labels that correspond to it. We illustrate this mapping in supplemental material for lack of space.

We use this set of behaviours, and the controller labels listed in Fig. 3a to compose a MIL-learning problem and learn an FSC with Controller Freak, as described in Sect. 4.1. The controller learned in this way is a non-deterministic FSC comprising 128 4-tuples in a subset of all 960 4-tuples in $Q \times O \times A \times Q$. We list this FSC in supplemental material for lack of space.

We test the learned FSC on the same planning problems as we tested the learned solver, using each of our four executors. Results are listed in the Experiment 2 rows of Fig. 9.

We make two observations. First, on the MaGe map the Backtracking executor (FSC-BT) returns paths with the same average number of steps as the solver. The solver is executed by DFS with backtracking like the Backtracking executor, so they find the same paths. Essentially the Backtracking executor plans, without a model. Second, the Backtracking-SLAM executor (FSC-BT(S)) takes a long time to solve some Lake maps because it keeps trying long, spiralling paths. We impose a time limit of 300 sec. to this executor only to measure the effect and find that it times out 8% of the time. With all other executors, the FSC learned from the solver, solves the same problems as the solver.

6 Conclusions and Future Work

We have shown how to train a model-based solver and use it to train a model-free controller with MIL. The two agents complement each other in that the solver can plan ahead but needs advance knowledge of an environment whereas the controller doesn't need advanced knowledge but can't plan and must explore the environment instead. The solver is learned from a single, generalised example and the controller from 15 examples automatically generated from the controller's observation labels. The controller is a new kind of Nondeterministic Finite State Controller and can solve the same problems as the solver when executed by the right kind of executor. A SLAM-ming executor is needed to avoid loops in environments with open areas. We have focused on solvers and controllers for navigation on grids and have implemented a pair of new Prolog libraries used to learn solvers and controllers and execute them on grid maps.

Limitations and Future Work We have only studied the ability of MIL systems to learn solvers and equivalent FSCs for grid navigation problems. It remains to be seen whether the approach we have described can be further applied to environments that are not grids, and tasks other than navigation. Further, connecting our solver and FSC to a robot's sensors and actors and solving problems in physical, rather than virtual, environments remains to be done.

Acknowledgement. The author would like to acknowledge the EPSRC grant no. EP/X030156/1 from which her post-doctoral research wass funded. The MIL team at the University of Surrey and Drs. Alan Hunter and Alfie Treloar of the University of Bath have provided patient, vital feedback during the development of this work.

Disclosure of Interests. No competing interests.

References

1. Bonet, B., Geffner, H.: Policies that generalize: solving many planning problems with the same policy. In: Yang, Q., Wooldridge, M.J. (eds.) IJCAI 2015 Proceedings, pp. 2798–2804. AAAI Press (2015)
2. Bonet, B., Palacios, H., Geffner, H.: Automatic derivation of memoryless policies and finite-state controllers using classical planners. In: ICAPS 2009 Proceedings (2009)
3. Dray, M.: r.oguelike v.0.1.0 (2023). https://github.com/matt-dray/r.oguelike
4. Geffner, H., Bonet, B.: A Concise Introduction to Models and Methods for Automated Planning: Synthesis Lectures on Artificial Intelligence and Machine Learning, 1st edn. Morgan & Claypool Publishers (2013)

5. Ghosh, D., Rahme, J., Kumar, A., Zhang, A., Adams, R.P., Levine, S.: Why generalization in RL is difficult: epistemic POMDPs and implicit partial observability. In: NeurIPS 2021 Proceedings, pp. 25502–25515 (2021)
6. Jurafsky, D., Martin, J.H.: Speech and Language Processing, 2nd edn. (2000)
7. Mealy, G.H.: A method for synthesizing sequential circuits. Bell Syst. Tech. J. **34**, 1045–1079 (1955)
8. Muggleton, S.: Inductive Logic Programming. N. Gener. Comput. **8**(4), 295–318 (1991)
9. Muggleton, S., Lin, D.: Meta-interpretive learning of higher-order dyadic datalog: predicate invention revisited. Mach. Learn. **100**(1), 49–73 (2015)
10. Muggleton, S., de Raedt, L.: Inductive logic programming: theory and methods. J. Logic Program. **19–20**(SUPPL. 1), 629–679 (1994)
11. Muggleton, S.H., Lin, D., Pahlavi, N., Tamaddoni-Nezhad, A.: Meta-interpretive learning: application to grammatical inference. Mach. Learn. **94**(1), 25–49 (2014)
12. Patsantzis, S., Muggleton, S.H.: Louise (2019). https://github.com/stassa/louise
13. Patsantzis, S., Muggleton, S.H.: Meta-interpretive learning as metarule specialisation. Machine Learning. arxiv:2106.07464 (2021)

Meta-Interpretive Learning as Second Order Resolution

James Trewern(✉), Stassa Patsantzis, and Alireza Tamaddoni-Nezhad

Department of Computer Science, University of Surrey, Guildford, UK
{jt00988,s.patsantzis,a.tamaddoni-nezhad}@surrey.ac.uk

Abstract. Meta-Interpretive Learning (MIL), a branch of Inductive Logic programming (ILP), has been shown to be an effective method for learning logic programs, through the use of higher-order 'meta-rules', from which first order clauses can be built using meta-substitutions. In this paper we propose a new framework for understanding MIL as Second Order SLD-Resolution which we prove is sound and complete for induction, as for deduction. We implement two new learning and reasoning engines for MIL, one called Vanilla implemented in Prolog, and the other, Prolog^2 implemented in Rust. We use Vanilla and Prolog^2 to implement Top Program Construction (TPC). TPC in Prolog^2 is a multi-threaded implementation, processing multiple instances of Second Order SLD-Resolution in parallel. Our results show that these systems can learn hundreds of clauses from over 600 examples in a matter of minutes for Vanilla-TPC, or Seconds in Prolog^2-TPC.

Keywords: Inductive Logic Programming · Meta-Interpretive Learning · SLD-Resolution · Top Program Construction · Second Order Resolution

1 Introduction

Meta-Interpretive Learning. Meta-Interpretive Learning (MIL) [12,14] is an advanced form of Inductive Logic Programming (ILP) [13] where first-order logic hypotheses are learned by inductive generalisation from examples and a higher-order background theory comprising both first- and Second-Order definite clauses. Examples, background theory and learned hypotheses are all in the form of logic programs in a logic programming language, typically, Prolog.

Second-Order SLD-Resolution. MIL systems are capable of learning, from a single positive example, complex logic programs with recursion and invented predicates (ones not included in the background theory, or examples [23]) and that generalise robustly to unseen instances. The present article formalises the understanding that this learning ability is the result of the use of SLD-Resolution

W.-Z. Dai (Ed.): ILP 2024, LNAI 16059, pp. 35–47, 2026.
https://doi.org/10.1007/978-3-032-09087-4_3

[8,10] as the learning procedure: by the soundness and completeness of SLD-Resolution [10,15], given that an example is a logical consequence of the higher-order background theory, a first order program can always be constructed, by applying to the clauses in the background theory substitutions of their Second-Order variables found by unification during SLD-Refutation of the example, and that program must necessarily entail the example with respect to the first-order background theory. Over-general hypotheses can be identified and rejected, or reformulated, by SLD-Refutation of negative examples. The inclusion of Second-Order definite clauses in the background theory raises SLD-Resolution to the second order of logic, where deduction and induction, learning and reasoning, become one.

Contributions. In this paper, we make the following contributions:

- **Theoretical results** A new recognition of MIL as Second-Order SLD-Resolution; proofs of *inductive* soundness and completeness of MIL.
- **Implementation** Two new learning and reasoning engines for MIL called *Vanilla* and *Prolog* ^{2} informed by the new understanding of MIL as Second-Order SLD-Resolution; Vanilla-TPC and Prolog^2-TPC , new implementations, of state-of-the-art MIL algorithm Top Program Construction.

2 Related Work

Meta-Interpretive Learning. Previous descriptions of MIL in the literature fail to clearly identify it as Second-Order SLD-Resolution. Such descriptions point instead to the implementation of MIL by means of a "Prolog meta-interpreter" modified to "fetch higher-order clauses" named "metarules" (e.g. in [2,4,9]). It is possible, for the discerning reader, to recognise MIL as Second-Order SLD-Resolution if only by "reading between the lines" of such descriptions: a "Prolog meta-interpreter" is a coding, in Prolog, of Prolog, and, therefore, of SLD-Resolution; and "fetching metarules" indicates that the "metarules" are *resolved with* as definite clauses, rather than acting as mere templates or syntactic bias—as they are described e.g. in [3], [7]). [17] define MIL as "metarule specialisation by SLD-Resolution"; which again fails to fully clarify the issue. In Sect. 3 we explicitly recognise MIL as Second-Order SLD-Resolution for the first time; and show, also for the first time, its soundness and completeness that follow from this new recognition.

Recursion and Predicate Invention. Demonstrations of learning of recursive logic programs with invented predicates, some from single examples, abound in the MIL literature, e.g. [11,12,14]. By contrast, earlier ILP approaches are only capable of limited forms of learning recursion and predicate invention. A comprehensive review of such limited capabilities of earlier systems is found in [5]. In Sect. 3 we prove that MIL is capable of learning arbitrary logic programs with no restriction to the structure of recursive clauses thanks to the soundness and completeness of SLD-Resolution. We leave an extension of our proof to programs with invented predicates for future work.

3 Framework

In this Section we introduce a novel framework for MIL as Second-Order SLD Resolution and prove its soundness and completeness.

3.1 Logical Notation

We start with the logical notation used throughout the Section. Our notation follows closely from [10] and [15], which we extend with definitions for Second-Order definite clauses.

FOL Language. We define a First-Order Logic (FOL) language as an alphabet consisting of sets of predicate symbols $\mathcal{P} = \{P, Q, R, ...\}$, function symbols $\mathcal{F} = \{f, g, h, ...\}$, constants $\mathcal{C} \subseteq \mathcal{F} = \{a, b, c, ...\}$, variables $\mathcal{V} = \{x, y, z, ...\}$, logical connectors $\neg, \wedge, \vee, \rightarrow, \Leftrightarrow$, quantifiers $\exists, \forall$ and punctuation symbols . , (and). Symbols have *arity*, a natural number; Constants have arity 0. *Terms* are defined inductively as follows: a variable is a term; a constant is a term; if f is a function symbol of arity n and $t_1, .., t_n$ are terms, $f(t_1, ..., t_n)$ is a term. *Formulae* are defined inductively as follows: if P is a predicate symbol of arity m and $t_1, ..., t_m$ are terms, $P(t_1, ..., t_m)$ is a formula, called an *atom*. If ϕ, ψ are formulae then $\neg\phi, \phi \wedge \psi, \phi \vee \psi, \phi \rightarrow \psi, \phi \Leftrightarrow \psi$ are formulae; if x is a variable in formula ϕ then $\exists x : \phi, \forall x : \phi$ are formulae. A formula is *ground* when it has no variables.

Logic Programming. A *literal* is an atom, or the negation of an atom; if A is an atom, A is a positive literal and $\neg A$ is a negative literal. A *clause* is a set of literals in disjunction: $\{L_1 \vee L_2 \vee L_3 \vee ...\}$; $\square$ is the empty clause. A clause is Horn if it has at most one positive literal and *Prolog* if all its variables are universally quantified; in which case we omit quantifiers. A Horn clause is a *definite program clause*, or simply *definite clause*, if it has exactly one positive literal, otherwise it is a Horn *goal*. A *definite program*, or *logic program*, is a set of definite clauses in conjunction: $\{C_1 \wedge C_2 \wedge C_3 \wedge ...\}$. By logic programming conventions we will write a definite clause, e.g., $\{P(x, y), \neg Q(x, z), \neg R(z, y)\}$ as an implication with the single positive literal first and the implication arrow reversed: $P(x, y) \leftarrow Q(x, z), R(z, y)$ under the standard semantics of disjunction where $A \vee \neg B \Leftrightarrow$ B $\rightarrow A$. We will call the single consequent literal, $P(x, y)$, the "head" of the clause and all other literals, $Q(x, z), R(z, y)$, the "body" of the clause. We will denote a Horn goal $G = \{\neg L_1 \vee \neg L_2 \vee ...\}$ as $\leftarrow G$.

Higher-Order Datalog. A Horn clause is *Datalog* if it has no function symbols other than constants and each variable in the head of the clause is also found in a literal in the body of the clause; we say the head and body literal "share" the variable. A Datalog clause is a *Second-Order clause* if it has variables existentially quantified over $\mathcal{P}$ in place of predicate symbols. A Second-Order clause may have variables existentially or universally quantified over $\mathcal{C}, \mathcal{V}$. A set of

Second-Order definite clauses is a *Second-Order definite program*. By MIL convention we will denote the quantification of variables in Second-Order clauses by type-case: lower-case for universally quantified variables, $x, y, z, ...$, upper-case for existentially quantified variables $P, Q, R, X, Y, Z, ...$

Resolution. Resolution [19] is a deductive inference rule: given a conjunction of two clauses, $\neg\phi \vee \psi \wedge \phi \vee \chi$, eliminate the pair $\{\neg\phi, \phi\}$ found in contradiction and *derive* a new clause $\psi \vee \chi$. $\{\neg\phi, \phi\}$ form a *complementary pair*. If C_1, C_2 are clauses from which C_3 is derived by resolution, C_3 is the *resolvent* of C_1, C_2; and $C_1 \cup C_2 \vdash_R C_3$ is the *Resolution-derivation* of C_3 from C_1, C_2. Let L be a literal. A substitution, ϑ, of variables in L is a set $\{v_1/t_1, ..., v_n/t_n\}$ denoting the simultaneous substitution of each variable v_i in L with a term t_i. $L\vartheta$ denotes the application of ϑ to L. If ϕ, ψ are two literals and ϑ is a substitution of variables in both so that $\phi\vartheta = \psi\vartheta$, ϑ is a *unifier* for ϕ, ψ. Let $\neg\phi \vee \psi \wedge \xi \vee \chi$ be a conjunction of clauses. If there exists a unifier ϑ such that $\phi\vartheta = \xi\vartheta$ then $\{\neg\phi\vartheta, \xi\vartheta\}$ form a complementary pair and can be eliminated by Resolution.

SLD-Resolution. SLD-Resolution is a variant of Resolution restricted to Horn clauses. Let $\Pi, \leftarrow G$ be a definite program and a Horn goal. $\Pi \cup \{\leftarrow G\} \vdash_{SLD} \square$, the derivation of the empty clause from $\Pi, \leftarrow G$ by SLD-Resolution is an *SLD-Refutation* of $\leftarrow G$ by Π. Let A, B be two sets of formulae; $A \models B$, read "A entails B", if and only if B is true when A is true, under the standard rules of logic. If $A \models \square$, A is *unsatisfiable*, meaning there is no substitution of the variables in A that can make A true. SLD-Resolution is sound: if there exists ϑ s.t. $\Pi\vartheta \cup \{\leftarrow G\vartheta\} \vdash_{SLD} \square$ then $\Pi \wedge \neg G \models \square$. SLD-Resolution is refutation-complete: if $\Pi \wedge \neg G \models \square$ then there exists ϑ s.t. $\Pi\vartheta \cup \{\leftarrow G\} \vdash_{SLD} \square$. Proofs of the soundness and completeness of SLD-Resolution are detailed in [10] and [15].

3.2 Second-Order SLD-Resolution

Definition 1 (MIL Problem). *Let* e^+ *be an atom that we call a positive example, and* $\mathcal{B} = \{B_{FO}, B_{SO}\}$ *be a higher-order definite program where* B_{FO} *is a set of definite clauses and* B_{SO} *is a set of Second-Order datalog clauses chosen s.t.* $\mathcal{B} \models e^+$ *(*Consistency Assumption*) The* MIL Problem *is to find substitutions* ϑ, Θ *of the variables in* $\mathcal{B}$ *s.t.* $H = B_{SO}\Theta$ *and* $B_{FO}\vartheta \wedge H \models e^+$ *(*Target Theory*). We call* $\{e^+, \mathcal{B}\}$ *the* elements of the MIL problem *and* H *a* solution to the MIL problem. *We call* H *the learned, or induced,* hypothesis. *Note that* H *is a set of First-Order definite clauses.*

Theorem 1 (Inductive Soundness and Completeness of MIL). *Let* $P_{MIL} = \{e^+, \mathcal{B}\}$. *If, and only if, the Consistency Assumption holds, then a solution to* P_{MIL} *will be found by SLD-Refutation of* e^+ *by* $\mathcal{B}$.

Proof. By the soundness and refutation completeness of SLD-Resolution:
$\exists\vartheta, \Theta : B_{FO}\vartheta \wedge B_{SO}\Theta \models e^+$ (Target Theory)
$\Leftrightarrow \exists\vartheta, \Theta : B_{FO}\vartheta \wedge B_{SO}\Theta \wedge \neg e^+ \models \square$
$\Leftrightarrow \exists\vartheta, \Theta : B_{FO}\vartheta \cup B_{SO}\Theta \cup \{\leftarrow e^+\} \vdash_{SLD} \square$
$\Leftrightarrow \mathcal{B} \models e^+$ (Consistency Assumption).

Remark 1. Theorem 1 states that, given a higher-order background theory $\mathcal{B}$ and a single atomic example e^+ that is a logical consequence of $\mathcal{B}$, a logic program H can always be learned by MIL that entails e^+ with respect to the first-order component of $\mathcal{B}$, i.e. B_{FO}. Theorem 1 makes no assumption about the extent to which H generalises to unseen examples, including negative examples. Thus, MIL is *inductively* sound and complete for one-shot learning.

4 Implementation

4.1 Vanilla-TPC

Vanilla. The results in the previous section inform our implementation of a new learning and reasoning engine for MIL that we call *Vanilla*[1], because it has the same structure as a "vanilla" Prolog meta-interpreter [25], but with added arguments for a) book-keeping (to collect the substitutions of existentially quantified variables in Second-Order clauses), b) filtering (to determine the symbols allowed in the heads of clauses in the learned program, possibly including invented predicate symbols) and, c), depth-limiting (to avoid infinite unifications between Second-Order definite clauses). Vanilla can be run in two modes. One mode uses Tabling (a.k.a. SLG-Resolution) [24] to control recursion, thus allowing left-recursive programs to be learned without going into infinite recursion. This mode also includes each new clause of a hypothesis to the background theory so that it can be resolved with itself, or other clauses in the hypothesis so-far. The second mode eschews tabling and instead controls recursion by a) constraints on the substitutions of existentially quantified variables in Second-Order clauses, to avoid construction of left-recursive clauses, and b) an upper limit on the number of resolution steps taken during an SLD-Refutation. Vanilla is developed in SWI-Prolog [26].

Vanilla-TPC. We use Vanilla to re-implement the MIL system Top Program Construction [16] and use this new version in comparisons with other systems in Sect. 5. We refer to this new system as Vanilla-TPC.

4.2 Prolog^2

Prolog^2 is a program for compiling and querying second order logic programs. This is achieved through implementing Second Order SLD-Resolution in the programming language Rust. The implementation is loosely inspired by the Warren Abstract Machine(WAM) [6], borrowing concepts such as heap term representation, argument registers, and a goal environment stack

Term Representation. When compiling programs or queries the terms must be translated from a text form into a data structure. This is stored in a heap structure, similar to the WAM, where each cell on the heap contains a tag and value.

[1] https://github.com/stassa/vanilla.

0	Func	3
1	Con	p
2	Ref	2
3	Ref	3

(a)

0	Func	3
1	Con	p
2	Arg	0
3	Arg	1

(b)

0	STR	1
1	p/2	
2	Ref	2
3	Ref	3

(c)

Fig. 1. Heap representation of the term $p(x, y)$ as in a goal(1a), in a clause (1b), and as a WAM term(1c). Each row represents 2 consecutive memory addresses. Func : n declares that the next n terms form a functor structure including (function or predicate). STR : n declares a structure starting at address n

Figure 1 Shows the Heap cells which represent the term $P(x, y)$.

One key difference from the WAM approach is to consider the predicate or function symbol as a term, which is part of a tuple of terms allowing variables to take the place of any functor. With this representation unification of second order terms becomes as straightforward as unifying tuples of terms in first order logic. This approach also differs from the WAM by storing clauses as compiled terms rather than as abstract machine instruction, necessitating the introduction of the Argument tag (ARG) to differentiate between query and clause variables.

Meta-Clauses. With Second Order Resolution we can see two types of clauses, first order and second order clauses. If we want to learn new clauses from Second Order clauses then we need both a substitution and a meta-substitution, the first used to create new goals, and the latter used to build new clauses. But we may not want to learn from all Second Order clauses such as a map clause which contains a predicate as an argument, but is not meant to provide a template for new clauses. To distinguish the two Prolog^2 uses the concept of meta-clauses, which would normally be called meta-rules in standard MIL, denoted by a set of universally quantified variables at the end of the clause, which may be empty.

After unifying a goal with the head of a clause, two values are produced, a set of bindings and a set of argument registers assigned heap addresses. To build a new goal or clause we copy the literals and replace the argument cells with the value at the address in the respective argument register, or introduce a new unbound ref cell if the register is not set. To allow newly learnt clauses to contain variables we use the concept of meta-variables, with an Arg$\forall$ tag. Meta-variables are substituted when building new goals, but replaced by normal variables when building new clauses. In meta-clauses, we must then single out the universally quantified variables by providing these in a set at the end of the clause, all other symbols are either existentially quantified variables, or constants. The Prolog^2 code shown in Formula 1 represents the higher order clause in Formula 2

$$P(X, Y) : -Q(X, Y)\{X, Y\}. \tag{1}$$

$$\exists PQ \forall xy P(x, y) \leftarrow Q(x, y) \tag{2}$$

The Clause Table. Prolog^2 stores all clauses within a clause table. Each clause in the clause table holds 2 key parts, the literals, stored as an array of heap addresses, and the clause type. The clause type can take 1 of 4 values, clause, body, meta, or hypothesis. The clause and body variants are both compiled before the execution of a query, may be either second order or first order clauses, and do not generate more clauses when matched with. The body clauses uniquely allow for goals with variable predicate symbols to match. The meta clauses as previously discussed are used to generate new clauses. finally, the hypothesis clauses which act as body clauses, are generated by matching with meta clauses. With these distinctions between clauses, Prolog^2 can handle the fetching of clauses when calling a goal, with 3 cases to consider, a goal with a variable predicate, a known constant predicate, or an unknown constant predicate.

Resolution. Resolution in Prolog^2 is handled by a 'Proof Stack' which stores the environment for each goal, with a pointer variable to the current environment. When an environment is created the only thing stored is a pointer to the goal atom on the heap. When the goal is tried, if a match is made to the head of a clause, 4 things are added. Firstly the list of clause indexes left to be matched against for that goal. Secondly, the bindings created by matching to a clause. Thirdly whether or not a new clause was introduced when matching, and if this new clause has an invented predicate. Finally, the environment stores the number of child goals that are created. These child goal environments are inserted at the index after the current pointer in the proof stack. With this information, if any goal fails, the effects of attempting a goal can be undone whilst backtracking. At each successful step, the solver increments the pointer, once the pointer exceeds the length of the proof stack then a solution is found, if whilst backtracking the pointer would be decremented before the first goal then a query has resolved to false. This approach is an adaptation of the one described for the WAM [6]

Advantages. By working directly with higher order terms, this implementation removes the need for a layer of meta-interpretation written on top of Prolog which can provide performance advantages. Additionally, this implementation benefits from simpler Meta-rule representation, allowing higher order predicate symbols to be recognised as variables if they start with a capital letter. With this, more complex or interesting meta-clauses can easily be included in the background knowledge, such as meta-clauses with both first order and higher order predicates, and predicate symbols in the arguments of literals. This can be extended to meta-clauses of higher order clauses allowing for the learning of higher-order programs, which was once considered an extension to MIL [2], but within this framework, this is a natural result of Second-Order SLD-Resolution.

4.3 Prolog^2-TPC

This implementation does not differ fundamentally from Vanilla-TPC, except that each positive example is learned from in parallel, and each sub-hypothesis is tested against negative examples in parallel. When generalising the Top Program each example is taken as an independent goal to begin a query of the second order logic program. This query then produces several hypotheses found whilst solving for the goal. A set of these hypotheses is collected from each of the instances of Second Order Resolution. This set of sub-hypotheses can then be specialised in parallel to produce the Top Program. By testing each Hypothesis in conjunction with the background knowledge against each negative example with 1st order resolution. Together with the other efficiency gains from Prolog^2, we expect this to provide a significant speed up to the learning.

5 Experiments

By removing the layer of meta-interpretation implemented on top of Prolog for Meta-Interpretive learning and instead implementing native Second Order Resolution we expect to see some improvement in efficiency. More significantly, by parallelising top program construction, we expect to see significant reductions in the time taken to solve learning problems with a large number of examples.

5.1 Materials and Methods

To evaluate *Vanilla-TPC* and *Prolog*^{2} *-TPC* we use the 'Grid World' and 'coloured graph' datasets, first used to test Louise [18]. We trained both systems with train test splits from $\{0.1, 0.2, 0.3, 0.4, 0.5, 0.6, 0.7, 0.8, 0.9\}$ with 0.1 having 10% of examples in the training split and 0.9 having 90%. For each split size, the experiment was run 10 times, randomising the split contents each time. For each experiment, we measure the time taken to learn a hypothesis, with a timeout set for 300 s, and the accuracy of the hypothesis against the remaining examples. If the experiment reaches the timeout, the accuracy was set to 0.[2]

Grid World. The grid world dataset is a challenge to learn a move/2 predicate, each example in the dataset is an example of a move from one position to another within a 4×4 grid world. The background knowledge includes 16 basic moves, with single steps in one of 4 directions and 12 double steps such as move right twice, or move right then up. Additionally a set of higher-order moves, listed in Fig. 2, are included. Given how many methods there are to move from one location to another this problem, by design, is combinatorially complex, as illustrated by Fig. 3, due to the large size of the hypothesis space, which increases exponentially with each example added to the set. This property makes the grid world experiment effective for measuring the efficiency of a learning system, as the cost to search for a hypothesis is so large.

[2] Experiment code and datasets:
https://github.com/JamesTrewern/louise-Testing/tree/Second-Order-Resolution-Tests
https://github.com/JamesTrewern/prolog2/tree/RunTests.

```
double_move(M,Ss,Gs):- move(M), M(Ss,Ss_1), M(Ss_1,Gs).
triple_move(M,Ss,Gs):-move(M), M(Ss,Ss_1), double_move(M,Ss_1,Gs).
quadruple_move(M,Ss,Gs):- move(M), double_move(M,Ss,Ss_1), double_move(M,Ss_1,Gs).
```

Fig. 2. Higher order move predicates

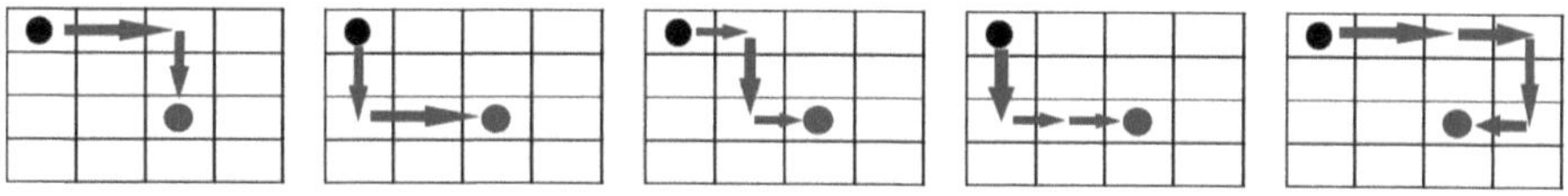

Fig. 3. Example of possible steps taken to go from 0,0 to 2,2 in 4×4 grid world

Coloured Graph. The coloured graph dataset describes two coloured graphs with the objective of learning the connected/2 predicate. This dataset includes the 4 variants: no noise, false positives, false negatives, and ambiguities. Each of these subsets describes the problem with differing types of noise in the examples, where ambiguities combines both false positives and negatives. Whilst this dataset is less expensive to learn from than the grid world example, it is effective at measuring the noise tolerance of a learner

5.2 Results

Accuracy. As shown in Figs. 4a and 4b, both implementations of TPC achieved similar accuracy though Prolog^2 under performed in accuracy for the coloured graph experiments with no noise and false positives. The major exception is in the final two splits when learning from 80% and 90% of the examples. Vanilla-TPC began to hit the 300-s threshold for the experiment with these sample sizes, leading to an accuracy of 0 in the very last split as there was no learnt hypothesis.

Time. Figures 5a and 5b, as expected, demonstrate that Prolog^2-TPC handled the largest split sizes significantly quicker than Vanilla-TPC. This was likely a result of the parallel nature. More surprisingly, even when handling the smallest split, there is still a large difference in the time taken to build the Top Program, which shows that the native implementation of second order resolution can achieve some significant gains in efficiency.

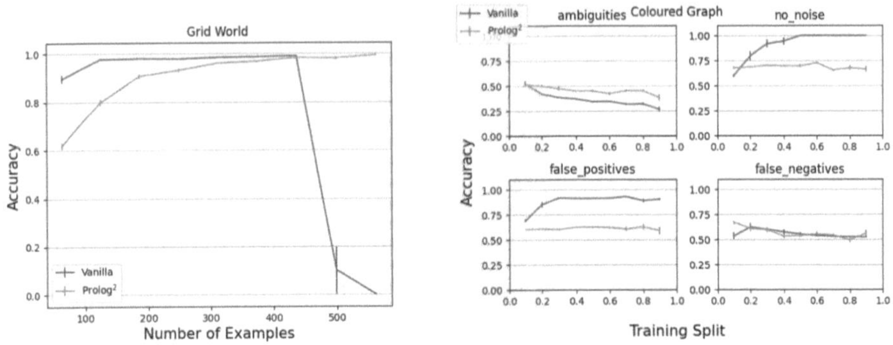

(a) (b)

Fig. 4. Average accuracy per number of examples for grid world (4a), and per training size ratio for coloured graph (4b). With vertical lines for standard error

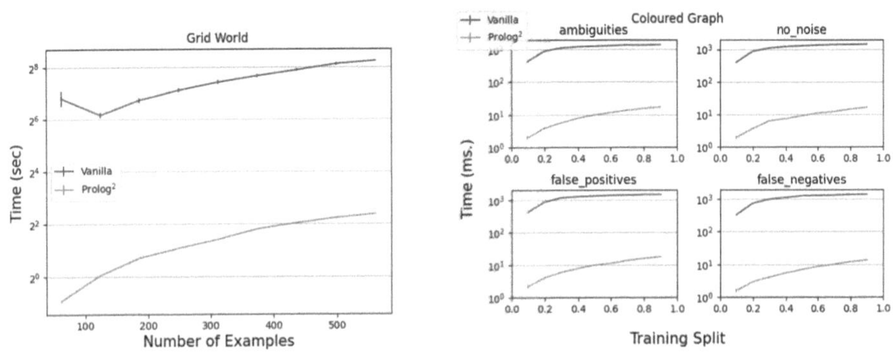

(a) (b)

Fig. 5. Average time taken to learn hypothesis per number of examples for grid world (4a), and per training size ratio for coloured graph (4b). With vertical lines for standard error

6 Conclusions and Future Work

6.1 Conclusions

Our work shows that considering MIL as a form of Second Order Resolution proves soundness and completeness and provides a useful framework for the understanding and implementation of MIL systems such as Vanilla and Prolog^2. We have also demonstrated that Prolog^2-TPC can learn from large numbers of examples within seconds where other MIL systems would take minutes, due to the parallel nature of its execution, and the lack of meta-interpretation needed to achieve Second Order Resolution.

6.2 Future Work

First Order Predicates in Meta-Rules. easy inclusion of first order predicate symbols in the Meta-Rules is an interesting result of considering MIL as Second Order Resolution. Similarly to the concept of interpreted background knowledge [2], the separation of Meta-Rules and background knowledge is not required when considering MIL as Second Order Resolution. This concept could potentially allow domain-specific experts help to inform learning. If applied properly this could bolster MIL's advantages in the areas of human-like computing, and understandable AI.

Alternative Approaches to Resolution. The goal of Prolog^2 and Prolog^2-TPC is to create an efficient MIL engine that could learn from large datasets in reasonable amounts of time. One approach to further increase the efficiency would be to try different approaches to Resolution. One approach is SLG-Resolution also called tabling [1,20], which can prevent left recursion loops by suspending certain goals, and increase efficiency by memoizing or tabling the results of goals. Another alternative approach to resolution is Multi-SLD-Resolution [21,22], where multiple binding environments exist concurrently, which could allow for Prolog^2 to utilise parallelism, even when learning from small numbers of examples. There are many approaches to Resolution with different advantages and disadvantages, though these have only been shown for First Order Resolution, so further work is needed to evaluate these approaches for Second Order Resolution, and expand the efficacy of this framework.

Acknowldegments. Trewern's PhD is supported by the Surrey Institute for People-Centred AI. The authors acknowledge the EPSRC grant on human-machine learning of ambiguities. The third author acknowledges the EPSRC Network Plus grant on Human-Like Computing (HLC).

References

1. Chen, W., Warren, D.S.: Tabled evaluation with delaying for general logic programs. J. ACM **43**(1), 20–74 (1996). https://doi.org/10.1145/227595.227597
2. Cropper, A., Muggleton, S.: Learning higher-order logic programs through abstraction and invention. In: Proceedings of the 25th International Joint Conference Artificial Intelligence (IJCAI 2016), pp. 1418–1424. IJCAI (2016). http://www.doc.ic.ac.uk/~shm/Papers/metafunc.pdf
3. Cropper, A.: Playgol: learning programs through play. CoRR arxiv:1904.08993 (2019)
4. Cropper, A., Muggleton, S.H.: Learning efficient logical robot strategies involving composable objects. In: Yang, Q., Wooldridge, M.J. (eds.) Proceedings of the Twenty-Fourth International Joint Conference on Artificial Intelligence, IJCAI 2015, Buenos Aires, Argentina, 25–31 July 2015, pp. 3423–3429. AAAI Press (2015). http://ijcai.org/Abstract/15/482

5. Flener, P., Yilmaz, S.: Inductive synthesis of recursive logic programs: achievements and prospects. J. Logic Program. **41**(2), 141–195 (1999). https://doi.org/10.1016/S0743-1066(99)00028-X. http://www.sciencedirect.com/science/article/pii/S074310669900028X
6. Hassan, A.K.: Warren's abstract machine: a tutorial reconstruction (1991)
7. Hocquette, C., Muggleton, S.: How much can experimental cost be reduced in active learning of agent strategies? In: Riguzzi, F., Bellodi, E., Zese, R. (eds.) ILP 2018. LNCS (LNAI), vol. 11105, pp. 38–53. Springer, Cham (2018). https://doi.org/10.1007/978-3-319-99960-9_3
8. Kowalski, R.A.: Predicate logic as programming language. In: IFIP Congress (1974). https://api.semanticscholar.org/CorpusID:10850205
9. Lin, D., Dechter, E., Ellis, K., Tenenbaum, J., Muggleton, S., Dwight, M.: Bias reformulation for one-shot function induction. In: Proceedings of the 23rd European Conference on Artificial Intelligence, pp. 525–530 (2014). https://doi.org/10.3233/978-1-61499-419-0-525
10. Lloyd, J.W.: Foundations of Logic Programming. Symbolic Computation. Springer Heidelberg (1987). https://doi.org/10.1007/978-3-642-83189-8
11. Muggleton, S., Dai, W.-Z., Sammut, C., Tamaddoni-Nezhad, A., Wen, J., Zhou, Z.-H.: Meta-interpretive learning from noisy images. Mach. Learn. **107**(7), 1097–1118 (2018). https://doi.org/10.1007/s10994-018-5710-8
12. Muggleton, S., Lin, D.: Meta-interpretive learning of higher-order dyadic datalog: predicate invention revisited. Mach. Learn. **100**(1), 49–73 (2015)
13. Muggleton, S., de Raedt, L.: Inductive logic programming: theory and methods. J. Logic Program. **19–20**(1), 629–679 (1994). https://doi.org/10.1016/0743-1066(94)90035-3
14. Muggleton, S.H., Lin, D., Pahlavi, N., Tamaddoni-Nezhad, A.: Meta-interpretive learning: application to grammatical inference. Mach. Learn. **94**(1), 25–49 (2013). https://doi.org/10.1007/s10994-013-5358-3
15. Nienhuys-Cheng, S.H., de Wolf, R.: Foundations of Inductive Logic programming. Springer, Berlin (1997)
16. Patsantzis, S., Muggleton, S.H.: Louise system (2019). https://github.com/stassa/louise
17. Patsantzis, S., Muggleton, S.H.: Meta-interpretive learning as metarule specialisation. CoRR arxiv:2106.07464 (2021)
18. Patsantzis, S., Muggleton, S.H.: Top program construction and reduction for polynomial time meta-interpretive learning. Mach. Learn. **110**(4), 755–778 (2021)
19. Robinson, J.A.: A machine-oriented logic based on the resolution principle. J. ACM **12**(1), 23–41 (1965). https://doi.org/10.1145/321250.321253
20. Sagonas, K., Swift, T.: An abstract machine for tabled execution of fixed-order stratified logic programs. ACM Trans. Program. Lang. Syst. (TOPLAS) **20**(3), 586–634 (1998)
21. Smith, D.A.: Multilog and data or-parallelism. J. Logic Program. **29**(1), 195–244 (1996) https://doi.org/10.1016/S0743-1066(96)00067-2. https://www.sciencedirect.com/science/article/pii/S0743106696000672
22. Smith, D.A., Hickey, T.J.: Multi-SLD resolution. In: Pfenning, F. (ed.) LPAR 1994. LNCS, vol. 822, pp. 260–274. Springer, Heidelberg (1994). https://doi.org/10.1007/3-540-58216-9_43
23. Stahl, I.: Predicate invention in ILP—an overview. In: Brazdil, P.B. (ed.) ECML 1993. LNCS, vol. 667, pp. 311–322. Springer, Heidelberg (1993). https://doi.org/10.1007/3-540-56602-3_144

24. Tamaki, H., Sato, T.: OLD resolution with tabulation. In: Shapiro, E. (ed.) ICLP 1986. LNCS, vol. 225, pp. 84–98. Springer, Heidelberg (1986). https://doi.org/10.1007/3-540-16492-8_66
25. Triska, M.: The power of Prolog (2005). https://www.metalevel.at/prolog
26. Wielemaker, J., Schrijvers, T., Triska, M., Lager, T.: SWI-prolog. Theory Pract. Logic Program. **12**(1–2), 67–96 (2012)

One-Shot Learning of Autonomous Behaviour: A Meta Inverse Entailment Approach

Dany Varghese[1(✉)], Daniel Cyrus[1], Stassa Patsantzis[1(✉)], James Trewern[1], Alfie Anthony Treloar[2], Alan Hunter[2], and Alireza Tamaddoni-Nezhad[1]

[1] University of Surrey, Guildford GU1 7XH, UK
{dany.varghese,d.cyrus,s.patsantzis,jt00988, a.tamaddoni-nezhad}@surrey.ac.uk

[2] University of Bath, Bath BA2 7AY, UK
{ajh210,aoat20}@bath.ac.uk

Abstract. "One-shot learning" traditionally refers to classifying a single instance using a machine learning model pre-trained on extensive datasets. In contrast, Inductive Logic Programming (ILP) approaches such as Meta-Interpretive Learning (MIL) and Meta Inverse Entailment (MIE), can generate complex logic programs from just a single positive example and minimal background knowledge without prior extensive training. This approach offers a human-centred form of machine learning that is more controllable, reliable, and comprehensible due to its small training data size and the inherent interpretability of logic programs. We use PyGol, a Python-based implementation of Meta Inverse Entailment, and compare its performance with ExpGen-PPO in learning autonomous behaviour. ExpGen-PPO is a state-of-the-art reinforcement learning framework designed to address the challenge of generalisation across diverse tasks through experience diversification and robust policy optimisation. Our experiments focus on two domains: maze-solving and obstacle avoidance for mobile robotics. In both domains, we first train the systems in simplified environments without obstacles and then test their ability to generalise to more complex environments with obstacles. Our results show that PyGol effectively learns generalisable solutions from a single example in both domains, whereas ExpGen-PPO requires more training and significantly more exploration to achieve similar performance.

Keywords: Meta Inverse Entailment (MIE) · Meta-Interpretive Learning (MIL) · One-shot learning · Autonomous Systems · Reinforcement Learning · PyGol

1 Introduction

Developing autonomous systems capable of rapidly learning and generalising complex behaviours from minimal data is a key challenge in Artificial Intelligence

D. Cyrus—Joint first author.

W.-Z. Dai (Ed.): ILP 2024, LNAI 16059, pp. 48–65, 2026.
https://doi.org/10.1007/978-3-032-09087-4_4

(AI) and robotics. Traditional machine learning methods often require large datasets and extensive training to achieve reliable performance in dynamic, real-world environments. In contrast, one-shot learning [6,11,20] aims to enable models to learn new tasks or behaviours from a single example, emulating the efficiency of human learning. This capability is crucial for applications such as autonomous navigation, robotics, and intelligent decision-making, where data is scarce, costly to obtain, or dynamically evolving.

This paper proposes a novel approach for one-shot learning of autonomous behaviour using Meta Inverse Entailment (MIE) [18,19], a symbolic machine learning technique that combines logic-based representations with inductive reasoning. By leveraging the inherent structure of logical rules and recursive predicates, MIE enables the automatic generation of compact, interpretable programs from minimal data. These programs can generalise learned behaviours to new, unseen environments while maintaining transparency and explainability.

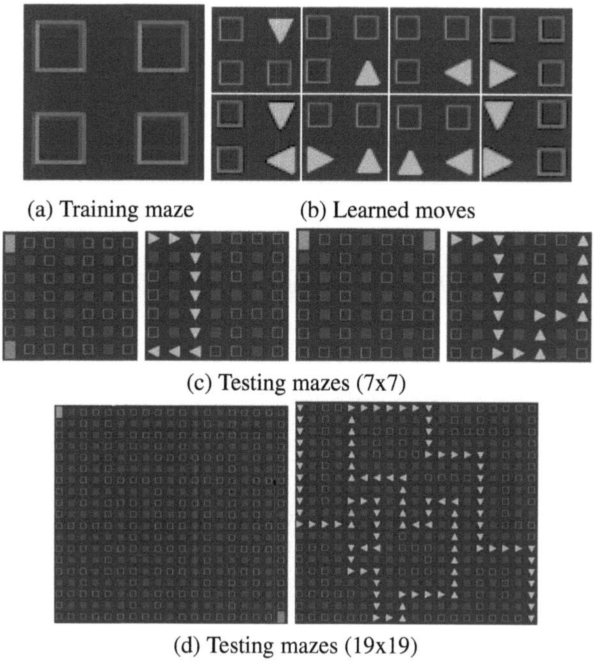

Fig. 1. One-shot learning of a maze-solving with PyGol. (a) PyGol is trained on a simplified maze with only floor tiles (green squares). (b) PyGol learns a program whose transitions are all moves possible in any maze (yellow arrows). (c-d) The learned program solves mazes of arbitrary size with walls, entrance, and exit tiles. (Color figure online)

We take advantage of Meta Inverse Entailment, implemented within PyGol [21], a Python-based system designed to support MIE's advanced learning capabilities. PyGol facilitates the automatic generation of language biases from background knowledge, eliminating the need for extensive pre-defined biases. By utilising bottom clauses of relevant literals and meta theory, PyGol enables the learning of target hypotheses in a flexible and adaptive manner, making it particularly effective in domains requiring one-shot learning. This framework enhances the generalisability of models, allowing them to solve complex tasks with minimal training data, as demonstrated in the autonomous behaviour experiments conducted in this study.

Table 1. The maze-solving program learned by PyGol from the training maze depicted in Fig. 1 (a) is shown here. The first four non-recursive clauses represent the agent's ability to exit the maze by taking a single step in each direction. The following four recursive clauses model continuous movement through the maze, enabling the agent to take multiple steps in one direction

One-shot maze-solving with PyGol
$solve(A, B) \leftarrow move\_down(A, B).$
$solve(A, B) \leftarrow move\_left(A, B).$
$solve(A, B) \leftarrow move\_right(A, B).$
$solve(A, B) \leftarrow move\_up(A, B).$
$solve(A, B) \leftarrow move\_down(A, C), solve(C, B).$
$solve(A, B) \leftarrow move\_left(A, C), solve(C, B).$
$solve(A, B) \leftarrow move\_right(A, C), solve(C, B).$
$solve(A, B) \leftarrow move\_up(A, C), solve(C, B).$

The one-shot generalisation capabilities of PyGol in a maze-solving domain are illustrated in Fig. 1. PyGol is trained in a simplified environment without walls, containing only four empty floor tiles, as depicted in Fig. 1a. Despite the simplicity of the training setup, PyGol learns all possible movement combinations in four directions, as represented by the red arrows in Fig. 1b. The learned program can solve more complex mazes featuring walls, entrances, and exits, as shown in Figs. 1c and 1d (with walls in red, entrances in blue, and exits in green), regardless of the maze's width or length. The underlying program, detailed in Table 1, demonstrates recursive calls to movement predicates: $move\_down/2$, $move\_up/2$, $move\_left/2$, and $move\_right/2$. These predicates enable the agent to take an arbitrary number of steps in any direction while ensuring that all moves are legal, i.e., the agent avoids crossing wall tiles. The move predicates are automatically generated based on the structure of the maze, highlighting PyGol's ability to efficiently generalise from minimal training data and solve a variety of maze configurations.

We compare MIE with ExpGen [22], a Deep Reinforcement Learning (Deep-RL) system designed for zero-shot generalisation. While Deep-RL is commonly used for path planning, most approaches struggle to generalise and are typically evaluated only on training instances [5]. In contrast, ExpGen is specifically developed to generalise to unseen instances and performs well in maze-solving—one of our experimental domains. It can also be adapted to our robot simulation domain, making it a suitable baseline for comparison with MIE.

2 Related Work

One-shot learning is a machine learning paradigm that enables models to learn new tasks or recognise new objects from a single or very few examples, contrasting sharply with traditional statistical approaches that require large datasets for effective training. Conventional methods, such as deep neural networks, typically require extensive data to generalise accurately, often involving hundreds of thousands or even millions of labelled examples. This heavy reliance on large-scale datasets stems from the statistical nature of these models, which use high-volume data to capture patterns and reduce overfitting. As a result, traditional approaches can struggle in domains where data collection is costly or scarce, such as medical diagnosis, rare event detection, or personalised applications, making them less feasible for scenarios that demand rapid adaptation or when data is limited. The inability to generalise from minimal data not only hampers flexibility but also highlights a fundamental limitation of such models, prompting the exploration of alternative methods. One-shot and few-shot learning methods address these challenges by leveraging prior knowledge and structured representations to learn efficiently from very few samples.

Recent efforts to bridge this gap include the concept of "in-context learning," introduced by Brown et al. (2020) with models like GPT-3 [2]. In-context learning enables large language models to perform tasks by conditioning on a few examples, but this is feasible only due to extensive pre-training on massive datasets involving billions of parameters. While this gives the appearance of one-shot or few-shot learning, the underlying reliance on large-scale pre-training raises concerns about scalability in truly resource-constrained settings. In contrast, one-shot learning techniques, such as Siamese networks [6], prototypical networks [16], and meta-learning algorithms like Model-Agnostic Meta-Learning (MAML) [4], focus on enabling models to generalise from minimal data. These methods often leverage prior knowledge and meta-level reasoning to enable more efficient learning from limited examples.

Meta-Interpretive Learning (MIL) [12] has emerged as a significant approach in the field of one-shot learning by leveraging logical and symbolic representations to learn efficiently from minimal examples. One-shot learning within the ILP framework was first introduced by Muggleton [14], proving the feasibility of positive-only learning in a Bayesian context. In a more recent development, Muggleton [9] extended this work by proving error bounds for one-shot learning, assuming a target theory of minimal generality. This extension introduced DeepLog, a new implementation of MIL capable of performing positive-only, one-shot learning to generate minimal-size and correct hypotheses within the same Bayesian framework.

3 Meta Inverse Entailment

This study uses a novel one-shot learning approach called Meta Inverse Entailment (MIE) which combines ideas from Inverse Entailment (IE) [10] and Meta-Interpretive Learning (MIL) [12]. Traditional IE and MIL approaches rely heavily on mode declarations or metarules, which serve as a declarative language bias to guide the hypothesis search. While this bias is essential for constraining and directing the learning process, it often demands significant human expertise and input, particularly in crafting domain-specific rules. This reliance on manually defined biases presents a challenge, as it limits the scalability and adaptability of MIL in various applications. MIE eliminates the need for manually defined declarative language biases by introducing two key mechanisms: the Bottom Clause of Relevant Literals (BCRL) and Meta Theory (MT). BCRL collects all literals relevant to a given example using background knowledge, thereby defining a focused yet complete hypothesis search space. MT serves as a higher-order language bias, automatically derived from the background, reducing reliance on human-crafted rules. Together, BCRL and MT enable flexible and automatic hypothesis generation, enhancing generalisation across domains with minimal manual input. Our formalism builds on established foundations of inductive logic programming [15] and is extended to incorporate ordered clauses and the notion of sequential subsumption. A summary of the logical notation is provided in Appendix A for reference.

Definition 1 ***(Relevant literals*** $(\overrightarrow{\mathcal{R}_e})$***).*** *Let B be the background knowledge, $\overrightarrow{\mathcal{B}}$ be the ordered clause of ground literals of B, and e be an example. Then the relevant literals of e is defined as $\overrightarrow{\mathcal{R}_e} = e \leftarrow L_1, L_2, \cdots, L_n$ if and only if $L_i \in \overrightarrow{\mathcal{B}}$ and L_i be related literal (See Definition 7 in Appendix B) of either L_j or e such that $1 \leq j < i$.*

Definition 2 ***(Bottom clause of relevant literals*** $(\bot_{e,B})$***).*** *Let B be the background knowledge, e be a definite clause representing an example, $\mathcal{K}$ be a set of constant terms and $\overrightarrow{\mathcal{R}_e}$ be the relevant literals of example e as defined in Definition 1. Then bottom clause of relevant literals of e, denoted as $\bot_{e,B}$ is $\overrightarrow{\mathcal{R}_e}$ where each unique occurrence of term $t_i \notin \mathcal{K}$ replaced with a new variable.*

The bottom clause of relevant literals introduced in MIE is similar to the bottom clause concept in Progol [10], however it does not use language bias such as mode declaration. The completeness and soundness of BCRL are beyond the scope of this paper and are discussed in detail in [18].

Definition 3 ***(Meta theory of relevant literals*** $(\mathcal{M}_e)$***).*** *Let e be an example, $\overrightarrow{\mathcal{R}_e}$ be the relevant literals of e. Then, a clause $\overrightarrow{C} \in \mathcal{M}_e$ if and only if;*

1. *$\exists\Theta$ such that $\overrightarrow{C}\Theta \succeq_s \overrightarrow{\mathcal{R}_e}$ (Refer Definition 6 in Appendix B) and*
2. *$\overrightarrow{C}$ is head_connected (Refer Definition 8 in Appendix B).*

The significant difference between a meta theory and a metarule is that a metarule specifies a relationship between the variables in the body of a rule. In meta theory, however, we avoid the tightly coupled nature of metarules to reduce computational complexity, deriving directly from background knowledge.

In MIE, we introduce a novel concept called the double-bounded hypothesis set. This set is defined as a sequential subsumption of meta theory, relative to the bottom clause of related literals. In this new framework (Refer Fig. 2), the hypothesis set of an example is constrained within specific boundaries: the bottom clause of relevant literals at the lower boundary and the encompassing meta theory at the upper boundary.

Definition 4 ***(Double-bounded hypothesis set*** $(HS(\bot_{e,B}, \mathcal{M}_e))$**).** *Let e be an example, $\bot_{e,B}$ be a bottom clause of relevant literals of e as defined in Definition 2, $\mathcal{M}_e$ be a meta theory as defined in Definition 3. Then*

$$HS(\bot_{e,B}, \mathcal{M}_e) = \{h| \text{ s.t: } (1)\ h \in \overrightarrow{\mathcal{L}_\bot},\ \text{and } (2)\ h \in \overrightarrow{\mathcal{L}_\mathcal{M}}\}$$

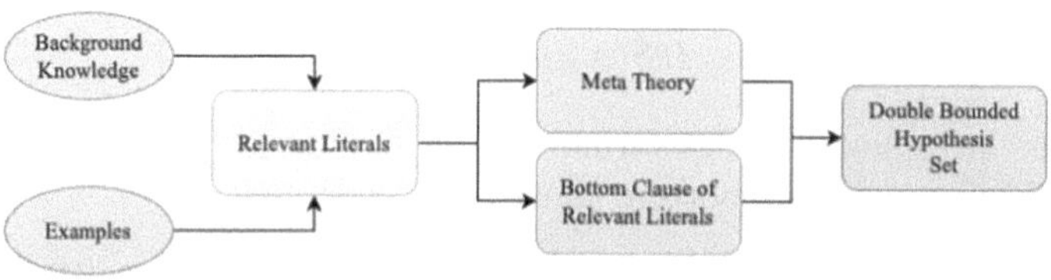

Fig. 2. Meta Inverse Entailment (MIE) framework. The process starts with background knowledge and examples from which relevant literals are extracted. These are used to construct the Bottom Clause of Relevant Literals (BCRL) and Meta Theory (MT), forming the lower and upper bounds of the hypothesis space, respectively. Together, they define a double bounded hypothesis set that supports flexible and automatic hypothesis generation, reducing reliance on manually defined language biases

Now, consider the problem specification of ILP. Suppose we are given a Horn program for a background knowledge B and a single Horn clause as an example E, then the hypothesis H should follow;

$$B \wedge H \models E \tag{1}$$

$$B \wedge H \text{ is consistent} \tag{2}$$

Equations 1 & 2 are equivalent to

$$B \wedge \neg E \models \neg H \tag{3}$$

$$B \not\models \neg H \tag{4}$$

Like inverse entailment, MIE generates some theories that are not derived from B alone but from $B \wedge \neg E$. Instead of the bottom clause, we consider a bridge formula CT. So, Eq. 3 can be written as

$$B \wedge \neg E \models CT \tag{5}$$

$$CT \models \neg H \tag{6}$$

Finally, Eq. 6 can also written as

$$H \models \neg CT \tag{7}$$

Also by Eqs. 4 and 6, we have

$$B \not\models CT \tag{8}$$

By Eq. 5, the set of clausal theories, CT, can be obtained by generating the double-bounded hypothesis set [18]. Further insight into the double-bounded hypothesis set can be obtained from the illustrative example presented in Example 1. Then

$$HS(\bot_{e,B}, \mathcal{M}_e) \models \neg CT \tag{9}$$

The candidate hypothesis (H) will be a subset of $HS(\bot_{e,B}, \mathcal{M}_e)$.

$$H = \{h | h \in HS(\bot_{e,B}, \mathcal{M}_e) \text{ and } h \models \neg CT\} \tag{10}$$

In Eq. 5, we introduce a bridge formula, a set of clausal theories as CT, which replaces the concept of the bottom clause.

Example 1. Let $\bot_{e,B}$ = eastbound(A) $\leftarrow$ has_car(A,B), short(B), closed(B), shape(B,rectangle), wheels(B,2). and $\mathcal{M}_e$ = {P(A) $\leftarrow$ Q(B,C), R(D)., P(A) $\leftarrow$ Q(B,C), R(D,E).}, then double bounded hypothesis set would be as follows;

$$HS(\bot_{e,B}, \mathcal{M}_e) = \begin{cases} eastbound(A) :- has\_car(A,B), short(B). \\ eastbound(A) :- has\_car(A,B), closed(B). \\ eastbound(A) :- has\_car(A,B), shape(B, rectangle). \\ eastbound(A) :- has\_car(A,B), wheels(B,2). \end{cases}$$

The MIE approach is implemented in a novel ILP engine named PyGol [21]. For a detailed description of both MIE and PyGol, the reader is referred to [18].

4 Experiments

We explore the potential of Meta Inverse Entailment for one-shot learning in autonomous robotic applications using positive-only learning. Our evaluation spans two experimental settings: (a) path planning in a maze, and (b) an obstacle avoidance robotics simulation[1]. In both environments, the physical constraints make negative examples redundant, as they are captured by the First-Order

[1] The code for this study is available on GitHub at https://github.com/hmlr-lab/One-Shot-Learning-autonomous-behavior.git.

background theory provided by the user. Specifically, the agent is allowed to take actions that do not result in crossing obstructions—walls in the maze and obstacles in the robotics simulation—ensuring that all movements are valid according to the physics of the environment.

In these settings, to learn how to navigate around obstacles, the agent only needs to master how to move between any two points while exploring all possible valid paths. This effectively demonstrates the agent's ability to generalise based solely on positive examples. If the physical laws governing the environment are not explicitly provided as background knowledge, negative examples, such as attempts to walk through a wall, would be required to define the boundaries of valid actions. Investigating how generalisation occurs with the presence of negative examples is an area left for future study.

4.1 Maze Solving

Mazes play a crucial role in the study of planning and navigation within artificial intelligence and robotics [8]. They provide a controlled and structured environment for testing algorithms that involve pathfinding, decision-making, and obstacle avoidance. Mazes challenge agents to find the most efficient route from a start point to a goal while navigating through various barriers and dead ends, making them ideal for evaluating an agent's ability to plan, learn, and adapt in complex environments [17]. The simplicity of a maze's design, combined with its potential complexity, allows researchers to study fundamental principles of planning and movement strategies that are applicable to real-world scenarios such as robotics, autonomous vehicles, and exploratory missions.

PyGol Setup. In our experiments, we first train the model within a simplified environment: an empty maze consisting of four passable "floor" tiles with no internal walls, as visualised in Fig. 1(a). This minimal setup is designed to reduce complexity and allow the model to focus on basic movement operations. We define four *move actions*—*move_down*/2, *move_up*/2, *move_left*/2, and *move_right*/2—which represent the agent's ability to move one step in each of the cardinal directions. PyGol uses these inputs to autonomously learn a generalised program for navigating the maze. The goal is for PyGol to identify all valid movement combinations and generalise a navigation strategy that can be applied in more complex mazes. During training, the model learns the movement operations as logical rules, which are then compiled into a formalised program, as shown in Table 1. By training in this controlled, empty maze environment, the model efficiently acquires the foundational rules necessary for path planning. These learned rules can later be transferred to more complex domains involving obstacles, walls, and varying maze sizes, enabling the agent to navigate and solve more intricate problems. This experimental setup demonstrates the ability of PyGol to generalise from minimal examples while building a robust movement strategy applicable across different scenarios. All source code required for setting up PyGol is available in the accompanying repository[2].

ExpGen-PPO Setup. For the Maze Solving experiment, we use the Maze environment from ProcGen Benchmark [3], a set of 16 computer game-like environments designed to test the "Zero-shot generalisation" ability of Reinforcement Learning (RL) systems. Each environment is divided into procedurally generated "levels" randomly assigned to training and testing sets. In the Maze environment, each level is one maze, with dimensions varying from 3×3 to 25×25, and with walls placed by Kruskal's algorithm [7]. Each maze has a start and end location, placed at random and an agent can navigate a maze by taking one of four discrete *move actions*: *moving up, down, left* or *right*. We modified the ProcGen environment[3], as it originally generates random mazes each time with a fixed total environment size. To make it compatible with the ILP approach, adjustments were made to ensure consistency and structure that aligns with ILP requirements. Figure 3 shows the original and modified ProcGen environments.

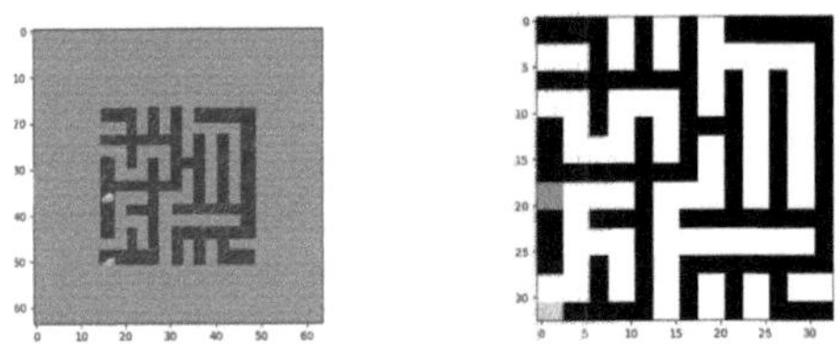

(a) (b)

Fig. 3. ProcGen maze environments: (3a) Original Environment (3b) Modified Environment

For the testing phase, we evaluated the performance of the two systems, PyGol and ExpGen-PPO, on a set of 15 mazes divided into three distinct sizes: 5×5, 10×10, and 15×15. Each size category contained five unique mazes, providing a comprehensive assessment of the systems' ability to generalise across varying complexity levels. The primary metric used for evaluation was the number of steps each system required to locate the exit in each test maze. This metric includes both forward steps and any backtracking actions taken during navigation.

The results of these tests are illustrated in Fig. 4, where the average number of steps is plotted for each system across the different maze sizes. Error bars are included to represent the standard error, providing insight into the variability of the performance across the test mazes. This evaluation allows us to compare the efficiency and consistency of both systems when solving mazes of increasing

[2] https://github.com/hmlr-lab/One-Shot-Learning-autonomous-behavior/tree/main/MIE.

[3] The modified version of ProcGen for fixed maze size is available at https://github.com/hmlr-lab/procgen.

complexity. We also reported the number of steps executed by a Prolog-based solver[4] that employs backtracking to find paths using the program generated by PyGol.

4.2 Obstacle Avoidance

We conducted a comparative analysis of PyGol and ExpGen-PPO for pathfinding and obstacle avoidance within a robotic simulation environment[5]. This simulator, developed in Python, models a survey mission in which an uncrewed surface vessel (USV) scans the bottom of a body of water using sonar to locate an object of interest. The simulation environment is depicted in Fig. 4a, which presents an example of a complete simulation run (or "episode") used during our experiments.

In this scenario, the USV operates in a river environment, where the dark central area represents the water, and the coloured regions above and below depict the riverbanks, which are impassable for the vessel. The USV itself is represented as a blue dot, while two red patches located to the south-west of the USV mark the areas that have been scanned by its sonar sensors. A narrow, unscanned strip, known as the "nadir," runs between the sonar's coverage areas. Users can interact with the simulator by clicking on a location in the window, directing the USV to travel to the selected coordinates. In the figure, the user has clicked on a point to the northeast of the USV's current position, and the simulation captures the vessel's movement towards that destination, as well as the regions that have already been scanned. This setup provides a controlled environment to test the pathfinding capabilities of the USV, including its ability to avoid obstacles while completing its mission.

Table 2. Obstacle avoidance training and test instances

Episode	Map	Variants	Islands	Distance
1 (training)	River	1	0	44.72
2 (testing)	River	6	1	210.95
3 (testing)	River	6	1	63.25
4 (testing)	Lake	6	2 or 3	174.93

PyGol Setup. In this experiment, similar to the maze-solving scenario, we manually define movement actions for the uncrewed surface vessel (USV). Instead of the four basic directional actions, we expand the agent's capability by introducing eight dyadic actions, enabling it to move in all eight compass directions:

[4] The code is available at https://github.com/hmlr-lab/IJCLR24_Planning_Datset/.
[5] The code for the simulator is available at https://github.com/aoat20/survey-simulation.

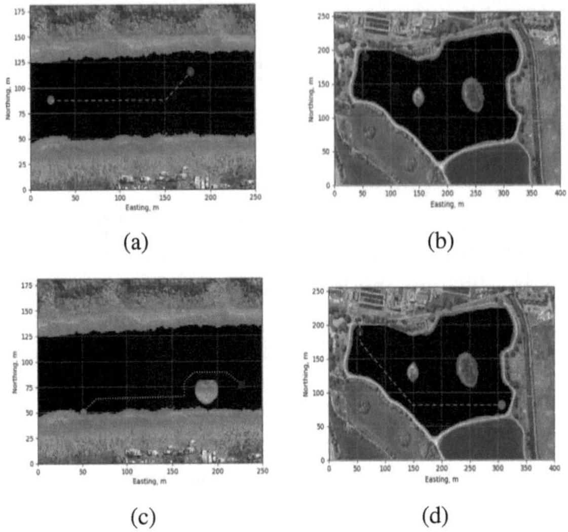

Fig. 4. Obstacle avoidance environments. 4a: Training on river map using random points. 4b: Lake map training. 4c & 4d: Paths learned by PyGol. White dots indicate the moved path, the red dot marking the starting position and the blue dot marking the ending position. (Color figure online)

$North$, $North - East$, $East$, $South - East$, $South$, $South - West$, $West$, and $North - West$. These expanded movement options allow for more flexible and precise navigation through the environment, particularly in avoiding obstacles and efficiently reaching the destination.

To complement the agent's movement capabilities, we have developed a Breadth-First Search (BFS) algorithm to find the shortest path in the given environment. The BFS algorithm systematically explores all possible paths from the USV's starting position, ensuring that the shortest and most optimal route is identified. This approach is particularly effective in environments where obstacles such as islands or other impassable areas are present, as it guarantees that the agent will always take the most efficient path to avoid these barriers while reaching the target destination. The use of BFS in this context not only ensures path efficiency but also improves overall performance in scenarios involving complex navigation tasks.

In this approach, we observed that using BFS during training often led to sub-optimal generalisation, as it typically produces a single shortest path—especially in obstacle-free environments—limiting the exposure to diverse action moves (Fig. 4a). To overcome this, we introduce *K-path learning*, which aims to discover *K distinct near-optimal paths* during training. This diversification helps ensure that the learned program captures a comprehensive range of valid actions. As shown in Table 3, varying K enriches the learned rules and improves both the completeness and robustness of the model. We further enhance realism through two constraints: a *passability constraint*, which prevents the USV from entering impassable regions like land or riverbanks, and a *directionality constraint*, which ensures each action reduces the Euclidean distance to the target.

We design four simulation episodes—one for training and three for testing—each featuring unique start and goal positions. Three episodes are set in a river environment and one in a lake, as illustrated in Fig. 4. To introduce complexity, we manually add one or two islands to each map; the lake map, which already contains two, is augmented with a third island. This setup results in one training scenario and 18 test variations, with differences in obstacle layout and goal distance, providing a robust evaluation of the learned model's generalisation and planning capabilities.

The USV cannot navigate through islands, so the agent must find an alternative path. Table 2 outlines the training and testing cases, where the "Distance" column lists the Euclidean distance between the initial and destination coordinates. To train PyGol, we use a single training example—a ground atom of the dyadic predicate $move/2$—with input and output state derived from the initial and final positions in Episode 1 from Table 1.

ExpGen-PPO Setup. Generalisation is a common challenge in reinforcement learning systems, where agents often fail to adapt to unseen environments. ExpGen-PPO is a state-of-the-art deep reinforcement learning framework specifically designed to enhance generalisation across a variety of tasks. It achieves this by incorporating explicit experience diversification and robust policy optimisation strategies. We train ExpGen-PPO using the OpenAI Gym toolkit for RL research [1]. The river map image, without any islands, is transformed into a binary matrix and incorporated into a Gym setting. The ExpGen-PPO training function creates 100 random destinations, equivalent to 100 training instances. We set the agent's reward to 10 for reaching the coordinates of an instance's destination, –1 for moving on impassable terrain, 1 for moving towards a training instance's destination and 0 for moving away from the destination. At test time, we set the starting position and destination to each of the 18 test instances and transform the lake image into a binary matrix for the 6 testing instances in the lake map.

Table 3. Program learned by PyGol for different values of K

$move(A, B) : -move\_east(A, B).$
$move(A, B) : -move\_east(A, C), move(C, B).$
$move(A, B) : -move\_south\_east(A, B).$
$move(A, B) : -move\_south\_east(A, C), move(C, B).$

(a) PyGol Program (K=1)

$move(A, B) : -move\_east(A, B).$
$move(A, B) : -move\_east(A, C), move(C, B).$
$move(A, B) : -move\_south\_east(A, B).$
$move(A, B) : -move\_south\_east(A, C), move(C, B).$
$move(A, B) : -move\_west(A, B).$
$move(A, B) : -move\_west(A, C), move(C, B).$
$move(A, B) : -move\_south(A, B).$
$move(A, B) : -move\_south(A, C), move(C, B).$

(b) PyGol Program (K=2)

We test PyGol and ExpGen-PPO on each of our 18 test instances. We measure the number of steps taken to find a path from the starting position to the destination of each episode, including backtracking steps. Figure 5b illustrates the results. The error bars show standard error.

5 Results and Discussion

The results, as illustrated in the Figs. 5a and 5b, compare the performance of PyGol and ExpGen-PPO across different maze sizes and simulation episodes. We additionally recorded the step count of a Prolog-based solver, which utilises backtracking to identify paths based on the program developed by PyGol. In Fig. 5a, representing the maze-solving experiment, PyGol demonstrates superior efficiency across all maze sizes, with significantly fewer moves required to solve the maze than ExpGen-PPO. As the maze size increases, the performance of ExpGen-PPO worsens, with a large increase in the number of moves, while PyGol remains relatively consistent, particularly in the 10×10 and 15×15 mazes. Moreover, the Prolog solver was able to solve the mazes in a relatively lower number of steps compared to ExpGen-PPO.

In Fig. 5b, which shows performance in the obstacle avoidance simulation, the trend continues. PyGol consistently outperforms ExpGen-PPO in all episodes, especially in more complex environments (Episode 3 and Episode 4). The number of moves required for ExpGen-PPO escalates with the complexity of the environment, whereas PyGol maintains (using BFS and Prolog solver)a low and stable move count, indicating its effectiveness in handling both simpler and more challenging map scenarios.

PyGol, from a single example, learns a recursive program capable of implementing a general path-finding strategy. This learned program enables the agent to navigate to any destination east of its starting position, as demonstrated in the training episode (Episode 1). By combining this general path-finding capability with the passability constraints provided by the user, PyGol efficiently guides the robot around obstacles to reach its destinations. The learned obstacle avoidance program is detailed in Table 4.

Both PyGol and ExpGen-PPO successfully solved all test instances in both the obstacle avoidance and maze-solving domains. However, a key distinction lies in their approaches when encountering unfamiliar environments. ExpGen-PPO, when its trained policy proves insufficient, resorts to a costly exploration-based strategy, significantly increasing the time required to solve most test instances. In contrast, PyGol, with its learned recursive path-finding program, efficiently navigates unseen environments.

Table 4. The final program learned by PyGol from obstacle avoidance (K=4)

$$move(A,B) : -move\_east(A,B).$$
$$move(A,B) : -move\_east(A,C), move(C,B).$$
$$move(A,B) : -move\_south\_east(A,B).$$
$$move(A,B) : -move\_south\_east(A,C), move(C,B).$$
$$move(A,B) : -move\_west(A,B).$$
$$move(A,B) : -move\_west(A,C), move(C,B).$$
$$move(A,B) : -move\_north\_west(A,B).$$
$$move(A,B) : -move\_north\_west(A,C), move(C,B).$$
$$move(A,B) : -move\_south(A,B).$$
$$move(A,B) : -move\_south(A,C), move(C,B).$$
$$move(A,B) : -move\_south\_west(A,B).$$
$$move(A,B) : -move\_south\_west(A,C), move(C,B).$$
$$move(A,B) : -move\_north(A,B).$$
$$move(A,B) : -move\_north(A,C), move(C,B).$$
$$move(A,B) : -move\_north\_east(A,B).$$
$$move(A,B) : -move\_north\_east(A,C), move(C,B).$$

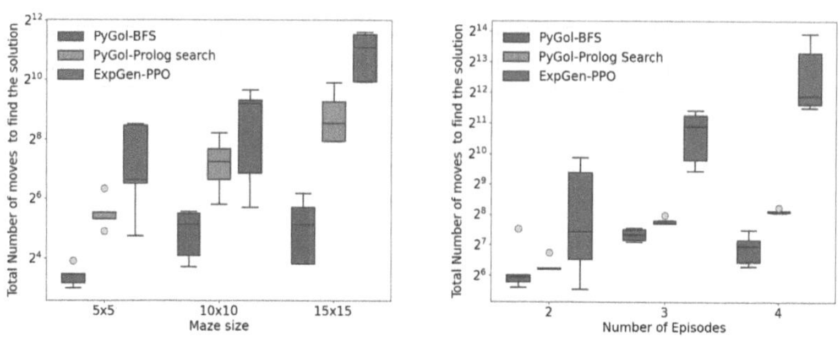

(a) (b)

Fig. 5. Maze Solving (a) and Obstacle Avoidance (b) performance.

The maze-solving results further emphasise this difference. As the maze size increased, PyGol consistently outperformed ExpGen-PPO by requiring significantly fewer moves to reach the goal. ExpGen-PPO's reliance on exploration led to a considerable increase in the number of moves, particularly in larger and more complex mazes. This raises questions about the generalisability and robustness of policies trained via reinforcement learning methods like ExpGen-PPO, especially when applied to environments beyond those encountered during training. PyGol's ability to generalise from minimal training examples suggests a more scalable and adaptable solution for both obstacle avoidance and maze-solving tasks in dynamic and novel environments.

6 Conclusions

This study has demonstrated the efficacy of Meta Inverse Entailment (MIL) as a powerful framework for learning generalised behaviours from minimal data. Through both theoretical validation and empirical evaluation, we introduced and evaluated PyGol, a novel MIE-based system, compared to the state-of-the-art Deep Reinforcement Learning (Deep-RL) approach, ExpGen-PPO. We applied these systems to two path-finding tasks: one in a simplified maze environment and another in a robotic simulation. Our results reveal that PyGol can efficiently learn complex behaviours from a single training example in simplified environments, such as an empty maze or a river simulation, and successfully generalise this knowledge to more complex test environments, including mazes with random dimensions and walls, as well as river and lake simulations containing obstacles like islands.

Although ExpGen-PPO demonstrated the ability to generalise behaviour, it required more extensive and task-specific training, such as exposure to additional maze levels or randomly varied destinations, to achieve similar performance to PyGol. The key advantage of PyGol lies in its capacity to generalise robustly from minimal input, reducing the need for exhaustive training across diverse scenarios.

These findings underscore the potential of MIE for applications where efficient learning from sparse data is critical. PyGol's performance highlights the adaptability and scalability of ILP approaches for solving complex tasks, making it a valuable tool for domains that involve dynamic, novel, or resource-constrained environments. This work contributes to advancing the field of machine learning by offering a more efficient alternative to data-intensive methods for path-finding and similar tasks.

Acknowledgement. The authors acknowledge the EPSRC grant on Human-machine learning of ambiguities to support safe, effective, and legal decision making (EP/X030156/1). ATN also acknowledges the EPSRC Network Plus grant on Human-Like Computing (HLC).

A Formal Structures and Semantics in First-Order Logic

A *First-Order Logic (FOL)* framework is defined using an alphabet composed of predicate symbols ($\mathcal{P}$), function symbols ($\mathcal{F}$), constants ($\mathcal{C}$), variables ($\mathcal{V}$), logical connectives ($\neg, \wedge, \vee, \rightarrow, \leftrightarrow$), quantifiers ($\forall, \exists$), and syntactic elements like parentheses and commas. Constants are function symbols of arity zero. Terms are built inductively: variables and constants are terms; if a function symbol f of arity n is applied to n terms $t_1, \ldots, t_n$, then $f(t_1, \ldots, t_n)$ is also a term. Atoms are expressions of the form $P(t_1, \ldots, t_m)$ where P is a predicate symbol of arity m and t_i are terms. Formulae can be constructed by combining atoms using logical connectives and quantifiers. A formula with no variables is called a ground formula. In the context of *logic programming*, an atom is treated as a basic assertion, while its negation forms a negative literal. A literal is thus either positive or negative. A clause is a finite disjunction of such literals, and it becomes a *Horn clause* if it contains at most one positive literal. When exactly one positive literal is present, the clause is referred to as a *definite clause*; otherwise, it serves as a goal clause. Logic programs are typically formed as conjunctions of definite clauses. These are commonly written in implication form, where the head (the positive literal) appears on the left and the body (a conjunction of conditions) on the right, e.g., $H \leftarrow B_1, B_2, \ldots, B_n$.

Definition 5 ***(Ordered clause).*** *An ordered clause $\overrightarrow{C}$ is a sequence of literals $L_1, L_2, .., L_n$ and denoted by $\overrightarrow{C} = L_1 \vee L_2 \vee .. \vee L_n$. The set of literals in $\overrightarrow{C}$ is denoted by C.*

Definition 6 ***(Sequential subsumption).*** *Let $\overrightarrow{C} = M_1 \vee M_2 \vee .. \vee M_m$ and $\overrightarrow{D} = N_1 \vee N_2 \vee .. \vee N_m$ be ordered clauses. $\overrightarrow{C}$ is said to be sequentially subsumes $\overrightarrow{D}$, denoted by $\overrightarrow{C} \succeq_s \overrightarrow{D}$, if there exists a substitution θ such that $\overrightarrow{C}\theta$ is a subsequence of $\overrightarrow{D}$. $\overrightarrow{C}$ and $\overrightarrow{D}$ are equivalent with respect to sequential subsumption denoted by $\overrightarrow{C} \sim_s \overrightarrow{D}$ if $\overrightarrow{C} \succeq_s \overrightarrow{D}$ and $\overrightarrow{D} \succeq_s \overrightarrow{S}$.*

B Extra Definitions and Examples Related to Meta Inverse Entailment

Definition 7 ***(Related literals).*** *Let $L_1 = P(s_1, s_2, \cdots, s_n)$ and $L_2 = Q(t_1, t_2, \cdots, t_m)$ be two ground literals and $\mathcal{K}$ be a set of user-defined constants then L_1 and L_2 are related literals if they have any common terms other than terms in $\mathcal{K}$.*

$\mathcal{K}$ represents a unique set of terms crucial for evaluating the relationship between two literals. While two literals might share a user-defined constant, this doesn't imply a conceptual connection (as illustrated in Example 2).

Example 2. Let $\mathcal{K}$ = {rectangle, triangle, 1} and L=

$$\begin{Bmatrix} L_1 = has\_car(train_1, car_1), \\ L_2 = has\_car(train_1, car_2), \\ L_3 = short(car_1), \\ L_4 = load(car_1, triangle), \\ L_5 = load(car_2, triangle), \end{Bmatrix}$$

Then, $\langle L_1, L_2 \rangle$ s a pair of related literals as they share the common term $train_1$ which is not in $\mathcal{K}$. Similarly, $\langle L_1, L_3 \rangle$, $\langle L_1, L_4 \rangle$ and $\langle L_3, L_4 \rangle$ are related literals as they share the term car_1 which is also not in $\mathcal{K}$. In contrast, $\langle L_4, L_5 \rangle$ are not related literals, even though they share the term *triangle*, as this term is present in $\mathcal{K}$.

Definition 8. ***(Head-connectedness*** *[13]**).*** *A definite ordered clause $h \leftarrow b_1, b_2, ..., b_n$ is said to be head-connected if and only if each body atom b_j contains at least one variable found either in h or in a body atom b_i, where $1 \leq i < j$.*

References

1. Brockman, G., et al.: Openai gym (2016)
2. Brown, T., Mann, B., et. al., R.: Language models are few-shot learners. In: Larochelle, H., Ranzato, M., Hadsell, R., Balcan, M., Lin, H. (eds.) Advances in Neural Information Processing Systems, vol. 33, pp. 1877–1901. Curran Associates, Inc. (2020)
3. Cobbe, K., Hesse, C., Hilton, J., Schulman, J.: Leveraging procedural generation to benchmark Reinforcement Learning. arXiv preprint arXiv:1912.01588 (2019)
4. Finn, C., Abbeel, P., Levine, S.: Model-agnostic meta-learning for fast adaptation of deep networks. In: Proceedings of the 34th International Conference on Machine Learning, ICML'17, vol. 70, pp. 1126–1135. JMLR.org (2017)
5. Kirk, R., Zhang, A., Grefenstette, E., Rocktäschel, T.: A survey of zero-shot generalisation in Deep Reinforcement Learning. J. Artif. Intell. Res. **76**, 201–264 (2023)
6. Koch, G., Zemel, R., Salakhutdinov, R., et al.: Siamese neural networks for one-shot image recognition. In: ICML Deep Learning Workshop, Lille, vol. 2:1, pp. 1–30 (2015)
7. Kruskal, J.B.: On the shortest spanning subtree of a graph and the Traveling Salesman Problem. Proc. Am. Math. Soc. **7**, 48–50 (1956)
8. LaValle, S.M.: Planning Algorithms. Cambridge university press, Cambridge (2006)
9. Muggleton, S.H.: Hypothesizing an algorithm from one example: the role of specificity. Phil. Trans. R. Soc. A: Math. Phys. Eng. Sci. **381**(2251), 20220046 (2023)
10. Muggleton, S.: Inverse entailment and Progol. N. Gener. Comput. **13**(3), 245–286 (1995)
11. Muggleton, S., Dai, W.Z., Sammut, C., Tamaddoni-Nezhad, A., Wen, J., Zhou, Z.H.: Meta-interpretive learning from noisy images. Mach. Learn. **107**(7), 1097–1118 (2018)
12. Muggleton, S., Lin, D., Pahlavi, N., Tamaddoni-Nezhad, A.: Meta-interpretive learning: application to grammatical inference. Mach. Learn. **94**(1), 25–49 (2014). https://github.com/metagol/metagol
13. Muggleton, S., Tamaddoni-Nezhad, A.: QG/GA: a stochastic search for progol. In: Inductive Logic Programming: 16th International Conference, ILP 2006, Santiago de Compostela, Spain, 24–27 August 2006, Revised Selected Papers, vol. 16. pp. 37–39. Springer, Heidelberg(2007). https://doi.org/10.1007/s10994-007-5029-3
14. Muggleton, S.H.: Learning from positive data. In: Inductive Logic Programming Workshop (1996). https://api.semanticscholar.org/CorpusID:18451163
15. Nienhuys-Cheng, S.-H., de Wolf, R.: Foundations of Inductive Logic Programming. LNCS, vol. 1228. Springer, Heidelberg (1997). https://doi.org/10.1007/3-540-62927-0
16. Snell, J., Swersky, K., Zemel, R.: Prototypical networks for few-shot learning. In: Advances in Neural Information Processing Systems, vol. 30. Curran Associates, Inc. (2017)
17. Thrun, S., Burgard, W., Fox, D.: Probabilistic robotics (massachusetts) (2005)
18. Varghese, D.: Explainable and Efficient Machine Learning using Meta Inverse Entailment. Ph.D. thesis, University of Surrey (2024)
19. Varghese, D., Barroso-Bergada, D., Bohan, D.A., Tamaddoni-Nezhad, A.: Efficient abductive learning of microbial interactions using meta inverse entailment. In Proceedings of the 31st International Conference on ILP (2022)

20. Varghese, D., Bauer, R., Baxter-Beard, D., Muggleton, S., Tamaddoni-Nezhad, A.: Human-like rule learning from images using one-shot hypothesis derivation. In: Inductive Logic Programming, pp. 234–250. Springer, Cham (2022). https://doi.org/10.1007/978-3-030-97454-1_17
21. Varghese, D., Tamaddoni-Nezhad, A.: PyGol (2022). https://github.com/PyGol/
22. Zisselman, E., Lavie, I., Soudry, D., Tamar, A.: Explore to generalize in zero-shot RL (2024)

Learning from Interpretation Transition with Unknowns

Tony Ribeiro[1,3,4](✉), Maxime Folschette[2], Morgan Magnin[1,3], Kotaro Okazaki[4], Kuo-Yen Lo[4], Antoine Roquilly[5,6], Jérémie Poschmann[6], and Katsumi Inoue[1,3]

[1] Centrale Nantes, CNRS, Laboratoire des Sciences du Numérique de Nantes, LS2N, UMR 6004, 44000 Nantes, France
tony.ribeiro@ls2n.fr

[2] Univ. Lille, CNRS, Centrale Lille, UMR 9189 CRIStAL, 59000 Lille, France

[3] National Institute of Informatics, 2-1-2 Hitotsubashi, Chiyoda-ku, Tokyo 101-8430, Japan

[4] SONAR Inc., 8-16-6, Chuo-Ku, Ginza, Tokyo 104-0061, Japan

[5] Nantes Université, CHU Nantes, INSERM, Anesthesie Réanimation, 44000 Nantes, France

[6] Nantes Université, CHU Nantes, Center for Research in Transplantation and Translational Immunology, UMR 1064, ITUN2, 44000 Nantes, France

Abstract. One major challenge when learning dynamical models from actual time series data consists in tackling partial data. Learning from interpretation transition (LFIT) automatically constructs a model of the dynamics of a system from the observation of its state transitions. In this paper, we extend the LFIT framework to learn from transitions between partial states where some variable values are unknown. By modeling the unknown, we achieve an overestimation of the real system regarding both its dynamics and variables interactions. We show through theoretical results the correctness of our approaches and its effectiveness through an experimental evaluation on benchmarks from biological literature.

Keywords: XAI · logical modeling · uncertainty · dynamic systems

1 Introduction

One major challenge when learning dynamical models from actual time series data consists in tackling partial data. For example, in Systems Biology, when trying to contribute to the identification of biological markers critical to the development of hospital-acquired pneumonia [10], a major challenge for modelers relies in overcoming the absence of some data in existing cohorts. Some data may be missing, because some variables were not accessible by experimental means (or were simply not considered of interest at the time of collecting data on real cohorts). Learning from partial data implies to extend existing learning approaches to data with unknowns among the state variables. This challenge

W.-Z. Dai (Ed.): ILP 2024, LNAI 16059, pp. 66–85, 2026.
https://doi.org/10.1007/978-3-032-09087-4_5

relates to a well-known problem in the field of discrete-event systems, which is opacity [8]. Since two decades, opacity has raised much interest in cryptography [9] and model-checking [1,6]. In these contexts, systems are analyzed to ensure that certain states or sequences of states remain hidden or protected from an external agent. For example, this implies that a system's secret state cannot be inferred by observing its behavior. When dealing with models of biological networks, opacity is relevant to understand how certain genes or pathways can be hidden from experimental observations. Despite being key for making a bridge between logical approaches and real-life data, opacity has been the subject of very few studies in the field of Boolean networks [15] and even less in the field of logic programs.

While the possibility of learning from transitions of partial interpretations has been briefly illustrated in [5], there has been neither details about its formal semantics (in particular for a multi-valued setting) nor implemented systems in the literature. Research regarding learning from incomplete transitions of (complete but possibly noisy) interpretations, in the context of neurosymbolic learning [3,4,12–14] exists, but their settings are not the same as learning from transitions of partial interpretations. In this paper, we aim to bring a first milestone to such a topic, opening the way to various applications hereafter. To achieve this goal, we propose to extend the Learning From Interpretation Transition (LFIT) framework [5,16], an inductive logic programming paradigm that automatically builds a model of the dynamics of a system from the observation of its state-transitions.

Figure 1 illustrates the general LFIT learning process. Given some raw data, like time-series of gene expression, a discretization of those data in the form of state transitions is assumed. From those state transitions, according to the semantics of the system dynamics, several inference algorithms modeling the system as a logic program have been proposed. In this paper, we extend the LFIT framework to learn from transitions between partial states where some variable values are unknown. We propose a formal modeling for learning from transitions of partial multi-valued interpretations, to realize the framework to incorporate into the General Usage LFIT Algorithm (GULA) [16]. By modeling the unknown, we achieve an overestimation of the real system regarding both its dynamics and variables interactions. We show through theoretical results the correctness of our approaches and its effectiveness through an experimental evaluation on benchmarks from biological literature.

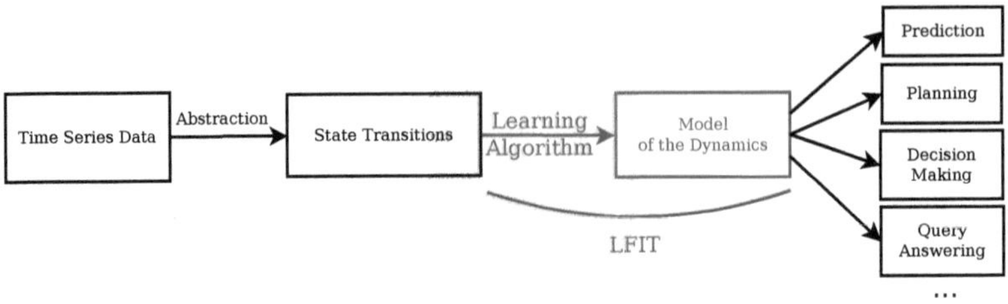

Fig. 1. Assuming a discretization of time series data of a system as state transitions, we propose a method to automatically model the system dynamics

2 Dynamical Multi-valued Logic Program

In this section, the concepts necessary to understand the modeling we propose in this paper are formalized. Let $\mathcal{V} = \{\mathrm{v}_1, \cdots, \mathrm{v}_n\}$ be a finite set of $n \in \mathbb{N}$ variables, $\mathcal{V}al$ the set in which variables take their values and $\mathsf{dom} : \mathcal{V} \to \{d \in \wp(\mathcal{V}al) \mid |d| \geq 2\}$ a function associating a domain (with at least two values) to each variable, with $\wp$ the power set. The atoms of multi-valued logic ($\mathcal{M}$VL) are of the form v^{val} where $\mathrm{v} \in \mathcal{V}$ and $val \in \mathsf{dom}(\mathrm{v})$. The set of such atoms is denoted by $\mathcal{A} = \{\mathrm{v}^{val} \in \mathcal{V} \times \mathcal{V}al \mid val \in \mathsf{dom}(\mathrm{v})\}$. Let $\mathcal{F}$ and $\mathcal{T}$ be a partition of $\mathcal{V}$, that is: $\mathcal{V} = \mathcal{F} \cup \mathcal{T}$ and $\mathcal{F} \cap \mathcal{T} = \emptyset$. $\mathcal{F}$ is called the set of feature variables, which values represent the state of the system at the previous time step $(t-1)$, and $\mathcal{T}$ is called the set of target variables, which values represent the state of the system at the current time step (t). A $\mathcal{M}$VL rule R is defined by:

$$R \quad = \quad \mathrm{v}_0^{val_0} \leftarrow \mathrm{v}_1^{val_1} \wedge \cdots \wedge \mathrm{v}_m^{val_m}$$

where $m \in \mathbb{N}$, and $\forall i \in [\![0;m]\!], \mathrm{v}_i^{val_i} \in \mathcal{A}$; furthermore, every variable is mentioned at most once in the right-hand part: $\forall j,k \in [\![1;m]\!], j \neq k \Rightarrow \mathrm{v}_j \neq \mathrm{v}_k$. The rule R has the following meaning: the variable v_0 can take the value val_0 in the next dynamical step if for each $i \in [\![1;m]\!]$, variable v_i has value val_i in the current dynamical step. The atom on the left side of the arrow is called the head of R, denoted $\mathrm{head}(R) := \mathrm{v}_0^{val_0}$, and is made of a target variable: $\mathrm{v}_0 \in \mathcal{T}$. The notation $\mathrm{var}(\mathrm{head}(R)) := \mathrm{v}_0$ denotes the variable that occurs in $\mathrm{head}(R)$. The conjunction on the right-hand side of the arrow is called the body of R, written $\mathrm{body}(R)$, and all variables in the body are feature variables: $\forall i \in [\![1;m]\!], \mathrm{v}_i \in \mathcal{F}$. In the following, the body of a rule is assimilated to the set $\{\mathrm{v}_1^{val_1}, \cdots, \mathrm{v}_m^{val_m}\}$; we thus use set operations such as $\in$ and $\cap$ on it, and we denote $\emptyset$ an empty body. A dynamical multi-valued logic program ($\mathcal{DM}$VLP) is a set of $\mathcal{M}$VL rules.

Definition 1 (Rule Domination). *Let R_1, R_2 be $\mathcal{M}$VL rules. R_1 dominates R_2, written $R_1 \geq R_2$ if* $\mathrm{head}(R_1) = \mathrm{head}(R_2)$ *and* $\mathrm{body}(R_1) \subseteq \mathrm{body}(R_2)$.

The dynamical system we want to learn the rules of, is represented by a succession of states as formally given by Definition 2. We also define the "compatibility" of a rule with a state in Definition 5, and with a transition in Definition 6.

Definition 2 (Discrete state). *A complete discrete state s on a set of variables $\mathcal{X}$ is a function from $\mathcal{X}$ to* $\mathsf{dom}(\mathrm{v})$*. It can be equivalently represented by the set of atoms* $\{\mathrm{v}^{s(\mathrm{v})} \mid \mathrm{v} \in \mathcal{X}\}$ *and thus we can use classical set operations on it. If s is a complete discrete state, s' is a partial discrete state iff $s' \subsetneq s$. We write $\mathcal{S}^{\mathcal{X}}$ to denote the set of all (partial or complete) discrete states on $\mathcal{X}$.*

Often, $\mathcal{X} \in \{\mathcal{F}, \mathcal{T}\}$. Moreover, we note $\mathrm{vars}(s) = \{\mathrm{v} \in \mathcal{X} \mid \exists val \in \mathsf{dom}(\mathrm{v}), \mathrm{v}^{val} \in s\}$ the set of variables that appear in a discrete state.

Example 1. Let $\mathcal{X} = \{a, b, c\}, dom(a) = dom(b) = \{0, 1\}$ and $dom(c) = \{0, 1, 2\}$.

- $\emptyset$ is a partial state, all variables value is unknown.
- $\{a^0\}$ is a partial state, both b and c value is unknown.
- $\{a^1, b^1\}$ is a partial state, c value is unknown.
- $\{a^1, b^0, c^2\}$ is a complete state, all variable have a value.
- $\{a^0, a^1, c^0\}$ is not a discrete state, a has multiple values.
- $\{a^0, b^0, c^0, c^2\}$ is not a discrete state, c has multiple values.

Definition 3 (States with Masking). *We call state with masking a couple $s = (s_p, s_c) \in \mathcal{S}^{\mathcal{X}} \times \mathcal{S}^{\mathcal{X}}$ so that s_c is complete and s_p is partial so that $s_p \subsetneq s_c$. We denote $\mathcal{S}_m^{\mathcal{X}}$ the set of all states with masking. Moreover, we define:* $\mathsf{observed}(s) = s_p$ *and* $\mathsf{actual}(s) = s_c$ *and we extend these notations to a pair of states and a set of states:* $\mathsf{observed}((s, s')) = (\mathsf{observed}(s), \mathsf{observed}(s'))$ *and* $\mathsf{actual}((s, s')) = (\mathsf{actual}(s), \mathsf{actual}(s'))$*;* $\mathsf{observed}(S) = \{\mathsf{observed}(s) \mid s \in S\}$ *and* $\mathsf{actual}(S) = \{\mathsf{actual}(s) \mid s \in S\}$.

In other words, the state with masking $s = (s_p, s_c)$ represents a state that we can choose to observe as the result of an partial/imperfect observation, or as the ground truth. In particular, a couple of (complete, partial or with masking) discrete states $(s, s') \in \mathcal{S}^{\mathcal{F}} \times \mathcal{S}^{\mathcal{T}}$ is called a transition.

In practice, the ground truth is not accessible, but interesting knowledge about the system dynamics could still be derived from the partial observation. Providing some interesting guaranties over these derived dynamics is the goal of the following formalization. To simplify the graphical representation of states, each discrete state will be depicted by a sequence of numbers corresponding to the value of each variable. For instance, the complete state $\{a^0, b^0, c^0\}$ is represented by the sequence 000, while $\{a^1, b^0, c^0\}$ is represented as 100, and $\{a^1, b^1, c^1\}$ as 111. Unknown values will be symbolized by '?', allowing us to see at a glance which variables are unknown in each state. For example, the state $\{a^0\}$ is represented as 0??, and $\{c^1\}$ as ??1. The transition graphs in Fig. 2 shows an illustration of a set T of state transitions involving three boolean variables, highlighting both complete and partial states. On the left the observed state transitions $\mathsf{observed}(T)$ with some unknown values and on the right the corresponding $\mathsf{actual}(T)$ with no unknown.

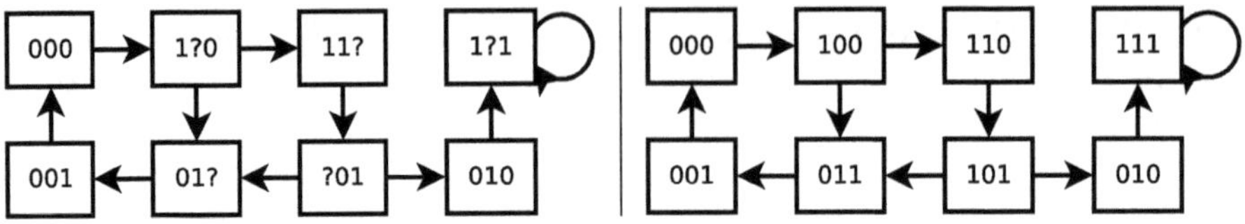

Fig. 2. Observed state transitions of a system with three boolean variables: discrete states represented by labeled boxes, arrows show transitions, and '?' denotes unknown values (left); the actual complete hidden state transitions (right)

Definition 4 (State uncertain equality). *Let $s, s' \in \mathcal{S}^{\mathcal{X}}$ be discrete states. The two states are* uncertain equal, *denoted $s \stackrel{\mathcal{X}}{\overset{\frown}{=}} s'$ when*

$$\forall \mathrm{v}^{val} \in s, \forall \mathrm{w}^{val'} \in s', \mathrm{v} = \mathrm{w} \implies val = val'$$

States with different values on the same variable cannot be the same since a variable has only one value at a time. But states without such conflicting atoms can potentially be the same state, missing values causing the uncertainty. Figure 3 show examples of equality relationship under unknown using graphical representation of discrete state.

Example 2. Let $\mathcal{X} = \{a, b, c\}, dom(a) = dom(b) = \{0, 1\}$ and $dom(c) = \{0, 1, 2\}$.

- $\{a^0, b^0, c^0\} \stackrel{\mathcal{X}}{=} \{a^0, b^0, c^0\}$, exactly the same state, usual equality.
- $\{a^0, b^0, c^0\} \stackrel{\mathcal{X}}{\neq} \{a^0, b^1, c^0\}$, one difference on b value, usual inequality.
- $\{a^0, b^0\} \stackrel{\mathcal{X}}{\overset{\frown}{=}} \{a^0, b^0, c^0\}$, c is unknown in first state, it could be c^0 or c^1.
- $\{a^0, b^0\} \stackrel{\mathcal{X}}{\overset{\frown}{\neq}} \{a^0, b^0\}$, c is unknown in both, can be same or different value.
- $\{a^0, b^0\} \stackrel{\mathcal{X}}{\neq} \{a^1, b^0\}$, a is different, cannot be the same hidden state.
- $\{a^0, b^1\} \stackrel{\mathcal{X}}{\overset{\frown}{=}} \{b^1, c^1\}$, c is unknown in first state and a is unknown in second state, no different value observed thus could be the same hidden state.

Property 1. Let $s1, s2$ be two discrete states with masking. From Definition 4 the following holds:

- $\mathsf{actual}(s1) \stackrel{\mathcal{X}}{=} \mathsf{actual}(s2) \implies \mathsf{observed}(s1) \stackrel{\mathcal{X}}{\overset{\frown}{=}} \mathsf{observed}(s2)$
  - but $\mathsf{observed}(s1) \stackrel{\mathcal{X}}{\overset{\frown}{=}} \mathsf{observed}(s2) \not\Leftarrow\!\!\!\Rightarrow \mathsf{actual}(s1) \stackrel{\mathcal{X}}{=} \mathsf{actual}(s2)$
- $\mathsf{observed}(s1) \stackrel{\mathcal{X}}{\not\overset{\frown}{=}} \mathsf{observed}(s2) \implies \mathsf{actual}(s1) \stackrel{\mathcal{X}}{\neq} \mathsf{actual}(s2)$
  - but $\mathsf{actual}(s1) \stackrel{\mathcal{X}}{\neq} \mathsf{actual}(s2) \not\Leftarrow\!\!\!\Rightarrow \mathsf{observed}(s1) \stackrel{\mathcal{X}}{\not\overset{\frown}{=}} \mathsf{observed}(s2)$

When two complete states are identical, their partial states are at least uncertain equal, as the introduction of unknowns cannot create differences. But observed states being uncertain equal does not mean that the actual states are

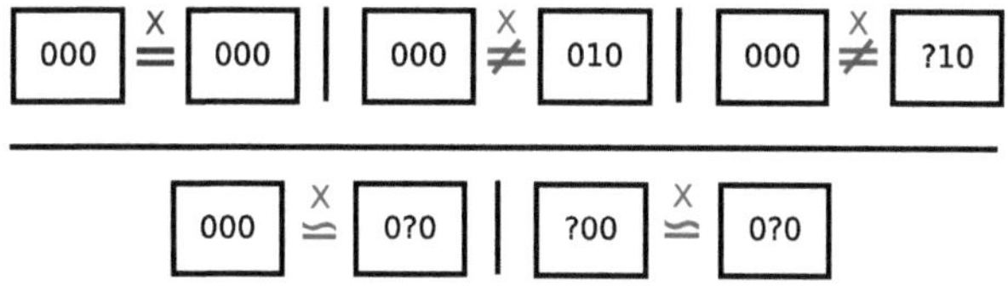

Fig. 3. Illustration of the concept of uncertain equality between discrete states. 000 and 000 are identical while 000 and 010 differ due to the second variable's value. Same for 000 and ?10, the unknown value does not matter here. States 000 and 0?0 are uncertain equal, as the '?' could be 0. Similarly, ?00 and 0?0 may represent the same state if both '?' are actually hiding 0.

certain equal since the unknown part can hide an actual difference. On the other hand, partial state inequality always corresponds to actual state inequality, because differences in observed variables are still present in the actual state. Once again, the reciprocal is not true since the difference between two complete states can be hidden by the masking.

Definition 5 (Rule-state matching). *Let $s \in \mathcal{S}^{\mathcal{F}}$. The $\mathcal{M}$VL rule R matches s, written $R \sqcap s$, if* $\text{body}(R) \subseteq s$.

The final program we want to learn should both: (1) match the observations in a complete (all transitions are learned) and correct (no spurious transition) way; (2) represent only minimal necessary interactions (no overly-complex rules). Regarding the actual hidden observations, the optimal program should concurrently: (1) match them all, tolerating spurious transitions due to unknown values; (2) ensure that all original minimal rules are dominated, and none exceeds their complexity, allowing spurious rules only when unknowns render them indistinguishable from true optimal ones. The idea behind this is that when learning from observations that include unknowns, the obtained program should be an over-approximation of the behaviors allowed by the actual system. Moreover, revealing the real value of some variables (that is, adding new observations that are less hidden than the original), we should be able to iterate the learning part and get closer to the optimal program of the actual transitions. The following definitions formalize these desired properties.

Definition 6 (Rule and program realization). *Let R be a $\mathcal{M}$VL rule and $(s, s') \in \mathcal{S}^{\mathcal{F}} \times \mathcal{S}^{\mathcal{T}}$. The rule R realizes the transition (s, s') if $R \sqcap s \wedge$* $\text{head}(R) \in s'$. *A $\mathcal{DM}$VLP P realizes (s, s') if $\forall \text{v}^{val} \in s', \exists R \in P$,* $\text{head}(R) = \text{v}^{val} \wedge R$ *realizes(s, s'). P realizes a set of transitions $T \subseteq \mathcal{S}^{\mathcal{F}} \times \mathcal{S}^{\mathcal{T}}$ if $\forall (s, s') \in T, P$ realizes(s, s').*

Property 2. Let $(s, s') \in \mathcal{S}_m^{\mathcal{F}} \times \mathcal{S}_m^{\mathcal{T}}$ be a transition of states with masking, and P a $\mathcal{DM}$VLP. If P realizes $\mathsf{observed}((s, s'))$ and $\forall \text{v} \in \mathcal{T}, \text{v} \notin \text{vars}(s') \implies \forall val \in \mathsf{dom}(\text{v}), \exists R \in P, R$ realizes $(\mathsf{observed}(s), \mathsf{observed}(s') \cup \{\text{v}^{val}\})$, then P realizes $\mathsf{actual}((s, s'))$.

Property 2 states that when in a transition a target variable value is unknown, a $\mathcal{DM}$VLP needs to have a rule matching for each possible value of the variable in order to ensure to realize the corresponding complete hidden target state.

Example 3. Let T be the set of transitions of Fig. 2 (left).

- $a^1 \leftarrow \emptyset$ realizes all transition to a^1.
- $a^1 \leftarrow a^0$ realizes 000 to 1?0 and 010 to 1?1.
- $c^0 \leftarrow a^0, b^0, c^0$ also realizes 000 to 1?0.
- $b^1 \leftarrow a^1, b^1, c^1$ realizes no transitions of T, never 111 is observed.
- $b^0 \leftarrow a^1, c^1$ realizes no transitions of T, never b^0 is observed after $\{a^1, c^1\}$.

Definition 7 (Conflict and Consistency). *A $\mathcal{M}$VL rule R conflicts with a set of transitions $T \subseteq \mathcal{S}^{\mathcal{F}} \times \mathcal{S}^{\mathcal{T}}$ when $\exists(s, s') \in T, (R \sqcap s \wedge \forall(s1, s2) \in T, s \overset{\mathcal{F}}{\simeq} s1, \text{var}(\text{head}(R)) \in \text{vars}(s2) \wedge \text{var}(\text{head}(R))^{val} \neq \text{head}(R)$. Otherwise, R is said to be consistent with T.*

Example 4. Let T be the set of transitions of Fig. 2.

- $a^1 \leftarrow \emptyset$ conflicts with T, since a^1 is not possible from 001.
- $a^1 \leftarrow a^0$ conflicts with T for the same reason.
- $a^1 \leftarrow c^0$ is consistent with T, as 000, 1?0, 010 all have a transition to a^1.
- $b^0 \leftarrow a^1, b^1, c^1$ is consistent with T, as it matches no state and thus there is no contradiction.

A rule is considered in conflict when its condition matches a feature state s, but the rule's outcome is not present in the target state of any transition from s or any other state that is uncertain equal to s (i.e., both states could be partial observations of the same actual state). However, if the variable in the rule's head is unknown in the target state, it's not considered a conflict, as the unknown could be the rule head. Furthermore, if a feature state that matches the rule's condition never transitions to the rule's head, yet has uncertain equality with a feature state that does, it's not considered a conflict. This is because the states might be actually the same, thus making the rule correct.

Property 3. Let R be a $\mathcal{M}$VL rule and $T \subseteq \mathcal{S}_m^{\mathcal{F}} \times \mathcal{S}_m^{\mathcal{T}}$ be a set of transitions with masking. It holds:

- R conflicts with $\mathsf{observed}(T) \implies R$ conflicts with $\mathsf{actual}(T)$.
  - but R conflicts with $\mathsf{actual}(T) \not\Longleftarrow R$ conflicts with $\mathsf{observed}(T)$.
- R consistent with $\mathsf{actual}(T) \implies R$ consistent with $\mathsf{observed}(T)$.
  - but R consistent with $\mathsf{observed}(T) \not\Longleftarrow R$ consistent with $\mathsf{actual}(T)$.

A rule consistent with a set of transitions remains consistent even when those transitions are masked by unknowns. The introduction of missing values cannot alter the original states, potentially reducing matches but not introducing new ones, thus preserving consistency. However, consistency with the observed transitions does not guarantee consistency with the actual ones, as different values might be concealed by unknowns.

A rule that conflicts with a set of transitions masked by unknowns will also conflict with the actual, corresponding hidden transitions. Revealing the missing values doesn't alter the visible atoms, so the rule condition will continue to be a subset of the feature state, maintaining the conflict. However, a rule conflicting with the actual transitions might not conflict with a masked version of them, introducing missing values in feature states can disrupt matching and remove conflict, while inserting unknowns in the target state could render the rule's head a feasible hidden value, rendering it consistent.

Definition 8 (Suitable and optimal program). *Let $T \subseteq \mathcal{S}^{\mathcal{F}}_m \times \mathcal{S}^{\mathcal{T}}_m$ a set of transitions with masking. A $\mathcal{DM}$VLP P is suitable for T if: P is consistent with* $\mathsf{observed}(T)$, *P realizes* $\mathsf{observed}(T)$, *P realizes* $\mathsf{actual}(T)$, *and for any possible $\mathcal{M}$VL rule R' consistent with* $\mathsf{observed}(T)$, *there exists $R \in P$ s.t. $R' \geq R$. If, in addition, for all $R \in P$, all the $\mathcal{M}$VL rules R' belonging to $\mathcal{DM}$VLP suitable for T are such that $R' \geq R$ implies $R \geq R'$, then P is called optimal and denoted $P_{\mathcal{O}}(T)$.*

Property 4. Let $T \subseteq \mathcal{S}^{\mathcal{F}}_m \times \mathcal{S}^{\mathcal{T}}_m$ a set of transitions with masking.

$$\forall R \in P_{\mathcal{O}}(\mathsf{actual}(T)), \exists R' \in P_{\mathcal{O}}(\mathsf{observed}(T)), R' \geq R$$
$$\forall R' \in P_{\mathcal{O}}(\mathsf{observed}(T)), \forall R \in P_{\mathcal{O}}(\mathsf{actual}(T)), R \geq R' \implies R = R'$$

The optimal program accounting for unknowns represents an over-approximation of the actual optimal program without unknowns, encompassing both dynamics and actual rules. All transitions realized by the optimal program of the ground truth are also realized by the optimal program considering unknowns. Actual optimal rules or their generalizations can be discovered among unknowns, as all optimal rules on the ground truth are specializations of those in the optimal program considering unknowns.

Additionally, the optimal program accounting for unknowns doesn't contain overly specific rules: none are more specific that the optimal rules on the ground truth. But it can also include rules not found in the optimal set on the ground truth, that were generated because of the unknown values. These additional rules cannot be discarded without risking the loss of actual optimal rules or their parts, as they remain indistinguishable from true optimal ones due to unknown values observed.

Example 5. Optimal $\mathcal{DM}$VLP of the actual transitions from Fig. 2 (right).

$$\begin{array}{lllll}
a_t^1 \leftarrow c_{t-1}^0 & a_t^0 \leftarrow a_{t-1}^0, c_{t-1}^1 & b_t^1 \leftarrow a_{t-1}^1, b_{t-1}^0 & b_t^0 \leftarrow a_{t-1}^0, b_{t-1}^0 & c_t^1 \leftarrow a_{t-1}^1 \\
a_t^1 \leftarrow a_{t-1}^1, b_{t-1}^1 & a_t^0 \leftarrow a_{t-1}^1, b_{t-1}^0 & b_t^1 \leftarrow a_{t-1}^1, c_{t-1}^1 & b_t^0 \leftarrow a_{t-1}^0, c_{t-1}^1 & c_t^1 \leftarrow b_{t-1}^1 \\
 & a_t^0 \leftarrow b_{t-1}^0, c_{t-1}^1 & b_t^1 \leftarrow a_{t-1}^0, b_{t-1}^1, c_{t-1}^0 & b_t^0 \leftarrow a_{t-1}^1, b_{t-1}^1, c_{t-1}^0 & c_t^0 \leftarrow b_{t-1}^0
\end{array}$$

Optimal $\mathcal{DM}$VLP of the transitions with unknowns from Fig. 2 (left).

$$\begin{array}{llllll}
a_t^1 \leftarrow c_{t-1}^0 & a_t^0 \leftarrow a_{t-1}^1 & b_t^1 \leftarrow \emptyset & b_t^0 \leftarrow \emptyset & c_t^1 \leftarrow a_{t-1}^1 & c_t^0 \leftarrow a_{t-1}^1 \\
a_t^1 \leftarrow a_{t-1}^1 & a_t^0 \leftarrow b_{t-1}^1 & & & c_t^1 \leftarrow b_{t-1}^1 & c_t^0 \leftarrow b_{t-1}^0 \\
a_t^1 \leftarrow b_{t-1}^1 & a_t^0 \leftarrow c_{t-1}^1 & & & c_t^1 \leftarrow c_{t-1}^1 & c_t^0 \leftarrow c_{t-1}^1
\end{array}$$

In this scenario, some actual optimal rules, such as $a_t^1 \leftarrow c_{t-1}^0$ and $c_t^1 \leftarrow a_{t-1}^1$, remain decipherable despite the presence of unknowns. Furthermore, we can see that all rules of the actual optimal program are dominated, as in $a_t^1 \leftarrow a_{t-1}^1, b_{t-1}^1$, which manifests partially through $a_t^1 \leftarrow a_{t-1}^1$ and $a_t^1 \leftarrow b_{t-1}^1$. The unknowns mask the'and' influence, yet we can deduce the constituent components of the influence. However, for variable b, the unknowns exert such significant influence that the empty rule emerges as the sole safe bet, revealing little about b's dynamic. For c, all the true optimal rules are revealed, yet the unknowns give rise to several spurious rules (in grey), which fail to dominate actual optimal rules and aren't compatible with the actual transitions. Nevertheless, with these unknowns present, they represent possible rules or components that might align with the concealed transitions.

According to Definition 8, we can obtain the optimal program by a trivial brute force enumeration algorithm: generate all rules consistent with T then remove the dominated ones. The purpose of the following section is to propose a non-trivial approach that is more efficient in practice to obtain the optimal program. In [16], we proposed the General Usage LFIT Algorithm (**GULA**) that guarantees to learn the optimal program of a set of transitions (without unknown at that time). In the following section, we extend the learning operation used in **GULA** to learn optimal program under unknowns.

2.1 Learning Operations

This section focuses on the manipulation of programs for the learning process. Definition 9 formalize the notion of positive and negative example of what we want to learn under unknowns. Definition 10 formalize the main atomic operations performed on a rule, whose objective is to make minimal modifications to a given $\mathcal{DM}$VLP in order to be consistent with a new set of transitions.

Definition 9 (Positive/Negative example). *Let $T \subseteq \mathcal{S}^{\mathcal{F}} \times \mathcal{S}^{\mathcal{T}}$, $s \in \mathcal{S}^{\mathcal{F}}$ and $\mathrm{v}^{val} \in \mathcal{A}$. When there exists $(s, s') \in T$ and $\mathrm{v}^{val} \in s'$, then s is called a positive example of v^{val} in T. When $\exists (s, s') \in T, \mathrm{v} \notin \mathrm{vars}(s')$ or $\exists s'' \in \mathcal{S}^{\mathcal{F}}, s \overset{\mathcal{F}}{\lesssim} s''$ and s'' is a positive example of v^{val} in T, then s is called a potentially positive example of v^{val} in T. When $\exists (s, s') \in T, s$ is neither a positive nor a potentially positive example, then s is called a negative example of v^{val} in T. We denote as $Pos_{\mathrm{v}^{val}}(T), Pos?_{\mathrm{v}^{val}}(T), Neg_{\mathrm{v}^{val}}(T)$ respectively the set of positive, potentially positive and negative examples of v^{val} in T.*

If the state s is never observed as a feature state in T then it is neither a positive, potentially positive or negative example: It is considered unobserved.

Property 5. Let $T \subseteq \mathcal{S}_m^{\mathcal{F}} \times \mathcal{S}_m^{\mathcal{T}}$ be a set of transition, $\mathrm{v}^{val} \in \mathcal{A}$. Let $(s1, s2) \in T$, it holds:

- $\mathsf{actual}(s1) \in Pos_{\mathrm{v}^{val}}(\mathsf{actual}(T)) \implies \mathsf{observed}(s1) \in Pos_{\mathrm{v}^{val}}(\mathsf{observed}(T)) \vee \mathsf{observed}(s1) \in Pos?_{\mathrm{v}^{val}}(\mathsf{observed}(T))$

- $\mathsf{observed}(s1) \in Pos_{\mathrm{v}^{val}}(\mathsf{observed}(T)) \implies \mathsf{actual}(s1) \in Pos_{\mathrm{v}^{val}}(\mathsf{actual}(T))$
  - but $\mathsf{observed}(s1) \in Pos?_{\mathrm{v}^{val}}(\mathsf{observed}(T)) \;\not\Longrightarrow\; \mathsf{actual}(s1) \in Pos_{\mathrm{v}^{val}}(\mathsf{actual}(T))$
- $\mathsf{observed}(s1) \in Neg_{\mathrm{v}^{val}}(\mathsf{observed}(T)) \implies \mathsf{actual}(s1) \in Neg_{\mathrm{v}^{val}}(\mathsf{actual}(T))$
  - $\mathsf{actual}(s1) \in Neg_{\mathrm{v}^{val}}(\mathsf{actual}(T)) \not\Longleftarrow\!\!\!\Rightarrow \mathsf{observed}(s1) \in Neg_{\mathrm{v}^{val}}(\mathsf{observed}(T))$

Theorem 1. *Let* $T \subseteq \mathcal{S}^{\mathcal{F}} \times \mathcal{S}^{\mathcal{T}}$, $\mathrm{v}^{val} \in \mathcal{A}$. *Let* $M := \{R \in \mathcal{M}\mathrm{VL} \mid \mathrm{head}(R) = \mathrm{v}^{val} \wedge \forall s \in Neg_{\mathrm{v}^{val}}(T), R \not\sqcap s\}$. *Then* $\{R \in P_{\mathcal{O}}(T) \mid \mathrm{head}(R) = \mathrm{v}^{val}\} = \{R \in M \mid \nexists R' \in \mathcal{M}\mathrm{VL}, R' \neq R \wedge R' \geq R\}$.

A positive example of a target atom v^{val} is a state from which a transition to v^{val} has been observed. A feature state in a transition where v is unknown in the target state is a potentially positive example, as the concealed value could indeed be v^{val}. Furthermore, states with uncertain equality to positive examples are also potentially positives, as the actual states could be the same, casting doubt on the observed transitions being unique outcomes. Negative examples, on the other hand, are states from which it's clear that a transition to the target atom is impossible in the actual complete state, thus falling outside both positive and potentially positive realms.

Figure 4 showcases the distinction between positive, potentially positive, and negative examples for the case of atom a^1. Here, a direct transition to a^1 is observed from states 000, 1?0, 1?1 and 010 (highlighted in blue), marking them as positive examples. From the state 01?, no explicit transition to a^1 is evident, though it might be an alternate outcome of the uncertainly equal state 010 that is positive, thus 01? is a potentially positive. Similarly, the state ?01, with transitions to both 01? and 010, doesn't definitively lead to a^1, as the actual state behind ?01 could be 101, implying other possibilities. Lastly, the state 001 stands alone as a negative example, as neither direct transitions nor uncertain equality with positive states point to its possibility in a^1. We can conclude that no a^1 outcome originates from 001 in our observed transitions. The state 11? is potentially positive from its transitions to ?01, where the ? could be a^1, and also from its uncertain equality with 1?0 and 1?1 that are positive examples.

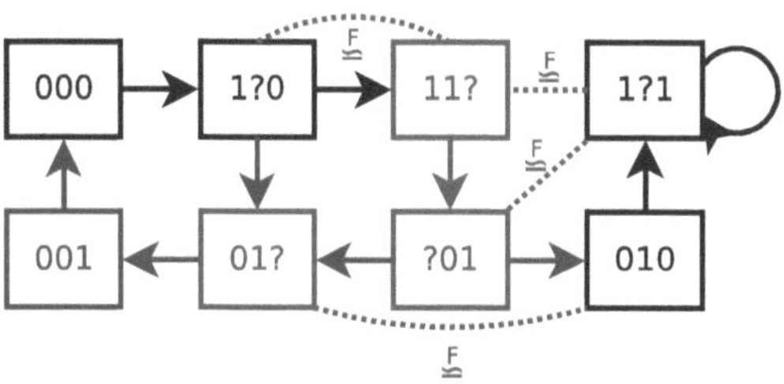

Fig. 4. Graphical classification regarding target a^1 of states/transitions in a transition graph. Blue arrows point to a^1, purple arrows to '?' values, while red arrows mark transitions to a^0. Blue states are positive examples, purple states are potentially positives and red states are negative example. Doted lines show uncertain equality between positive examples and potentially positive examples. (Color figure online)

Theorem 1 states that the optimal rules of a given target atom v^{val} can be obtained by simply avoiding the matching of negative examples. The optimal program can thus be obtain in a brute force manner by enumerating all possible rules and checking this simple property. A more efficient solution is to reduce space search by doing iterative rule specialization exploiting the following notions.

Definition 10 (Rule least specialization). *Let R be a $\mathcal{M}$VL rule and $s \in \mathcal{S}^{\mathcal{F}}$ such that $R \sqcap s$. The* <u>*least specialization*</u> *of R by s according to $\mathcal{F}$ and $\mathcal{A}$ is:*

$$L_{\text{spe}}(R, s, \mathcal{A}, \mathcal{F}) := \{\text{head}(R) \leftarrow \text{body}(R) \cup \{\mathrm{v}^{val}\} \mid \\ \mathrm{v} \in \mathcal{F} \wedge \mathrm{v}^{val} \in \mathcal{A} \wedge \mathrm{v}^{val} \notin s \wedge \forall val' \in \mathbb{N}, \mathrm{v}^{val'} \notin \text{body}(R)\}.$$

Property 6. Let s be a discrete state and R a $\mathcal{M}$VL rule. It holds that:

- (1) $\forall R' \in L_{\text{spe}}(R, s, \mathcal{A}, \mathcal{F}), R' \not\sqcap s.$
- (2) $\forall s' \in \mathcal{S}^{\mathcal{F}}, R \sqcap s' \wedge s \overset{\mathcal{F}}{\neq} s' \wedge s \overset{\mathcal{F}}{\not\leq} s' \implies \exists R' \in L_{\text{spe}}(R, s, \mathcal{A}, \mathcal{F}), R' \sqcap s';$

Property 6 illustrates the interests of the least specialization, $L_{\text{spe}}(R, s, \mathcal{A}, \mathcal{F})$, which generates a rule set that matches all the states that R covers, excluding s. This is because each modified rule is crafted with a single additional condition, carefully considering all compatible possibilities.

The next properties are directly used in the learning algorithm. Proposition 1 gives an explicit definition of the optimal program for an empty set of transitions, which is the starting point of the algorithm. Theorem 2 gives a method to iteratively compute $P_{\mathcal{O}}(T)$ for any $T \subseteq \mathcal{S}^{\mathcal{F}} \times \mathcal{S}^{\mathcal{T}}$, starting from $P_{\mathcal{O}}(\emptyset)$. Finally, Proposition 2 gives a method to obtain the optimal program from any suitable program by simply removing the dominated rules.

Proposition 1 (Optimal Program of Empty Set). $P_{\mathcal{O}}(\emptyset) = \{\mathrm{v}^{val} \leftarrow \emptyset \mid \mathrm{v} \in \mathcal{T} \wedge val \in \mathsf{dom}(\mathrm{v})\}$.

Theorem 2 (Least Specialization and Suitability). *Let $\mathrm{v}^{val} \in \mathcal{A}$, $s \in \mathcal{S}^{\mathcal{F}}$ and $T, T' \subseteq \mathcal{S}^{\mathcal{F}} \times \mathcal{S}^{\mathcal{T}}$ such that,* $\text{first}(T') = \{s\} \wedge s \notin \text{first}(T)$. *Let $R_P := \{R \in P_{\mathcal{O}}(T) \mid R \sqcap s, \text{head}(R) = \mathrm{v}^{val}, s \in Neg_{\mathrm{v}^{val}}(T \cup T')\}$. Then $(P_{\mathcal{O}}(T) \setminus R_P) \cup \bigcup_{R \in R_P} L_{\text{spe}}(R, s, \mathcal{A}, \mathcal{F})$ is suitable for $T \cup T'$.*

Proposition 2 (From Suitable to Optimal). *Let $T \subseteq \mathcal{S}^{\mathcal{F}} \times \mathcal{S}^{\mathcal{T}}$. If P is a $\mathcal{DM}$VLP suitable for T, then $P_{\mathcal{O}}(T) = \{R \in P \mid \forall R' \in P, R' \geq R \implies R' = R\}$.*

3 Algorithm

In this section we present a new version of **GULA**: the General Usage LFIT Algorithm previously introduced in [16]. Here we extend the algorithm to learn optimal program under unknowns. **GULA** learns a logic program from the observations of its state transitions. Given as input a set of transitions $T \subseteq \mathcal{S}^{\mathcal{F}} \times \mathcal{S}^{\mathcal{T}}$,

GULA iteratively constructs a $\mathcal{DMVLP}$ that models the dynamics of the observed system by applying the method formalized in the previous section as shown in Algorithm 1. The algorithm will learn the optimal logic program $P_{\mathcal{O}}(T)$. As compared to its previous version, the algorithm's core mechanism remains unchanged, except for the revised calculation of negative examples tailored to account for observations featuring unknown values.

Algorithm 1. GULA

- **INPUT:** a set of atoms $\mathcal{A}$, a set of transitions $T \subseteq \mathcal{S}^{\mathcal{F}} \times \mathcal{S}^{\mathcal{T}}$, two sets of variables $\mathcal{F}$ and $\mathcal{T}$.
- For each atom $\mathrm{v}^{val} \in \mathcal{A}$ of each variable $\mathrm{v} \in \mathcal{T}$:
  - Extract all states from which a transition to v^{val} **does** exist:
    $Pos_{\mathrm{v}^{val}} := \{s \in \mathrm{first}(T) \mid \exists (s, s') \in T \wedge \mathrm{v}^{val} \in s'\}$
  - Extract all states from which a transition to v^{val} **could** exist:
    $Pos?_{\mathrm{v}^{val}} := \{s \in \mathrm{first}(T) \mid \exists (s, s') \in T, \mathrm{v} \notin \mathrm{vars}(s') \vee \exists pos \in Pos_{\mathrm{v}^{val}}, s \stackrel{\mathcal{F}}{\simeq} pos\}$
  - $Neg_{\mathrm{v}^{val}} := \mathrm{first}(T) \setminus (Pos_{\mathrm{v}^{val}} \cup Pos?_{\mathrm{v}^{val}})$
  - Initialize $P_{\mathrm{v}^{val}} := \{\mathrm{v}^{val} \leftarrow \emptyset\}$.
  - For each state $s \in Neg_{\mathrm{v}^{val}}$:
    - * Extract and remove the rules of $P_{\mathrm{v}^{val}}$ that match s:
      $M_{\mathrm{v}^{val}} := \{R \in P \mid \mathrm{body}(R) \subseteq s\}$
    - * $P_{\mathrm{v}^{val}} := P_{\mathrm{v}^{val}} \setminus M_{\mathrm{v}^{val}}$.
    - * $LS := \emptyset$
    - * For each rule $R \in M_{\mathrm{v}^{val}}$:
      - · Compute its least specialization $P' = L_{\mathrm{spe}}(R, s, \mathcal{A}, \mathcal{F})$.
      - · Remove rules in P' dominated by a rule in $P_{\mathrm{v}^{val}}$.
      - · $LS := LS \cup P'$.
    - * Add all remaining rules of LS to $P_{\mathrm{v}^{val}}$: $P_{\mathrm{v}^{val}} := P_{\mathrm{v}^{val}} \cup LS$.
  - $P := P \cup P_{\mathrm{v}^{val}}$
- **OUTPUT:** P (P is $P_{\mathcal{O}}(T)$).

From the set of transitions T, **GULA** learns the conditions under which each $\mathrm{v}^{val} \in \mathcal{A}, \mathrm{v} \in \mathcal{T}$ may appear in the next state. The algorithm starts by computing the set of all negative examples of the appearance of v^{val} in next state: all states such that v never takes the value val in the next state of a transition of T, accounting for the hidden possibility introduced by unknowns value. Those negative examples are then used during the following learning phase to iteratively learn the set of rules $P_{\mathcal{O}}(T)$. The learning phase starts by initializing a set of rules $P_{\mathrm{v}^{val}}$ to $\{R \in P_{\mathcal{O}}(\emptyset) \mid \mathrm{head}(R) = \mathrm{v}^{val}\} = \{\mathrm{v}^{val} \leftarrow \emptyset\}$. $P_{\mathrm{v}^{val}}$ is iteratively revised against each negative example neg in $Neg_{\mathrm{v}^{val}}$. All rules R_m of $P_{\mathrm{v}^{val}}$ that match neg have to be revised. In order for $P_{\mathrm{v}^{val}}$ to remain optimal, the revision of each R_m must not match neg but still matches every other state that R_m matches. To ensure that, the least specialization (see Definition 10) is used to revise each conflicting rule R_m. For each variable of $\mathcal{F}$ so that $\mathrm{body}(R_m)$ has no condition over it, a condition over another value than the one observed in state neg can be added. None of those revision match neg and all states matched by R_m are still matched by at least one of its revisions. Each revised rule can be dominated by a rule in $P_{\mathrm{v}^{val}}$ or another revised rules and thus dominance must be checked from both. The non-dominated revised rules are then added to $P_{\mathrm{v}^{val}}$. Once $P_{\mathrm{v}^{val}}$ has been revised against all negatives example of $Neg_{\mathrm{v}^{val}}$, $P_{\mathrm{v}^{val}} = \{R \in P_{\mathcal{O}}(T) \mid \text{head}(R) = \mathrm{v}^{val}\}$. Finally, $P_{\mathrm{v}^{val}}$ is added to P and the loop restarts with another atom. Once all values of each variable have been treated, the algorithm outputs P which is then equal to $P_{\mathcal{O}}(T)$. The source code of the algorithm is available at https://github.com/Tony-sama/pylfit under GPL-3.0 License.

Theorem 3 from [16] still holds: **GULA** terminates and **GULA** is sound, complete and optimal w.r.t. its input, i.e., all and only non-dominated consistent rules appear in its output program which is the optimal program of its input ($\textbf{GULA}(\mathcal{A}, T, \mathcal{F}, \mathcal{T}) = P_{\mathcal{O}}(T)$). The complexity of **GULA** remains unchanged compared to previous versions, we refer to [16] for the detail complexity analysis. Its scalability is evaluated in Sect. 4 with brute force enumeration as baseline.

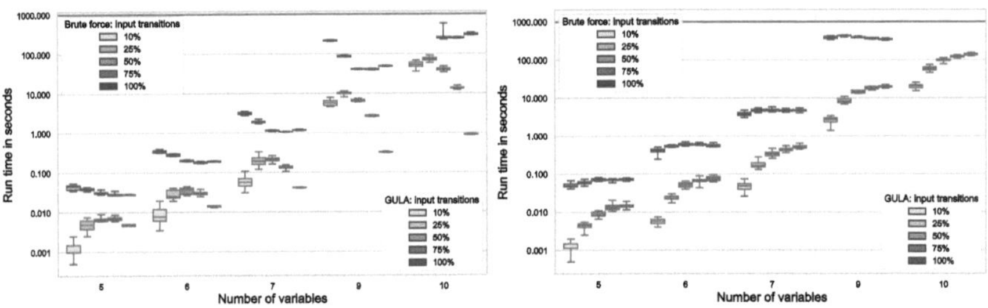

Fig. 5. Runtime in seconds (log scale) for one call of **GULA** (blue) and **brute force enumeration** (red) on a random subset of 10% to 100% of transitions from Boolean networks with 5 to 10 variables. 10 runs for each scenario with a time-out of 1,000 s. Left: only complete states appears. Right: Each state includes a random number of unknown values, not exceeding 50% of the state. (Color figure online)

4 Evaluation

In this section, the scalability of **GULA** is evaluated using Boolean network benchmarks from the biological literature (Boolenet [2] and Pyboolnet [7]). All experiments[1] were conducted on one core of an AMD Ryzen 9 (7950X, 4.5 GHz) with 64 Gb of RAM. Boolean networks are converted to $\mathcal{DM}$VLP where $\forall v \in \mathcal{V}, \mathsf{dom}(v) = \{0, 1\}$. In [2,7] file formats, for each variable, Boolean functions are

[1] Available at: https://github.com/Tony-sama/pylfit. Using command "`python evaluations/ijclr2024/ijclr2024.py`" from the repository's `tests` folder. All experiments were run with the release version 0.4.0 of pylfit.

given in disjunctive normal form (DNF), a disjunction of conjunction clauses that can be considered as a set of Boolean atoms of the form v or ¬v. Each clause c of the DNF of a variable v is directly converted into a rule R such that, head(R) = v_t^1 and $\mathrm{v}'^1_{t-1} \in \mathrm{body}(R) \iff \mathrm{v}' \in c$ and $\mathrm{v}'^0_{t-1} \in \mathrm{body}(R) \iff \neg\mathrm{v}' \in c$. For each such $\mathcal{DM}$VLP the set T of all transitions are generated using the synchronous semantics. Then for each $(s, s') \in T$, states s and s' are subsequently obscured by unknown values; these unknowns represent up to 50% of each state.

Figure 5 show the differences of performance between **GULA** and **brute force enumeration** when learning the optimal $\mathcal{DM}$VLP from different subset of transitions of each benchmarks size. For all benchmarks, **GULA** is clearly more efficient (both for observation with and without unknowns). The difference exponentially increasing with the number of variables: about 10 times faster with 6 variables and 100 times faster with 9 variables. The **brute force enumeration** reaches the time out for 10 variables benchmarks and beyond. **GULA** succeeds in learning a $\mathcal{WDM}$VLP from the benchmarks with up to 10 variables before the time-out of 1,000 seconds for all considered sub-sets of transitions. We observe different trends in runtime performance between complete/partial observations. For complete observations, runtime improves with increasing proportion of transitions, likely due to the proximity of optimal rules in the observed subset to the system's actual optimal rules, allowing for quicker pruning of spurious candidates. In contrast, with partial observations, this pattern disappears, as the additional spurious rules introduced by unknown values may offset any speed gains from more powerful rules. Future work could explore the impact of spurious rules on computation time, potentially leading to heuristic design. For now, it's worth noting that in practice, many spurious rules may not match observed states and could be disregarded, depending on the application.

5 Conclusion

In this paper, we proposed a modeling approach that tackles the challenge of learning from partially observable systems by extending the LFIT framework to model unknown values. We formalized theoretical properties and guarantees allowing to model a system observed though partial data as a $\mathcal{DM}$VLP that is an over-approximation of the actual system regarding both its dynamics and rules. We also proposed a novel extension of **GULA** that enables the learning of such logic programs and demonstrate through experimental results the efficiency and effectiveness of this approach. This contribution marks a significant step towards bridging the gap between logical approaches and real-world applications in fields like Systems Biology. While our approach ensures an over-approximation of the original rules, it may be too conservative for certain applications, limiting its utility for large-scale systems. Moreover, the scalability of GULA restricts its use to smaller domains. In practice, there might be benefits to searching for more precise rules at the risk of specialization beyond the ground truth rules or missing certain relationships. However, studying this trade-off between approximation quality, rule complexity, and runtime is outside the scope of this paper. Future work could focus on developing heuristics to improve the pertinence of learned rules in real-world scenarios, possibly approaching the ground truth rules more effectively through clever combinations of the rules found. Additionally, adapting the **PRIDE** algorithm [17] to the modeling proposed in this paper would enable finding a subset of the optimal program in polynomial time, suitable for real-world scenarios and datasets.

Acknowledgements. Funded by the European Union This research has been funded by the European Union. Views and opinions expressed are however those of the author(s) only and do not necessarily reflect those of the European Union or ERCEA.Neither the European Union nor the granting authority can be held responsible for them.
This work has also been supported by JSPS KAKENHI Grant Number JP21H04905 and JST CREST Grant Number JPMJCR22D3, Japan.
The English quality of this manuscript was enhanced by Yumi, a virtual assistant hosted locally, using the large language model "Hathor" [11] from Nitral-AI on a Nvidia RTX4090 using Koboldcpp (https://github.com/LostRuins/koboldcpp) and SillyTavern (https://github.com/SillyTavern/SillyTavern).

A Appendix: Proofs of Section 2

Property 7. Let $s1, s2$ be two discrete states with masking. From Definition 4 the following holds:

- $\mathsf{actual}(s1) \overset{\mathcal{X}}{=} \mathsf{actual}(s2) \implies \mathsf{observed}(s1) \overset{\mathcal{X}}{\simeq} \mathsf{observed}(s2)$
  - but $\mathsf{observed}(s1) \overset{\mathcal{X}}{\simeq} \mathsf{observed}(s2) \not\Longrightarrow \mathsf{actual}(s1) \overset{\mathcal{X}}{=} \mathsf{actual}(s2)$
  - $\mathsf{observed}(s1) \overset{\mathcal{X}}{\not\simeq} \mathsf{observed}(s2) \implies \mathsf{actual}(s1) \overset{\mathcal{X}}{\neq} \mathsf{actual}(s2)$
  - but $\mathsf{actual}(s1) \overset{\mathcal{X}}{\neq} \mathsf{actual}(s2) \not\Longrightarrow \mathsf{observed}(s1) \overset{\mathcal{X}}{\not\simeq} \mathsf{observed}(s2)$

Proof.

- $\mathsf{actual}(s1) \overset{\mathcal{X}}{=} \mathsf{actual}(s2) \implies \forall \mathrm{v}^{val} \in s1, \mathrm{v}^{val} \in s2$, thus $s1 \overset{\mathcal{X}}{\simeq} s2$ from Definition 4.
  - Let $s1 := (\{a^0\}, \{a^0, b^0\})$ and $s2 := (\{b^0\}, \{a^1, b^0\})$ two states with masking. Then $\mathsf{actual}(s1) \neq \mathsf{actual}(s2)$ but $\mathsf{observed}(s1) \overset{\mathcal{X}}{\simeq} \mathsf{observed}(s2)$.
- $\mathsf{observed}(s1) \overset{\mathcal{X}}{\not\simeq} \mathsf{observed}(s2) \implies \exists \mathrm{v}^{val} \in s1, \exists \mathrm{v}^{val'} \in s2, val \neq val'$ thus $\mathrm{v}^{val} \in \mathsf{actual}(s1), \mathrm{v}^{val'} \in \mathsf{actual}(s2)$ and $\mathsf{actual}(s1) \neq \mathsf{actual}(s2)$.
  - Let $s1 := (\{a^0\}, \{a^0, b^0\})$ and $s2 := (\{b^0\}, \{a^1, b^0\})$ two states with masking. Then $\mathsf{observed}(s1) \overset{\mathcal{X}}{\simeq} \mathsf{observed}(s2)$ but $\mathsf{actual}(s1) \neq \mathsf{actual}(s2)$. □

Property 8. Let $(s, s') \in \mathcal{S}_m^{\mathcal{F}} \times \mathcal{S}_m^{\mathcal{T}}$ be a transition of states with masking, and P a $\mathcal{DMVLP}$. If P realizes $\mathsf{observed}((s, s'))$ and $\forall \mathrm{v} \in \mathcal{T}, \mathrm{v} \notin \mathrm{vars}(s') \implies \forall val \in \mathsf{dom}(\mathrm{v}), \exists R \in P, R$ realizes $(\mathsf{observed}(s), \mathsf{observed}(s') \cup \{\mathrm{v}^{val}\})$, then P realizes $\mathsf{actual}((s, s'))$.

Proof.

- Let R be a $\mathcal{M}$VL rule, by Definition 5, $R \sqcap \mathsf{observed}(s) \implies R \sqcap \mathsf{actual}(s)$.
- By Definition 6, P realizes $\mathsf{observed}((s, s'))$ implies that $\forall \mathrm{v}^{val} \in \mathsf{observed}(s'), \exists R \in P, \mathrm{head}(R) = \mathrm{v}^{val}, R$ realizes $\mathsf{actual}((s, s'))$.
- Let $\mathrm{v} \in \mathcal{T}$ so that $\mathrm{v} \notin \mathrm{vars}(\mathsf{observed}(s'))$. This imples that $\forall val \in \mathsf{dom}(\mathrm{v}), \exists R \in P, \mathrm{head}\, R = \mathrm{v}^{val} \wedge R \sqcap s$. Thus $\forall \mathrm{v}^{val} \in \mathsf{actual}(s') \setminus \mathsf{observed}(s'), \exists R \in P, \mathrm{head}(R) = \mathrm{v}^{val}, R$ realizes $\mathsf{actual}((s, s'))$.
- Thus $\forall \mathrm{v}^{val} \in \mathsf{actual}(s'), \exists R \in P, \mathrm{head}\, R = \mathrm{v}^{val}, R$ realizes $\mathsf{actual}((s, s'))$.

Thus P realizes $\mathsf{actual}((s, s'))$. □

Property 9. Let R be a $\mathcal{M}$VL rule and $T \subseteq \mathcal{S}_m^{\mathcal{F}} \times \mathcal{S}_m^{\mathcal{T}}$ be a set of transitions with masking. It holds:

- R conflicts with $\mathsf{observed}(T) \implies R$ conflicts with $\mathsf{actual}(T)$.
  - but R conflicts with $\mathsf{actual}(T) \not\Longleftarrow R$ conflicts with $\mathsf{observed}(T)$.
- R consistent with $\mathsf{actual}(T) \implies R$ consistent with $\mathsf{observed}(T)$.
  - but R consistent with $\mathsf{observed}(T) \not\Longleftarrow R$ consistent with $\mathsf{actual}(T)$.

Proof.

- From Definition 7, R conflicts with $\mathsf{observed}(T) \implies \exists (s, s') \in T, (R \sqcap \mathsf{observed}(s) \wedge \forall (s1, s2) \in \mathsf{observed}(T), \mathsf{observed}(s) \backsimeq s1 \vee \mathsf{observed}(s) = s1, \exists \mathrm{var}(\mathrm{head}(R))^{val} \in s2, \mathrm{var}(\mathrm{head}(R))^{val} \neq \mathrm{head}(R)$. From Definition 5, $R \sqcap \mathsf{actual}(s)$. Thus $\exists (\mathsf{actual}(s), s'') \in \mathsf{actual}(T), R \sqcap \mathsf{actual}(s) \wedge \forall (\mathsf{actual}(s), s2) \in \mathsf{actual}(T), \mathrm{head}(R) \notin s2$ thus R in conflict with $\mathsf{actual}(T)$ by Definition 7.
  - For example, let $T = \{((\{a^0, b^0\}, \{a^0, b^0\}), (\{b^1\}, \{a^0, b^1\}))\}$ a set of transitions with masking, and $R := a^1 \leftarrow b^0$. R conflicts with $\mathsf{actual}(T)$ but R does not conflict with $\mathsf{observed}(T)$.
- Let R consistent with $\mathsf{actual}(T)$. Suppose that R conflicts with $\mathsf{observed}(T)$, then R conflicts with $\mathsf{actual}(T)$, which is a contradiction.
  - For example, let $T = \{((\{a^0, b^0\}, \{a^0, b^0\}), (\{b^1\}, \{a^0, b^1\}))\}$ a set of transitions with masking, and $R := a^1 \leftarrow b^0$. R consistent with $\mathsf{observed}(T)$ but R does conflict with $\mathsf{actual}(T)$. □

Property 10. Let $T \subseteq \mathcal{S}_m^{\mathcal{F}} \times \mathcal{S}_m^{\mathcal{T}}$ a set of transitions with masking.

$$\forall R \in P_{\mathcal{O}}(\mathsf{actual}(T)), \exists R' \in P_{\mathcal{O}}(\mathsf{observed}(T)), R' \geq R$$
$$\forall R' \in P_{\mathcal{O}}(\mathsf{observed}(T)), \forall R \in P_{\mathcal{O}}(\mathsf{actual}(T)), R \geq R' \implies R = R'$$

Proof.

- By Definition 8, $\forall R \in P_{\mathcal{O}}(\mathsf{actual}(T)), R$ consistent with $\mathsf{actual}(T)$, thus from Proposition 3, R consistent with $\mathsf{observed}(T)$. By Definition 8, for any possible $\mathcal{M}$VL rule $R1$ consistent with $\mathsf{observed}(T)$, there exists $R2 \in P_{\mathcal{O}}(\mathsf{observed}(T))$ s.t. $R2 \geq R1$. Thus $\exists R' \in P_{\mathcal{O}}(\mathsf{observed}(T)), R' \geq R$.
- Let $R' \in P_{\mathcal{O}}(\mathsf{observed}(T)), R \in P_{\mathcal{O}}(\mathsf{actual}(T)), R \geq R'$. By Proposition 3, since R consistent with $\mathsf{actual}(T)$ then R consistent with $\mathsf{observed}(T)$. Thus by Definition 8, $\exists R'' \in P_{\mathcal{O}}(\mathsf{observed}(T)), R'' \geq R$ and from Definition 1, $R'' \geq R'$ since $R \geq R'$. Since $\forall R1 \in P$, all the $\mathcal{M}$VL rules $R2$ belonging to $\mathcal{DM}$VLP suitable for $\mathsf{observed}(T)$ are such that $R2 \geq R1$ implies $R1 \geq R2$, thus $R'' = R = R'$. □

Property 11. Let $T \subseteq \mathcal{S}^{\mathcal{F}}_m \times \mathcal{S}^{\mathcal{T}}_m$ be a set of transition, $\mathrm{v}^{val} \in \mathcal{A}$. Let $(s1, s2) \in T$, it holds:

- $\mathsf{actual}(s1) \in \mathit{Pos}_{\mathrm{v}^{val}}(\mathsf{actual}(T)) \implies \mathsf{observed}(s1) \in \mathit{Pos}_{\mathrm{v}^{val}}(\mathsf{observed}(T)) \lor \mathsf{observed}(s1) \in \mathit{Pos?}_{\mathrm{v}^{val}}(\mathsf{observed}(T))$
- $\mathsf{observed}(s1) \in \mathit{Pos}_{\mathrm{v}^{val}}(\mathsf{observed}(T)) \implies \mathsf{actual}(s1) \in \mathit{Pos}_{\mathrm{v}^{val}}(\mathsf{actual}(T))$
  - but $\mathsf{observed}(s1) \in \mathit{Pos?}_{\mathrm{v}^{val}}(\mathsf{observed}(T)) \;\not\Longrightarrow\; \mathsf{actual}(s1) \in \mathit{Pos}_{\mathrm{v}^{val}}(\mathsf{actual}(T))$
- $\mathsf{observed}(s1) \in \mathit{Neg}_{\mathrm{v}^{val}}(\mathsf{observed}(T)) \implies \mathsf{actual}(s1) \in \mathit{Neg}_{\mathrm{v}^{val}}(\mathsf{actual}(T))$
  - $\mathsf{actual}(s1) \in \mathit{Neg}_{\mathrm{v}^{val}}(\mathsf{actual}(T)) \not\Longrightarrow \mathsf{observed}(s1) \in \mathit{Neg}_{\mathrm{v}^{val}}(\mathsf{observed}(T))$

Proof.

- Let $\mathsf{actual}(s1) \in \mathit{Pos}_{\mathrm{v}^{val}}(\mathsf{actual}(T))$, then by Definition 9, $\exists(\mathsf{actual}(s1), \mathsf{actual}(s2)) \in \mathsf{actual}(T), \mathrm{v}^{val} \in \mathsf{actual}(s2)$. Thus $\mathrm{v}^{val} \in \mathsf{observed}(s2') \lor \mathrm{v} \notin \mathrm{vars}(\mathsf{observed}(s2'))$ thus $\mathsf{observed}(s1) \in \mathit{Pos}_{\mathrm{v}^{val}}(\mathsf{observed}(T)) \lor \mathsf{observed}(s1) \in \mathit{Pos?}_{\mathrm{v}^{val}}(\mathsf{observed}(T))$.
- Let $\mathsf{observed}(s1) \in \mathit{Pos}_{\mathrm{v}^{val}}(\mathsf{observed}(T))$, then by Definition 9, $\exists(\mathsf{observed}(s1), \mathsf{observed}(s2)) \in \mathsf{observed}(T), \mathrm{v}^{val} \in \mathsf{observed}(s2)$. Thus $\mathrm{v}^{val} \in \mathsf{actual}(s2)$ and $\mathsf{actual}(s1) \in \mathit{Pos}_{\mathrm{v}^{val}}(\mathsf{actual}(T))$.
  - For example, let $T = \{((\{a^0, b^0\}, \{a^0, b^0\}), (\{b^1\}, \{a^0, b^1\}))\}$ a set of transitions with masking. Here, $\{a^0, b^0\} \in \mathit{Pos?}_{a^1}(\mathsf{observed}(T))$ but $\{a^0, b^0\} \notin \mathit{Pos}_{a^1}(\mathsf{actual}(T))$.
- Let $s1 \in \mathit{Neg}_{\mathrm{v}^{val}}(\mathsf{observed}(T))$ then by Definition 9, $s1 \notin \mathit{Pos}_{\mathrm{v}^{val}}(\mathsf{observed}(T))$ and $s1 \notin \mathit{Pos?}_{\mathrm{v}^{val}}(\mathsf{observed}(T))$. Thus $\mathsf{actual}(s1) \notin \mathit{Pos}_{\mathrm{v}^{val}}(\mathsf{actual}(T))$ otherwise contradict with first point.
  - For example, let $T = \{((\{a^0, b^0\}, \{a^0, b^0\}), (\{b^1\}, \{a^0, b^1\}))\}$ a set of transitions with masking. Here, $\{a^0, b^0\} \in \mathit{Neg}_{a^1}(\mathsf{actual}(T))$ but $\{a^0, b^0\} \notin \mathit{Neg}_{a^1}(\mathsf{observed}(T))$. □

Theorem 3. *Let* $T \subseteq \mathcal{S}^{\mathcal{F}} \times \mathcal{S}^{\mathcal{T}}$, $\mathrm{v}^{val} \in \mathcal{A}$. *Let* $M := \{R \in \mathcal{M}\mathrm{VL} \mid \mathrm{head}(R) = \mathrm{v}^{val} \land \forall s \in \mathit{Neg}_{\mathrm{v}^{val}}(T), R \not\sqcap s\}$. *Then* $\{R \in P_{\mathcal{O}}(T) \mid \mathrm{head}(R) = \mathrm{v}^{val}\} = \{R \in M \mid \nexists R' \in \mathcal{M}\mathrm{VL}, R' \neq R \land R' \geq R\}$.

Proof. Let suppose $\exists R \in P_{\mathcal{O}}(T), R \notin \{R \in M \mid \nexists R' \neq R, R' \geq R\}$. If $R \notin M$ then $\exists s \in Neg_{\mathrm{v}^{val}}(T), R \sqcap s$ and thus by Definition 9, R is in conflict with T thus $R \notin P_{\mathcal{O}}(T)$, which is a contradiction. If $R \in M$ but $\exists R' \in M, R' \neq R, R' \geq R$ then by Definition 8, $R \notin P_{\mathcal{O}}(T)$ since it is dominated by another consistent rule, which is a contradiction. □

Property 12. Let s be a discrete state and R a $\mathcal{M}$VL rule. It holds that:

- (1) $\forall R' \in L_{\text{spe}}(R, s, \mathcal{A}, \mathcal{F}), R' \not\sqcap s$.
- (2) $\forall s' \in \mathcal{S}^{\mathcal{F}}, R \sqcap s' \wedge s \overset{\mathcal{F}}{\neq} s' \wedge s \overset{\mathcal{F}}{\not\succeq} s' \implies \exists R' \in L_{\text{spe}}(R, s, \mathcal{A}, \mathcal{F}), R' \sqcap s'$;

Proof.

- (1) By Definition 10, $\forall R' \in L_{\text{spe}}(R, s, \mathcal{A}, \mathcal{F}), \exists \mathrm{v}^{val} \in \text{body}(R'), \mathrm{v}^{val} \notin s$ thus $R' \not\sqcap s$ by Definition 5.
- (2) Let $s' \in \mathcal{S}^{\mathcal{F}}, R \sqcap s', s \neq s', s \overset{\mathcal{F}}{\not\succeq} s'$ thus $\exists \mathrm{v}^{val} \in s', \mathrm{v}^{val'} \in s, val \neq val'$. By Definition 10, $\exists R' \in L_{\text{spe}}(R, s, \mathcal{A}, \mathcal{F}), \text{body}(R') = \text{body}(R) \cup \mathrm{v}^{val}$, since $\mathrm{v}^{val} \notin s$ thus $\text{body}(R') \subseteq s'$ and $R' \sqcap s'$. Then $\exists R' \in L_{\text{spe}}(R, s, \mathcal{A}, \mathcal{F}), \mathrm{v}^{val'} \in$ body R' and thus $R' \not\sqcap \mathsf{actual}(s)$. □

Proposition 3. *(Optimal Program of Empty Set)* $P_{\mathcal{O}}(\emptyset) = \{\mathrm{v}^{val} \leftarrow \emptyset \mid \mathrm{v} \in \mathcal{T} \wedge val \in \mathsf{dom}(\mathrm{v})\}$.

Proof. By construction from Definition 8.

Theorem 4. *(Least Specialization and Suitability) Let* $\mathrm{v}^{val} \in \mathcal{A}$, $s \in \mathcal{S}^{\mathcal{F}}$ *and* $T, T' \subseteq \mathcal{S}^{\mathcal{F}} \times \mathcal{S}^{\mathcal{T}}$ *such that,* $\text{first}(T') = \{s\} \wedge s \notin \text{first}(T)$. *Let* $R_P := \{R \in P_{\mathcal{O}}(T) \mid R \sqcap s, \text{head}(R) = \mathrm{v}^{val}, s \in Neg_{\mathrm{v}^{val}}(T \cup T')\}$. *Then* $(P_{\mathcal{O}}(T) \setminus R_P) \cup \bigcup_{R \in R_P} L_{\text{spe}}(R, s, \mathcal{A}, \mathcal{F})$ *is suitable for* $T \cup T'$.

Proof. Let $P = (P_{\mathcal{O}}(T) \setminus R_P) \cup \bigcup_{R \in R_P} L_{\text{spe}}(R, s, \mathcal{A}, \mathcal{F})$. Since $P_{\mathcal{O}}(T)$ is consistent with T, by Definition 7, $(P_{\mathcal{O}}(T) \setminus R_P)$ and R_P are consistent with T. Furthermore, $\forall R \in R_P, \forall R' \in L_{\text{spe}}(R, s, \mathcal{A}, \mathcal{F}), R'$ is also consistent with T and thus P consistent with T. And P also consistent with T' from Proposition 6 since all conflicting rule of R_P have been made into consistent rules, thus P consistent with $T' \cup T$. Since $P_{\mathcal{O}}(T)$ realizes $T, s \notin T, s \in Neg_{\mathrm{v}^{val}}(T \cup T')$ thus by Definition 9, $\nexists s1 \in \text{first}(T), s1 \overset{\mathcal{F}}{\succeq} s$ thus from Proposition 6, $\forall (s1, s2) \in T, \exists R \in R_P, R$ realizes $(s1, s2)$ then $\exists R' \in L_{\text{spe}}(R, s, \mathcal{A}, \mathcal{F}), R'$ realizes $(s1, s2)$, thus P realize T. Since $s \notin \text{first}(T)$, a $\mathcal{M}$VL rule R such that $\text{body}(R) = s$ does not conflict with T. By definition of suitable program, $\forall \mathrm{v}^{val}, s \in Pos_{\mathrm{v}^{val}}(T \cup T'), \exists R' \in P_{\mathcal{O}}(T), R' \geq R$, thus $P_{\mathcal{O}}(T)$ realizes T' and P still realize T' from Proposition 6. We then also have P realizes $T \cup T'$ and from Proposition 4, let $TT \in \mathcal{S}^{\mathcal{F}}_m \times \mathcal{S}^{\mathcal{T}}_m$ such that $\mathsf{observed}(TT) = T$, then P realizes $\mathsf{actual}(TT)$. To prove that P verifies the last point of the definition of a suitable $\mathcal{M}$VLP, let R be a $\mathcal{M}$VL rule not conflicting with $T \cup T'$. Since R is also not conflicting with T, there exists $R' \in P_{\mathcal{O}}(T)$ such that $R' \geq R$. If R' is not conflicting with T', then R' will not be revised and $R' \in P$, thus R is dominated by a rule of P. Otherwise, R' is in conflict with T', thus $R' \sqcap s$ and $\forall (s, s') \in T', \exists \mathrm{v}^{val} \in s', \mathrm{v}^{val} \neq \text{head}(R')$. Since R is not in conflict with T' and $\text{head}(R) = \text{head}(R')$, since $R' \geq R$ then $\text{body}(R) = \text{body}(R') \cup I, \exists \mathrm{v}^{val} \in I, \mathrm{v}^{val} \notin s$. By definition of least specialization, there is a rule $R'' \in L_{\text{spe}}(R', s, \mathcal{A}, \mathcal{F})$ such that $\text{v}^{val} \in \text{body}(R'')$ and since $R'' = \text{head}(R') \leftarrow \text{body}(R') \cup \text{v}^{val}$ thus $R'' \geq R$. Thus R is dominated by a rule of P. □

Proposition 4. *(From Suitable to Optimal) Let $T \subseteq \mathcal{S}^{\mathcal{F}} \times \mathcal{S}^{\mathcal{T}}$. If P is a $\mathcal{DM}$VLP suitable for T, then $P_{\mathcal{O}}(T) = \{R \in P \mid \forall R' \in P, R' \geq R \implies R' = R\}$.*

Proof. By Definition 8.

References

1. Bérard, B., Haar, S., Schmitz, S., Schwoon, S.: The complexity of diagnosability and opacity verification for petri nets. Fund. Inf. **161**(4), 317–349 (2018)
2. Dubrova, E., Teslenko, M.: A SAT-based algorithm for finding attractors in synchronous Boolean networks. IEEE/ACM Trans. Comput. Biol. Bioinform. (TCBB) **8**(5), 1393–1399 (2011)
3. Gao, K., Wang, H., Cao, Y., Inoue, K.: Learning from interpretation transition using differentiable logic programming semantics. Mach. Learn. **111**(1), 123–145 (2022)
4. Gentet, E., Tourret, S., Inoue, K.: Learning from interpretation transition using feed-forward neural networks. In: CEUR Workshop Proceedings, vol. 1865, pp. 27–33. CEUR-WS.org (2016)
5. Inoue, K., Ribeiro, T., Sakama, C.: Learning from interpretation transition. Mach. Learn. **94**(1), 51–79 (2014)
6. Jacob, R., Lesage, J.J., Faure, J.M.: Overview of discrete event systems opacity: models, validation, and quantification. Ann. Rev. Control. **41**, 135–146 (2016)
7. Klarner, H., Streck, A., Siebert, H.: PyBoolNet: a python package for the generation, analysis and visualization of Boolean networks. Bioinformatics **33**(5), 770–772 (2016)
8. Lafortune, S., Lin, F., Hadjicostis, C.N.: On the history of diagnosability and opacity in discrete event systems. Ann. Rev. Control. **45**, 257–266 (2018)
9. Ma, Z., Cai, K.: Optimal secret protection in discrete event systems with dynamic clearance levels. IFAC-PapersOnLine **56**(2), 3579–3584 (2023)
10. Montassier, E., et al.: Robust airway microbiome signatures in acute respiratory failure and hospital-acquired pneumonia. Nat. Med. **29**(11), 2793–2804 (2023)
11. Nitral-AI: Hathor, a finetuned LLM model based on the llama 3 instruct (2024). https://huggingface.co/Nitral-AI/Hathor_Aleph-L3-8B-v0.72
12. Phua, Y.J., Inoue, K.: Learning logic programs from noisy state transition data. In: Kazakov, D., Erten, C. (eds.) ILP 2019. LNCS (LNAI), vol. 11770, pp. 72–80. Springer, Cham (2020). https://doi.org/10.1007/978-3-030-49210-6_7
13. Phua, Y.J., Inoue, K.: Learning logic programs using neural networks by exploiting symbolic invariance. In: Inductive Logic Programming - 30th International Conference, ILP 2021, Virtual Event, 25–27 October 2021, Proceedings. LNCS, vol. 13191, pp. 203–218. Springer, Heidelberg (2021). https://doi.org/10.1007/978-3-030-97454-1_15
14. Phua, Y.J., Ribeiro, T., Inoue, K.: Learning representation of relational dynamics with delays and refining with prior knowledge. FLAP **6**(4), 695–708 (2019)

15. Reveliotis, S.: Strongly infinite-step opaque boolean networks. In: 17th IFAC Workshop on Discrete Event Systems WODES 2024 (2024)
16. Ribeiro, T., Folschette, M., Magnin, M., Inoue, K.: Learning any memory-less discrete semantics for dynamical systems represented by logic programs. Mach. Learn. (1), 1–78 (2021). https://doi.org/10.1007/s10994-021-06105-4
17. Ribeiro, T., Folschette, M., Magnin, M., Inoue, K.: Polynomial algorithm for learning from interpretation transition. In: 1st International Joint Conference on Learning & Reasoning, pp. 1–5 (2021)

Towards an Automatic Student Supervisor System Using Declarative Languages

Nikolai-Iraj Sanamrad(✉), Cristina Padró-Ferragut, Carlos Monserrat, and M. José Ramírez-Quintana

Valencian Research Institute for Artifiial Intelligence (VRAIN), Universitat Politécnica de Valéncia, Valencia, Spain
insanamr@upv.es, {cpadro,cmonserr,mramirez}@dsic.upv.es

Abstract. Tasks with high complexity levels, such as cooking, surgical suturing, and the operation of sophisticated machinery, typically entail various learning stages. These stages may include individual study, observation of task execution, and hands-on practice under expert supervision. However, this supervision demands the presence and commitment of an expert, which is both time-consuming and expensive. This paper presents an automated student supervisor system that addresses these challenges, making supervision more cost-effective and scalable. We formally specify the behaviour of the supervisor system as a transition system that models how the configuration of the system changes with each action performed by the learner according to a given pattern/model that synthesises how the task must be executed. In this way, our system can supervise new student's executions by using conformance checking, thus comparing the current student action with the model. This allows the system to identify the correct and incorrect actions performed by the student during the execution of the task. We have implemented a prototype of the supervision system using the programming language Maude. Maude is a declarative formalism (based on rewriting logic) that has been shown to be suitable for specifying and reasoning about systems. The prototype was evaluated using a small dataset comprising samples of surgical suturing.

Keywords: Automated supervision system · Conformance checking · Formal specification · Declarative programming

1 Introduction

Human learning of complex tasks usually involves several distinct processes: individually learning about the task and its components, watching the performance of the task and finally executing the task under expert supervision [8].

W.-Z. Dai (Ed.): ILP 2024, LNAI 16059, pp. 86–100, 2026.
https://doi.org/10.1007/978-3-032-09087-4_6

Supervision of students is an expensive and time-consuming process usually involving an expert supervising the student individually, as it requires the attention of the expert during training. This leads to limited teaching scalability, as more experts are required to supervise more students. Besides, the scarcity of experts limits the scale to which learning can be expanded.

The solution to these limitations is to offer an automatic supervision system, which would provide real-time feedback as a student executes a task, similar to the feedback given by a supervising expert. An automatic supervision system should consist of multiple components responsible for storing and collecting information about a task and supervising a student using the available information.

This paper presents an automatic supervision system formally defined as a transition system and implemented in Maude [7], which is a powerful high-level formal reasoning tool using rewriting logic. Maude has been chosen for this task due to the particular requirements of conformance checking, for which formal reasoning and first-order logic provide an optimal set of tools for verification of systems based on configuration properties. In addition, Maude is capable of backtracking, which is useful for further expansion of the system. Maude has been used to verify critical code, as it can show states or configurations that could be reached but are not desired or not planned for. The automatic supervision system uses Dependency Graphs (DGs) as notation to represent the patterns that capture the know-how of experts by doing the task. In this way, supervision is carried out by matching the sequence of actions performed by the student with the pattern (conformance checking). We validated the Maude prototype using the JIGSAWS dataset [15], that includes examples of a surgical suturing task. This is a perfect example of a complex task that must be learned under expert supervision.

The contributions of this paper are twofold:

- The formal definition of an automated supervision system able to perform conformance checking of the task execution of a student represented by the sequence of performed activities. The system will provide the list of correctly and incorrectly executed activities and whether the task has been successfully completed (despite errors, if any). The list of errors will allow the evaluation of the learner and, for the learner, to know in which parts of the task he/she needs to improve.
- The implementation of the supervision system in Maude. The prototype is able to interactively (on-line) monitor the students' execution of the task by indicating, at any time, whether the activity to be performed (or being performed) complies with the pattern or not.

The paper is organised as follows: Sect. 2 presents some related work, Sect. 3 introduces the formalism of Dependency Graphs for representing complex tasks, Sect. 4 defines the supervisor system as a Transition System, Sect. 5 briefly describes the Maude implementation of the prototype, and Sect. 6 concludes the paper and offers potential pathways for prospective research by highlighting areas of potential future work.

2 Background

Learning complex tasks under expert supervision has long been considered an integral part of learning methods in multiple domains, which include professional training, apprenticeships, academia, and sports. Despite these significant benefits that experts bring to the learning process, studies over the years have indicated that there are notable difficulties involved [9]. This can be due to, among many factors, the limitations associated with experts' abilities to effectively transfer skills, costs and expert availability [13]. This has led to the exploration of automated solutions for learning complex tasks [4]. Among similar proposals, one such solution offers the prediction of an action based on last known action [3], but without task correctness analysis or feedback. A robotic cooperative manipulation system presented in another similar paper [5] uses a similar task model, offering varying ways to execute a task and recognises actions as they are being performed, but doesn't take into account complex relations between actions in a task. None of these systems utilise task models inferred from alternative ways of performing a task, unlike the system presented in this paper.

Process Mining (PM) has been pivotal in analyzing business processes through a data-driven approach. PM [1] uses event logs from information systems to extract data, preprocess it, discover process models, check their conformance, enhance them with performance metrics, and visualize the results. Various PM methods include declarative approaches that specify desired process properties or constraints. These approaches are flexible, allowing for process variations and additional constraints, typically using graphical languages and logic formalisms (e.g., ConDec [11] and Declare [12] with Linear Temporal Logic). Some methods directly use logic languages and inductive logic programming (ILP) techniques [2]. The hypothesis posited is that, similar to PM, logic-based languages like Maude can effectively model and supervise complex tasks performed by humans.

3 Modelling Tasks Performed by Humans

In this section, we first present Dependency Graphs as a suitable formalism for representing tasks performed by humans, which will serve as one of the inputs to our system. Then, we summarise the inference process described in [10] for inferring patterns/models representing different ways of performing a given task from several executions of the task performed by experts. These models, which are also described as Dependency Graphs, will be used in Sect. 5.2 to experimentally evaluate how our supervisor system is applied for the automatic monitoring of trainees. Finally, we introduce the notation used in the paper.

3.1 Representing Tasks by Dependency Graphs

A Dependency Graph [14] is a directed graph that represents the dependencies among a set of entities. In a Dependency Graph, nodes represent the entities such as actions, modules, or variables, and directed edges represent the dependencies between these entities. Thus, Dependency Graphs are a valuable tool for visualizing, analyzing, and managing dependencies within complex systems in an explainable and concise way.

In process mining [1], Dependency Graphs are instrumental for understanding the relationships and dependencies between various activities or events within a business process. Similarly to business processes, a task performed by humans can also be seen as a set of activities/actions that can exhibit dependencies among them. Thus, given the set of activities $\mathcal{A}$ that can be used to fulfill a task, an execution example is a finite sequence of these activities $(A_1, A_2, \ldots, A_m), A_i \in \mathcal{A}$, meaning that activity A_i is performed before A_{i+1}, $\forall i, 1 \leq i < m$. Thus, a sequence $(A_1, A_2, \ldots, A_m)$ can be represented as the Dependency Graph whose nodes are the activities A_i and whose edges are defined by each pair of consecutive nodes A_i and A_{i+1}, that is $A_i \rightarrow A_{i+1}$.

3.2 Learning Task Models

In [10], the authors present an inductive procedure to infer a collection of patterns/models of a task from a small set of execution examples performed by experts. Thus, each model represents a different way of performing the task. The approach uses Dependency Graphs (DGs) for representing the models demonstrating that DGs are robust enough to model tasks performed by humans for supervision purposes. DGs gerenalise the execution of tasks and thus inevitably lose some information from task examples, such as the exact number of loops and the relation of actions beyond those executed immediately before or after each other. Some of these limitations are addressed by the introduction of node types.

Figure 1 shows the complete process for obtaining multiple models from a collection of execution traces.

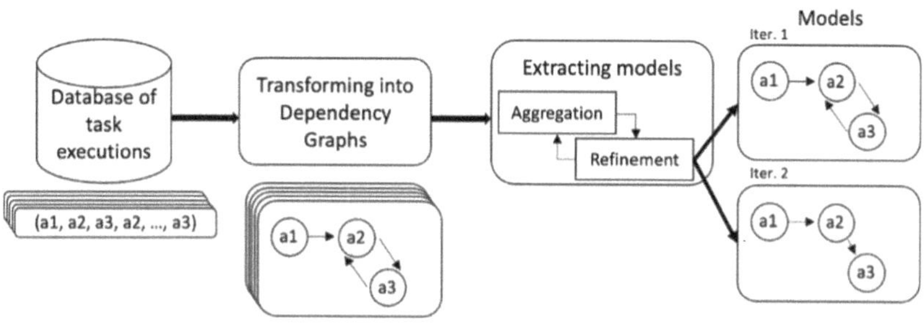

Fig. 1. Task model learning process

The process starts by converting the task execution traces into Dependency Graphs. Then, the model inference takes place by applying an inductive algorithm that combines a generalisation operator with a refinement operator. The generalisation operator generates the most general graph by aggregating all the Dependency Graphs. Then, the refinement operator specialises it to get the least general graph that is valid (there is at least one path in the graph that allows us to fulfill the task) and that covers at least one of the examples (that is, all the edges and nodes of the example are included in it). The generated graph that satisfies the two above conditions is considered a model and the examples covered are removed for the next iteration. The removal of the covered examples is aimed at letting the algorithm find a new general model covering the remaining examples, as they are intended to be applied in the order in which they were generated, in order to cover all examples. The process is repeated, generating one model in each iteration, until covering all the examples.

3.3 Dependency Graph Notation

A Dependency Graph is a directed graph $G = (V, E)$, where V is a set of labelled vertices v_{l_i}(representing actions or events l_i), and $E \subseteq V \times V$ is a set of directed edges. For the sake of readibility, each $(v_i, v_j) \in E$ is represented as $v_i \rightarrow v_j$. In order to be able to easily check the validity of the models, in [10] the set of labels $\mathcal{L}$ is extended to include two special labels S and F associated to the vertices v_S and v_F, respectively. These artificial nodes represent the first node/action to be executed (v_S) and the last node/action to be executed (v_F). Any possible path from (v_S) to (v_F) can be considered a correct or valid task execution.

One of the limitations of the algorithm for model generation outlined in the previous section is that some dependencies between nodes are lost in the inferred models, such as which sub-sequences of nodes are to be executed in mutual exclusion. In our approximation, we consider three possible dependencies between nodes (see Fig. 2).

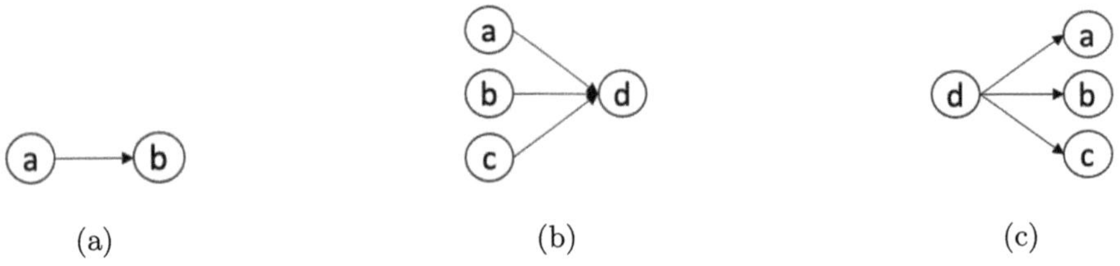

Fig. 2. Different types of dependencies between nodes in Dependency Graphs. (a) Sequential nodes. (b) Nodes with multiple input edges. (c) Nodes with several outgoing edges

The first case (Fig. 2.a) corresponds to consecutively executed events. The nodes with multiple input edges (Fig. 2.b) and the ones with several outgoing edges (Fig. 2.c) can be affected by the logical operators *AND*, *OR*, and *XOR*.

We assume that an expert extends the models by adding information at the nodes. For that, V is extended to include the type of the nodes (*N*ormal node,

AND node, *OR* node, *XOR* node) defined by the experts. For example, two subsequences that must run in mutual exclusion are indicated by stating that the common node at the beginning of the subsequences is an *XOR* node.

In what follows, we denote the nodes in V as (v_{l_i}, t_i), where t_i and l_i are the type and the label of node v_{l_i}, respectively. A path in a directed Dependency Graph can be defined as a sequence of nodes connected by edges. More formally, given a Dependency Graph $G = (V, E)$, a simple path from node v_i to v_j in G is defined as:

$$\begin{aligned} p_G(v_i, v_j) = (v_{k_1}, v_{k_2}, \ldots, v_{k_n}) \text{ such that} & \\ & (v_{k_r}, t_{k_r}) \in V, \forall 1 \leq r \leq n \\ & v_i = v_{k_1}, v_j = v_{k_n} \\ & v_{k_r} \neq v_{k_s} \forall 1 \leq r, s \leq n, r \neq s \\ & \forall 1 \leq r < n, (v_{k_r} \to v_{k_{r+1}}) \in E \end{aligned}$$

We denote the set of all simple paths from v_i to v_j in G as $P_G(v_i, v_j)$. Analogously, $in\_path(p_G(v_i, v_j))$ denotes the set of labels of the nodes in path $p_G(v_i, v_j)$, that is

$$in\_path(p_G(v_i, v_j)) = \{k | v_k \in p_G(v_i, v_j)\}$$

In that follows, the subscript G will be omitted when it is clear from the context.

4 Supervisor System Specification

In this section, we formally specify the supervisor system whose aims is to process the activities that a learner has performed in order to complete a given task. The system must check not only that all the activities necessary to successfully complete the task have been performed, but also that they have been executed in the correct order according to the model. To do this, the system takes the sequence of activities of the learner (in the order of execution) and analyses them sequentially. In this way, the system is also able to detect incorrectly performed activities, either because they have not been executed in the right order (according to the model) or because they do not belong to the model.

The supervision systems is modeled as a transition system describing its behavior. The transition system consists of a set of configurations $\mathcal{C}$, a transition relation $\Rightarrow$, and a set of rules $\mathcal{R}$ that determine how the transitions can be executed. To detect that the sequence of activities carried out by the learner conforms the model (that is, it corresponds to a valid path in the model) an activation indicator is assigned to each node. Formally,

$$path(v_i, v_j, G) = \{v_{k_1}, v_{k_2}, \ldots, v_{k_m} | v_{k_1} = v_i \wedge v_{k_m} = v_j \wedge \forall 1 \leq l < m : (v_{k_l} \to v_{k_{l+1}}) \in G\}$$

Definition 1. System Configuration
The system configuration is defined as the tuple

$$\langle A, LS, LR, LW, G, St \rangle$$

where $A = [A_i, \ldots, A_f]$ is a sequence of actions performed by the student, LS is the set whose elements are pairs of the form (l_k, f_k) being l_k the labels of all nodes in V and $f_k \in \{1, 0, -1\}$ an activation indicator denoting whether A_{l_k} has already been executed, not executed yet, or the paths from l_k must be executed in mutual exclusion or are blocked (respectively), LR and LW are the list of correct and incorrect actions (respectively) performed before A_i, G is the Dependency Graph (the model), and St is the status (that indicates whether it is starting, executing, or whether it has successfully or unsuccessfully completed the task).

Definition 2. Initial and Final System Configurations
Let $\mathcal{A} = \{A_1, \ldots, A_n\}$ be the set of activities for a given task, $[A_i, \ldots, A_f]$ the sequence of activities performed by a student augmented with the S and F artificial activities denoting the start and end of the task, respectively. Then, the initial configuration is

$$\langle [S, A_i, \ldots, A_f, F], [(S, 0), (A_1, 0), \ldots, (A_n, 0), (F, 0)], [], [], G, starting \rangle$$

Analogously, the final configuration is

$$\langle [], LS, LR, LW, G, final\_st \rangle$$

being the status $final\_st$ either *correct* or *incorrect* depending on whether the student has completed the task or not.

Without loss of generality, in the formalisation of the transition system sometimes a node (v_i, t_i) will be denoted as v_i when the node type t_i is not relevant to the definition of the rule.

The transition system composed of 11 rules is presented in Table 4. The rules are categorized to handle different types of nodes and conditions within the pattern:

- **Initialization**: Rule 1 sets the conditions under which a trace begins. This rule is essential for establishing the initial state of the system that allows the processing of the sequence of activities carried out by the student, enabling its supervision.
- **Task Completion**: Rules 2 and 3 define the conditions under which a trace ends, indicating successful task completion (rule 2) or failure to complete the task (rule 3).
- **Sequentiality**: Rule 4 handles the normal execution of activities that occur consecutively in the pattern, under the condition that neither the node corresponding to the current activity nor its parent node are logical operators.

- **Rejection**: Rule 5 specifies the conditions under an activity performed by the student is rejected either because it does not belong to the pattern or it cannot be executed due to the preceding activity according to the pattern not being performed or blocked.
- **AND Node Processing**: Rules 6 and 7 handle the execution of activities corresponding to AND nodes in the pattern. Rule 6 is applied when all the conditions for an AND node are met (i.e., the activities of all parent nodes in the pattern have been executed). Rule 7 reflects the invalid execution attempt of the AND node because the activities of some of its parent nodes have not been yet executed.
- **OR Node Processing**: Rule 8 processes activities that correspond to OR nodes in the pattern by checking that at least the activity of one of its parent nodes has already been executed.
- **XOR Node Processing**: Rule 9 handles XOR nodes, ensuring that the logical meaning of the XOR operator is satisfied, i.e., the child nodes of an XOR nodes are executed in mutual exclusion. The condition for identifying an XOR node is verified when an activity associated with one of its child nodes is processed, specifically when this is the first child node that is executed after the XOR node. To guarantee mutual exclusion, both the XOR node and all its alternative child nodes are blocked for further executions by setting their activation indicator to the value of -1.
- **LOOP Processing**: Rules 10 and 11 handle loops and activities that are repeated in the student sequence. Rule 10 ensures that the trace adheres to the loop conditions: there is a cycle in the pattern and all the activities in it has been executed by the student. If it is the case, the activation indicators of the nodes in the cycle are reset to 0, allowing for a new execution of the loop. Rule 11 detects when a student attempts to execute an activity that has already been done and that must be rejected based on one of the following conditions:
  - Potential Cycle Detection: The activity could be part of an existing cycle in the pattern. However, this cycle either has not been executed completely or contains nodes that has been previously blocked (meaning that the path is also blocked).
  - Absence of Cycles in the Pattern: There is no cycle in the pattern that includes this activity, and therefore, it cannot be repeated.

  This rule ensures that activities are executed in accordance with the defined patterns and prevents improper repetitions.

Table 1 illustrates an example of a trace using the supervision system. To facilitate the understanding of the trace, we label the symbol of the transition relation with the reference of the rule applied in each transition step. We use a toy example in that the activity labels are coded as natural numbers. We assume that the set of activities defining a given task t is $\mathcal{A} = \{1, 3, 2, 4, 4, 5\}$ and that G is the model of task t shown in Fig. 3. Finally, the sequence of activities performed by the student doing t is $(1, 3, 2, 4, 4, 5)$.

The supervisor system processes the student activities from the initial configuration (as defined in Definition 2). As displayed in Table 1, the final status indicates that task t has been successfully completed by the student. Also, the supervisor system has been able to identify the list $[S, 1, 3, 4, 5, F]$ as the correct activities according to pattern G (which constitute a valid path from S to F) and the list $[2, 4]$ as the incorrect activities performed by the student.

$$\frac{}{\langle [S|T], LS, LR, LW, G, starting\rangle \Rightarrow \langle T, LS \setminus \{(S,n)\} \cup \{(S, n+1)\}, LR + [S], LW, G, executing\rangle} \tag{1}$$

$$\frac{F \in LR}{\langle [], LS, LR, LW, G, executing\rangle \Rightarrow \langle [], LS, LR, LW, G, correct\rangle} \tag{2}$$

$$\frac{F \in LW}{\langle [], LS, LR, LW, G, executing\rangle \Rightarrow \langle [], LS, LR, LW, G, incorrect\rangle} \tag{3}$$

$$\frac{\begin{array}{c}(v_M \rightarrow v_A) \in G \ \wedge \ \{(v_A, t_A), (v_M, t_M)\} \subseteq V \wedge t_A \notin \{AND, OR\} \\ \wedge t_M \notin \{XOR\} \wedge (M, m) \in LS \wedge (A, 0) \in LS \wedge m > 0\end{array}}{\langle [A|T], LS, LR, LW, G, executing\rangle \Rightarrow \langle T, (LS \setminus \{(A, 0)\}) \cup \{(A, 1)\}, LR + [A], LW, G, executing\rangle} \tag{4}$$

$$\frac{\begin{array}{c}(\nexists\, v_M (v_M \rightarrow v_A) \in G) \\ \vee\ (\forall\, v_M (v_M \rightarrow v_A) \in G\ (\{(M, m)\} \subseteq\ LS \wedge (m \leq 0))\end{array}}{\langle [A|T], LS, LR, LW, G, executing\rangle \Rightarrow \langle T, LS, LR, LW + [A], G, executing\rangle} \tag{5}$$

$$\frac{(A, 0) \in LS \wedge (v_A, AND) \in V \wedge \forall v_M\ (v_M \rightarrow v_A) \in G\ ((M, m) \in LS \wedge m > 0)}{\langle [A|T], LS, LR, LW, G, executing\rangle \Rightarrow \langle T, LS \setminus \{(A, 0)\} \cup \{(A, 1)\}, LR + [A], LW, G, executing\rangle} \tag{6}$$

$$\frac{(A, 0) \in LS \wedge (v_A, AND) \in V \wedge \exists v_M\ (v_M \rightarrow v_A) \in G((M, m) \in LS \wedge m \leq 0)}{\langle [A|T], LS, LR, LW, G, executing\rangle \Rightarrow \langle T, LS, LR, LW + [A], G, executing\rangle} \tag{7}$$

$$\frac{(A, n) \in LS \wedge (v_A, OR) \in G \wedge \exists v_M\ (v_M \rightarrow v_A) \in G\ ((M, m) \in LS \wedge m > n)}{\langle [A|T], LS, LR, LW, G, executing\rangle \Rightarrow \langle T, LS \setminus \{(A, n)\} \cup \{(A, n+1)\}, LR + [A], LW, G, executing\rangle} \tag{8}$$

$$\frac{(v_M \rightarrow v_A) \in G \wedge (v_M, XOR) \in V \wedge (M, 1) \in LS}{\begin{array}{l}\langle [A|T], LS, LR, LW, G, executing\rangle \Rightarrow \langle T, LS \setminus\ (\{(M, 1)\} \cup \{(F, f) | (v_M \rightarrow v_F) \in G\}) \\ \qquad \cup\ \{(A, 1), (M, -1)\} \cup \{(F, -1) | (v_M \rightarrow v_F) \in G, F \neq A\}, \\ \qquad LR + [A], LW, G, executing\rangle\end{array}} \tag{9}$$

$$\frac{\begin{array}{c}(v_M \rightarrow v_A) \in G \wedge \{(M, m), (A, n)\} \subseteq\ LS \wedge (n \neq 0) \wedge (m \neq 0) \\ \wedge \exists p \in P_G(v_A, v_M)\ (\forall v_J \in in\_path(p)((J, j) \in LS \wedge j \neq 0)) \\ \wedge(\nexists v_K, v_L \in in\_path(p)(v_K \rightarrow v_L \in G, \{(K, -1), (L, -1)\} \subseteq LS))\end{array}}{\begin{array}{l}\langle [A|T], LS, LR, LW, G, executing\rangle \Rightarrow \langle T, (LS\setminus\ \{(V, f) |\ \forall p \in P_G(v_A, v_M)(V \in in\_path(p))\} \\ \qquad \cup\{(V, 0) |\ \forall p \in P_G(v_A, v_M)(V \in in\_path(p))(V \neq A)\} \\ \qquad \cup\{(A, 1)\}, LR + [A], LW, G, executing\rangle\end{array}} \tag{10}$$

$$\frac{\begin{array}{l}\forall\, v_M (v_M \rightarrow v_A) \in G \wedge \{(M, m), (A, n)\} \subseteq\ LS \wedge n \neq 0 \wedge m \neq 0 \\ \wedge(\ (\bigcup_{v_M} P_G(v_A, v_M) = \emptyset) \vee (\forall p \in \bigcup_{v_M}\ P_G(v_A, v_M) \\ \qquad (\exists v_J \in in\_path(p)\ \ ((J, 0) \in LS))\vee \\ \qquad (\exists v_K, v_L \in in\_path(p)(v_K \rightarrow v_L \in G, \{(K, -1), (L, -1)\} \subseteq LS)))\end{array}}{\langle [A|T], LS, LR, LW, G, executing\rangle \Rightarrow \langle T, LS, LR, LW + [A], G, executing\rangle} \tag{11}$$

Table 1. Execution trace of the student sequence $(1, 3, 2, 4, 4, 5)$ using the model in Fig. 3 and the rules of the Transition System in Table 4

$\langle [S, 1, 3, 2, 4, 4, 5, F], [(S, 0), (1, 0), (2, 0), (3, 0), (4, 0), (5, 0), (F, 0)], [], [], G, starting\rangle \stackrel{1}{\Rightarrow}$
$\langle [1, 3, 2, 4, 4, 5, F], [(S, 1), (1, 0), (2, 0), (3, 0), (4, 0), (5, 0), (F, 0)], [S], [], G, executing\rangle \stackrel{4}{\Rightarrow}$
$\langle [3, 2, 4, 4, 5, F], [(S, 1), (1, 1), (2, 0), (3, 0), (4, 0), (5, 0), (F, 0)], [S, 1], [], G, executing\rangle \stackrel{9}{\Rightarrow}$
$\langle [2, 4, 4, 5, F], [(S, 1), (1, -1), (2, -1), (3, 1), (4, 0), (5, 0), (F, 0)], [S, 1, 3], [], G, executing\rangle \stackrel{5}{\Rightarrow}$
$\langle [4, 4, 5, F], [(S, 1), (1, -1), (2, -1), (3, 1), (4, 0), (5, 0), (F, 0)], [S, 1, 3], [2], G, executing\rangle \stackrel{4}{\Rightarrow}$
$\langle [4, 5, F], [(S, 1), (1, -1), (2, -1), (3, 1), (4, 1), (5, 0), (F, 0)], [S, 1, 3, 4], [2], G, executing\rangle \stackrel{11}{\Rightarrow}$
$\langle [5, F], [(S, 1), (1, -1), (2, -1), (3, 1), (4, 1), (5, 0), (F, 0)], [S, 1, 3, 4], [2, 4], G, executing\rangle \stackrel{8}{\Rightarrow}$
$\langle [F], [(S, 1), (1, -1), (2, -1), (3, 1), (4, 1), (5, 1), (F, 0)], [S, 1, 3, 4, 5], [2, 4], G, executing\rangle \stackrel{4}{\Rightarrow}$
$\langle [], [(S, 1), (1, -1), (2, -1), (3, 1), (4, 1), (5, 1), (F, 1)], [S, 1, 3, 4, 5, F], [2, 4], G, executing\rangle \stackrel{2}{\Rightarrow}$
$\langle [], [(S, 1), (1, -1), (2, -1), (3, 1), (4, 1), (5, 1), (F, 1)], [S, 1, 3, 4, 5, F], [2, 4], G, correct\rangle$

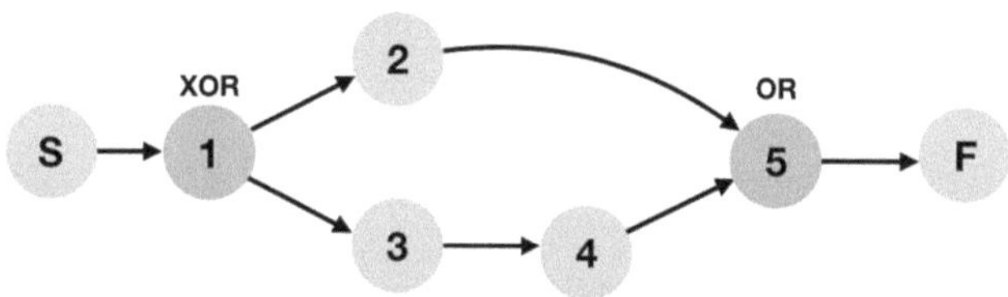

Fig. 3. An example of a task model represented as a Dependency Graph

5 Automated Supervision Prototype

In this section, we briefly describes the main characteristics of the supervision system prototype we have implemented in Maude, and some experiments carried out to show how the prototype works in practice.

5.1 Implementation Using Maude

The formal definition of the automatic supervision system defined in the previous section has been implemented using Maude and uploaded to a GitHub repository[1]. We have defined the following data structure to implement the system configuration: $Config = ActionList$ — $TupleList$ — $ActionList$ — $ActionList$ — $Graph$ — $Status$, which is a tuple of six elements. Each element corresponds to a component and occupies its designated position in a specific order separated by |. The first component represents the student's sequence of actions, the second is the list of pairs (the action's label and an activation indicator), and so on.

[1] https://github.com/supervision-systems-development/graph-models.

The rules of the Transition System shown in Table 4 are implemented in Maude using rewriting rules. This is because unlike functional equations, rewriting rules in Maude do not have to terminate, making them ideal for saving the system's configurations. Thus, similar to how transition rules are applied to the system configuration, Maude rewriting rules are also applied to the configuration. These rewriting rules work by matching patterns of specified components, performing transitions according to the transition system. Due to space constraints, we include the *start* rewriting rule that implements rule 1 in Table 4. This rule (shown in Fig. 4) is applied when the system status is set to *starting*, as indicated by the *Status* variable. Once the *start* rewriting rule is applied, the input action $a[i]$ is added to the list of correct actions LR, and function *activateCookie* is called to add the tuple $t(i, 1)$ to the list of activation indicators LS. Following this, the system status in the configuration is changed to *executing*, ensuring that this rule cannot be applied to subsequent configurations.

```
rl [start]:
  a[i] ; AList | TupleCookies | CList | EList | G | starting
  =>
  if isStartingNode( a[i] , G )
    then
      AList | activateCookie( i , TupleCookies) | ( CList ; (a[i]) ) |
        EList | G | executing
    else
      AList | TupleCookies | CList | ( EList ; (a[i]) ) | G | starting
  fi .
```

Fig. 4. The *start* rewriting rule implementing the system transition rule 1

5.2 Experimental Evaluation

To evaluate the behaviour of our supervisor prototype, two experiments were conducted. The experiments are aimed at demonstrating that our system functionality is correct and conforms to the formal definition of the supervision system. In the first experiment, we replicated the configuration used in Table 1 in Sect. 4 to demonstrate identical behaviour with the system specification. In the second experiment, we assessed the system's conformance checking capabilities using the JIGSAWS dataset [15].

Showing Maude Supervisor Functionality with a Toy Example. First, we have replicated the configuration used in Table 1 in Sect. 4 with the toy example in Fig. 3. The result of the Maude program is shown on Fig. 5. It shows a default *rewrite* command with the starting configuration used in Table 1 as an argument. Without arguments, the *rewrite* command returns the last configuration after all rewrites have been performed. The last configuration is identical to the final configuration shown in Table 1.

```
rewrite in GRAPH-RL : (a(-5) ; a(1) ; a(3) ; a(2) ; a(4) ; a(4) ;
a(5) ; a(-7)) | nil | nil | nil | (((((n[1]: nxor -> n[3]: nseq
;; n[-5]: nseq -> n[1]: nxor) ;; n[1]: nxor -> n[2]: nseq) ;;
n[3]: nseq -> n[4]: nseq) ;; n[2]: nseq -> n[5]: nor) ;; n[5]:
nor -> n[-7]: nseq) ;; n[4]: nseq -> n[5]: nor | starting .
rewrites: 1721 in 0ms cpu (0ms real) (~ rewrites/second)
result Config: nil | (-5,1),t(3,1),t(1,-1),t(2,-1),t(4,1),t(5,1),
t(-7,1) | a(-5) ; a(1) ; a(3) ; a(4) ; a(5) ; a(-7) | a(2) ; a(4) |
n[1]: nxor -> n[2]: nseq ;; n[1]: nxor -> n[3]: nseq ;; n[2]: nseq
-> n[5]: nor ;; n[3]: nseq -> n[4]: nseq ;; n[4]: nseq -> n[5]: nor
;; n[5]: nor -> n[-7]: nseq ;; n[-5]: nseq -> n[1]: nxor | correct
```

Fig. 5. Maude output for the input sequence $S = (1, 3, 2, 4, 4, 5)$ and the graph model in Fig. 3, with a correct result. This output expresses S as -5 and F as -7 due to the internal implementation of labels as integers.

Conformance Checking Using the JIGSAWS Dataset. The JIGSAWS dataset [15] offers a set of samples for surgical suturing from four different professional surgeons. Surgical suturing is an optimal complex task to use and consists of clear atomic actions that can be performed with variations to complete the task. These atomic actions are clear for non-professionals, which makes this a great explainable example. A subsample of this dataset was used in [10] to infer several models (expressed as Dependency Graphs) applying the inference procedure we outlined in Sect. 3.

In this section we used the sequences of actions in JIGSAW and the models from prior work [10] to perform a conformance checking analysis. Conformance checking [6] is a technique used in process mining to compare a given process model with the actual execution of the process.

In conformance checking, we are only interested in determining which sequences can perform the task according to a model, so we are only interested in the final value of the $final_st$ component of the configuration after the execution, as it is either *correct* or *incorrect*, indicating the success of the task execution. Due to the large dataset size, only part of the results is shown. In particular, Table 2 shows the trace logs for sequences 13, 14, 15, and 16.

Table 2. Subsample of the dataset

Sequence	Sequence of actions (log)
13	1,5,8,2,3,6,9,4,2,3,6,9,2,4,2,3,6,9,4,2,3,6,9,11
14	1,4,8,2,3,6,9,4,2,3,6,9,6,2,3,6,9,4,2,3,6,9,11
15	1,5,8,2,3,6,9,4,2,3,6,9,4,2,3,6,9,4,2,3,6,9,11
16	1,5,2,3,6,4,2,3,6,4,2,3,6,4,2,3,6,11

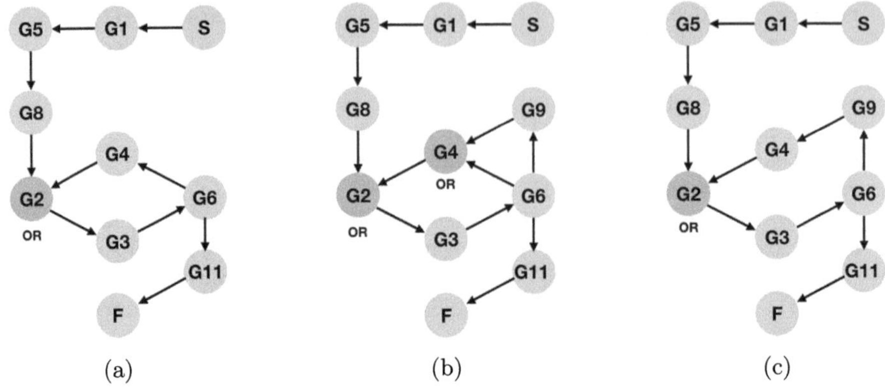

Fig. 6. Dependency Graphs [10] used for conformance checking. Starting nodes are labelled with S, ending nodes are labelled with F, nodes with logical functionality are marked in cyan and have their logical function indicated

Table 3. Conformance checking results for the sequences shown in Table 2 with task models shown on Fig. 6

	Sequence conformance and rejection proportion for each model					
Sequence	Graph (a)	% Rejected	Graph (b)	% Rejected	Graph (c)	% Rejected
13	Correct	20%	Correct	4%	Correct	4%
14	Incorrect	95%	Incorrect	95%	Incorrect	95%
15	Correct	17%	Correct	0%	Correct	0%
16	Incorrect	88%	Incorrect	88%	Incorrect	88%

The results for the four sequences in Table 2 are shown in Table 3. For each model (columns (a), (b) and (c)) we indicate whether the sequence conforms to the model. Additionally, it shows the proportion of rejected actions (columns %Rejected).

From the four sequences, two conform all three models, and two do not conform to any model. Sequence 13 conforms each model, but with different proportions of incorrect actions. In particular, with model (a), 20% of the actions are considered incorrect, but only 4% are considered incorrect with models (b) and (c). This is caused by the absence of the node $G9$ in model (a), which sequence 13 executes several times. Sequence 14 does not conform to any model due to the absence of mandatory action $G5$. Sequence 15 conforms to all models. However, due to the absence of the node $G9$ in model (a), the rate of incorrect actions for model is higher. Sequence 16 does not conform to all models with a high rate of incorrect actions due to the absence of the mandatory $G8$ in it.

The conformance analysis of the entire JIGSAWS dataset containing 39 sequences with respect to the models in Fig. 6 resulted in 20 sequences conforming models (a) and (b), and 21 sequences conforming model (c). The same sequences that conform (a) also conform (b) and (c), with model (c) having only one additional conforming sequence that does not conform (a) nor (b).

6 Conclusion and Future Work

In this paper, we formally defined an automatic supervisor system able to monitor trainees doing tasks using Maude. It uses Dependency Graphs [10] as the formalism to express task models, giving us a simple but clear understanding of complex tasks made up of separate actions. We extended the notation of Dependency Graphs to include the dependencies between the nodes expressed as the logical operators *And*, *Or*, and XOR. The defined supervisor system is able not only of detecting that the learners have completed the task or not, but also monitoring the learner doing the task by identifying which of the actions carried out are correct (because they are included in the model and have been executed in the right order), and which ones are incorrect. This information is crucial for supervisory duties.

Despite us using inferred task models for behaviour demonstration, the developed system is general enough to be used with any task model consisting of clearly defined atomic actions, including hand-generated models based on the expert knowledge about the task, with the only restriction that models must be expressed in the dependency graph notation. The model resolution can vary based on the detail to which the atomic actions are specified.

Another future work will involve benchmark comparisons or large-scale testing and applying iterative learning for continuous improvement could be beneficial. System evaluation using more real-world examples is also intended to be performed in future work.

Future research should prioritize support of high-level description of a task (for instance, in natural language), from which (semi-)automatically get other restrictions and dependencies between the nodes of the model.

Acknowledgement. This work was funded by CIPROM/2022/6 (FASSLOW) funded by Generalitat Valenciana, the EC H2020-EU grant agreement No. 952215 (TAILOR), and Spanish grant PID2021-122830OB-C42 (SFERA) funded by MCIN/AEI/10.13039/ 501100011033 and "ERDF A way of making Europe". NS is supported by grant Generalitat Valenciana (European funds 2014–2020 REACT-EU). CPF is supported by Universitat Politècnica de València under FPI grant PAID-01-22.

References

1. van der Aalst, W.M.P.: Process Mining: Data Science in Action, 2 edn. Springer, Heidelberg (2016). https://doi.org/10.1007/978-3-662-49851-4
2. Alman, A., Maggi, F.M., Montali, M., Peñaloza, R.: Probabilistic declarative process mining. Inf. Syst. **109**, 102033 (2022)

3. Both, F., Hoogendoorn, M., Treur, J.: Model-based ambient analysis of human task execution. In: Proceedings of the 1st international conference on PErvasive Technologies Related to Assistive Environments, PETRA '08, pp. 1–8. Association for Computing Machinery, New York (2008). https://doi.org/10.1145/1389586.1389690
4. Brynjolfsson, E., M.A.: The Second Machine Age: Work, Progress, and Prosperity in a Time of Brilliant Technologies. WW Norton & Company, New York (2014)
5. Cacace, J., Caccavale, R., Finzi, A., Lippiello, V.: Interactive plan execution during human-robot cooperative manipulation. IFAC-PapersOnLine **51**(22), 500–505 (2018)
6. Carmona, J., Van Dongen, B., Solti, A., Weidlich, M.: Conformance Checking: Relating Processes and Models. Springer, Cham (2018). https://doi.org/10.1007/978-3-319-99414-7
7. Clavel, M., et al.: Maude: specification and programming in rewriting logic. Theor. Comput. Sci. **285**(2), 187–243 (2002). https://doi.org/10.1016/S0304-3975(01)00359-0. https://www.sciencedirect.com/science/article/pii/S0304397501003590
8. Ericsson, K.A.: Development of Professional Expertise: Toward Measurement of Expert Performance and Design of Optimal Learning Environments. Cambridge University Press, Cambridge (2009)
9. Ericsson, K. A., Krampe, R. T., Tesch-Römer, C.: The role of deliberate practice in the acquisition of expert performance. Psychol. Rev. **100**(3), 363 (1993)
10. Nieves, D., Ramírez-Quintana, M., Monserrat, C., Ferri, C., Hernández-Orallo, J.: Learning alternative ways of performing a task. Expert Syst. Appl. **148**, 113263 (2020)
11. Pesic, M., van der Aalst, W.M.P.: A declarative approach for flexible business processes management. In: Eder, J., Dustdar, S. (eds.) BPM 2006. LNCS, vol. 4103, pp. 169–180. Springer, Heidelberg (2006). https://doi.org/10.1007/11837862_18
12. Pesic, M., Schonenberg, H., Van der Aalst, W.M.: Declare: full support for loosely-structured processes. In: 11th IEEE International Enterprise Distributed Object Computing Conference (EDOC 2007), pp. 287–287. IEEE (2007)
13. Sweller, J.: Cognitive load during problem solving: effects on learning. Cogn. Sci. **12**(2), 257–285 (1988)
14. Van Steen, M.: Graph theory and complex networks. Introduction **144**, 1–287 (2010)
15. Gao, Y., et al.: The JHU-ISI gesture and skill assessment working set (JIGSAWS): a surgical activity dataset for human motion modeling. In: MICCAI Workshop (2014)

Learning Rules Explaining Interactive Theorem Proving Tactic Prediction

Liao Zhang[1(✉)], David M. Cerna[2], and Cezary Kaliszyk[1,3]

[1] University of Innsbruck, Innsbruck, Austria
Liao.Zhang@student.uibk.ac.at
[2] Czech Academy of Sciences, Prague, Czechia
dcerna@cas.cs.cz
[3] University of Melbourne, Melbourne, Australia
cezary.kaliszyk@unimelb.edu.au

Abstract. Formally verifying the correctness of mathematical proofs is more accessible than ever, however, the learning curve remains steep for many of the state-of-the-art interactive theorem provers (ITP). Deriving the most appropriate subsequent proof step, and reasoning about it, given the multitude of possibilities, remains a daunting task for novice users. To improve the situation, several investigations have developed machine learning based guidance for *tactic* selection.

Such approaches struggle to learn non-trivial relationships between the chosen tactic and the structure of the proof state and represent them as symbolic expressions. To address these issues we (i) We represent the problem as an *Inductive Logic Programming (ILP)* task, (ii) Using the ILP representation we enriched the feature space by encoding additional, computationally expensive properties as *background knowledge* predicates, (iii) We use this enriched feature space to learn rules explaining when a tactic is applicable to a given proof state, (iv) We use the learned rules to filter the output of an existing tactic selection approach and empirically show improvement over the non-filtering approaches.

Keywords: Inductive logic programming · Interactive theorem proving

1 Introduction

Interactive Theorem Provers (ITP), such as Coq [27], Lean [20], and Isabelle [22], are powerful tools that combine human instruction with computer verification to construct formal mathematical proofs, providing a reliable means of certification and ensuring safety in critical applications.

These systems operate as follows: the user specifies a goal to prove, *the initial proof state*. Then the user specifies *tactics* (an operation transforming a proof state into proof states). Certain tactics close proof states. The proof is complete if there are no remaining open proof states, i.e., the goal has been proved.

W.-Z. Dai (Ed.): ILP 2024, LNAI 16059, pp. 101–116, 2026.
https://doi.org/10.1007/978-3-032-09087-4_7

Given the complexity of ITP systems, a fully automated approach to proving user specified goals is intractable. Numerous investigations have instead focused on providing the user with guidance through tactic suggestion.

The methods used in practice by ITP users are statistical machine learning methods such as k-nearest neighbors (k-NN) and naive Bayes [9]. These methods take a goal g, select a goal g' most similar goal to g, and rank the particular tactics relevant for solving g' based on their likelihood of solving g.

Neural network and LLM-based approaches addressing the task include: CoqGym [29] trains tree neural networks to automatically construct proofs for *Coq*. Thor [14] combines LLMs and external symbolic solvers to search for proofs for Isabelle. LLMs are also applied to synthesising training data to enhance the performance of theorem proving [28]. Despite showing slight improvement in performance during machine learning evaluations, in practice these methods require long training for each new theory, which makes them less useful for day to day proof development.

Additionally, they lack interpretability. When a user receives predictions, they may want to know why a particular tactic was chosen over another tactic to better understand what actions they should take in the future.

Furthermore, guidance based on statistical learning approaches often requires propositionalisation of features, calculated based on the structure of the *abstract syntax tree (AST)* of a proof state [30], e.g., *there is a path between nodes X and Y in tree T*. For complex and precise features, pre-computation is prohibitively expensive.

Moreover, logical inference is significantly influenced by the small error margins present in the statistical inferencing mechanisms of LLMs and similar models. Thus, predictions based on chained logical inferences will quickly suffer a loss of predicative accuracy [17].

In contrast to pre-computed features, we represent such features as logic programs and compute them only when needed for learning. For example, we define logic programs for the existence of two particular nodes on a path (of arbitrary length) from the root of the tree as ($above(AST, X, Y)$). Below, we present a learned rule for the simplification tactic which states that the tactic is applicable to a proof state when the goal node of the proof state contains a constant above two constructs (also in the goal) which differ.

```
tac(A,"simpl") :-
  goal_node(const,A,B,C), goal_node(construct,A,D,E),
  goal_above(A,B,D), goal_node(construct,A,F,E),dif(F,D),
  goal_above(A,B,F).
```

The rules, as presented above, are learned using inductive logic programming (ILP), in particular, *Aleph* [26]. In addition to providing rules explaining tactic prediction, we use the resulting rules to filter the output of k-NN, in particular, the classifier presented in [3,9] (Tactician and TacticToe). Essentially, we want to determine whether $ps, r \models p_t$ where ps is a logic program representing the proof state, r is a learned rule for the tactic t, and p_t is the head predicate of

r denoting that t should be applied to ps. Thus, given the list of recommended tactics by a k-NN classifier, we can further filter this list using the learned rules. Our hypothesis is that features of proof state defined through logic programs can be used to learn rules which can be used to filter the output of a k-NN model to improve accuracy.

In addition to improved performance, our approach produces rules to explain the predictions. Consider again the aforementioned rule of `simpl` that specifies that the goal may be simplified if it contains a constant above two constructors with different positions. Here, the constructor and the constant denote the datatypes of Coq's terms. The same variable E confirms that the two constructors must correspond to the same identifier in Coq. This rule may suit the Coq structure $S\ x - S\ y$ which denotes $(1 + x) - (1 + y)$. It can be simplified to $x - y$. S denotes a constructor, and $-$ denotes a constant. The first argument of `goal_node` is a constant that is constrained by us via mode declarations [26].

We use the ILP system Aleph [26] together with a user-defined cost function to evaluate the learned rules on Coq's standard library. We chose Aleph because it has empirically good results [5]. We refrain from using modern ILP approaches such as *Popper* [6] as the underlying ASP solvers have difficulty generating models when many variables are required and high-arity definitions are included in the background. We develop representation predicates (`goal_node`) to efficiently denote the nodes of the AST. We also develop feature predicates (`goal_above`) which denote the properties of the AST calculated based on the representation predicates. The motivation for developing feature predicates is that propositionalization of it would significantly enlarge the representation making it impractical to use. Our experiments confirm that feature predicates can learn more precise rules (rules with higher F-1 scores [25]) compared to representation predicates. Additionally, the experiments demonstrate that the combination of ILP and k-NN can improve the accuracy of tactic suggestions in Tactician, the main tactic prediction system for Coq.

Contributions First, we express the task of predicting the best tactic to apply to the given proof state as an ILP task. Second, using the ILP representation we enriched the feature space by encoding additional, computationally expensive features as *background knowledge* predicates, allowing us to avoid grounding the features which are computationally expensive. Third, We use this enriched feature space to learn rules explaining when a tactic is applicable to a given proof state and filter the output of an existing tactic selection approach using these rules. Finally, We empirically show improvement over the non-filtering approaches.

This is the first time an investigation has considered ILP as a tool for improving tactic suggestion methods for ITPs.

2 Background

Theorem Proving in Coq. Coq is one of the most popular proof assistants and has been widely used for building trustworthy software [18] and verifying the

```
Inductive nat : Type :=
  | O
  | S (n : nat).

Theorem add_assoc : ∀ n m p : nat,
  n + (m + p) = (n + m) + p.
Proof.
  induction n.
  - intros. simpl. reflexivity.
  - intros. simpl. rewrite IHn. reflexivity.
Qed.
```

```
n : nat
IHn : ∀ m p : nat, n + (m + p) = n + m + p
m, p : nat
______________________________________(1/1)
S n + (m + p) = S n + m + p
```

Fig. 1. A Coq proof of the associative property of addition and the proof state before `simpl`.

correctness of mathematical proofs [10]. Coq tactics are proof state transformations that provide a high-level combination of underlying logical inferences. To illustrate how theorems are formalized in Coq, we present a simple example in Fig. 1. Here, we want to prove the associative property of addition. The natural numbers in Coq are defined by two constructors `O` and `S`. `O` denotes 0, and `S n` denotes $n + 1$. Here, the initial proof state is the same as the statement of the theorem. We first apply induction on `n` and obtain two cases corresponding to the two constructors. In the first case, `n` equals 0. After some simplifications, we can prove $0 = 0$ by the tactic `reflexivity`. The second case is a bit more complicated, and we need to apply the induction hypothesis `IHn` to finish the proof. Figure 1 also presents a concrete example of a proof state. A proof state consists of a *goal* to prove and several *hypotheses*. The goal is below the dashed line. `IHn`, `n`, `m`, and `p` are the names of hypotheses. A proof state is often represented as a sequent $E \vdash g$ where E and g denote the hypotheses and the goal, respectively.

Adaptations of k-NN to Theorem Proving. Several machine learning algorithms have been adapted to theorem proving tasks. In most cases, simpler algorithms adapted to formal reasoning tasks perform better than deep learning based methods in practice. For this reason, modified k-NN (explained in [2]) is the main algorithm for TacticToe and Tactician. Even if evaluations with deep learning or large tree-based classifiers have shown some theoretical improvements, the simpler algorithms training for the particular theories developed by users, give a larger practical advantage to the users. As such, we focus on the modified k-NN in this work. Standard k-NN starts by calculating the distance between a new proof state and all known proof states in the database. The distance is measured by the similarity between the features of the proof states, usually using tree walks in the AST of the proof state [16]. The dependencies of such selected neighbours, with additional scaling by their distances, inclusion of the neighbours themselves, and further modifications exhibit commendable empirical performance [24], and are therefore the default algorithm both in Tactictoe and Tactician.

3 Background Knowledge

To utilize ILP, we need to appropriately define the background knowledge. We start this section by encoding the nodes of AST as representation predicates. Then we propose new feature predicates that will allow leveraging the power of ILP. We finally add predicate anonymization, already very useful in automated reasoning systems, to representation and feature predicates.

3.1 Representation Predicates

Every node in the AST of the proof state is converted to a fact. There are two categories of nodes: identifiers of existing objects and constructors of Coq's datatype. A node in the goal is converted to $goal\_node(name, nat, goal\_idx)$. The argument *name* refers to the value of the node. A unique natural number is assigned to every proof state to identify it. The argument $goal\_idx$ uses a sequence of natural numbers to specify the position of the node in the goal. A node in a hypothesis is converted to a fact $hyp\_node(name, nat, hyp\_name, hyp\_idx)$. Compared to a $goal\_idx$, a hyp_idx starts with the name of a hypothesis so that two hyp_idx from different hypotheses have different prefixes. The $goal\_node$ and hyp_node predicates are called *representation predicates* in this work.

3.2 Feature Predicates

We also define two categories of *feature predicates* which represent the properties of AST based on the representation predicates.

Positional Predicates represents the relative relationships between nodes' positions. The predicate `goal_left(Goal_idx1, Goal_idx2)` and `goal_above(Nat, Goal_idx1, Goal_idx2)` respectively checks whether the node is left (above) to another node in the goal. They are inspired by the horizontal features and vertical features used in previous works [4,30]. Similarly, we define `hyp_left(Hyp_idx1, Hyp_idx2)` and `hyp_above(Nat, Hyp_idx1, Hyp_idx2)`. Previous works have confirmed the usefulness of using the occurrence numbers of features in feature characterization, which inspires us to develop the predicate `dif(Goal_idx1, Goal_idx2)`. It denotes that the same node multiply occurs in different positions in the goal.

Equational Predicates check the equality between two terms. The predicate `eq_goal_term(Nat, Goal_idx1, Goal_idx2)` checks that the two subterms in the goal are the same. The root nodes of the two subterms are located in the positions `Goal_idx1` and `Goal_idx2`, respectively. It pertains to `reflexivity` which proves a goal of the equation if the equality holds after some normalization. Thus, it can prove $x = x$ and inspires us to develop `eq_goal_term`. The predicate `eq_goal_hyp_term(Nat, Goal_idx, Hyp_idx)` is inspired by a number of tactics that check the equality between the goal and the hypotheses, such as `assumption`, `apply`, and `auto`. For instance, `assumption` proves a goal if it equals

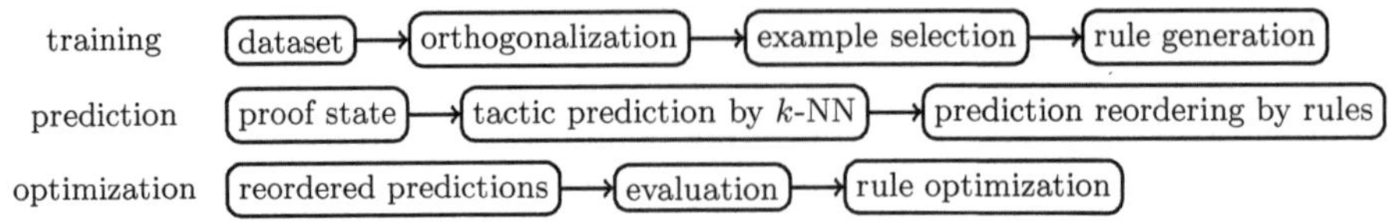

Fig. 2. An overview of the procedures of the learning framework.

a hypothesis. Assume a proof state $H_1 : Q\ x, H_2 : P\ x \rightarrow Q\ x \vdash Q\ x$ which can be proved by `assumption`. The predicate `eq_goal_hyp_term` checks the equality between the goal and $Q\ x$ in a hypothesis. The predicate `is_hyp_root(Nat, Hyp_idx)` ensures the node is the root of a hypothesis. Thus, it can show the equality only holds between the goal and H_1 instead of H_2. With a reason akin to that of `is_hyp_root`, we define `is_goal_root(Nat, Goal_idx)`. The equality between two terms in different hypotheses is checked by `eq_hyp_term(Nat, Hyp_idx1, Hyp_idx2)`. It is useful for tactics that can apply hypotheses several times, e.g., `auto`. Assume a proof state $H_1 : P\ x, H_2 : P\ x \rightarrow Q\ x \vdash Q\ x$. First, `auto` applies H_2 to the goal and changes the goal to $P\ x$. Then, it applies H_1 to prove the new goal. The description of the operation requires to show that H_1 equals to the premise of H_2.

3.3 Anonymous Predicates

We also substitute identifiers with more abstract descriptions to facilitate the generalization ability of ILP. The substitution is similar to that in ENIGMA anonymous [13]. The predicates that accept original nodes and abstract nodes as their first arguments are called *original predicates* and *anonymous predicates*, respectively. We substitute identifiers with their categories, consisting of inductive types, constants, constructors, and variables. Besides the abstract nodes, we also include the original nodes as arguments in `goal_node` and `hyp_node`. We need them because when checking the equality, we want to compare the original nodes. Afterward, the anonymous predicates of nodes change to $goal\_node(anonym\_name, nat, goal\_idx, origin\_name)$ and $hyp\_node(anonym\_name, nat, hyp\_name, hyp\_idx, origin\_name)$. Some basic identifiers are not substituted, which consist of `logic_false`, `logic_true`, `and`, `or`, `iff`, `not`, `eq`, `bool_true`, and `bool_false`. There are both logic and boolean values of true and false because Coq can represent objects in logic or programs. Concerning the constructors of Coq's datatypes, we only retain four important constructors: `rel`, `prod`, `lambda`, and `evar`.

4 Method

Figure 2 presents an overview of our learning framework. During the training, we first perform orthogonalization, a technique introduced in TacticToe, to clean the dataset. Then, we select examples and apply ILP to generate rules. To make predictions, first, k-NN predicts a sequence of likely helpful tactics. Afterward, the rules are used as a filter to reorder the predictions. The optimization procedure denotes removing some low-quality rules. This is achieved by evaluating the reordered predictions in the validation dataset and removing the low-quality ones. In the next subsections, we describe these parts.

4.1 Orthogonalization

In some cases, different tactics could transform the same proof state in the same way. This raises ambiguity and makes learning difficult. Orthogonalization is used to reduce such ambiguity. In the orthogonalization, we only focus on four very popular tactics in Coq's standard library: `assumption`, `reflexivity`, `trivial`, and `auto`. We denote the sets of proof states which can be closed by `assumption`, `reflexivity`, `trivial`, and `auto` as AS, R, T, and AT, respectively. There exist the relations $AS \subsetneq T$, $R \subsetneq T$, and $T \subsetneq AT$. For each proof state ps to which the tactic t is applied, the above four automation tactics are sequentially tried. If ps can be finished by the automation tactic t', we replace t by t'. If none of the four tactics can finish the proof state, the original t is preserved. The orthogonalization procedure is simpler than in TacticToe, which orthogonalizes all tactics. This is because our current predicates can only capture a part of the usage of tactics. We leave full orthogonalization as future work.

4.2 Example Selection

Choosing appropriate training examples is crucial for learning reasonable rules. For a specific tactic tac, the proof states to which it is applied are regarded as the positive examples. The proof states to which the tactics different from tac are applied are regarded as the negative examples. We experimentally determine the number of positive and negative examples for learning rules. We develop a clustering mechanism to split positive examples into roughly equal-sized clusters. We experimentally evaluate the combinations of different numbers of negative examples and different numbers of positive examples.

We choose an implementation of a constrained k-means algorithm [19] to split positive examples into clusters of roughly the same size. The original k-means algorithm [11] can only split examples into a certain number of clusters. In contrast, constrained k-means can also specify the lower bound and the upper bound of the size of the clusters, which is important to give good sizes of training examples for each ILP learning task.

We apply k-NN to discover negative examples for each positive example. As this pre-processing step is not theorem-proving specific, we use the general k-NN from the scikit-learn library [23]. We use the same features as Tactician [30]. For each positive example, k-NN calculates the distance between it and every negative example in the training data. Then, we rank the negative examples in an ascending order of distance.

Algorithm 1 Preselection Reorder

Input: a sequence of tactics $tac_{1..50}$ preselected by k-NN for a proof state
Output: a sequence of tactics which is a reorder of the preselection
goods ← [ ]
bads ← [ ]
for all $i \in \{1..50\}$ **do**
  if tac_i is accepted by learned rules **then**
    append tac_i to the end of *goods*
  else
    append tac_i to the end of *bads*
  end if
end for
reorder ← the sequence of appending *bads* to the end of *goods*
return *reorder*

4.3 Training and Prediction

For each tactic, we use Aleph to generate ILP rules for each cluster of positive examples and its associated negative examples. Afterwards, all the rules are merged together, and duplicated rules are removed. Finally, we remove the rules of tactics that are logically subsumed by other rules of the same tactic.

Algorithm 1 illustrates the procedures of making predictions. We use the state-of-the-art k-NN in Tactician. The features are the same as those used in Sect. 4.2. Assume a pair of a proof state and a tactic (ps, tac). To make predictions, first, k-NN preselects a sequence of likely tactics $tac_{1..50}$. For each tac_i, we use the learned rules to determine whether to accept it. During the evaluation, the prediction tac_i is expected (unexpected) if tac_i is equal (unequal) to tac. If the rules accept (reject) a tactic, the prediction is a declared positive (negative). If the rules reject a tac_i equal to tac, we regard the prediction made by the rules as a false negative (FN). Based on the expected tactics and acceptances, we also obtain true positives (TPs), true negatives (TNs), and false positives (FPs).

4.4 Rule Optimization

The idea of rule optimization is to remove some low-quality rules to increase the overall performance of rules. For the evaluation of all rules, we chose the F-1 score as the metric, defined as $\frac{2TP}{2TP+FP+FN}$, because it is a standard metric for evaluating imbalanced data. As an illustration of the imbalance, given a pair of a proof state and a tactic tac, rules make predictions for 50 preselected tactics. However, at most one is the same as tac. If a rule is overly general, which means that the number of FPs introduced by it is much larger than the number of TPs introduced by it, removing it will increase the overall F-1 score.

Although a large number of negative examples prevents generating overly general rules, using them may not produce the best rules for two reasons. First, our background can merely capture a portion of the usage of the tactics; thus, a significantly large number of negative examples cannot produce perfect rules but may produce overly specific rules. Second, some negative examples in our dataset are actually false negatives. A mathematician may be able to choose the next step from a couple of tactics that make different proof transformations. Orthogonalization in Sect. 4.1 can only partially remove such overlaps between tactics, thereby decreasing the number of false negatives. It is computationally prohibitive to perform full orthogonalization of our data. Observe that, our experiments still show an increase in accuracy in light of the noisy data.

Our approach allows us to learn many rules explaining a particular tactic. Over the training set, some of these rules capture the usage of the given tactic better than others. Before, moving to testing on unseen data, we prune the learned rules and keep only those that performed well on the validation set.

To determine which rules to include, we evaluate the quality of each rule in the validation dataset and remove those with low qualities. The left rules are used for the evaluation on the test dataset. We measure the quality of each rule and remove it if its quality is below a certain threshold. We set different thresholds and choose the threshold leading to the highest F-1 score via experiments. For the metric of the quality of a single rule, we use *precision*, defined as $\frac{TP}{TP+FP}$. Here, FP and TP are produced by a single rule. Precision is a good metric because if a rule is too general, its precision will be low and we will be able to remove it to improve the overall F-1 score.

5 Experiments

We conducted the experiments on Coq's standard library [7]. We chose Coq's standard library as the benchmark because it is a standard dataset for evaluating machine learning for Coq. Moreover, it comprises well-crafted proofs developed by Coq experts and has been optimized for decades. Coq's standard library consists of 41 theories and 151,678 proof states in total. The code for this paper is available at https://github.com/Zhang-Liao/ilp_coq.

Most parameters of Aleph were left as default besides three parameters. We set the maximal length of a clause to 1,000, the upper bound of proof depth to 1,000, and the largest number of nodes to be explored during the search to 30,000. We define a cost function similar to the default cost function because, by default, Aleph cannot learn with no negative examples or only one positive example. The user-defined cost function was only used when there were no negative examples or exactly one positive example. We set a timeout of ten minutes for learning.

We conducted the experiments in the transfer-theory setting, which means different Coq theories are used for training, validation, and testing. We use this setting because it simulates a practical application scenario of ILP. Mathematicians develop new theories based on the definitions and proven theorems in the developed theories. To be practically beneficial, ILP should also learn rules from training theories, and the learned rules should help make tactic suggestions for theories that do not depend on the training theories. The training theory should be carefully chosen before conducting experiments. The theory `Structures` was

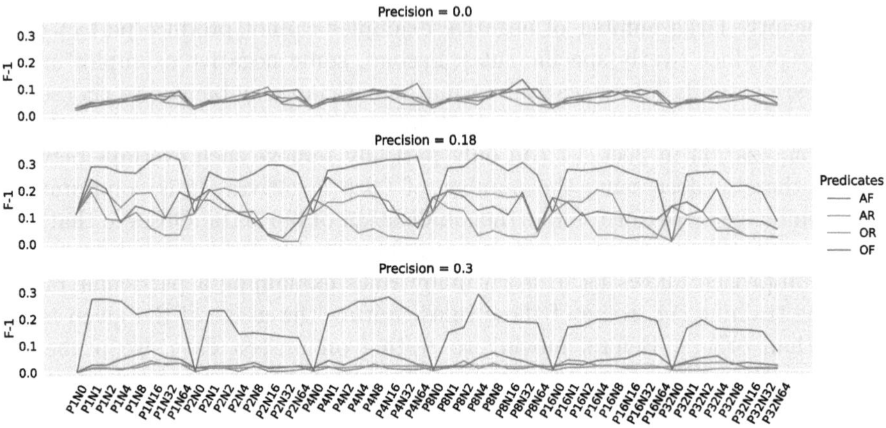

Fig. 3. F-1 scores of different parameters when *qualt* is set to 0, 0.18, or 0.30. *AF*, *AR*, *OF*, and *OR* denote the anonymous feature predicates, the anonymous representation predicates, the original feature predicates, and the original representation predicates, respectively. In the x-axis caption *P* and *N* denote *pos* and *neg*, respectively.

chosen for training because it has a balanced distribution of various tactics. To be consistent with the transfer-theory setting, the testing theories should not depend on `Structures`. From Coq's standard library, we chose all theories which do not depend on `Structures` for testing including `rtauto`, `FSets`, `Wellfounded`, `funind`, `btauto`, `nsatz`, and `MSets`. Afterward, from all the theories that do not depend on the testing theories, we randomly chose five theories: `PArith`, `Relations`, `Bool`, `Logic`, and `Lists`, merged as the validation dataset.

5.1 Parameter Optimization

In Sect. 4, we introduced three additional hyper-parameters beyond those already present in Aleph. They are the size of the cluster of positive examples (*pos*), the number of negative examples of each positive example (*neg*), and the quality-theshold (*qualt*) below which the rule should be removed.

We evaluated the F-1 scores of different predicate categories with different parameters. There are four predicate categories AF, AR, OF, and OR, respectively denoting the anonymous feature predicates, the anonymous representation predicates, the original feature predicates, and the original representation predicates. *AF* and *OF* contain both representation predicates and feature predicates, while *AF* and *AR* only contain anonymous predicates. We chose *pos* between 0 and 32. For *neg*, we chose it between 0 and 64. For all the combinations of *pos* and *neg*, rules were generated. Afterward, the learned rules were evaluated in the validation dataset. Finally, we calculated the F-1 scores with different values of *qualt*. The range of *qualt* was set between 0 and 0.30, with intervals of 0.06.

Table 1. The best parameters of each predicate category.

Parameter	AF	AR	OF	OR
Precision	0.18	0.12	0.18	0.12
Positive	1	16	4	1
Negative	32	1	1	1

Table 2. The F-1 scores in the test dataset.

Theory	AF	AR	OF	OR
rtauto	**0.564**	0.401	0.502	0.440
FSets	**0.266**	0.125	0.193	0.144
Wellfounded	**0.229**	0.049	0.134	0.135
funind	**0.545**	0.0	0.0	0.0
btauto	**0.339**	0.125	0.162	0.122
nsatz	**0.164**	0.070	0.163	0.116
MSets	**0.272**	0.084	0.143	0.095

Figure 3 depicts the F-1 scores when $qualt = \{0, 0.18, 0.30\}$. The significance of *qualt* is evident. When $qualt = 0$, the best F-1 scores of all predicate categories hover around 0.10. The best scores become significantly higher than 0.10 when $qualt = 0.18$. The low F-1 scores of $qualt = 0$ are caused by some overly general rules which are discussed in Sect. 4.4. An example of such an overly general rule is provided below, showing the necessity of employing an appropriate *qualt*.

```
tac(A,"reflexivity") :- goal_node(coq_Init_Logic_eq,A,B,C).
```

The above rule denotes that `reflexivity` is appropriate whenever there is an equal sign in the goal. It is too general and irrelevant to the usage of `reflexivity` as explained in Sect. 3.2. With $qualt = 0.30$, the best F-1 scores decrease again. The decline is attributed to the fact that most rules remained by a very high *qualt* are excessively specific, thereby producing a limited number of TPs.

Afterward, we analyze the results obtained with $qualt = 0.18$ since the F-1 scores are notably higher than those with $qualt = \{0, 0.30\}$. None of the predicate categories obtains the highest F-1 score with $pos = 32$. We assume the reason is that an overly large *pos* may gather many irrelevant positive examples, which causes difficulties in choosing negative examples. If two positive examples significantly differ, an appropriate negative example for one of them may be inappropriate for the other. A large value of *neg* generally decreases the F-1 scores of all predicates except for *AF*. A possible explanation is that too many negative examples cause *AR*, *OF*, and *OR* to learn overly specific rules. Due to the expressivity of *AF*, it can still learn some reasonable rules.

Table 1 displays the optimal parameters of all predicate categories. The generalization does not work well for *OF* and *OR*, but already with *AF* its F-1 score peak necessitates a large *neg*, indicating its superior ability to distinguish positive examples from negative examples and to learn precise rules. Perhaps due to the reason that our background knowledge is incapable of perfectly capturing the usage of tactics, *AF* also uses $pos = 1$. A small *pos* allows *AF* to learn many rules for diverse situations. *AR* requires $pos = 16$ to achieve its peak F-1 score, possibly due to its limitation of representing AST in a highly generalized manner.

The training times for each category of predicates are presented in Fig. 4. The total training time is calculated by summing the training times for the examples

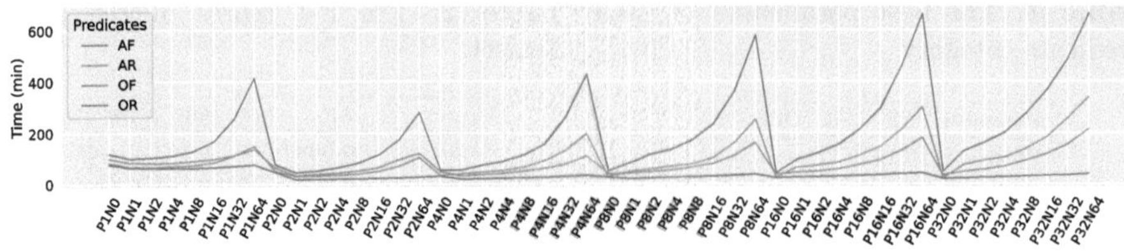

Fig. 4. Training times for different categories of predicates.

associated with each cluster of tactics. Learning definitions of feature predicates is computationally more costly than learning definitions of representation predicates, likely due to the resource overhead required for the former. Moreover, learning anonymous predicates requires more time than original predicates. We hypothesize that obfuscating some of the structure of the proof terms (when learning anonymous predicates) correlates with an increase in the size of the search space and thus longer learning times when searching for programs distinguishing a large number of positive examples from negative examples. In some cases the learning phase took more than ten hours, indicating potential future work to improve the computational efficiency. Nevertheless, our learning is still significantly faster than contemporary neural networks trained to solve similar problems and, in addition, we provide an explanation of our decisions (in the form of a logic program).

5.2 Testing

According to parameter optimization, we choose the rules with the best parameter and test the performance in the test dataset. Table 2 shows the F-1 scores in the test dataset. Using a background knowledge consisting of AF predicate definitions during training results in rules which perform best during testing. This owes to that AF can learn precise rules to characterize the usage of tactics. In comparison, the rules learned by AR are too general, and the rules learned by OF and OR are too specific. In all theories, except those consisting of only a few proof states (`funind` has only 14 proof states), training with OF, OR, and AR background knowledge results in rules performing well on the test data F-1 scores. We also evaluated whether the combination of ILP and k-NN can improve the accuracy of k-NN. The algorithm of reordering is explained in Sect. 4.3. Figure 5 shows the results of the top-k accuracies in different theories. In all the theories, the combination of ILP and k-NN increases the accuracies of k-NN.

6 Case Studies and Limitations

To illustrate that we indeed learn precise rules, besides the example of `simpl` presented in Sect. 1, we present three more examples in this section. The rule of

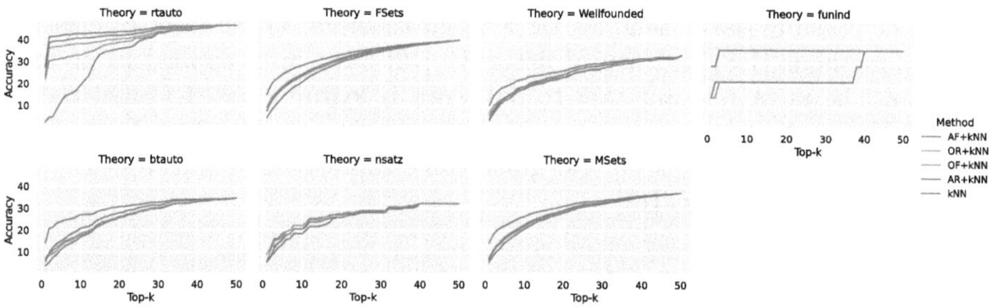

Fig. 5. Top-k accuracies in the test theories. It denotes how often the label is predicted in the first k predictions. The symbol $+$ denotes using the rules learned by a certain predicate category to reorder the preselections.

`trivial` suits the goal $A \rightarrow B = B$. First, `trivial` introduces A as a hypothesis, changing the proof state to $H : A \vdash B = B$. Next, `trivial` can automatically prove $B = B$. The rule of `auto` aligns the proof state of the structure $H : B \vdash A \vee B$. The tactic `auto` decomposes the disjunction, and the goal changes to either proving A or proving B. Then, it proves B with the hypothesis. In contrast, `trivial` cannot decompose the disjunction. The rule of `intuition` suits the goal $A \leftrightarrow A$ which cannot be proved by `auto`. In comparison, `intuition` can perform stronger automation than `auto` and can prove it.

```
tac(A,"trivial") :-
  goal_node(prod,A,B,C),goal_node(const,A,D,E), goal_above(A,B,D),
  goal_node(const,A,F,E),goal_above(A,B,F),eq_goal_term(A,F,D).
tac(A,"auto") :-
  goal_node(coq_Init_Logic_or,A,B,C),goal_node(const,A,D,E),
  goal_above(A,B,D),hyp_node(const,A,F,G,E),eq_goal_hyp_term(A,D,G).
tac(A,"intuition") :-
  goal_node(coq_Init_Logic_iff,A,B,C),goal_node(const,A,D,E),
  goal_above(A,B,D),goal_node(const,A,F,E),eq_goal_term(A,F,D)
```

Albeit we can learn several reasonable rules, many tactics are difficult to describe. There are several reasons for the difficulties. First, our current work cannot generalize tactics with different arguments. For instance, assume there are two tactics `apply H1` and `apply H2` where `H1` and `H2` are names of hypotheses. They are regarded as different tactics but may have the same behavior. Second, the usage of some tactics such as `induction` is inherently complicated [21]. Third, the same mathematical theorem can proved in various ways which leads to many overlaps between the usage of tactics.

7 Related Work

There are several tasks of machine learning for theorem proving. *Premise selection* is probably the most well-discovered task. It studies the question of how to predict possibly useful lemmas for a given theorem. Quite a lot of classical learning methods [1,8] and neural networks [12] have been applied to premise selection. The most relevant task to our work is learning-based formal theory proving. Researchers have investigated both employing machine learning to learn from human-written proofs [9] and guide some sophisticated software to automatically construct proofs [15].

8 Conclusion and Future Work

We have developed the first application of ILP to interactive theorem proving. For this, we have developed new feature predicates, able to dynamically calculate features based on the representation of AST of the proof state. We proposed a method for using ILP effectively for tactic prediction. We experimentally evaluated the rules learned by ILP and compared them to practically used prediction mechanisms in ITPs. The experiments confirm that the method gives explainable tactic predictions. Our work shows the potential of applications of ILP to improve ITP tactic suggestion methods.

Several improvements are possible. We would like to use our work with stronger ILP systems, such as Popper. However, given that our background knowledge includes predicates with high arity and our method builds large rules with many variables, the underlying ASP (SAT) solver used by Popper struggles with the generation of models. Improvements to our encoding and recent work on improving the performance of Popper can make this research direction viable in the near future. Next, it is interesting to use ILP to capture the relations between arguments of tactics and the objects to which the arguments refer. Finally, we plan to investigate the application of ILP to other ITP tasks [31].

Acknowledgments and Disclosure of Funding. This work was supported by the Czech Science Foundation Grant No. 22-06414L, the Cost action CA20111 EuroProofNet, the ERC PoC project *FormalWeb3* no. 101156734, Amazon Research Awards, the EU ICT-48 2020 project no. 952215 TAILOR, the ERC CZ project no. LL1902 POSTMAN, and the University of Innsbruck doctoral scholarship *promotion of young talent*.

References

1. Alama, J., et al.: Premise selection for mathematics by corpus analysis and kernel methods. J. Autom. Reason. **52**, 191–213 (2014)
2. Blaauwbroek, L., Urban, J., Geuvers, H.: Tactic learning and proving for the coq proof assistant. arXiv preprint arXiv:2003.09140 (2020)
3. Blaauwbroek, L., Urban, J., Geuvers, H.: The tactician: a seamless, interactive tactic learner and prover for coq. In: Benzmüller, C., Miller, B. (eds.) CICM 2020. LNCS (LNAI), vol. 12236, pp. 271–277. Springer, Cham (2020). https://doi.org/10.1007/978-3-030-53518-6_17

4. Chvalovský, K., Jakubův, J., Suda, M., Urban, J.: ENIGMA-NG: efficient neural and gradient-boosted inference guidance for E. In: Fontaine, P. (ed.) CADE 2019. LNCS (LNAI), vol. 11716, pp. 197–215. Springer, Cham (2019). https://doi.org/10.1007/978-3-030-29436-6_12
5. Cropper, A., Dumančić, S.: Inductive logic programming at 30: a new introduction. J. Artif. Intell. Res. **74**, 765–850 (2022)
6. Cropper, A., Morel, R.: Learning programs by learning from failures. Mach. Learn. **110**, 801–856 (2021)
7. Czajka, Ł, Kaliszyk, C.: Hammer for coq: automation for dependent type theory. J. Autom. Reason. **61**, 423–453 (2018)
8. Gauthier, T., Kaliszyk, C.: Premise selection and external provers for hol4. In: CPP, pp. 49–57 (2015)
9. Gauthier, T., Kaliszyk, C., Urban, J., Kumar, R., Norrish, M.: Tactictoe: learning to prove with tactics. J. Autom. Reason. **65**, 257–286 (2021)
10. Gonthier, G., et al.: Formal proof-the four-color theorem. Not. AMS **55**(11), 1382–1393 (2008)
11. Hartigan, J.A., Wong, M.A.: Algorithm as 136: a k-means clustering algorithm. J. R. Stat. Soc. Ser. c (Appl. Stat.) **28**(1), 100–108 (1979)
12. Irving, G., Szegedy, C., Alemi, A.A., Eén, N., Chollet, F., Urban, J.: Deepmath-deep sequence models for premise selection. NIPS **29** (2016)
13. Jakubův, J., Chvalovský, K., Olšák, M., Piotrowski, B., Suda, M., Urban, J.: ENIGMA anonymous: symbol-independent inference guiding machine (system description). In: Peltier, N., Sofronie-Stokkermans, V. (eds.) IJCAR 2020. LNCS (LNAI), vol. 12167, pp. 448–463. Springer, Cham (2020). https://doi.org/10.1007/978-3-030-51054-1_29
14. Jiang, A.Q., et al.: Thor: wielding hammers to integrate language models and automated theorem provers. NIPS **35**, 8360–8373 (2022)
15. Kaliszyk, C., Urban, J., Michalewski, H., Olšák, M.: Reinforcement learning of theorem proving. Adv. Neural Inf. Process. Syst. **31** (2018)
16. Kaliszyk, C., Urban, J., Vyskočil, J.: Efficient semantic features for automated reasoning over large theories. In: Yang, Q., Wooldridge, M. (eds.) IJCAI, pp. 3084–3090. AAAI Press (2015)
17. LeCun, Y.: Do large language models need sensory grounding for meaning and understanding. In: Workshop on Philosophy of Deep Learning (2023)
18. Leroy, X.: The CompCert C verified compiler: documentation and user's manual. Ph.D. thesis, Inria (2021)
19. Levy-Kramer, J.: k-means-constrained (2018). https://github.com/joshlk/k-means-constrained
20. de Moura, L., Kong, S., Avigad, J., van Doorn, F., von Raumer, J.: The lean theorem prover (system description). In: Felty, A.P., Middeldorp, A. (eds.) CADE 2015. LNCS (LNAI), vol. 9195, pp. 378–388. Springer, Cham (2015). https://doi.org/10.1007/978-3-319-21401-6_26
21. Nagashima, Y.: `LiFtEr`: language to encode induction heuristics for Isabelle/HOL. In: Lin, A.W. (ed.) APLAS 2019. LNCS, vol. 11893, pp. 266–287. Springer, Cham (2019). https://doi.org/10.1007/978-3-030-34175-6_14
22. Paulson, L.C.: Isabelle: A Generic Theorem Prover. Springer, Heidelberg (1994). https://doi.org/10.1007/bfb0030558
23. Pedregosa, F., et al.: Scikit-learn: machine learning in python. J. Mach. Learn. Res. **12**, 2825–2830 (2011)
24. Rute, J., et al.: Graph2tac: learning hierarchical representations of math concepts in theorem proving. arXiv preprint arXiv:2401.02949 (2024)

25. Sasaki, Y., et al.: The truth of the f-measure. Teach. Tutor Mater. **1**(5), 1–5 (2007)
26. Srinivasan, A.: The aleph manual (2001)
27. The Coq Development Team: Coq reference manual 8.11.1 (2020). https://coq.github.io/doc/v8.11/refman/index.html
28. Xin, H., et al.: Lego-prover: neural theorem proving with growing libraries. arXiv preprint arXiv:2310.00656 (2023)
29. Yang, K., Deng, J.: Learning to prove theorems via interacting with proof assistants. In: ICML, pp. 6984–6994. PMLR (2019)
30. Zhang, L., Blaauwbroek, L., Piotrowski, B., Černý, P., Kaliszyk, C., Urban, J.: Online machine learning techniques for coq: a comparison. In: Kamareddine, F., Sacerdoti Coen, C. (eds.) CICM 2021. LNCS (LNAI), vol. 12833, pp. 67–83. Springer, Cham (2021). https://doi.org/10.1007/978-3-030-81097-9_5
31. Zhang, L., et al.: Learning proof transformations and its applications in interactive theorem proving. In: FroCos, pp. 236–254 (2023)

Active Learning of Digenic Functions with Boolean Matrix Logic Programming

Lun Ai[1(✉)], Stephen H. Muggleton[2], Shi-Shun Liang[1], and Geoff S. Baldwin[1]

[1] Department of Life Sciences, Imperial College London, London, UK
{lun.ai15,shishun.liang20,g.baldwin}@imperial.ac.uk
[2] Department of Computing, Imperial College London, London, UK
s.muggleton@imperial.ac.uk

Abstract. We apply logic-based machine learning techniques to facilitate cellular engineering and drive biological discovery, using a comprehensive knowledge base of metabolic processes called a genome-scale metabolic network model (GEM). Predicted host behaviours are not always correctly described by GEMs. Learning the intricate genetic interactions within GEMs presents computational and empirical challenges. To address these difficulties, we describe a novel approach called Boolean Matrix Logic Programming (BMLP) by leveraging boolean matrices to evaluate large logic programs. We introduce a new system, $BMLP_{active}$, which efficiently explores the genomic hypothesis space by guiding informative experimentation through active learning. In contrast to sub-symbolic methods, $BMLP_{active}$ encodes a state-of-the-art GEM of a widely accepted bacterial host in an interpretable and logical representation using datalog logic programs. Notably, $BMLP_{active}$ can successfully learn the interaction between a gene pair with 90% fewer training examples than random experimentation, overcoming the increase in experimental design space. $BMLP_{active}$ enables rapid optimisation of metabolic models and offers a realistic approach to a self-driving lab for microbial engineering.

Keywords: Logic Programming · Boolean Matrices · Systems Biology · Genome-Scale Metabolic Networks

1 Introduction

Our study explores the applicability of abductive reasoning and active learning to extensive biological systems. We expand the scope of logic-based gene function learning by looking at a genome-scale metabolic model. The genome-scale metabolic model (GEM), iML1515 [19], encompasses 1515 genes and 2719 metabolic reactions of the *Escherichia coli* (*E. coli*) strain K-12 MG1655, a versatile host organism in metabolic engineering to produce valuable compounds. In iML1515, interactions between gene pairs have been identified as a key error

W.-Z. Dai (Ed.): ILP 2024, LNAI 16059, pp. 117–125, 2026.
https://doi.org/10.1007/978-3-032-09087-4_8

source [3]. Learning these interactions requires exploring a combinatorial hypothesis space. Given that biological relationships are commonly described logically, Inductive Logic Programming (ILP) [20] is particularly adept at operating on biological knowledge bases. We propose Boolean Matrix Logic Programming (BMLP) where we employ boolean matrices as underlying bottom-up evaluation mechanisms of large datalog programs. This approach allows us to classify phenotypic effects using a datalog encoding of the state-of-the-art GEM iML1515. We focused on re-discovering the function associated with the key gene *tyrB* in the Tryptophan biosynthesis pathways. Overlapping functions between two genes *tyrB* and *aspC* is a digenic interaction since they are responsible for producing the same amino acid. To learn from a combinatorial hypothesis space with high data efficiency, we create an active learning system $BMLP_{active}$ to learn this digenic interaction, requiring 90% fewer experiments than random experimentation. Abductive reasoning and active learning via ILP were successfully demonstrated in biological discovery by the prominent Robot Scientist [14]. However, this demonstration was limited to only 17 genes in the aromatic amino acid pathways of yeast. In contrast, $BMLP_{active}$ is the first logic programming system to learn digenic interaction on the genome scale from GEMs (Fig. 1).

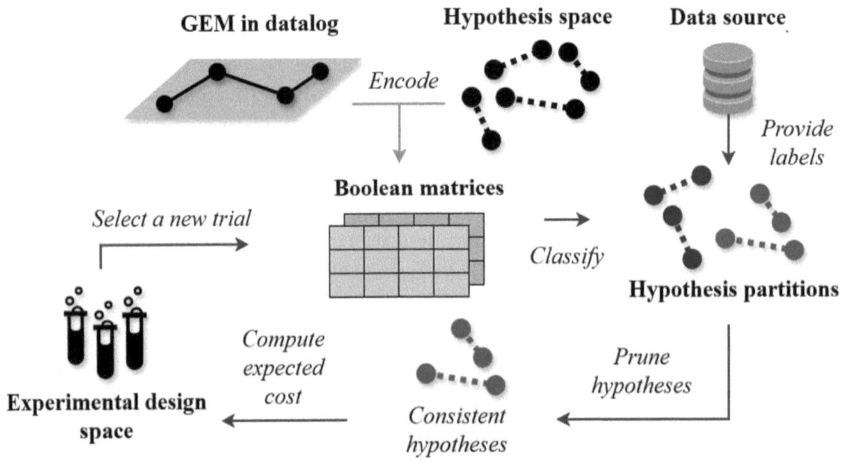

Fig. 1. Certain genetic mutations would block pathways, causing cells to die (positive label). $BMLP_{active}$ finds a gene-reaction association hypothesis to explain the pathway blockage and lethality. It encodes the GEM iML1515 as boolean matrices and uses them to classify genetic mutation experiment labels for every hypothesis. It consults a data source to request ground truth labels. $BMLP_{active}$ iteratively refutes hypotheses inconsistent with the labels.

2 Related Work

Many computational scientific discovery systems [4,12,16,24,30] were designed to formulate symbolic hypotheses from experimental results. One cannot directly employ these systems for experimental planning. In contrast, the Robot Scientist [14,15] automatically proposed hypotheses, designed experiments and performed them using laboratory robotics. Experiments were actively selected to minimise the expected cost of experimentation for learning gene functions in yeast [5]. Notably, we apply $BMLP_{active}$ to the GEM iML1515 which represents a significant increase in complexity compared to the aromatic amino acid pathways investigated by the Robot Scientist platforms.

BMLP uses boolean matrices to compute the least model. Obtaining the least Herbrand model of linear recursive datalog programs can be reduced to computing the transitive closure of boolean matrices [8,23]. Fischer and Meyer [10] and Ioannidis [13] showed a divide-and-conquer boolean matrix computation technique by viewing relational databases as graphs. An ILP system called DeepLog [21] employed boolean matrices for choosing optimal background knowledge to derive a compact bottom clause. In contrast to BMLP, a great body of work [6,11,17,27–29] only studied approximated evaluations of logic program in tensor spaces. Solving certain recursive programs is difficult whereas these can be solved by an iterative bottom-up evaluation approach [27] such as BMLP.

3 Modelling a GEM with a Petri Net

In an auxotrophic mutant experiment, genes are deleted from a cell. Thus, key metabolic reactions might be no longer viable due to the gene removal, leading to insufficient cell growth. We model the metabolic mechanisms using a GEM. A GEM contains biochemical reactions of substances. Each reaction involves chemical substances x_i and y_j:

$$\text{Irreversible: } x_1 + x_2 + ... + x_m \longrightarrow y_1 + y_2 + ... + y_n$$
$$\text{Reversible: } x_1 + x_2 + ... + x_m \longleftrightarrow y_1 + y_2 + ... + y_n$$

which is often represented by a Petri net [26]. The reactions in a GEM are transitions (edges in a Petri net) between reactants and products (nodes in a Petri net). We associate *binary* phenotypic effects – normal or reduced cell growth of auxotrophic mutants compared to the wild-type, with reachability to key substances in the metabolic network. To evaluate this reachability problem, we look at Petri nets with restrictions, namely *one-bounded elementary nets* (OEN) [25] where nodes are marked with at most one token (Example 1). The reachability problem is evaluated as a recursive datalog program with two arguments. Each argument of our transformed datalog program concatenates multiple constants, e.g. $h2\_o2$. This results in a hypergraph [2], a directed graph where an edge can connect to any number of nodes. To construct this datalog program, we consider a hypergraph that describes the association between substances and reactions.

Example 1. *$\mathcal{P}_1$ represents a metabolic network as an OEN and hypergraph. The clauses reaction_1, reaction_2 and reaction_3 are the three transitions t_1, t_2 and t_3. c1_c2 and c3_c4 are two hypernodes. Both graphs show that the node c_5 is reachable from $\{c_1, c_2\}$ via t_1 and t_2. We can evaluate the groundings of pathway(m1, Y) in the Herbrand model which includes pathway(m1, c5). The OEN and hypergraph are illustrated below:*

$$\mathcal{P}_1 : \left\{ \begin{array}{r} metabolites(m1, c1\_c2). \\ metabolites(m1, c1). \\ metabolites(m1, c2). \\ reaction\_1(c1\_c2, c3\_c4). \\ reaction\_1(c1\_c2, c3). \\ reaction\_1(c1\_c2, c4). \\ reaction\_2(c3\_c4, c5). \\ reaction\_3(c5, c4). \\ reaction(X, Y) \leftarrow metabolites(X, Y). \\ reaction(X, Y) \leftarrow reaction\_1(X, Y). \\ reaction(X, Y) \leftarrow reaction\_2(X, Y). \\ reaction(X, Y) \leftarrow reaction\_3(X, Y). \\ pathway(X, Y) \leftarrow reaction(X, Y). \\ pathway(X, Y) \leftarrow reaction(X, Z), \\ pathway(Z, Y). \end{array} \right\}$$

4 Boolean Matrix Logic Programming

We propose the Boolean Matrix Logic Programming (BMLP) problem. In contrast to traditional logic program evaluation, BMLP uses boolean matrices to evaluate recursive datalog programs with arity at most two (at most two arguments) and at most two body literals, namely the H_2^2 program class [22]. The H_2^2 program class has the Universal Turing Machine expressivity when extended with functional symbols [31].

Definition 1 (Boolean Matrix Logic Programming (BMLP) problem). *Let $\mathcal{P}$ be a datalog program containing a set of clauses with the predicate symbol r. The goal of Boolean Matrix Logic Programming (BMLP) is to find a boolean matrix $\boldsymbol{R}$ encoded by a datalog program such that $(\boldsymbol{R})_{i,j} = 1$ if $\mathcal{P} \models r(c_i, c_j)$ for constants c_i, c_j and $(\boldsymbol{R})_{i,j} = 0$ otherwise.*

Consider a ground term u that concatenates n constant symbols $c_1, c_2, ..., c_n$. We can represent u using a n-bit binary vector. When c_k is in u, the k-th bit of the binary vector is 1. All reactions in iML1515 are encoded this way to form rows in two boolean matrices $\mathbf{R}_1$ and $\mathbf{R}_2$ (Fig. 2a).

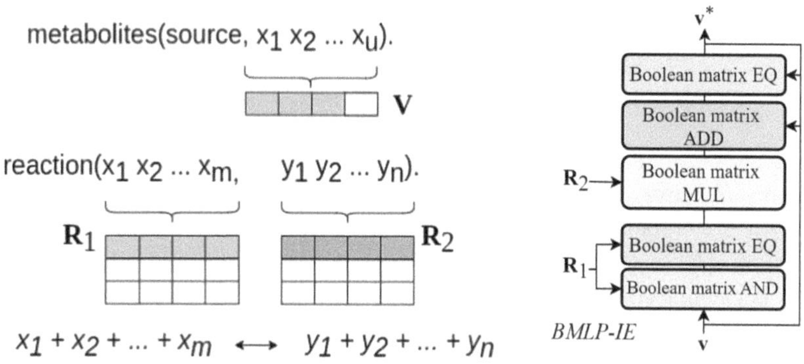

(a) (b)

Fig. 2. (a) The vector **v** encodes source chemical metabolites. All reactions are represented in the boolean matrices $\mathbf{R}_1$ and $\mathbf{R}_2$. (b) The module BMLP-IE computes $\mathbf{v}^*$, the closure of reaction products, using binary AND over rows and boolean matrix addition (ADD), multiplication (MUL) and equality (EQ) [8].

We implement a BMLP module in SWI-Prolog [32] called iterative extension (BMLP-IE) for the task of bottom-up evaluation of reachability in metabolic networks. Each binary vector is represented as an integer. BMLP-IE (Fig. 2b) iteratively expands the set of facts derivable from a partially grounded query $r(u, Y)$. For $\mathcal{P}$ containing n constant symbols, we represent u as a $1 \times n$ row vector $\mathbf{v}$. $\mathbf{R}_1$ and $\mathbf{R}_2$ can be multiplied with boolean vectors to turn transitions "on" or "off" in the OEN to modify the network connectivity. This module gives a 170x runtime boost for this task compared to SWI-Prolog [1], showing the benefit of a special-purpose module.

5 Active Learning

Our active learning system $BMLP_{active}$ selects experiments to minimise the expected value of a user-defined cost function and iteratively prunes hypotheses inconsistent with experimental outcomes. $BMLP_{active}$ uses the compression score of a hypothesis h [5] based on the Minimal Description Length principle [7] to compute the posterior probability:

$$compression(h, E) = |E^+| - \frac{|E^+|}{pc_h}(size(h) + fp_h)$$

$$p'(h|E) = \frac{2^{compression(h,E)}}{\sum_{h_i \in H} 2^{compression(h_i,E)}}$$

E are labelled examples and E^+ are positive examples. pc_h and fp_h are the number of positive predictions and false positive coverage. This compression function favours a general hypothesis with high coverage and penalises overgeneral hypotheses that incorrectly predict negative examples. $BMLP_{active}$ uses the following heuristic function [5] to select an experiment from candidate experiments T with an approximated minimum expected cost:

$$EC(H,T) \approx min_{t \in T} [C_t + p(t)(mean_{t' \in T-\{t\}} C_{t'}) J_{H_t} \\ + (1 - p(t))(mean_{t' \in T-\{t\}} C_{t'}) J_{\overline{H_t}}]$$

H_t and $\overline{H_t}$ are subsets of hypotheses H consistent and inconsistent with t's label. $J_{H_t} and J_{\overline{H_t}}$ are calculated according to the entropy $-\sum_{h \in H} p'(h|E)\, log_2(p'(h|E))$ where H is replaced by H_t or $\overline{H_t}$. The probability $p'(h|E)$ is calculated from the compression function. $p(t)$ is the probability that the label of the experiment t is positive and is computed by the probability sum of consistent hypotheses $\sum_{h \in H_t} p'(h|E)$. C_t is the cost of t from a user-defined experiment cost function.

For some hypothesis space H and background knowledge BK, V_s is the version space consistent with s training examples with the assumption that an active version space learner selects one instance per iteration. The shrinkage of the hypothesis space is $\frac{|V_{s+1}|}{|V_s|}$ after querying the label of the s-th instance. The minimal reduction ratio $p(x_s, V_s)$ is the minority ratio of the version space V_s partitioned by an instance x_s.

$$p(x_s, V_s) = \frac{min(|\{h \in V_s |\, h \cup BK \models x_s\}|, |\{h \in V_s |\, h \cup BK \not\models x_s\}|)}{|V_s|}$$

The optional selection strategy is to select instances with minimal reduction ratios as close as possible to $\frac{1}{2}$ to eliminate up to 50% of the hypothesis space [18]. A passive learner is considered a learner using random example selection since it does not have control over which training examples it uses.

Theorem 1 *(Active learning sample complexity bound [1]). For some $\phi \in [0, \frac{1}{2}]$ and a small hypothesis error $\epsilon > 0$, if an active version space learner can select instances to label from an instance space $\mathcal{X}$ with minimal reduction ratios greater than or equal to ϕ, the sample complexity s_{active} of the active learner is*

$$s_{active} \leq \frac{\epsilon}{\epsilon + \phi} s_{passive} + c \tag{1}$$

where c is a constant and $s_{passive}$ is the sample complexity of learning from randomly labelled instances.

Theorem 1 says that the number of instances needed by active learning should be always smaller than the number of randomly sampled examples given a positive ϕ. Recent work [1] has theoretically and empirically supported Theorem 1. This means the biological experiment sequence needed to arrive at a finding can be shortened by active learning.

We applied BMLP-IE to obtain predicted phenotypic effects for all combinations of candidate experiments and hypotheses. These predictions were compared with experimental data. Labels of experiment instances were requested from a data source, e.g. a laboratory or an online dataset. We have only considered labels from synthetic or online phenotype data. However, $BMLP_{active}$ can request data from a laboratory to automate experiments.

6 Experiments

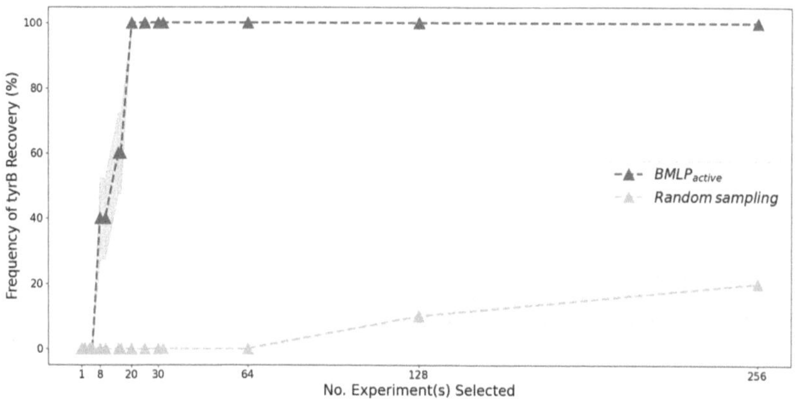

Fig. 3. tyrB isoenzyme function recovery frequency. The experimental space had $(\binom{33}{2}+33) \times 7 = 3927$ instances for double gene-knockout synthetic data and single gene-knockout experimental data of key 33 genes in 7 conditions. The hypothesis space contained $(27 \times 32 + 6 \times 31) + 2 = 1052$ candidate gene-enzyme associations related to 27 single-function genes, 6 double-function genes, the tyrB original function and an empty hypothesis.

We removed the metabolic reaction associated with *tyrB* from iML1515. This GEM model iML1515 [19] was first represented as a datalog program and then as boolean matrices for computation. The random selection strategy randomly sampled N instances from the instance space. $BMLP_{active}$ selected N experiments from this instance space to actively learn from the hypothesis space. Both methods output the hypothesis with the highest compression.

In Fig. 3 we observed that $BMLP_{active}$ successfully guarantees the recovery of the correct gene function with as few as 20 experiments. Random sampling failed to effectively prune competitive hypotheses even with 250+ experiments. This result also shows that $BMLP_{active}$ significantly reduced the number of experiments needed by 90% compared to random experiment sampling.

7 Conclusion and Future Work

We explored abductive reasoning and active learning using Boolean Matrix Logic Programming (BMLP), which utilises boolean matrices encoded in SWI-Prolog to compute datalog programs. We applied our active learning system $BMLP_{active}$ to learn a key digenic function in a state-of-the-art genome-scale metabolic network. Though we focused on a reduced set of hypotheses in the experiment, the combinatorial space was sufficiently large that random experiment selection was not viable as an experimentation strategy in a discovery process. The remarkable increase in the data efficiency of $BMLP_{active}$ demonstrates its potential even as the experimental design space grows exponentially.

Petri nets complement knowledge representation with dynamic analysis [26]. However, the simulation of Petri nets in logic programming has been much less explored. Future work will explore the link between Petri nets and Probabilistic Logic Programming [9]. Transitions could have firing likelihood constraints and this uncertainty can be modelled by probabilistic logic programs.

Acknowldegement. The first, third and fourth authors acknowledge support from the UKRI 21EBTA: EB-AI Consortium for Bioengineered Cells and Systems (AI-4-EB) award (BB/W013770/1). The second author acknowledges support from the UK's EPSRC Human-Like Computing Network (EP/R022291/1), for which he acts as Principal Investigator.

References

1. Ai, L., Muggleton, S.H., Liang, S.S., Baldwin, G.S.: Boolean matrix logic programming for active learning of gene functions in genome-scale metabolic network models. arXiv (2024)
2. Berge, C.: Hypergraphs: Combinatorics of Finite Sets. North-Holland Mathematical Library (1989)
3. Bernstein, D.B., Akkas, B., Price, M.N., Arkin, A.P.: Evaluating E. coli genome-scale metabolic model accuracy with high-throughput mutant fitness data. Mol. Syst. Biol. **19**(12) (2023)
4. Brunton, S.L., Proctor, J.L., Kutz, J.N.: Discovering governing equations from data by sparse identification of nonlinear dynamical systems. Proc. Natl. Acad. Sci. **113**(15), 3932–3937 (2016)
5. Bryant, C.H., Muggleton, S.H., Oliver, S.G., Kell, D., Reiser, P., King, R.D.: Combining inductive logic programming, active learning and robotics to discover the function of genes. Electron. Trans. Artif. Intell. 1–36 (2001)
6. Cohen, W., Yang, F., Mazaitis, K.R.: TensorLog: a probabilistic database implemented using deep-learning infrastructure. J. Arti. Intell. Res. **67**, 285–325 (2020)
7. Conklin, D., Witten, I.H.: Complexity-based induction. Mach. Learn. **16**(3), 203–225 (1994)
8. Copilowish, I.M.: Matrix development of the calculus of relations. J. Symb. Log. **13**(4), 193–203 (1948)
9. De Raedt, L., Kimmig, A.: Probabilistic (logic) programming concepts. Mach. Learn. **100**(1), 5–47 (2015). https://doi.org/10.1007/s10994-015-5494-z
10. Fischer, M.J., Meyer, A.R.: Boolean matrix multiplication and transitive closure. In: 12th Annual Symposium on Switching and Automata Theory, pp. 129–131 (1971)
11. Grefenstette, E.: Towards a formal distributional semantics: simulating logical calculi with tensors. In: Proceedings of the Second Joint Conference on Lexical and Computational Semantics, pp. 1–10 (2013)
12. Guimerà, R., et al.: A Bayesian machine scientist to aid in the solution of challenging scientific problems. Sci. Adv. **6**(5) (2020)

13. Ioannidis, Y.E.: On the computation of the transitive closure of relational operators. In: Proceedings of the 12th International Conference on Very Large Data Bases, pp. 403–411 (1986)
14. King, R.D., et al.: Functional genomic hypothesis generation and experimentation by a robot scientist. Nature **427**, 247–252 (2004)
15. King, R.D., et al.: The automation of science. Science **324**(5923), 85–89 (2009)
16. Langley, P.W., Simon, H.A., Bradshaw, G., Zytkow, J.M.: Scientific Discovery: Computational Explorations of the Creative Process (1987)
17. Lin, F.: From satisfiability to linear algebra. Hong Kong University of Science and Technology, Technical report (2013)
18. Mitchell, T.M.: Generalization as search. Artif. Intell. **18**, 203–226 (1982)
19. Monk, J.M., et al.: iML1515, a knowledgebase that computes escherichia coli traits. Nat. Biotechnol. **35**(10), 904–908 (2017)
20. Muggleton, S.H.: Inductive logic programming. N. Gener. Comput. **8**, 295–318 (1991)
21. Muggleton, S.H.: Hypothesizing an algorithm from one example: the role of specificity. Philos. Trans. Roy. Soc. A: Math. Phys. Eng. Sci. **381**(2251) (2023)
22. Muggleton, S.H., Lin, D., Tamaddoni-Nezhad, A.: Meta-interpretive learning of higher-order dyadic datalog: predicate invention revisited. Mach. Learn. **100**(1), 49–73 (2015). https://doi.org/10.1007/s10994-014-5471-y
23. Peirce, C.S.: Collected Papers of Charles Sanders Peirce, Volumes II (1932)
24. Petersen, B.K., Larma, M.L., Mundhenk, T.N., Santiago, C.P., Kim, S.K., Kim, J.T.: Deep symbolic regression: Recovering mathematical expressions from data via risk-seeking policy gradients. In: Proceedings of the 9th International Conference on Learning Representations (2020)
25. Rozenberg, G., Engelfriet, J.: Elementary net systems. In: Reisig, W., Rozenberg, G. (eds) Lectures on Petri Nets I: Basic Models. ACPN 1996. Lecture Notes in Computer Science, vol. 1491 (1998)
26. Sahu, A., Blätke, M.A., Szymański, J.J., Töpfer, N.: Advances in flux balance analysis by integrating machine learning and mechanism-based models. Comput. Struct. Biotechnol. J. **19**, 4626–4640 (2021)
27. Sato, T.: A linear algebraic approach to datalog evaluation. Theory Pract. Logic Program. **17**(3), 244–265 (2017)
28. Sato, T., Inoue, K.: Differentiable learning of matricized DNFs and its application to Boolean networks. Mach. Learn. **112**(8), 2821–2843 (2023)
29. Sato, T., Kojima, R.: Boolean network learning in vector spaces for genome-wide network analysis. In: Proceedings of the Eighteenth International Conference on Principles of Knowledge Representation and Reasoning, pp. 560–569 (2021)
30. Todorovski, L., Džeroski, S.: Integrating knowledge-driven and data-driven approaches to modeling. Ecol. Model. **194**(1), 3–13 (2006)
31. Tärnlund, S.: Horn clause computability. BIT Numer. Math. **17**(2), 215–226 (1977)
32. Wielemaker, J., Schrijvers, T., Triska, M., Lager, T.: SWI-prolog. Theory Pract. Logic Program. **12**(1–2), 67–96 (2012)

Learning and Reasoning with Uncertainty

An Algebraic Framework for Hierarchical Probabilistic Abstraction

Nijesh Upreti(✉) and Vaishak Belle

The University of Edinburgh, 10 Crichton Street, Edinburgh EH8 9AB, UK
n.upreti@ed.ac.uk

Abstract. Abstraction is essential for reducing the complexity of systems across diverse fields, yet designing effective abstraction methodology for probabilistic models is inherently challenging due to stochastic behaviors and uncertainties. Current approaches often distill detailed probabilistic data into higher-level summaries to support tractable and interpretable analyses, though they typically struggle to fully represent the relational and probabilistic hierarchies through single-layered abstractions. We introduce a hierarchical probabilistic abstraction framework aimed at addressing these challenges by extending a measure-theoretic foundation for hierarchical abstraction. The framework enables modular problem-solving via layered mappings, facilitating both detailed layer-specific analysis and a cohesive system-wide understanding. This approach bridges high-level conceptualization with low-level perceptual data, enhancing interpretability and allowing layered analysis. Our framework provides a robust foundation for abstraction analysis across AI subfields, particularly in aligning System 1 and System 2 thinking, thereby supporting the development of diverse abstraction methodologies.

Keywords: probabilistic abstraction · hierarchical models · algebra

1 Introduction

Abstraction serves as a core concept across knowledge domains, simplifying complex relationships into more comprehensible forms by focusing on essential details and discarding irrelevant ones [4,14,33]. In probabilistic models, abstraction is challenging due to inherent uncertainties and the stochastic nature of the systems involved [16,26]. Various methodologies have been developed to summarize detailed probabilistic information into higher-level representations while preserving essential characteristics and relationships, making such frameworks tractable and interpretable under uncertainty [4,21,22,25,31]. Yet, single-layered probabilistic abstractions are often inadequate for capturing the full relational and probabilistic hierarchy in a single low-to-high-level mapping.

Recent works emphasize multi-layered representations to model real-world hierarchical complexities, such as in disease diagnosis [18] and epidemic modeling [15]. These layered approaches are essential for analyzing phenomena across

W.-Z. Dai (Ed.): ILP 2024, LNAI 16059, pp. 129–146, 2026.
https://doi.org/10.1007/978-3-032-09087-4_9

multiple levels, providing interpretable insights into complex interactions and uncertainties [12,16,17]. Further, hierarchical modeling using directed acyclic graphs (DAGs) has become instrumental in fields like cognitive science, where hierarchical DAGs model complex concepts across layers [9]. However, constructing interpretable high-level theories from low-level data requires a structured framework for hierarchical relational and probabilistic information. A formal mathematical treatment of abstraction hierarchies is thus critical, offering a robust foundation for reasoning in complex spaces. Starting from single-layer mappings and progressing to multi-layered models captures complexities at each level while clarifying relationships between different layers [17]. Such a framework would further enable the development of methods to learn abstraction hierarchies in diverse contexts, supporting detailed decomposition for in-depth analysis [23,35].

To position our work within this existing research landscape, we draw upon several foundational studies. First, Hofmann and Belle's work established an abstraction framework for robot programs with probabilistic beliefs, utilizing the DS logic and bisimulation in probabilistic dynamic systems to demonstrate sound and complete abstraction [20]. Second, Beckers et al. contributed a framework for analyzing abstraction and approximation within causal models, providing formal definitions and results for approximate causal abstractions [3]. Third, Segal et al.'s study on probabilistic abstraction hierarchies (PAH) introduced a principled approach for learning abstraction hierarchies from data, addressing complexities in modeling multi-level systems [35]. Our work is inspired by these research endeavors and directly builds on Holtzen et al.'s papers on probabilistic program abstraction, which establishes single-layered mappings from concrete programs to their abstract versions with soundness properties [21,22].

In this paper, we propose a hierarchical probabilistic abstraction framework that generalizes the measure-theoretic approach as introduced by Holtzen et al. to multi-layered settings while providing a structured, modular foundation for abstraction in complex systems. By decomposing abstraction into layered mappings, the framework supports detailed, layer-specific analysis alongside a comprehensive system-level understanding, enabling dual-level reasoning: individual transformations and probabilistic relationships at each layer, and cumulative effects across layers. This structured approach facilitates exploration of abstractions across AI subfields, notably in System 1 and System 2 cognition, by connecting high-level conceptual reasoning with low-level perceptual data [24]. This comprehensive perspective is vital for advancing research in cognitive AI, statistical relational learning, and neurosymbolic AI, laying a solid foundation for the development of diverse abstraction methodologies.

2 Motivating Example

Imagine a personalized learning system designed to optimize educational outcomes for students with diverse backgrounds and abilities. The goal is to create an adaptive education platform that tailors learning experiences based on individual cognitive profiles, learning environments, and behavioral patterns. This example is a slightly more complex version of examples as outlined in Belle's work [4]. Towards modeling such a system, consider a probabilistic relational model (PRM) for a university database U, representing student learning and performance. The model instantiates constraints for a parameterized Bayesian network as follows:

Environmental Factors $\longrightarrow$ Cognitive Processes $\longleftarrow$ Learning Behaviors $\longrightarrow$ Educational Outcomes

Low-Level Theory U_l:

- $\square$ **0.7** HLE(x, High)
- $\square$ **0.2** HLE(x, Medium)
- $\square$ **0.1** HLE(x, Low)
- $\square$ **0.6** PI(x, High)
- $\square$ **0.3** PI(x, Medium)
- $\square$ **0.1** PI(x, Low)
- $\square$ **0.5** SES(x, High)
- $\square$ **0.3** SES(x, Medium)
- $\square$ **0.2** SES(x, Low)
- $\square$ **0.4** WM(x, High) $\wedge$ HLE(y, High) $\wedge$ PI(z, High) $\wedge$ SES(w, High) $\Longrightarrow$ cogAbility(x, y, z, w, u) for $u \in$ {Strong, Moderate}
- $\square$ **0.6** WM(x, Medium) $\wedge$ HLE(y, Medium) $\wedge$ PI(z, Medium) $\wedge$ SES(w, Medium) $\Longrightarrow$ cogAbility(x, y, z, w, u) for $u \in$ {Moderate, Weak}

High-Level Theory U_h:

- $\square$ **0.7** engagement(x, High)
- $\square$ **0.3** engagement(x, Low)
- $\square$ **0.5** cogAbility(x, Strong) $\wedge$ engagement(y, High) $\wedge$ adaptation(z, High) $\Longrightarrow$ academicPerformance(x, y, z, u) for $u \in$ {Excellent, Good}
- $\square$ **0.5** cogAbility(x, Weak) $\wedge$ engagement(y, Low) $\wedge$ adaptation(z, Low) $\Longrightarrow$ academicPerformance(x, y, z, u) for $u \in$ {Average, Poor}

In the given example case, while a two-layer abstraction from U_l to U_h captures some relationships between variables, it falls short due to the complexity and interdependencies in educational systems. In the formal model, we see numerous variables such as Home Learning Environment (HLE), Parental Involvement (PI), and Socioeconomic Status (SES), each affecting Cognitive Abilities (WM) and Learning Styles (LS). The interaction of these variables in a two-layer mapping is insufficient to capture the nuanced impacts across all layers. For instance, a high-quality home learning environment (HLE = High) might significantly enhance working memory (WM = High), which in turn influences engagement (engagement = High) and ultimately leads to better academic performance (academicPerformance = Excellent). However, this pathway also intersects with other variables like parental involvement and socioeconomic status, creating a web of interdependencies that a two-layer model cannot fully address.

To address complex interdependencies, we can use hierarchical abstractions to decompose the problem into multiple layers, each capturing specific relationships and interactions. This approach accommodates detailed representations that reflect the complex interdependencies among variables, such as those between home learning environment, parental involvement, and socioeconomic status. By maintaining probabilistic integrity across layers, this hierarchical model breaks down these complexities, providing interpretable insights that can guide educators and policymakers in addressing the nuanced factors impacting educational outcomes.

2.1 New Directions in Hierarchical Probabilistic Abstraction

In exploring probabilistic abstraction, we encounter pivotal questions that challenge our understanding of hierarchical models. These largely unexplored questions require a structured methodology to articulate the foundational principles of hierarchical abstraction. Our approach—constructing complex abstraction layers from foundational taxonomy—serves as a starting point to address these inquiries, offering a systematic way to navigate and clarify the complexities of such models.

Before delving into a detailed examination of hierarchical abstractions, it is essential to outline the key questions guiding our inquiry:

1. *Defining Hierarchical Abstraction:* What defines a hierarchical abstraction within probabilistic systems, and how can this definition be systematically applied across layers?
2. *Validating Hierarchical Structures:* How do we ascertain the accuracy of a hierarchical model in abstracting its underlying probabilistic layers?
3. *Navigating Abstraction Layers:* What mechanisms facilitate the effective translation and navigation between different levels of abstraction within a hierarchical model?
4. *Managing Complexity:* How does hierarchical abstraction aid in the simplification and management of the inherent complexity in probabilistic systems?
5. *Operationalizing Hierarchical Compositions:* How can operations and compositions across various hierarchical layers be conceptualized and applied to enhance probabilistic modeling?

3 Foundational Taxonomy for Probabilistic Abstraction

In this section[1], we delineate the taxonomy of abstraction processes by examining one-layered mappings, which we use subsequently to build multi-layered hierarchies in compositional manner. Firstly, we analyze the transition from a concrete state to an abstract state without considering subsequent layers of abstractions. This focused approach clarifies and classifies foundational abstraction methods, forming a basis for more complex, multi-layered abstractions. Restricting our examination to one-layered mappings, we categorize abstraction processes based on their structural characteristics and the nature of mappings. These include direct abstraction (each concrete state maps to a unique abstract state), divergent abstraction (a single concrete state maps to multiple abstract states), and convergent abstraction (multiple concrete states aggregate into a single abstract state). Each type offers insights into how information and characteristics from the concrete domain are represented, reduced, or combined in the abstract domain.

[1] For any schematic representation presented in this paper, the upward arrow ($\uparrow$) symbolizes an abstraction operation, indicating the transformation from a lower-level probability space to a higher-level abstracted probability space. Each step in the chain, represented by a unique abstraction operation $\mathcal{A}_i$, transitions the system from one probabilistic space $(\Omega_{i-1}, \Sigma_{i-1}, P_{i-1})$ to another $(\Omega_i, \Sigma_i, P_i)$.

By focusing on these initial mappings, we establish a foundational taxonomy, facilitating the systematic exploration of abstraction strategies and laying the groundwork for investigating multi-layered hierarchical abstractions.

3.1 Direct Abstraction (One-to-One)

In our taxonomy, the first category, direct abstraction, entails a one-to-one mapping between each concrete state and its abstract counterpart. Holtzen et al.'s work on probabilistic program abstraction exemplifies this approach, using direct abstraction specifically in the context of probabilistic programs [22]. Building on this example and retaining the same measure-theoretic approach, we generalize the framework to encompass a wider range of one-to-one mappings that extend beyond program-specific applications, thereby broadening the applicability of probabilistic abstraction, as outlined schematically below.

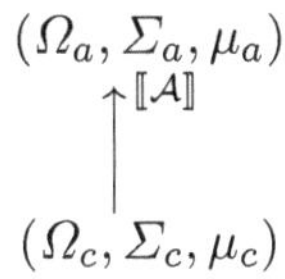

Definition 1. (Direct Abstraction): Let $(\Omega_c, \Sigma_c, \mu_c)$ be a concrete probability space and $(\Omega_a, \Sigma_a, \mu_a)$ an abstract probability space. Direct abstraction is facilitated by a bijective measurable function $\mathcal{A} : \Omega_c \to \Omega_a$, ensuring a one-to-one correspondence between elements of Ω_c and Ω_a.

Formally, $\mathcal{A}$ is a measurable function such that for any measurable set $B \in \Sigma_a$, the pre-image $\mathcal{A}^{-1}(B)$ is measurable in Σ_c, i.e., $\forall B \in \Sigma_a, \mathcal{A}^{-1}(B) \in \Sigma_c$. The abstract measure μ_a is the pushforward of the concrete measure μ_c via $\mathcal{A}$, defined by $\mu_a(B) = \mu_c(\mathcal{A}^{-1}(B))$ for all $B \in \Sigma_a$, ensuring the preservation of probabilistic information through the abstraction process.

3.2 Divergent Abstraction (One-to-Many)

Divergent abstraction allows a single set of low-level evidence to be abstracted into multiple high-level theories or concepts, as illustrated below:

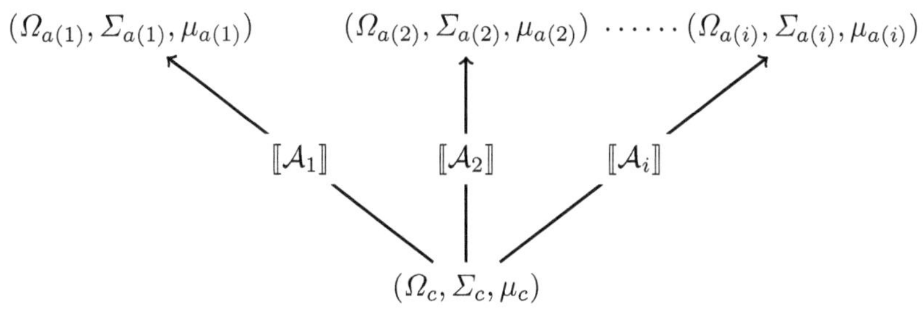

Definition 2 (Divergent Abstraction): Given a concrete probability space $(\Omega_c, \Sigma_c, \mu_c)$, divergent abstraction maps this space to a collection of abstract probability spaces $\{(\Omega_{a(i)}, \Sigma_{a(i)}, \mu_{a(i)})\}_{i\in I}$, where I is an index set, via measurable functions $\{\mathcal{A}_i : \Omega_c \to \Omega_{a(i)}\}_{i\in I}$. Each $\mathcal{A}_i$ is measurable, ensuring that for every $i \in I$ and $A_i \in \Sigma_{a(i)}$, $\mathcal{A}_i^{-1}(A_i) \in \Sigma_c$. The unified abstract sigma-algebra $\Sigma^{'}$ is defined as $\sigma\left(\bigcup_{i\in I} \mathcal{A}_i(\Sigma_c)\right)$, the smallest sigma-algebra containing the union of the images of Σ_c under all $\mathcal{A}_i$. A unified abstract measure $\mu^{'}$ on $\Sigma^{'}$ is constructed such that for any $E \in \Sigma^{'}$, $\mu^{'}(E)$ integrates or aggregates $\mu_{a(i)}(E \cap \Omega_{a(i)})$ for all $i \in I$, normalized to ensure $\mu^{'}$ is a probability measure.

3.3 Convergent Abstraction (Many-to-One)

Conversely, in convergent abstraction, multiple sets of low-level evidence are integrated into a single high-level theory, allowing for a comprehensive synthesis of low-level evidence through the abstraction process as illustrated below:

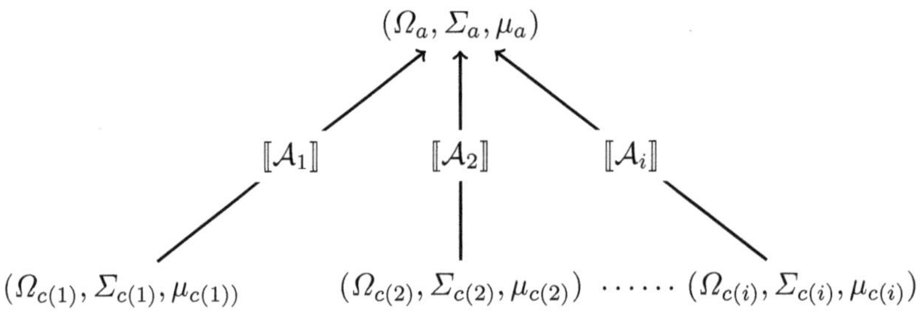

Definition 3 (Convergent Abstraction): Let $\{(\Omega_{c(i)}, \Sigma_{c(i)}, \mu_{c(i)})\}_{i\in I}$ be a collection of concrete probability spaces and $(\Omega_a, \Sigma_a, \mu_a)$ an abstract probability space. Convergent abstraction is achieved through measurable functions $\{\mathcal{A}_i : \Omega_{c(i)} \to \Omega_a\}_{i\in I}$, which map elements from $\Omega_{c(i)}$ to Ω_a, thereby aggregating disparate concrete spaces into a single abstract space. The formal characterization includes two main criteria: first, each $\mathcal{A}_i$ must be measurable, ensuring that for every $B \in \Sigma_a$, the pre-image $\mathcal{A}_i^{-1}(B)$ is measurable in $\Sigma_{c(i)}$; formally, $\forall i \in I, \forall B \in \Sigma_a, \mathcal{A}_i^{-1}(B) \in \Sigma_{c(i)}$. Second, the abstract measure μ_a integrates the measures from all concrete spaces, defined for any $B \in \Sigma_a$ as $\mu_a(B) = \sum_{i\in I} \mu_{c(i)}(\mathcal{A}_i^{-1}(B))$, with appropriate normalization to ensure μ_a remains a probability measure, thus coherently consolidating probabilistic information from multiple concrete spaces into the abstract space.

4 Advancing Into Hierarchical Probabilistic Abstraction

Using the foundational types of abstraction (direct, convergent, and divergent) various hierarchical taxonomies can be constructed by combining these single-layered abstractions into structured, tree-like models. Layering direct abstractions sequentially creates a multi-layered hierarchy known as sequential abstraction, where each level builds directly on the previous one, enabling a systematic progression from low-level details to high-level concepts.

Beyond simple sequential structures, hybrid hierarchical probabilistic abstractions introduce more complex configurations. For instance, a model beginning with a divergent layer followed by sequential direct abstractions is termed a divergent sequential abstraction. A divergent sequential abstraction enables multiple sequential abstractions on the same foundational data, whereas a convergent sequential abstraction starts with different foundational spaces, applies sequential abstractions to each, and unifies them at higher levels.

This structured approach enables the construction of hierarchical models that maintain consistency and interpretability across abstraction layers, supporting diverse modeling needs. In certain cases, divergent abstractions may even simplify into a sequential form when no further divergent paths exist, underscoring the importance of understanding structural relationships between abstraction types. By grounding higher-level abstractions in low-level details, we ensure that the entire hierarchy retains coherence and accuracy across layers.

In our approach to representing hierarchical abstract representations, we categorize into two types of Hierarchical Probabilistic Abstraction Models (HPAMs) based on the complexities they capture:

1. HPAM-DAG (Directed Acyclic Graphs)[2]: Uses a tree-like structure for systems with clear, sequential progressions and no cycles. This type is ideal for unidirectional hierarchical relationships, simplifying analysis.
2. HPAM-CD (Cyclical and Dynamic): Captures systems with feedback loops, cycles, and dynamic interactions, reflecting real-world complexity. Due to these complexities, this type requires more formal and mathematical treatment and is reserved for future work.

For now, we focus exclusively on HPAM-DAGs to simplify and analyze complex probabilistic systems, ensuring coherent, unidirectional mapping and maintaining clear hierarchical relationships.

Definition 4 (HPAM-DAG): A Hierarchical Probabilistic Abstraction, denoted as $\mathcal{H}$, is defined as a triple $(\mathcal{V}, \mathcal{E}, \{\mathcal{P}_v\}_{v \in \mathcal{V}})$ where:

- $\mathcal{V}$ is a set of vertices in a Directed Acyclic Graph (DAG), each corresponding to a distinct probabilistic space.
- $\mathcal{E} \subseteq \mathcal{V} \times \mathcal{V}$ is a set of directed edges in the DAG, each representing an abstraction mapping between probabilistic spaces.
- $\{\mathcal{P}_v\}_{v \in \mathcal{V}}$ is a family of probabilistic spaces associated with vertices in $\mathcal{V}$. For each vertex v, the probabilistic space $\mathcal{P}_v$ is a tuple $(\Omega_v, \Sigma_v, P_v)$, where:

[2] The decision to employ DAG-based models is motivated by their ability to enable a clear, systematic transition from concrete to abstract representations in a unidirectional manner, facilitating straightforward analysis and interpretation of probabilistic relationships.

- Ω_v is the sample space for vertex v, representing all possible outcomes.
- Σ_v is a σ-algebra over Ω_v, defining the set of events for which probabilities are assigned.
- $P_v : \Sigma_v \rightarrow [0,1]$ is a probability measure that assigns probabilities to events in Σ_v.

For every directed edge $(v_i, v_j) \in \mathcal{E}$ within the DAG, there exists an abstraction mapping $\mathcal{A}_{ij} : \Omega_{v_i} \rightarrow \Omega_{v_j}$ that facilitates a transformation between probabilistic spaces $\mathcal{P}_{v_i}$ and $\mathcal{P}_{v_j}$. This mapping satisfies the condition:

$$P_{v_j}(A_{v_j}) = P_{v_i}(\mathcal{A}_{ij}^{-1}(A_{v_j})), \tag{1}$$

for all $A_{v_j} \in \Sigma_{v_j}$, where $\mathcal{A}_{ij}^{-1}(A_{v_j})$ is the pre-image of A_{v_j} under $\mathcal{A}_{ij}$, ensuring the preservation of probabilistic measures through the abstraction process.

4.1 Boundary of Abstraction

Establishing a clear boundary for abstraction in probabilistic models is essential, and the Highest Possible Abstraction (HPoA) serves to mark this boundary. Beyond the HPoA, further abstraction risks obscuring critical probabilistic or relational details, diminishing the model's essence as an abstractive method, interpretability and analytical rigor. The HPoA thus defines the upper limit of meaningful abstraction, ensuring that each layer within the abstraction hierarchy contributes substantively to the model's integrity. This approach preserves essential information at every level, supporting the construction of hierarchical models that are both robust and interpretable.

Definition 5 (HPoA). Let's consider a HPAM-DAG denoted as $\mathcal{H} = (\mathcal{V}, \mathcal{E}, \{\mathcal{P}_v\}_{v \in \mathcal{V}})$. Within this framework, HPoA is formalized as a specific probabilistic space $(\Omega_{HPoA}, \Sigma_{HPoA}, P_{HPoA})$ that meets the following rigorously defined criteria:

1. **Preservation of Probabilistic Integrity:** For every set $A_{HPoA} \in \Sigma_{HPoA}$, it holds that $P_{HPoA}(A_{HPoA})$ is congruent with the probabilistic measure assigned to its corresponding set in any precursor probabilistic space within $\mathcal{H}$. Formally, this means:
$$\forall A_{HPoA} \in \Sigma_{HPoA}, \exists A_{\mathcal{P}_v} \in \Sigma_{\mathcal{P}_v} \text{ for } \mathcal{P}_v \in \{\mathcal{P}_v\}_{v \in \mathcal{V}} : \\ P_{HPoA}(A_{HPoA}) = P_{\mathcal{P}_v}(\mathcal{A}_{v \rightarrow HPoA}^{-1}(A_{HPoA})),$$
where $\mathcal{A}_{v \rightarrow HPoA}$ denotes the abstraction mapping from Ω_v to Ω_{HPoA}.
2. **Maximal Generalization:** $(\Omega_{HPoA}, \Sigma_{HPoA}, P_{HPoA})$ achieves the highest degree of abstraction permissible under the constraints of probabilistic integrity. No further abstraction (Ω', Σ', P') can be derived from HPoA without a resultant loss in the preservation of essential probabilistic relationships. This is expressed as: $\nexists(\Omega', \Sigma', P') : \Sigma_{HPoA} \subsetneq \Sigma' \wedge \forall A' \in \Sigma', P'(A') \neq P_{HPoA}(\mathcal{A}_{HPoA \rightarrow'}^{-1}(A'))$.

In essence, the HPoA, $(\Omega_{HPoA}, \Sigma_{HPoA}, P_{HPoA})$, encapsulates the terminus of the abstraction process within $\mathcal{H}$, marking the juncture beyond which no additional abstraction can be achieved without compromising the model's fundamental probabilistic structure.

Proposition 1 (Existence of the HPoA in HPAM-DAG). Given a HPAM-DAG $\mathcal{H} = (\mathcal{V}, \mathcal{E}, \{\mathcal{P}_v\}_{v \in \mathcal{V}})$, there exists at least one HPoA, $(\Omega_{HPoA}, \Sigma_{HPoA}, P_{HPoA})$, such that for any probabilistic space (Ω', Σ', P') that can be derived from $(\Omega_{HPoA}, \Sigma_{HPoA}, P_{HPoA})$ via an abstraction mapping, it results in the loss of at least one essential probabilistic relationship.

5 HPAM-DAG Types

Different types of HPAM-DAGs emerge as we combine foundational abstraction types in various ways. Each variant of HPAM-DAG has unique properties based on the specific combination and configuration of these foundational mappings. By arranging these mappings into multilayered structures, we can create HPAM-DAGs that represent increasing levels of complexity within probabilistic systems.

In this section, we outline two types of HPAM-DAGs: sequential abstraction and a more complex hybrid variant. While these examples provide a foundation, it is important to note that many other types of HPAM-DAGs can be formally defined by varying combinations of foundational abstraction types. These additional configurations offer potential avenues for exploration in future works.

5.1 Sequential Abstraction

Sequential abstraction represents the simplest form of HPAM, as it layers direct abstractions in a straightforward, linear progression from low-level to high-level concepts, without incorporating branching or merging complexities.

Definition 6 (Sequential Abstractions): Let $(\Omega_0, \Sigma_0, P_0)$ represent the foundational probability space. Sequential abstraction is characterized by a finite series of probability spaces $\{(\Omega_i, \Sigma_i, P_i)\}_{i=0}^{n}$, where each space $(\Omega_{i+1}, \Sigma_{i+1}, P_{i+1})$ is derived from $(\Omega_i, \Sigma_i, P_i)$ via an abstraction operation $\mathcal{A}_i$. The culmination of this process, the HPoA, $(\Omega_{HPoA}, \Sigma_{HPoA}, P_{HPoA})$, is distinguished as the endpoint of the sequence. For each i, ranging from 1 to n, this is formally represented as:

$$\mathcal{A}_i : (\Omega_{i-1}, \Sigma_{i-1}, P_{i-1}) \to (\Omega_i, \Sigma_i, P_i),$$

under the stipulations that: (1) for every measurable set $A \in \Sigma_{i-1}$, the condition $P_{i-1}(A) = P_i(\mathcal{A}_i(A))$ holds true (Preservation of Probability Mass), and (2) there is no σ-algebra smaller than Σ_i, denoted as $\Sigma' \subsetneq \Sigma_i$, for which the preservation of probability mass criteria remains valid (Minimality).

Proposition 2 (Uniqueness of HPoA in Sequential Abstractions): Given a concrete probability space $(\Omega_0, \Sigma_0, P_0)$, the HPoA, $(\Omega_{HPoA}, \Sigma_{HPoA}, P_{HPoA})$, achieved through a sequential abstraction process is unique. This implies that for any two HPoAs, $(\Omega_{HPoA}, \Sigma_{HPoA}, P_{HPoA})$ and $(\Omega'_{HPoA}, \Sigma'_{HPoA}, P'_{HPoA})$ derived from $(\Omega_0, \Sigma_0, P_0)$ via any sequence of abstraction operations, it must hold that $\Sigma_{HPoA} = \Sigma'_{HPoA}$.

Proposition 3 (Existence of Intermediate States): Given a concrete probability space $(\Omega_0, \Sigma_0, P_0)$ and a HPoA, $(\Omega_{HPoA}, \Sigma_{HPoA}, P_{HPoA})$, obtained through a sequential abstraction process, for any intermediate abstraction $(\Omega_i, \Sigma_i\ , P_i)$ where $0 < i < n$ and $(\Omega_i, \Sigma_i, P_i) \neq (\Omega_{HPoA}, \Sigma_{HPoA}, P_{HPoA})$, there exists at least one intermediate state $(\Omega_{int}, \Sigma_{int}, P_{int})$ that facilitates the decomposition of the abstraction sequence into:

$$[\![\mathcal{A}_{\text{pre}}]\!] : \Omega_0 \to \Omega_{int} \quad \text{and} \quad [\![\mathcal{A}_{\text{post}}]\!] : \Omega_{int} \to \Omega_{HPoA}.$$

Property 1 (Comprehensibility): Given the existence of an intermediate abstraction state $(\Omega_{int}, \Sigma_{int}, P_{int})$, there exists a structured pathway, $[\![\mathcal{A}_{\text{pre}}]\!] : \Omega_0 \to \Omega_{int}$ and $[\![\mathcal{A}_{\text{post}}]\!] : \Omega_{int} \to \Omega_{HPoA}$, that enhances the comprehensibility of the abstraction process. This is formalized as the ability to sequentially deconstruct the abstraction hierarchy into comprehensible steps, each represented by measurable transformations preserving essential probabilistic structures.

Inspired by Ai et al. findings on sequential learning tasks, our abstraction process is designed with intermediate stages to enhance comprehensibility [1]. Ai et al. noted that structured and sequential presentation of concepts improves human understanding. By preserving intermediate abstraction states, we ensure each step remains comprehensible and accessible.

Property 2 (Tractability): The identification and utilization of the intermediate abstraction state $(\Omega_{int}, \Sigma_{int}, P_{int})$ within the sequential abstraction process confirm the modular nature of the abstraction and significantly improve the tractability of conducting analyses across the hierarchy. This modularity allows for targeted adjustments and refinements at specific levels of abstraction, effectively navigating and understanding probabilistic relationships at each hierarchical level.

Ensuring tractability is vital for the practical application of abstraction methodologies. Results from Holtzen et al. demonstrate that maintaining computational manageability at each step allows for efficient analysis and reasoning, making the overall process more effective [21,22].

5.2 Hybrid HPAMs

Hybrid HPAM-DAGs amalgamate sequential, divergent, and convergent abstraction methodologies within hierarchical probabilistic modeling to adeptly capture the complexities of intricate systems. Defined over a base probability space $(\Omega_0, \Sigma_0, P_0)$, Hybrid HPAM-DAG employs a dynamic mix of abstraction operations that either progress linearly, branch out divergently, and/or converge from various sequences into a unified model. This integration allows for a nuanced exploration and understanding of the system's probabilistic behaviors from multiple perspectives, ensuring the model comprehensively reflects the system's dynamics and dependencies. By leveraging the strengths of each abstraction method, Hybrid HPAM-DAG offers a versatile framework that maintains the system's probabilistic integrity while navigating through its complex landscape, making it a powerful tool for modeling sophisticated systems with high fidelity.

To exemplify, consider a hybrid model that combines direct, sequential, divergent, and convergent abstraction processes to model the dynamic nature of complex systems like Alzheimer's disease. It begins with a foundational concrete space $(\Omega_0, \Sigma_0, P_0)$, where Ω_0 represents the population at risk for Alzheimer's disease, Σ_0 includes measurable events indicating risk factors for Alzheimer's, and P_0 quantifies the initial distribution of these risk factors. For more details, refer to the appendix section for a pseudocode algorithm.

Sequential Abstraction: On the first layer, the abstraction transitions the model from broad risk factors to specific biological markers indicative of Alzheimer's:

$$\mathcal{A}_1 : (\Omega_0, \Sigma_0, P_0) \rightarrow (\Omega_1, \Sigma_1, P_1)$$

where $(\Omega_1, \Sigma_1, P_1)$ focuses on biological markers such as amyloid-beta levels and tau protein tangles. The model employs sequential abstractions to refine the understanding of how these biological markers influence disease progression:

$$\mathcal{A}_2 : (\Omega_1, \Sigma_1, P_1) \rightarrow (\Omega_2, \Sigma_2, P_2)$$

where $(\Omega_2, \Sigma_2, P_2)$ might include cognitive decline metrics and early symptoms of Alzheimer's disease.

Divergent Abstraction: From this point, the model branches into distinct intervention pathways:

$$\mathcal{A}_{3,i} : (\Omega_2, \Sigma_2, P_2) \rightarrow (\Omega_{3,i}, \Sigma_{3,i}, P_{3,i}), \quad i \in \{1, 2\}$$

Each path i represents a different intervention strategy, such as cognitive therapy or medication, with outcomes specific to those treatments. For example:

1. $\mathcal{A}_{3,1}$ could represent cognitive therapy, focusing on improving cognitive functions through exercises and mental activities.
2. $\mathcal{A}_{3,2}$ could represent medication, focusing on pharmacological treatments aimed at slowing the progression of the disease.

Convergent Abstraction: The insights from these divergent paths are then synthesized into a unified model:

$$\mathcal{A}_4 : (\Omega_{3,1} \cup \Omega_{3,2}, \Sigma_{3,1} \cup \Sigma_{3,2}, P_{3,1} \oplus P_{3,2}) \rightarrow (\Omega_4, \Sigma_4, P_4)$$

resulting in a comprehensive understanding of the efficacy and outcomes of various Alzheimer's disease management strategies.

This hybrid methodology can be applied in several contexts: integrating genetic, environmental, and clinical data to study Alzheimer's disease progression and treatment effectiveness in research; developing personalized treatment plans that consider multiple intervention strategies in clinical practice; and informing healthcare policies based on comprehensive models that incorporate various risk factors and treatment outcomes in policy making. The Hybrid HPAM-DAG framework effectively integrates sequential, divergent, and convergent abstraction processes, providing a structured approach to understanding and managing Alzheimer's disease. It progressively abstracts and refines data, offering valuable insights at each hierarchical level.

6 Related Works

Abstraction serves as a critical tool for simplifying and understanding the complexity inherent in drawing analogies, parsing through inherent relational information, employing reasoning by formally representing uncertainty [13,16,33]. The work of Saitta and Zucker, for instance, provides a comprehensive exploration of abstraction, from its fundamental role in planning and solving constraint satisfaction problems to its implementation in the coordination of multi-agent systems [33]. Moreover, abstraction plays a crucial role in domains such as program analysis and verification, probabilistic games, labeled transition systems, probabilistic programs, complex systems, and inductive logic programming, enhancing the innovative problem-solving capabilities and methodological developments within each field [2,7,8,17,29,30,34]. While some research has concentrated on the specific challenges and opportunities presented by probabilistic settings, others have offered theoretical insights on ideal specifications and the dynamics of mappings within abstractions more generally [11,25,27]. Through these diverse treatments, abstraction emerges not only as a key concept for theoretical exploration but also as a practical tool for accommodating complex problem-solving methodologies across a spectrum of scientific inquiries [31].

Numerous fields have developed sophisticated frameworks to formalize abstraction, providing a mathematical foundation for this complex concept and offering structured analyses of the abstraction process [2,14]. Milner's work on the semantics of concurrent processes has significantly influenced our exploration of algebraic formalisms for probabilistic abstraction [28]. Similarly, Hennessy and Milner's algebraic laws, which introduce observational congruence to study nondeterministic and concurrent programs, offer valuable insights into comparing different levels of abstractions within probabilistic abstraction hierarchies [19]. Further, studies on probabilistic bisimulation and cocongruence for probabilistic systems could inspire novel approaches in this area as exemplified by the work by Hofmann and Belle on abstracting noisy robot programs [5,10,20,32]. The algebraic tools as discussed, developed for defining and verifying concurrent program properties, hold promise for extending into designing and verifying probabilistic abstraction hierarchies. However, practical application of these theories has been mixed—some have been successfully integrated into real-world applications, while others face challenges in bridging theoretical insights with practical implementation [6,14,27].

In Belle's work, for instance, a novel semantic framework for analyzing and abstracting probabilistic models is unveiled, significantly contributing to the discourse on abstraction [4]. This research builds upon and extends the foundational work of Banihashemi et al., which investigated isomorphism and thorough abstractions in the context of situation calculus agent programs, primarily from a non-probabilistic perspective [2]. Belle aims to adapt these foundational concepts to probabilistic settings, such as in probabilistic relational models (PRMs), through the introduction of unweighted abstractions that are compatible with categorical settings in terms of satisfaction and entailment [2,4]. This foundation facilitates the advancement of weighted abstractions and the integration of evidence, while also examining the linkage between these abstractions and stochastic models, notably through the lens of weak exact abstractions and the automation of abstraction generation.

Moreover, Belle also highlights the potential of incorporating methodologies from Giunchiglia and Walsh's research on logical theory operations into the probabilistic framework, necessitating some adjustments [4,14]. Albeit with some limitations in the unweighted and weighted approaches outlined, Belle provides detailed discussions on Banihashemi et al.'s approach of abstraction in knowledge representation and automated planning, especially hierarchical planning. Belle's work opens new avenues for both theoretical exploration and practical application within probabilistic modeling and planning [2,4,14,23]. We start our inquiry by following up on the call for newer approaches in representing abstraction hierarchies as Belle and Banihashemi et al. outline [2,4].

Further, Holtzen et al. explores the concept of abstraction within probabilistic programming, specifically investigating how to abstract a probability distribution defined by such a program [21,22]. The study identifies and automatically generates abstractions that semantically represent conditional independence assumptions, thereby aiding in the design of algorithms for simplifying inference processes. This is achieved by adapting techniques from program verification to analyze deterministic code, applying a refined form of predicate abstraction to create abstract probabilistic programs that preserve the essential characteristics of the original programs [21] . A key contribution of their work is the introduction of the concept of distributional soundness, which ensures the consistency of probability distributions between abstract and concrete programs. Holtzen et al. outlines a theory and methodology for developing distributionally sound abstractions across a broad range of probabilistic programs, leveraging complex independence structures to streamline the original program [21]. Through this approach, Holtzen et al. illustrates the practical advantages of abstraction, such as enhanced efficiency in inference procedures, across various statistical models formulated as probabilistic programs [21,22].

7 Discussion

Our approach seeks to unify diverse theoretical perspectives while advancing the understanding and practical application of abstraction, bridging the gap between theoretical foundations and real-world utility in hierarchical representations. Despite its strengths, our framework has several limitations. The integration of multiple abstraction layers and the hybrid nature of our framework can lead to increased computational complexity, potentially making it less scalable for very large datasets or highly complex systems. While our approach aims to enhance interpretability by structuring abstractions hierarchically, there is a trade-off between the level of detail retained and the simplicity of the abstracted models, making it challenging to balance these aspects. Furthermore, our framework, though robust in the contexts we've explored, may face challenges when generalized to entirely new domains or types of data that were not considered during its development.

The effectiveness of our framework heavily relies on the quality and completeness of the initial data. Poor quality data can lead to inaccurate abstractions and potentially flawed conclusions. Additionally, the hierarchical nature and the need for intermediate abstractions require significant computational resources, which may not be readily available in all settings. The current use of Directed Acyclic Graphs (DAGs) for representation, while useful for capturing dependencies and causal relationships, can be limiting in expressing more complex, multi-layered abstractions. A more rigorous and holistic framework is necessary to represent abstraction hierarchies effectively, ensuring that multi-layered representations are comprehensively understood and utilized.

This work introduces the concepts of hierarchical probabilistic abstraction and a specific hybrid approach, yet many other taxonomies and abstraction methods remain unexplored and warrant further study to fully understand abstraction frameworks. Recognizing the importance of hierarchical representations for interpreting multi-layered abstractions, future work will provide a formal treatment of this framework by developing a rigorous mathematical foundation and delivering a comprehensive analysis of the Hybrid HPAM-DAG approach. We also intend to address current limitations by refining computational strategies, investigating additional taxonomies of abstraction, and conducting extensive testing across diverse domains and applied settings. These efforts will enhance our approach, expand its applicability, and ultimately lead to a more robust and holistic representation of abstraction hierarchies.

8 Conclusion

In this paper, we introduce a conceptual framework for hierarchical probabilistic abstraction that extends a measure-theoretic foundation to address challenges in modeling complex systems. By structuring the abstraction process into layered mappings, this framework supports modular problem-solving and allows for both detailed layer-specific analysis and a cohesive, system-wide understanding. This dual-level approach enhances model development by bridging high-level conceptual insights with low-level perceptual data. The modular structure ensures that each layer of the abstraction hierarchy can be independently developed, analyzed, and comprehended, fostering the construction of interpretable models. Additionally, this hierarchical framework provides flexibility in integrating multiple abstraction levels, facilitating the exploration of complex phenomena with both depth and breadth.

A Hybrid HPAM for Alzheimer's Disease Management

In this section, we provide a high-level pseudocode algorithm to illustrate the application of HPAM-DAGs in Alzheimer's disease management. The algorithm demonstrates how direct, divergent, and convergent abstractions can model the relationships among risk factors, biological markers, treatment pathways, and patient outcomes.

Pseudocode Algorithm

Initialize DAG G with initial probability space $(\Omega_0, \Sigma_0, P_0)$.
Initialize $(\text{Final\_Model}, \text{HPoA}) = \{\}$, HPoA = undefined.
while True **do**
  Step 1: Apply Direct Abstraction to map low-level risk factors to biological markers.
  for each risk_factor in $(\Omega_0, \Sigma_0, P_0)$ **do**
    Define Direct Abstraction:

$$(\Omega_1, \Sigma_1, P_1) = \mathcal{A}_{\text{Direct}}((\Omega_0, \Sigma_0, P_0))$$

    Add Node $G : (\Omega_1, \Sigma_1, P_1)$.
    Add Edge $G : (\Omega_0, \Sigma_0, P_0) \to (\Omega_1, \Sigma_1, P_1)$.
  end for
  Step 2: Apply Divergent Abstraction to generate multiple treatment pathways.
  for each $(\Omega_1, \Sigma_1, P_1)$ in Bio_Markers **do**
    Define Divergent Abstraction:

$$(\Omega_{2_i}, \Sigma_{2_i}, P_{2_i}) = \mathcal{A}_{\text{Divergent}}((\Omega_1, \Sigma_1, P_1))$$

    Add Node $G : (\Omega_{2_i}, \Sigma_{2_i}, P_{2_i})$.
    Add Edge $G : (\Omega_1, \Sigma_1, P_1) \to (\Omega_{2_i}, \Sigma_{2_i}, P_{2_i})$.
  end for
  Step 3: Apply Convergent Abstraction to unify treatment outcomes.

Combine using Convergent Abstraction:

$$(\Omega_3, \Sigma_3, P_3) = \mathcal{A}_{\text{Convergent}}(\{(\Omega_{2_1}, \Sigma_{2_1}, P_{2_1}), \ldots, (\Omega_{2_n}, \Sigma_{2_n}, P_{2_n})\})$$

Add Node $G : (\Omega_3, \Sigma_3, P_3)$.
Add Edge $G : \{(\Omega_{2_1}, \Sigma_{2_1}, P_{2_1}), \ldots, (\Omega_{2_n}, \Sigma_{2_n}, P_{2_n})\} \rightarrow (\Omega_3, \Sigma_3, P_3)$.
Step 4: Calculate Highest Possible Abstraction (HPoA).
Construct HPoA:

$$(\Omega_{\text{HPoA}}, \Sigma_{\text{HPoA}}, P_{\text{HPoA}}) = \mathcal{A}_{\text{HPoA}}((\Omega_3, \Sigma_3, P_3))$$

Step 5: Validate if HPoA matches observed outcomes in Alzheimer's patients.
if P_{HPoA} matches observed outcomes O **then**
    return Success: Valid HPoA achieved for Alzheimer's Disease Management.
else if no further abstractions can be made
    return Failure: HPoA cannot be constructed.
else
    Perform interventions or update models and iterate.
    Update DAG G with new treatment data.
end if
end while

References

1. Ai, L., Langer, J., Muggleton, S.H., Schmid, U.: Explanatory machine learning for sequential human teaching. Mach. Learn. **112**(10), 3591–3632 (2023)
2. Banihashemi, B., De Giacomo, G., Lespérance, Y.: Abstraction in situation calculus action theories. In: Proceedings of the AAAI Conference on Artificial Intelligence, vol. 31 (2017)
3. Beckers, S., Eberhardt, F., Halpern, J.Y.: Approximate causal abstractions. In: Uncertainty in Artificial Intelligence, pp. 606–615. PMLR (2020)
4. Belle, V.: Abstracting probabilistic models: relations, constraints and beyond. Knowl.-Based Syst. **199**, 105976 (2020)
5. Castellani, I.: Bisimulations and abstraction homomorphisms. In: Ehrig, H., Floyd, C., Nivat, M., Thatcher, J. (eds.) CAAP 1985. LNCS, vol. 185, pp. 223–238. Springer, Heidelberg (1985). https://doi.org/10.1007/3-540-15198-2_14
6. Clarke, E., Grumberg, O., Jha, S., Lu, Y., Veith, H.: Counterexample-guided abstraction refinement. In: Emerson, E.A., Sistla, A.P. (eds.) CAV 2000. LNCS, vol. 1855, pp. 154–169. Springer, Heidelberg (2000). https://doi.org/10.1007/10722167_15
7. Cousot, P., Monerau, M.: Probabilistic abstract interpretation. In: Seidl, H. (ed.) ESOP 2012. LNCS, vol. 7211, pp. 169–193. Springer, Heidelberg (2012). https://doi.org/10.1007/978-3-642-28869-2_9
8. Cropper, A., Muggleton, S.: Learning higher-order logic programs through abstraction and invention. In: Twenty-Fifth International Joint Conference on Artificial Intelligence. Association for the Advancement of Artificial Intelligence (2016)

9. Danks, D.: Unifying the Mind: Cognitive Representations as Graphical Models. MIT Press (2014)
10. Danos, V., Desharnais, J., Laviolette, F., Panangaden, P.: Bisimulation and cocongruence for probabilistic systems. Inf. Comput. **204**(4), 503–523 (2006)
11. Dehnert, C., Gebler, D., Volpato, M., Jansen, D.N.: On abstraction of probabilistic systems. In: International Autumn School on Rigorous Dependability Analysis Using Model Checking Techniques for Stochastic Systems, pp. 87–116 (2012)
12. Fagin, R., Halpern, J.Y.: Reasoning about knowledge and probability. J. ACM (JACM) **41**(2), 340–367 (1994)
13. Gentner, D., Hoyos, C.: Analogy and abstraction. Top. Cogn. Sci. **9**(3), 672–693 (2017)
14. Giunchiglia, F., Walsh, T.: A theory of abstraction. Artif. Intell. **57**(2–3), 323–389 (1992)
15. Gubar, E., Taynitskiy, V., Fedyanin, D., Petrov, I.: Hierarchical epidemic model on structured population: diffusion patterns and control policies. Computation **10**(2), 31 (2022)
16. Halpern, J.Y.: Reasoning About Uncertainty. MIT press (2017)
17. Halpern, J.Y., Koller, D.: Representation dependence in probabilistic inference. J. Artif. Intell. Res. **21**, 319–356 (2004)
18. Han, W., Kang, X., He, W., Jiang, L., Li, H., Xu, B.: A new method for disease diagnosis based on hierarchical brb with power set. Heliyon **9**(2) (2023)
19. Hennessy, M., Milner, R.: Algebraic laws for nondeterminism and concurrency. J. ACM (JACM) **32**(1), 137–161 (1985)
20. Hofmann, T., Belle, V.: Abstracting noisy robot programs. In: Proceedings of the 2023 International Conference on Autonomous Agents and Multiagent Systems, pp. 534–542 (2023)
21. Holtzen, S., Broeck, G., Millstein, T.: Sound abstraction and decomposition of probabilistic programs. In: International Conference on Machine Learning, pp. 1999–2008. PMLR (2018)
22. Holtzen, S., Millstein, T., Van den Broeck, G.: Probabilistic program abstractions. In: Proceedings of the 33rd Conference on Uncertainty in Artificial Intelligence (UAI) (2017)
23. Junges, S., Spaan, M.T.: Abstraction-refinement for hierarchical probabilistic models. In: Shoham, S., Vizel, Y. (eds.) CAV 2022. LNCS, vol. 13371, pp. 102–123. Springer, Cham (2022). https://doi.org/10.1007/978-3-031-13185-1_6
24. Kahneman, D.: Thinking, Fast and Slow. Farrar, Straus and Giroux (2011)
25. Koller, D., Friedman, N.: Probabilistic Graphical Models: Principles and Techniques. MIT Press (2009)
26. Lüdtke, S., Schröder, M., Krüger, F., Bader, S., Kirste, T.: State-space abstractions for probabilistic inference: a systematic review. J. Artif. Intell. Res. **63**, 789–848 (2018)
27. McIver, A., Morgan, C.: Abstraction, Refinement and Proof for Probabilistic Systems. Springer, Cham (2005)
28. Milner, R.: Operational and algebraic semantics of concurrent processes. In: Formal Models and Semantics, pp. 1201–1242. Elsevier (1990)
29. Monniaux, D.: An abstract Monte-Carlo method for the analysis of probabilistic programs. In: Proceedings of the 28th ACM SIGPLAN-SIGACT Symposium on Principles of Programming Languages, pp. 93–101 (2001)
30. Muggleton, S., De Raedt, L.: Inductive logic programming: theory and methods. J. Logic Program. **19**, 629–679 (1994)

31. Murphy, K.P.: Machine Learning: A Probabilistic Perspective. MIT Press (2012)
32. Panangaden, P.: Probabilistic bisimulation. ACM SIGLOG News **2**(3), 72–84 (2015)
33. Saitta, L., Zucker, J.D.: Abstraction in Artificial Intelligence. Springer, Cham (2013)
34. Sandholm, T., Singh, S.: Lossy stochastic game abstraction with bounds. In: Proceedings of the 13th ACM Conference on Electronic Commerce, pp. 880–897 (2012)
35. Segal, E., Koller, D., Ormoneit, D.: Probabilistic abstraction hierarchies. In: Advances in Neural Information Processing Systems, vol. 14 (2001)

Differentiable Inductive Logic Programming in High-Dimensional Space

Stanisław J. Purgał[2], David M. Cerna[1(✉)], and Cezary Kaliszyk[3]

[1] Czech Academy of Sciences Institute of Computer Science, Prague, Czechia
dcerna@cs.cas.cz
[2] University of Innsbruck, Innsbruck, Austria
[3] University of Melbourne, Melbourne, Australia
cezary.kaliszyk@unimelb.edu.au

Abstract. Synthesizing large logic programs through symbolic Inductive Logic Programming (ILP) typically requires intermediate definitions. However, cluttering the hypothesis space with invented predicates typically degrades performance. In contrast, gradient descent provides an efficient method to find solutions within high-dimensional spaces; a property not fully exploited by neuro-symbolic ILP approaches. We propose extending the *differentiable* ILP framework by large-scale (extending its small-scale) predicate invention to emulate search through a high-dimensional space, and thus allowing us to exploit the efficacy of gradient descent. We show that large-scale predicate invention is beneficial to differentiable inductive synthesis and results in learning capabilities beyond existing neuro-symbolic ILP systems. Furthermore, we achieve these results without specifying the precise structure of the solution within the *inductive bias*.

Keywords: Inductive Logic Programming · Differentiable Logics · Predicate Invention

1 Introduction

Neuro-symbolic ILP is quickly becoming one of the most important research domains in inductive synthesis [5]. Such systems can aid explainability research by providing logical representations of what was learned and providing noise-handling capabilities to symbolic learners. Systems such as δILP can consistently learn solutions for many standard inductive synthesis problems [12,25]. Nonetheless, searching through the hypothesis space remains a challenging task. To deal with this difficulty, inductive learners introduce problem-specific restrictions that reduce the size of the respective search space [24,26]; what is commonly referred to as *language bias*. While this is conducive to solving simple learning tasks, more complex synthesis tasks or tasks where the required language bias is not easily specifiable remain a formidable challenge.

W.-Z. Dai (Ed.): ILP 2024, LNAI 16059, pp. 147–162, 2026.
https://doi.org/10.1007/978-3-032-09087-4_10

Predicate invention (PI) is a technique that enables the creation of new predicates, thereby adding shortened programs to the hypothesis space and circumventing the limitations imposed by the user-provided background knowledge. However, in purely symbolic inductive synthesis, reliance on large-scale PI is avoided, as it is time- and space-wise too demanding [19], and has only been used effectively in very restricted settings [1].

This paper introduces a novel approach to neuro-symbolic inductive synthesis, compatible with large-scale predicate invention, that leverages the power of the highly influential differentiable ILP [12]. We show that a few changes to the original architecture is enough to train models using a reduced language bias that tests with a significantly higher success rate. Our extension synthesizes a user-provided number of invented predicates during the learning process. Large-scale PI is either intractable for most systems due to memory requirements or results in a performance drop as it clutters the hypothesis space. In contrast, gradient descent methods generally benefit from large search spaces (high dimensionality). Thus, we propose introducing a large number of invented predicates to improve performance. We evaluate the approach on several standard ILP tasks (many derived from [12]), including several which existing neuro-symbolic ILP systems find to be a significant challenge (see *Hypothesis 1*).

Solutions found by our extension of δILP, in contrast to the usual ILP solutions, include large numbers of invented predicates. We posit the usefulness of large-scale PI for synthesizing complex logic programs. While adding many invented predicates can be seen as a duplication of the search space and, therefore, equivalent to multiple initializations of existing neuro-symbolic ILP systems, we demonstrate that our extension of δILP easily outperforms the re-initialization approach on a particularly challenging task (see *Hypothesis 2*). We compare to the most relevant existing approach, δILP (presented in [12]).

Unlike the experiments presented in [12], which specify the solution's precise structure, we assume a generic shape for all predicate definitions. Thus, our experiments force the learner to find both the correct predicates to reference within an invented predicate's definition and the structure of the definition. In this experimental setting, our approach is on par with δILP and, for challenging tasks, outperforms it. In particular, we outperform δILP on tasks deemed difficult in [12] such as *0=X mod 3* and *0=X mod 5.*

Furthermore, we propose an adjusted measure of task difficulty. In [12], the authors proposed the number of *learned* predicate definitions as a measure of learning complexity. While our results do not contradict this assertion, it is more precise to focus on the relation between input variables and body-only variables, i.e., we solve *0=X mod 5* (requires learning four predicate definitions) consistently but perform poorly on the seemingly simpler task $Y = X + 4$ which requires learning two predicates (*Hypothesis 3*). Improving our understanding of task difficulty will aid future investigations.

Our contributions are as follows: **(i)** an extension of δILP capable of large-scale PI (*Hypothesis 1*)[1], **(ii)** experimental verification of improved performance on challenging tasks (*Hypothesis 1*), **(iii)** experimental verification that large-scale PI differs from weight re-initialization (*Hypothesis 2*), **(iv)** proposing a novel complexity criterion and experimentally validating it (*Hypothesis 3*).

2 Related Work

We briefly introduce Inductive logic programming [5], cover aspects of δILP [12] directly relevant to our increase in dimensionality, and compare our approach to related systems inspired by δILP. We assume familiarity with basic logic and logic programming; see [23].

2.1 Inductive Logic Programming (ILP)

ILP is traditionally a form of symbolic machine learning whose goal is to derive explanatory hypotheses from sets of examples (denoted E^+ and E^-) together with background knowledge (denoted BK). Investigations often represent explanatory hypotheses as logic programs [6,7,14,21,22]. A benefit of this approach is that only a few examples are typically needed to learn an explanatory hypothesis [9].

The most common learning paradigm implemented within ILP systems is *learning from entailment* [23]. The systems referenced above, including δILP, use this paradigm, which is succinctly stated as follows: A hypothesis H explains E^+ and E^- through the BK, if

$$\forall e \in E^+, BK \wedge H \models e \quad \text{and} \quad \forall e \in E^-, BK \wedge H \not\models e$$

Essentially, the hypothesis, together with the background knowledge, entails all the positive examples and none of the negative examples. In addition to the learning paradigm, one must consider how to search through the *hypothesis space*, the set of logic programs constructible using definitions from the BK together with the predicates provided as examples. Many approaches exploit *subsumption* ($\leq_{sub}$), which has the following property in relation to entailment: $H_1 \leq_{sub} H_2 \Rightarrow H_1 \models H_2$ where H_1 and H_2 are plausible hypotheses. Subsumption provides a measure of specificity between hypotheses and, thus, is used to measure progress. The FOIL [22] approach (*top-down*) iteratively builds logic programs using this principle. *Bottom-up* approaches, i.e., Progol [17], build the subsumptively most specific clause for each positive example and use FOIL to extend more general clauses towards it.

The ILP system *Metagol* [7] implements the meta-learning approach to search. It uses second-order Horn templates to restrict and search the hypothesis space. An example template would be $P(x, y)\text{:-}Q(x, z), R(z, y)$ where P, Q, and R are variables ranging over predicate symbols. This approach motivates the *template* representation of δILP and our work.

[1] Our implementation can be found at the following repository: github.com/Ermine516/DILP2.

2.2 Differentiable ILP

Given that δILP plays an integral role in our work, we go into some detail concerning the system architecture. We refer the reader to the paper introducing δILP [12] for more details.

The δILP system provides a framework for differentiable *learning from entailment* ILP. Logic programs are represented by vectors whose components encode whether a particular code fragment is likely to be part of the solution. Such programs are "executed" in fuzzy logic, using a weighted average of fuzzy evaluations of code fragments. The hypothesis space consists of all possible combinations of these code fragments captured by user-provided *templates*, a generalization of *metarules* [7]. In our setting *metarules* take the following form:

Definition 1 (V-Metarule). *Let x, y, z_1, z_2, z_3, z_4 be first-order variables, V a set of first-order variables such that $x, y \in V$ and $z_1, z_2, z_3, z_4 \notin V$, and P, Q, and R second-order variables ranging over predicate symbols. Then $P(x,y)$:-$Q(z_1,z_2), R(z_3,z_4)$ is a V-metarule.*

Unlike standard metarules, V-Metarules can have various instances.

Definition 2 (V-Metarule Instance). *Let M be a V-Metarule of the form $P(x,y)$:-$Q_1(\ x_1,x_2)$, $R_1(x_3,x_4)$. Then $P(x,y)$:- $Q_1(\ y_1,y_2)$, $R_1(y_3,y_4)$ is an Instance of M if $y_1, y_2, y_3,\ y_4 \in V$.*

Essentially, V-metarules are a generalization of metarules that allows for different variable configurations. A (V,p)-template is defined using V-Metarules as follows:

Definition 3 ((V,p)-template). *Let p be a predicate symbol, $M = P(x,y)$:-$Q_1(x_1,x_2)$, $R_1(x_3,x_4)$ and $M' = P'(x,y)$:- $Q_2(x_1,x_2)$, $R_2(x_3,x_4)$ be V-metarules. Then the (V,p)-template constructed from M and M' is $(M\{P \mapsto p\}, M'\{P' \mapsto p\})$.*

An instance of a (V,p) -template (M_1,M_2) is the pair (M_1',M_2') where M_1' and M_2' are V-Metarule Instances of M_1 and M_2.

An instantiation of a (V,p)- template (M_1,M_2) is $(M_1'\sigma,\ M_2'\sigma)$ where (M_1',M_2') is an instance of (M_1,M_2) and σ maps the second-order variables to predicate symbols.

Observe that we use templates consisting of two metarules as this is the minimal size, which allows for recursion and disjunction in the predicate definition.

In [12], additional restrictions were put on the instantiations of the second-order variables to simplify the hypothesis space for harder tasks. The authors designed the templates to allow precise descriptions of the solution structure, thus simplifying the search. We took a more general approach, which allowed us to define templates uniformly. This results in a larger hypothesis space and, thus, a more challenging experimental setting.

Example 1. Consider a $(\{x, y, z\}, p)$-template. Possible instances of the contained $(\{x, y, z\})$-metarules include

$$p(x, y)\text{:-}Q_1(x, y), R_1(x, y) \qquad p(x, y)\text{:-}Q_2(x, z), R_2(x, z)$$

A program fitting this template would be the following:

$$p(x, y) : \text{-}succ(x, y) \qquad p(x, y) : \text{-}succ(x, z), p(x, z)$$

where R_2 maps to p and Q_1, R_1, and Q_2 map to *succ*.

Templates are generalizable to higher-arity predicates; learning such predicates is theoretically challenging for this ILP setting [18]. It is common to restrict learning to dyadic predicates. Reducing template complexity is important when introducing many templates (up to 150). From now on, by template, we mean (V, p)-template.

As input, δILP requires a set of templates T (using pairwise distinct symbols, $p_1, \cdots, p_n$) and *BK*. From the input, it derives a satisfiability problem where each disjunctive clause $C_{i,j}$ denotes the range of possible choices for clause j given template $t \in T$, i.e., overall instantiations of t. The logical models satisfying this formula denote logic programs modulo the clauses derivable using the template instantiated by the *BK* and the symbols $p_1, \cdots, p_n$. Switching from a discrete semantics over $\{0, 1\}$ to a continuous semantics allows the use of differentiable logical operators when implementing differentiable deduction. Solving ILP tasks, in this setting, is reduced to minimizing loss through gradient descent.

δILP uses E^+ and E^- as training data for a binary classifier to learn a model attributing *true* or *false* to ground instances of predicates. This model implements the conditional probability $p(\lambda|\alpha, W, T, L, BK)$, where $\lambda \in \{true, false\}$, α is a ground instance, W a set of weights, T the templates, and L the symbolic language used to describe the problem containing a finite set of atoms.

Each $(\{x, y, z\}, p_i)$-template $(t_1, t_2) \in T$ is associated with a weight matrix whose shape is $d_1 \times d_2$ where d_j denotes the number of clauses constructible using the *BK* and L modulo the constraints of t_j. The number of weights may be roughly approximated (*quintic*) in terms of the number of templates (considering possible instances and the four second-order variables to instantiate). The weights denote δILP's confidence in an instantiation of a template being part of the solution; so-called *per template* assignment. We provide a detailed discussion of weight assignment in Sect. 3.

δILP implements differentiable inferencing by providing each clause c with a function $f_c : [0, 1]^m \rightarrow [0, 1]^m$ whose domain and range are valuations of grounded instantiations of templates. Note, m is not the number of templates; rather, it is the number of groundings of each template, a much larger number dependent on the *BK*, language bias, and the *atoms* of the symbolic language L. Consider a template (t_1, t_2) admitting the clause pair (c_1, c_2), and let the current valuation be $\mathcal{EV}_i$ and $g : [0, 1] \times [0, 1] \rightarrow [0, 1]$ a function computing $\vee$-*clausal* (disjunction between clauses). Assuming we have a definition of f_c, then $g(f_{c_1}(\mathcal{EV}_i), f_{c_2}(\mathcal{EV}_i))$ denotes one step of *forwards-chaining*. Computing the weighted average over all clausal combinations admitted by (t_1, t_2), using the *softmax* of the weights, and finally performing $\vee$-*step* (disjunction between inference steps) between their sums, in addition to $\mathcal{EV}_i$, results in $\mathcal{EV}_{i+1}$. This process is repeated n times (the number of forward-chaining steps), where $\mathcal{EV}_0$ is derived from the BK.

The above construction still depends on a precise definition of f_c. Let

$$c_g = p(x, y)\text{:-}Q_1(y_1, y_2), Q_2(y_3, y_4)$$

where $y_1, y_2, y_3, y_4 \in \{x, y, z\}$. We want to collect all ground predicates p_g for which a substitution θ into $Q_1, Q_2, y_1, y_2, y_3, y_4$ exists s.t. $p_g \in \{Q_1(y_1, y_2)\theta, Q_2(y_3, y_4)\theta\}$. These ground predicates are then paired with the appropriate grounding of the lefthand side of c_g. The result of this process can be reshaped into a tensor emphasizing which pairs of ground predicates derive various instantiations of $p(x_1, x_2)$. In the case of body-only variables, there is one pair per atom in the language. Pairing this tensor with some valuation $\mathcal{EV}_i$ allows one to compute $\wedge$-*literal* (conjunction between literals of a clause) between predicate pairs. As a final step, we compute $\vee$-*exists* (disjunction between variants of literals with body-only variables) between the variants and thus complete computation of the tensor required for a step of *forward-chaining*.

Four operations parameterize the above process for conjunction and disjunction. We leave discussion to Sect. 4.

2.3 Related Approaches

To the best of our knowledge, three recent investigations are related to δILP and build on the architecture. The *Logical Neural Network* (LNN) [24] uses a similar templating, but only to learn non-recursive *chain rules*, i.e. of the form $p_0(X, Y)\text{:-}p_1(X, Z_1), \cdots, p_n(Z_n, Y)$; this is simulatable using δILP templates, especially for the short rules presented by the authors. They introduced particular parameterized, differentiable, logical operators that are optimizable for ILP.

Another system motivated by δILP is αilp [25]. The authors focused on learning logic programs that recognize visual scenes rather than general ILP tasks. The authors restricted the BK to predicates explaining aspects of the visual scenes used for evaluation. To build clauses, the authors start from a set of initial clauses and use a *top-k beam search* to iteratively extend the body of the clauses based on evaluation with respect to E^+. In this setting, predicate invention and recursive definitions are not considered. Additionally, learning a relation between two variables is not considered.

Feed-Forward Neural-Symbolic Learner [8] does not directly build on the δILP architecture but provides an alternative approach to one of the problems the δILP investigation addressed, namely developing a neural-symbolic architecture that can provide symbolic rules when presented with noisy input. In this work [8], rather than softening implication and working with fuzzy versions of logical operators, compose the Inductive *answer set programming* learners

ILASP [14] and *FASTLAS* [13] with various pre-trained neural architectures for classification tasks. This data is then transformed into a weighted knowledge for the symbolic learner. While this work is to some extent relevant to the investigation outlined in this paper, we focus on improving the differentiable implication mechanism developed by the authors of δILP rather than completely replacing it. Furthermore, the authors focus on tasks with simpler logical structures, similar to the approach taken by αilp.

Earlier investigations, such as NeuralILP [29], experimented with various *T-norms*, and part of the investigation reported in [12] studied their influence on learning. The authors leave scaling their approach to larger, possibly recursive programs as future work, a limitation addressed herein.

In [26], the authors built upon δILP but further restricted templating to add a simple term language (at most term depth 1). Thus, even under the severe restriction of at most one body literal per clause, they can learn predicates for list *append* and *delete*. Nonetheless, scalability remains an issue. *Neural Logical Machines* [11], in a limited sense, addressed the scalability issue. The authors modeled propositional formulas using multi-layer perceptrons wired together to form a circuit. This circuit is then trained on many (10000 s) instances of a particular ILP task. While the trained model was accurate, interpretability is an issue, as it is unclear how to extract a symbolic expression. Our approach provides logic programs as output, similar to δILP.

Some related systems loosely related to our work are *Logical Tensor Networks* [10], *Lifted Relational Neural Networks* [27], *Neural theorem prover* [16], and *DeepProbLog* [15]. While some, such as Neural theorem prover, can learn rules, it also suffers from scaling issues. Overall, these systems were not designed to address learning in an ILP setting. Concerning the explainability aspects of systems similar to δILP, one notable mention is *Logic Explained Networks* [4], which adapts the input format of a neural learner to derive explanations from the output. However, the problem they tackle is only loosely connected to our work.

3 Contributions

The number of weights used by δILP is approximately *quintic* in the number of templates used, thus incurring a significant memory footprint (See Sect. 2.2). This issue is further exacerbated as computing evaluations requires grounding the hypothesis space. As a result, experiments performed in [12] use task-specific templates precisely defining the structure of the solution; this is evident in their experiments as certain tasks, i.e., the *even* predicate (See Fig. 1), list multiple results, with different templating. These restrictions result in only a few of the many possible solutions being present in the search space. Furthermore, this *language bias* greatly influences the success rate of δILP on tasks such as *length*; the authors report low loss in **92.5%** of all runs, which significantly differs from our reduced *language bias* experiments, i.e. **0%** correct solutions and **0%** achieving low loss.

```
e(A,B):-i7(B,B),i7(B,B)
e(A,B):-i7(B,A),i7(A,B)
i7(A,B):-z(C,B),z(C,B)
i7(A,B):-i13(A,C),s(C,B)
i13(A,B):-s(C,B),i7(C,C)
i13(A,B):-z(A,B),z(C,A)
```

```
e(A,B):-i2(C,B),i2(C,B)
e(A,B):-i18(B,C),i2(C,A)
i2(A,B):-i2(C,C),i18(B,C)
i2(A,B):-z(A,B),z(A,B)
i18(A,B):-z(C,A),z(A,A)
i18(A,B):-s(B,C),s(C,A)
```

Fig. 1. *even* (*e* above) solutions trimmed to used templates. Note, *s* denotes successor, and *z* denotes zero

To achieve low loss, in addition to the chosen *language bias*, δILP's authors assign weights *per template* resulting in a large vector v of learnable parameters, see Sect. 4. This seems to imply high dimensionality; however, intuitively, *softmax* is applied to v during differentiable inferencing and thus transforms v into a distribution, effectively reducing its dimensionality.

Our investigation aims to: **(i)** increase the dimensionality of the search space while maintaining the efficacy of the differentiable inferencing, and **(ii)** minimize the *bias* required for effective learning. We proceed by adding many ({x,y,z},p)-templates (each with a unique symbol p) as discussed in Subsect. 2.2; this largely reduces the biases towards solutions of a particular shape. Nonetheless, given the significant number of weights required, large-scale PI remains highly intractable. Thus, we amend how weights are assigned to templates (See Sect. 4).

Assigning weights *per template* is the main source of the significant memory footprint. The authors discuss this design choice in Appendix F of [12]. In this Appendix, the authors describe assignment *per clause*, i.e., the weight denotes the likelihood of a given instantiation of a metarule instance occurring within an instantiation of a template. This approach was abandoned as it was "incapable of escaping local minima on harder tasks". Assigning weights *per clause* results in roughly a quadratic reduction in the number of weights.

Our system (δILP$_2$) assigns weights *per literal*, i.e., the weight denotes the likelihood of a given literal occurring within an instantiation of a template. Assignment *per literal* results in another roughly quadratic reduction in the number of assigned weights.

We observed that the most challenging tasks require learning a binary relation whose solution requires using a third (non-argument) variable, an additional body-only variable. This observation differs from the observations presented in [12] where complexity was measured purely in terms of the number of *learned predicate definitions* required. For example, consider *0=X mod 5*-hard and *Y=X+4*; our approach solves the former 61% of the time and the latter 4% of the time. Note, *0=X mod 5*-hard requires four learned predicate definitions while *Y=X+4* requires two, yet unlike *0=X mod 5*-hard, both predicates relate two variables through a third non-argument variable.

We test δILP_2 and support our observation through experimentally testing the following hypotheses (see Sect. 5):

- Hypothesis 1: Differentiable ILP benefits from increasing the number of templates used during training.
- Hypothesis 2: The benefit suggested by *hypothesis 1* is not solely due to the relationship between increasing the number of templates and training a multitude of times with a task-specific number of templates.
- Hypothesis 3: Learning binary predicates using body-only variables remains a challenge regardless of the weight assignment approach.

4 Methodology

We now outline the methodological differences between our implementations of differentiable inferencing and δILP; We **(i)** assign weights *per literal*, **(ii)** use slightly different logical operators, **(iii)** use more precise measures of training outcomes, and **(iv)** use a slightly different method of batching examples.

Weight Assignment. To exploit the benefits of large-scale PI, we need to reduce the large memory footprint incurred by δILP's weight assignment, *per template* assignment. We distinguish three types of weight assignment:

- *per template*: weight encodes the likelihood that a pair of clauses is the correct choice for the given template.
- *per clause*: weight encodes the likelihood that a clause occurs in the correct choice of clauses for the given template.
- *per literal*: weight encodes the likelihood a literal occurs in one of the correct clauses for the given template.

Per literal assignment is the coarsest of the three but also has the least memory footprint, thus allowing for large-scale PI. Our system, δILP_2, implements *per Literal* assignment.

T-Norm for Fuzzy Logic. Differentiable inferencing (Sect. 2) requires four differentiable logic operators. The choice of these operators greatly impacts overall performance. The Author's of δILP experimented with various *t-norms*, continuous versions of *classical* conjunction [2], from which continuous versions of other logical operators are derived. The standard t-norms are *max* ($x \wedge y \equiv \max\{x, y\}$), *product* ($x \wedge y \equiv x \cdot y$) and łukasiewicz ($x \wedge y \equiv \max\{x+y-1, 0\}$). For simplicity, we refer to all operators derived from a t-norm by **the conjunctive operator**, i.e., $x \vee y \equiv \min\{x, y\}$ is referred to as *max* when discussing the chosen t-norm.

	δILP	δILP_2
$\wedge$-Literal	product	product
$\vee$-Exists	max	max
$\vee$-Clausal	max	max
$\vee$-Step	product	max

When computing many inference steps, *product* produces vanishingly small gradients. Large programs require more inferencing, see Fig. 3, thus, we use *max* for $\vee$-step.

Batch Probability. We require computing values for all predicates over all combinations of atoms, thus motivating an alternative approach to typical *mini-batching*. Instead of parameterization by *batch size*, we use a *batch probability* – the likelihood of an example contributing to gradient computation. When computing the loss, the example sets E^+ and E^- equally contribute. Regardless of the chosen examples, the loss is balanced (divided by the number of examples contributing). If batching results in no examples from E^+ (E^-), we set that half of the loss to 0 (with 0 gradient). Performance degrades when the *batch probability* is near 0.0 or 1.0. In our experiments, we used 0.5.

4.1 Considered Outcomes

The experiments outlined in Sect. 5 (See Table 1A & 1B) allow for five possible outcomes: *Correct on Test* (**C**), *Fuzzily Correct on Test* (***F***), *Correct on Training* (***CT***), *Fuzzily Correct on Training* (***FT***), and **FAIL**. We differentiate between test and training to cover the possibility of **overfitting** and differentiate between correct and fuzzy to cover the possibility of learning programs only correct using fuzzy logic.

Overfitting. δILP avoids overfitting as the search space is restricted enough to exclude overfitting programs. However, this is no longer the case when 100 s of templates are used. For example, when learning *even*, it is possible, when training with enough invented predicates, to remember all even numbers provided in E^+. Thus, we add a validation step to test our solutions on unseen data (i.e., numbers up to 20 after training on numbers up to 10). Given the types of tasks we evaluated and the structure of the resulting model, a relatively large number of unseen examples is enough to validate. Learning over-fitting solutions for large, unseen input is highly unlikely as the programs would be very large. During experimentation, we observed that δILP$_2$ rarely overfits, even when it clearly could. A plausible explanation is that shorter, precise solutions have a higher frequency in the search space.

Fuzzy Solutions. Another class of solutions observed in both our and earlier experimental designs is *fuzzy solutions*; that is, programs that made correct predictions using fuzzy logic but incorrect predictions when evaluated using classical logic (selected predicates with the highest weight). Typically, fuzzy solutions are worse at generalizing – they are correct when tested using the training parameters (for example, inference steps) and break on unseen input. Entirely correct solutions for *even* are translatable into a program correct for all numbers, while a fuzzy solution fails to generalize beyond training.

5 Experiments

We compare δILP$_2$ (*per Literal*) to δILP (*per Template*) on tasks presented in [12][2] plus additional tasks to experimentally test *Hypothesis 2 & 3*. The tasks are separated into four domains: *numeric*, *list*, *ancestors*, and *graphs*. Results are shown in Table 1A & 1B. Tasks annotated by *easy* contain extra background knowledge, simplifying the learning process, while *hard* versions do not use the extra background knowledge. Concerning *experimental parameters*, we ran δILP$_2$ (*Per Literal* assignment) using 150 templates to produce Table 1. For δILP (*Per Template* assignment) [12], we ran it with the precise number of templates needed to solve the task. Using more templates was infeasible for many tasks due to the large memory footprint of *per template* assignment. In both cases, we used $(\{x, y, z\}, p_i)$-templates with pairwise distinct p_i.

Other parameters are as follows: $2k$ gradient descent steps, early finish when loss reaches 10^{-3}, differentiable inference is performed for 25 steps, batch probability of 0.5, weights are initialized using a normal distribution, output programs are derived by selecting the highest weighted literals for each template.

We ran the experiments producing Fig. 2 on a computational cluster with 16 nodes, each with 4 GeForce RTX 2070 (with 8 GB of RAM) GPUs. We ran the experiments producing Table 1A & 1B on a GPU server with 8 NVIDIA A40 GPUs (46 GB each). We implemented both δILP and δILP$_2$ using PyTorch [20] (version 2.0). Our implementation can be found at the following repository: github.com/Ermine516/DILP2.

[2] Section 5 and Appendix G of [12].

Table 1. **(A)** *Per Literal* results: difference computed with respect to Table 1 (B). Significance computed using t-test and $p < e^{-4}$. We use † to denote differences that are not significant. Tasks are denoted *name/arity*, i.e. task *even* has arity 1 and *length* has arity 2. **(B)** *Per Template* result. Due to significant memory requirements, neither *(0=X mod 5)* task fits in GPU memory (46 GB). Problems annotated with * are easy for *Per template* as the hypothesis space fits in one weight matrix.

Task	C	F	CT	FT	diff C	diff CT
predecessor/2	100	100	100	100	**+2%**†	**+2%**†
even/1	92	99	92	99	**+32%**	**+32%**
$(X \leq Y)$/2*	30	31	35	38	-70%	-65%
(0=X mod 3)/1	91	97	91	97	**+91%**	**+91%**
(0=X mod 5)/1-easy	77	80	97	100	**+77%**	**+97%**
(0=X mod 5)/1-hard	61	65	61	65	**+61%**	**+65%**
(Y=X+2)/2	99	100	99	100	-1% †	-1% †
(Y=X+4)/2	4	12	5	13	**+4%**†	**+5%**†
member/2*	17	19	37	43	-67%	-67%
length/2	25	26	31	38	**+25%**	**+31%**
grandparent/2	38	38	92	94	**+38%**	**+89%**
undirected_edge/2	94	94	100	100	**+75%**	**+81%**
adjacent_to_red/1	94	99	94	99	**+48%**	**+48%**
two_children/1	74	100	74	100	**+13%**	**+13%**
graph_colouring/1	83	85	96	100	-15%	-2% †
connectedness/2*	40	41	98	99	**+16%**	**+74%**
cyclic/1	19	19	90	100	**+18%**	**+89%**

(A)

Task	C	F	CT	FT
predecessor/2	98	100	98	100
even/1	70	94	70	94
$(X \leq Y)$/2*	100	100	100	100
(0=X mod 3)/1	0	0	0	0
(0=X mod 5)/1-easy	-	-	-	-
(0=X mod 5)/2-hard	-	-	-	-
(Y=X+2)/2	100	100	100	100
(Y=X+4)/2	0	0	0	0
member/2*	84	100	84	100
length/2	0	0	0	0
grandparent/2	0	0	3	3
undirected_edge/2	19	100	19	100
adjacent_to_red/1	46	90	46	90
two_children/1	61	100	61	100
graph_colouring/1	98	100	98	100
connectedness/2*	24	100	24	100
cyclic/1	0	0	1	1

(B)

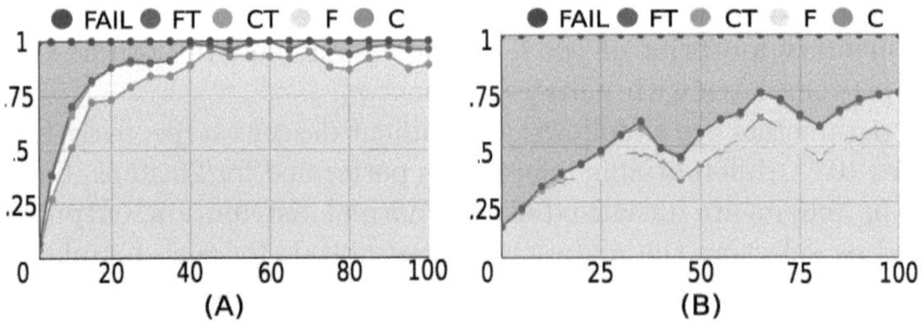

Fig. 2. Learning $0 = Xmod\ 3$ **(A)** and $X \leq Y$ **(B)** varying the number of templates (X-axis). The Y-axis is the proportion of solutions in each category. All considered tasks show this pattern

5.1 Hypothesis 1

Figure 2 illustrates the proportion of runs within each of our five categories (**C**, **CT**, **F**, **FT**, **FAIL**). As the number of templates increases, the proportion of the runs categorized as correct and generalizing increases. This pattern emerges even for tasks that remain hard to learn. Figure 2 clearly provides strong evidence supporting **Hypothesis 1**.

When comparing with δILP, out of the 17 tasks we tested δILP and δILP$_2$ on, δILP$_2$ showed improved performance on 13 tasks, and the improved performance was statistically significant for 12 of these tasks. Of the four remaining tasks, δILP showed a statistically significant performance difference on two, namely $X \leq Y$ and *member*. Both benefit from *per template* assignment as the entire search space fits into one weight matrix. Thus, δILP is essentially performing brute force search. While one would expect the same issue to occur for *connectedness*, there are fewer solutions to *member* and $X \leq Y$ in the search space than in the case of *connectedness*; it is a more general concept. Thus, even when δILP has an advantage, δILP$_2$ outperforms it when training on more complex learning tasks.

Notably, δILP$_2$ outperforms δILP on many challenging tasks. For example, *0=X mod 5* cannot be solved by δILP in our experimental setting. In [12], low loss was attained only 14% of the time when +2 and +3 are in the *BK* [12]. In contrast, we achieved a 61% success rate on this task even when the *BK* contained only *successor* and *zero*; for the dependency graphs of a solution learned, see Fig. 3.

5.2 Hypothesis 2

To illustrate that large-scale predicate invention is not equivalent to re-initialization of weights, we ran δILP$_2$ on the *0=X mod 6* while varying the numbers of templates used during training (results shown in Fig. 3**B**), i.e. improved performance is not the result of randomly initializing a small number of templates many times. Note, *0=X mod 6* is slightly more challenging than *0=X mod 5* and thus aids in illustrating the effect of larger-scale PI. According to Fig. 3**B**, when training with three templates (minimum required), we would need to run δILP$_2$ 5000 times to achieve a similar probability of success (**F** solution) as a single 50 predicate run.

When using five invented predicates, which is minimum required to avoid constructing binary predicates (see Hypothesis 3), we would need to run δILP$_2$ 750 times to achieve a similar probability of success (finding a fuzzily correct solution) as a single 50 predicate run. These results do not necessarily imply that using more predicates is always beneficial over doing multiple runs; however, they show that repeated training with intermediary weight re-initialization is not a sufficient explanation of the observed benefits of large-scale PI.

5.3 Hypothesis 3

In Table 1**A** & 1**B**, one can observe that some tasks that require learning a relatively simple program (i.e., *length*) are more challenging than tasks such as *0=X mod 6* that require learning a much larger program.

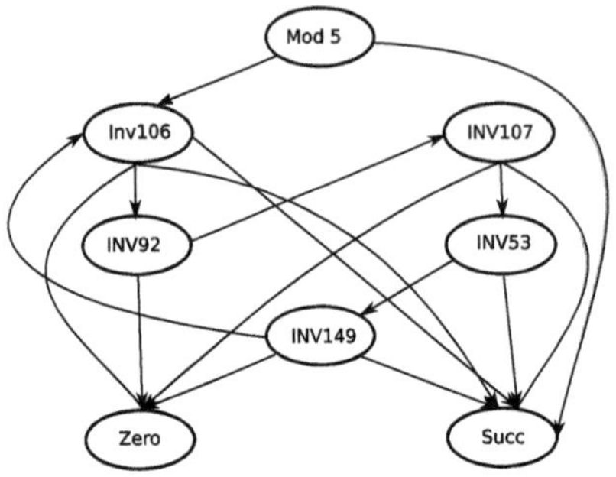

task	C	F	CT	FT
3 templates	0%	0.02%	0%	0.02%
5 templates	0.11%	0.13%	0.11%	0.14%
50 templates	60%	65%	60%	65%

Fig. 3. (A) Template dependency graph of a correct program learned by δILP_2 for the $(0 = \text{X mod } 5)$-hard task. **(B)** δILP_2 learning *0 = X mod 6*. Ran 10k times for 3 and 5 templates and 100 for 50

As stated above, we hypothesize this is due to propagating the gradient through an existential quantification. This results in difficulties when learning predicates that relate two input variables through a body-only variable. The difficulty increases with the number of such predicates required to solve the task.

We introduced a task explicitly designed to test this hypothesis: $(Y = X+4)$. This task requires only one more predicate than $Y = X + 2$, yet the success rate drops significantly with respect to $Y = X + 2$ (from 99% to 4%). For *0=X mod 2 (even)* and *0=X mod 5*, the change is gradual (from 92% to 61%). Thus, the number of relational predicate definitions that a given task requires learning is a more precise measure of complexity than the number of learned predicate definitions.

6 Conclusion and Future Work

The main contribution of this work (***Hypothesis*** 1) is strong evidence that additional templating (beyond what is necessary) improves performance. Verification of this hypothesis used δILP_2, our modified version of δILP. We performed our experiments using reduced language bias compared to the experiments presented in [12]. Furthermore, we used the same generic template for all predicate definitions learned by the system. This choice makes some tasks significantly more difficult. Additionally, we verified that the performance gains were not simply due to properties shared with weight re-initialization when using a task-specific number of templates during learning (***Hypothesis*** 2).

During experimentation, we noticed that the difficulty of the task did not correlate well with the number of learned predicate definitions needed to solve it but rather with the arity and the necessity of a body-only variable. Therefore, we tested this conjecture using the tasks $Y = X + 2$ and $Y = X + 4$. While both systems solve $Y = X + 2$, performance drastically drops for $Y = X + 4$, which only requires learning two invented predicates. Note, *0=X mod 5* requires learning four invented predicates and is easily solved by δILP$_2$. This observation highlights the challenging tasks for such synthesis approaches (*Hypothesis* 3) and suggests a direction for future investigation.

As a continuation of our investigation, we plan to integrate ILP with Deep Neural Networks as a hybrid system that is trainable end-to-end through back-propagation. The Authors of δILP presented the first steps in [12]. One can imagine the development of a network inferring a discrete set of objects in an image [3], or integration with Transformer-based [28] language models that produce atoms δILP$_2$ can process. This research direction can lead to a network that responds to natural language queries based on a datalog database. Also, as part of planned investigations, we consider an ablation study to show that the improved performance is indeed due to large-scale predicate invention and a scalability analysis to test the limits of the approach.

Acknowledgments. Supported by the ERC starting grant no. 714034 SMART, Czech Science Foundation Grant No. 22-06414L, Math$_{LP}$ project (LIT-2019-7-YOU-213) of the Linz Institute of Technology and the state of Upper Austria, Cost action CA20111 EuroProofNet, and the Doctoral Stipend of the University of Innsbruck. We would also like to Thank David Coufal (CAS ICS) for setting up and providing access to the institute's GPU Server.

Disclosure of Interests. The authors have no competing interests.

References

1. Supplementary material from "hypothesizing an algorithm from one example: the role of specificity"
2. Monoidal t-norm based logic: towards a logic for left-continuous t-norms. Fuzzy Sets and Systems **124**(3), 271–288 (2001), fuzzy Logic
3. Carion, N., Massa, F., Synnaeve, G., Usunier, N., Kirillov, A., Zagoruyko, S.: End-to-end object detection with transformers. CoRR **abs/2005.12872** (2020)
4. Ciravegna, G., et al.: Logic explained networks. Artif. Intell. **314**, 103822 (2023)
5. Cropper, A., Dumancic, S.: Inductive logic programming at 30: a new introduction. J. Artif. Intell. Res. **74**, 765–850 (2022)
6. Cropper, A., Morel, R.: Learning programs by learning from failures. Mach. Learn. **110**(4), 801–856 (2021). https://doi.org/10.1007/s10994-020-05934-z
7. Cropper, A., Muggleton, S.: Metagol system (2016). https://github.com/metagol/metagol
8. Cunnington, D., Law, M., Lobo, J., Russo, A.: FFNSL: feed-forward neural-symbolic learner. Mach. Learn. **112**(2), 515–569 (2023)
9. Dai, W.Z., Muggleton, S., Wen, J., Tamaddoni-Nezhad, A., Zhou, Z.H.: Logical vision: one-shot meta-interpretive learning from real images. In: Lachiche, N., Vrain, C. (eds.) Inductive Logic Programming. ILP 2017. LNCS, vol. 10759, pp. 46–62. Springer, Cham (2018). https://doi.org/10.1007/978-3-319-78090-0_4
10. Donadello, I., Serafini, L., d'Avila Garcez, A.S.: Logic tensor networks for semantic image interpretation. In: Sierra, C. (ed.) Proceedings of the Twenty-Sixth International Joint Conference on Artificial Intelligence, IJCAI 2017, pp. 1596–1602. ijcai.org (2017)

11. Dong, H., Mao, J., Lin, T., Wang, C., Li, L., Zhou, D.: Neural logic machines. In: 7th International Conference on Learning Representations, ICLR 2019. OpenReview.net (2019)
12. Evans, R., Grefenstette, E.: Learning explanatory rules from noisy data. J. Artif. Intell. Res. **61**, 1–64 (2018)
13. Law, M., Russo, A., Bertino, E., Broda, K., Lobo, J.: Fastlas: scalable inductive logic programming incorporating domain-specific optimisation criteria. In: The Thirty-Fourth AAAI, pp. 2877–2885. AAAI Press (2020)
14. Law, M., Russo, A., Broda, K.: Inductive learning of answer set programs. In: Fermé, E., Leite, J. (eds.) Logics in Artificial Intelligence. JELIA 2014. LNCS, vol. 8761, pp. 311–325. Springer, Cham (2014). https://doi.org/10.1007/978-3-319-11558-0_22
15. Manhaeve, R., Dumancic, S., Kimmig, A., Demeester, T., Raedt, L.D.: Neural probabilistic logic programming in deepproblog. Artif. Intell. **298**, 103504 (2021)
16. Minervini, P., Bosnjak, M., Rocktäschel, T., Riedel, S., Grefenstette, E.: Differentiable reasoning on large knowledge bases and natural language. In: The Thirty-Fourth AAAI, pp. 5182–5190. AAAI Press (2020)
17. Muggleton, S.: Inverse entailment and progol. N. Gener. Comput. **13**(3&4), 245–286 (1995)
18. Muggleton, S.H., Lin, D., Tamaddoni-Nezhad, A.: Meta-interpretive learning of higher-order dyadic datalog: predicate invention revisited. Mach. Learn. **100**(1), 49–73 (2015). https://doi.org/10.1007/s10994-014-5471-y
19. Muggleton, S.H., et al.: ILP turns 20 - biography and future challenges. Mach. Learn. **86**(1), 3–23 (2012)
20. Paszke, A., et al.: Pytorch: an imperative style, high-performance deep learning library. In: Wallach, H., Larochelle, H., Beygelzimer, A., d' Alché-Buc, F., Fox, E., Garnett, R. (eds.) Advances in Neural Information Processing Systems 32, pp. 8024–8035. Curran Associates, Inc. (2019)
21. Purgal, S.J., Cerna, D.M., Kaliszyk, C.: Learning higher-order logic programs from failures. In: Raedt, L.D. (ed.) Proceedings of the Thirty-First International Joint Conference on Artificial Intelligence, IJCAI 2022, pp. 2726–2733. ijcai.org (2022)
22. Quinlan, J.R.: Learning logical definitions from relations. Mach. Learn. **5**, 239–266 (1990)
23. Raedt, L.D.: Logical and Relational Learning. Cognitive Technologies. Springer, Berlin, Heidelberg (2008). https://doi.org/10.1007/978-3-540-68856-3
24. Sen, P., de Carvalho, B.W.S.R., Riegel, R., Gray, A.G.: Neuro-symbolic inductive logic programming with logical neural networks. In: Thirty-Sixth AAAI, pp. 8212–8219. AAAI Press (2022)
25. Shindo, H., Pfanschilling, V., Dhami, D.: αilp: thinking visual scenes as differentiable logic programs. Mach. Learn. (2023)
26. Shindo, H., Nishino, M., Yamamoto, A.: Differentiable inductive logic programming for structured examples. In: Thirty-Fifth AAAI, pp. 5034–5041. AAAI Press (2021)
27. Sourek, G., Svatos, M., Zelezný, F., Schockaert, S., Kuzelka, O.: Stacked structure learning for lifted relational neural networks. In: Lachiche, N., Vrain, C. (eds.) Inductive Logic Programming. ILP 2017. LNCS, vol. 10759, pp. 140–151. Springer, Cham (2018). https://doi.org/10.1007/978-3-319-78090-0_10
28. Vaswani, A., et al.: Attention is all you need. CoRR **abs/1706.03762** (2017)
29. Yang, F., Yang, Z., Cohen, W.W.: Differentiable learning of logical rules for knowledge base reasoning. In: Guyon, I., et al. (eds.) Advances in Neural Information Processing Systems 30: Annual Conference on Neural Information Processing Systems 2017, pp. 2319–2328 (2017)

Pre-Training Meta-Rule Selection Policy for Visual Generative Abductive Learning

Yu Jin[1], Jingming Liu[1], Zhexu Luo[1], Yifei Peng[1], Ziang Qin[1], Wang-Zhou Dai[2], Yao-Xiang Ding[1](✉), and Kun Zhou[1]

[1] State Key Lab of CAD&CG, Zhejiang University, Hangzhou, China
dingyx.gm@gmail.com, kunzhou@acm.org

[2] National Key Lab of Novel Software Technology, Nanjing University, Nanjing, China
daiwz@lamda.nju.edu.cn

Abstract. Visual generative abductive learning studies jointly training symbol-grounded neural visual generator and inducing logic rules from data, such that after learning, the visual generation process is guided by the induced logic rules. A major challenge for this task is to reduce the time cost of logic abduction during learning, an essential step when the logic symbol set is large and the logic rule to induce is complicated. To address this challenge, we propose a pre-training method for obtaining meta-rule selection policy for the recently proposed visual generative learning approach AbdGen [20], aiming at significantly reducing the candidate meta-rule set and pruning the search space. The selection model is built based on the embedding representation of both symbol grounding of cases and meta-rules, which can be effectively integrated with both neural model and logic reasoning system. The pre-training process is done on pure symbol data, not involving symbol grounding learning of raw visual inputs, making the entire learning process low-cost. An additional interesting observation is that the selection policy can rectify symbol grounding errors unseen during pre-training, which is resulted from the memorization ability of attention mechanism and the relative stability of symbolic patterns. Experimental results show that our method is able to effectively address the meta-rule selection problem for visual abduction, boosting the efficiency of visual generative abductive learning. Code is available at https://github.com/jinyuaaa/Metarule_Select.

Keywords: Neurosymbolic visual generation · Abductive learning · Inductive logic programming

1 Introduction

Building neuro-symbolic visual generation model with logic symbol groundings, where the visual generative process is guided by logic rules, has been an emerging research topic recently [17,20]. The symbol-grounded neural visual generator is appearing not only because the generation results are interpretable and stable,

W.-Z. Dai (Ed.): ILP 2024, LNAI 16059, pp. 163–180, 2026.
https://doi.org/10.1007/978-3-032-09087-4_11

but also because they lead to strong rule-based generalization ability and capability of inducing logical generative rules from data. Among the initial researches, AbdGen [20] promotes the idea of abductive learning [7,31] into visual generative learning, enjoying the advantage of doing neural visual generator learning, symbol grounding, and logic rule induction simultaneously from dataset with limited labeling information for symbol grounding.

For further enabling AbdGen to handle large sets of logical symbols and complicated logic generation rules, which is common in visual generation tasks with complicated spacial and temporal dependencies, a major obstacle is the time cost of logical abduction during training. The logic abduction process of AbdGen is done by Prolog-based logic programming system, which is non-differentiable. Even though it is advantageous for its stability and interpretability, the efficiency is an issue especially compared with the neural module, which is differentiable and computationally efficient. The logical abduction process of AbdGen follows the framework proposed in MetaAbd [6], which involves both symbol grounding and rule induction. The learning process integrates symbol grounding abduction, and meta-interpretative learning [18], such that the induction of the rule is transformed into the search over the possible rule space induced by the meta-rule set. The size of the meta-rule set significantly affects the time cost of rule induction. The smaller the size, the more efficient the abduction process. On the other hand, for supporting inducing general logic rules without too much tweaking and hand-tuning, a general and larger-sized meta-rule set is preferrable. This trade-off is the main technical challenge to deal with for our work.

In this paper, we propose a pre-training strategy for learning the meta-rule selection policy aiming at boosting the efficiency of logical abduction during AbdGen training. The pre-trained selection policy is the key to deal with the trade-off between generality and efficiency for meta-rule set. For AbdGen training, a general meta-rule set with complete meta-rules can be kept. Given a training instance which includes positive and negative cases of images without symbol grounding labels, the meta-rule selection policy chooses a small set of meta-rules for inputting into the logical reasoning module, hence boosting the abduction efficiency. Utilizing the embedding representation of symbol groundings in AbdGen model, our selection model further builds embedding representations of meta-rules, and utilizes the attention module for meta-rule selection, which can be effectively integrated with both neural model and logic reasoning system. Furthermore, benefited from the disentanglement of symbol and sub-symbol representations of AbdGen, the meta-rule selection policy can be pre-trained under pure symbolic data, which does not involve symbol grounding learning process, thus is of low time cost. Finally, a potentially technical issue for the pre-trained selection policy is that unseen symbol grounding errors can appear during the AbdGen training stage, especially at the beginning of training. While it is interesting to observe that the pre-trained selection policy has relatively strong toleration ability for the errors. This verifies the memorization ability of attention mechanism as well as the relative stability of symbolic patterns. Experimental results show that our method can be utilized to significantly reduce the time cost of abduction, even when the abductive learning task is unseen during the pre-training stage.

2 Related Work

2.1 Neuro-Symbolic Visual Generative Learning

Visual generative learning has received great attention in recent years, in particular multi-modal generation such as text-to-vision generation [22,24,25]. Despite the great success, the generation results suffer from hallucination, still lacking strong controllability, interpretability, and stability. One promising solution is to augment the generation process with symbolic modules to utilize their reasoning power instead of solely relying on black-box neural models.

One possible solution is fully end-to-end differentiable neuro-symbolic models, which is still not quite common for generative models, but is common for addressing inference tasks such as visual question answering [11,30]. Such models are relatively efficient due to the fully differentiable properly. On the other hand, the neural part usually needs specific designs to achieve particular functionality. In comparison, traditional logic reasoning models usually enjoys the benefit of generality, while the efficiency is usually a major issue to utilize them in complicated tasks. While in our view, this issue can be addressed by guiding the search-based reasoning process based on the data-driven neural model. The method proposed in this work pursuits this idea.

Building neuro-symbolic visual generative model is still an emerging research topic, in special logic-based models. One pioneer work is VAEL [17], which integrates the DeepProblog [15] framework with autoencoder visual generators, achieving impressive ability for visual objects generation based on logic rules, as well as strong generalization when the training and testing logic rules differ. On the other hand, AbdGen [20] is based on the visual generative abductive learning framework, which enables both symbol grounding and rule induction, two central tasks in neuro-symbolic visual generation. Our work is built on AbdGen due to its strong disentanglement ability of symbolic and sub-symbolic representations and its effective and general logic induction functionality.

2.2 Meta-Rule Selection

Designing proper inductive bias is known as a grand challenge for inductive logic programming (ILP) [2], which is also the situation for visual generative abductive learning, as a neuro-symbolic extension to the ILP problem. One of the major formulations of the inductive bias is the choice of the meta-rules [8,9,12,18]. Meta-rules are second-order rules which define the structure of learnable programs, whose choice significantly affects the learning performance. As discussed in Sect. 1, there is a trade-off for universality and efficiency in deciding the size of the meta-rule set. Even though a number of pioneer researches have been conducted on identifying the suitable meta-rule set [3,5,27], this problem is still under-explored and remain unaddressed. Our work builds upon the idea of learning meta-rule selection model from data, which is also studied in previous researches [10,16,21] under pure symbolic learning tasks. While our method faces neuro-symbolic learning scenario, and builds upon the benefits of both neural models and symbol modules, with no previous researches existing on this direction.

3 Problem Setup

3.1 Visual Generative Abductive Learning

Symbol-grounded Conditional Generation. We first formalize the neuro-symbolic visual generation task for our learned model to address. An example is illustrated in Fig. 1. The generation process takes one or more input images x as conditions. The input images have their logical symbol groundings z_{ground} and sub-symbolic style z_{sub}. The generation is controlled by a set of background logic rules B, and the output is a new set of images $\hat{x}$ with their corresponding symbol groundings $\hat{z}_{ground}$ and $\hat{z}_{sub}$, satisfying following constraints:

$$B \cup z_{ground} \models \hat{z}_{ground}, \; \hat{z}_{sub} = z_{sub}, \tag{1}$$

where $\models$ denotes logical entailment, ensuring that the symbol groundings $\hat{z}_{ground}$ of the generated images are consistent with the logic rule R and the symbol grounding z_{ground} of the input image. Furthermore, the generated images maintain the sub-symbolic style z_{sub} of the input.

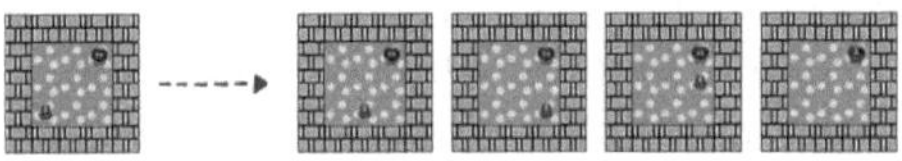

Fig. 1. Example of symbol-grounded conditional generation. Given the first picture and the symbolic rule *Mario moves with right priority followed by up priority towards the target*, a sequence of images would be generated. Here the symbol to be grounded for each image is the position of Mario, and the sub-symbolic style includes all visual features unchanged among images.

Neuro-symbolic Visual Generator. The generation model builds upon the neuro-symbolic visual generator proposed in AbdGen [20], which consists of both neural and symbolic parts. The neural part (E_{sym}, E_{sub}, V, G) consists of a symbolic encoder E_{sym}, a sub-symbolic encoder E_{sub}, a symbol grounding module V, and a decoder G. The encoders E_{sym} and E_{sub} are responsible for transforming input image x into latent symbolic representation z_{sym}, which preserves symbolic information *but remains ungrounded*, and sub-symbolic style representation z_{sub}. The symbol grounding module V, which builds upon vector-quantized structure [28], is responsible for grounding z_{sym} into grounded representations z_{ground}. All the representations are assumed to be vector embeddings. This encoding process can be expressed with

$$z_{sym} = E_{sym}(x), \; z_{ground} = V(z_{sym}), \; z_{sub} = E_{sub}(x). \tag{2}$$

Once z_{ground} and z_{sub} are identified, they are provided into the logical reasoning system, which is *non-differentiable and Prolog-based*, with the background knowledge B inside. Then $\hat{z}_{ground}$ and $\hat{z}_{sub}$ are identified based on Eq. 1. Given $\hat{z}_{ground}$ and $\hat{z}_{sub}$ as inputs, the decoder G generates the output image $\hat{x}$: $G(\hat{z}_{ground} \oplus \hat{z}_{sub}) = \hat{x}$, where $\oplus$ denotes the embedding concatenation. The above model structure reveals the essentialness of building embedding representations of symbol groundings, as well as the disentanglement between symbolic and sub-symbolic information, which are guaranteed by on the training mechanism proposed in AbdGen.

Visual Generative Abductive Learning: The learning process for AbdGen involves both training the above symbol-grounded neuro-symbolic visual generator and inducing the background knowledge B from data. Following classical ILP learning scenario, the data is assumed to include both positive and negative cases of raw images, which are generated w.r.t. the hidden background knowledge B. Furthermore, we assume that the symbol groundings of only a very small subset of images are labeled, which are denoted as Z^L_{ground}. Furthermore, only a subset of B, which is denoted as B_L, is given to the learner. The learning problem can formulated into

$$\arg\max_{\theta, Z^U_{ground}, B_U} \mathcal{L}(X, Z^L_{ground}, B_L | \theta, Z^U_{ground}, B_U), \tag{3}$$

where $\mathcal{L}$ is the data likelihood, θ is the parameters of the neuro-visual generator, Z^U_{ground} is the unlabeled symbol groundings in the dataset, and B_U is the missing logic rules in B to induce. This learning problem is solved by the contrastive meta-abduction method proposed in [20], which pursuits meta-interpretative and meta-abductive learning [6,18] to visual generative abductive learning. We omit the details of this method due to space limitations. The key is that the method iteratively generates *pseudo groundings* z^{pseudo}_{ground} for the unlabeled cases, which are gradually rectified during the learning process, and conducts logic induction to obtain B_U based on z^{pseudo}_{ground} and a set of candidate meta-rules $M \subset B_L$ in the given background knowledge. The target of our work is to pre-train a meta-rule selection policy to obtain a shrinked set of meta-rules adaptively w.r.t. different z^{pseudo}_{ground}, instead of using a fixed set of M throughout the learning process.

3.2 Meta-Rule Selection Policy

We provide the concrete formulation of the meta-rule selection policy. During the training process of AbdGen, each unlabeled training instance consists of a fixed number of positive and negative cases, whose pseudo-groundings are prediced by the model and denoted z^{pseudo}_{ground} as above. Furthermore, a *meta-rule pool* M is prepared, which consists of all candidate meta-rules for learning. The meta-rule selection policy $\pi(z^{pseudo}_{ground}) : \mathcal{Z} \mapsto 2^M$ is a mapping from the symbol grounding space $\mathcal{Z}$ to the product space of the meta-rule pool, for selecting a proper subset $\mathtt{m} \subset M$ of meta-rules for z^{pseudo}_{ground}. The rules in $\mathtt{m}$ are considered as the most relevant to the current pseudo groundings. The meta-rule selection policy is obtained from a pre-training process as introduced below.

Selection Policy Pre-training. For obtaining the selection policy π, during the pre-training stage, we assume there exist a pure symbolic dataset, which is generated from a set of background knowledge sets $\mathbf{B} = \{B'_1, B'_2, \ldots, B'_K\}$. Each of the instances in the dataset is generated by first sampling a background knowledge set B' from $\mathbf{B}$, and then sampling positive and negative cases with their symbol groundings z_{ground}. Different from the visual generative abductive learning in AbdGen, 1) the instances consist of only symbol groundings without raw image inputs; 2) the groundings are fully labeled. Such dataset is easier to be collected than raw image data, or even can be directly synthesized in applications. Furthermore, each $B' \in \mathbf{B}$ indicates a different latent generation rule. The learner is given the same meta-rule pool M, and targeting at obtaining the selection policy π from the dataset. The learned policy is expected to be applied on the AbdGen learning task where the background knowledge set B is outside of $\mathbf{B}$. In the experiments, we verify that our approach indeed achieves this ability.

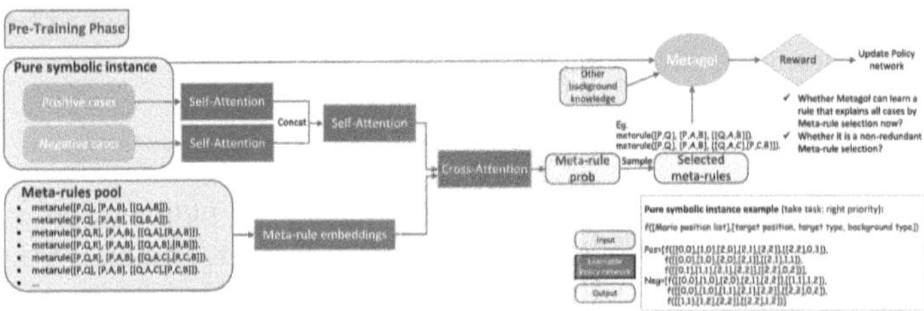

Fig. 2. The pre-training phase for learning the meta-rule selection policy.

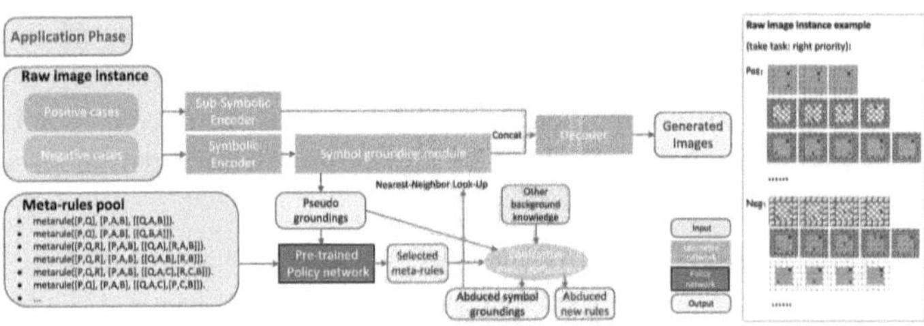

Fig. 3. The application phase for applying the policy in AbdGen training.

4 Proposed Method

In this section, we introduce the pre-training strategy for learning the meta-rule selection policy and its application in AbdGento accelerate the logical programming system by selecting meta-rules from meta-rules pool. The process is divided into two main phases: the pre-training phase and the application phase, as illustrated in Fig. 2 and Fig. 3.

The pre-training phase is illustrated in Fig. 2, which is designed to teach the model to identify and select relevant meta-rules based on the symbol values extracted from various cases. The selection policy is designed a neural model, which employs multiple attention mechanisms to process the symbol grounding representations, and utilizes a cross-attention mechanism to generate the probabilities for meta-rule selection. Bernoulli sampling is then applied to these probabilities to select the meta-rules that will be used in the logical programming system. Since only pure symbol data is involved in pre-training, we can utilize meta-interpretative learning method (Metagol [4]), which is much more time-efficient than meta-abduction method in AbdGen since no symbol grounding learning is involved. The performance of the selected meta-rules is evaluated based on whether Metagol can learn a rule that explains all cases and the number of selected meta-rules. This evaluation informs the reward calculation, which is utilized to update the policy model via neural policy optimization algorithm.

The application phase is illustrated in Fig. 3, which leverages the pre-trained model to expedite the meta-rule selection process for the training instances, which are presented as raw images, with only a small subset of their symbol groundings being labeled. The pre-trained policy takes pseudo-groundings that the neuro-symbolic visual generator predicts, and output a shrinked subset of meta-rule pool for abductive learning, hence significantly reduces the rule search space and saves the time cost of AbdGen training.

4.1 Model Design

To facilitate meta-rule selection, a series of attention mechanisms [1] are employed (Fig. 2). The input to this process is a pure symbol cases bag adhering to specific task rules, including both positive and negative cases. The output is the meta-rule selection most relevant to the case patterns, sampled by meta-rule probabilities, which is calculated by the following process.

Self-attention. Recall that each instance consists of positive and negative cases. For the set of positive cases, a self-attention mechanism is applied to their symbol embedding representations. This mechanism is designed to identify internal correlations within the positive cases, capturing important patterns and dependencies that are crucial for subsequent processing. Similarly, the negative cases undergo a self-attention process to uncover internal relationships among them. After processing both positive and negative cases individually, the resultant tensor embeddings from the self-attention mechanisms are concatenated to form a combined tensor. This combined tensor embodies the interactions between positive and negative cases. To delve deeper into these interactions, another layer of self-attention is applied to the combined tensor. This step enhances the model's understanding of the correlations between the cases, integrating information from both positive and negative cases to create a comprehensive representation.

Cross-attention. Cross-attention mechanism, which further involves the learnable embeddings of meta-rules, aims to link the combined tensor of instance with the meta-rules to generate selection probabilities for each meta-rule. The cross-attention mechanism takes the combined tensor and meta-rule embeddings as inputs and outputs a probability for each meta-rule, incorporating information from the cases within the instance. This mechanism allows the model to assess the relevance of each meta-rule to the given cases.

Sampling. Based on the selection probabilities obtained from the cross-attention mechanism, Bernoulli sampling is performed to select the most relevant meta-rules. The sampling strategy is crucial as it determines which meta-rules will be used in the logical reasoning process. By assigning higher probabilities to promising meta-rules, the model enhances the efficiency of the selection process, ensuring that only the most pertinent meta-rules are chosen.

4.2 Training Method

Policy Optimization in Pre-training Stage. We regard the selection of meta-rules as a decision-making process. Specifically, based on the positive and negative samples of the current task, we choose a subset of meta-rules for subsequent rule learning through a selection policy. Our insight is that when the negative and positive cases are sufficiently provided, if the meta-rule selection is inappropriate, it is even impossible to induce a rule by Metagol. Therefore, we set the reward R based on whether rules can be successfully learned:

$$R = \begin{cases} 0, & \text{if Metagol cannot induce a rule,} \\ 2^{n-n_s}, & \text{otherwise,} \end{cases} \tag{4}$$

where n is the total number of meta-rules in the meta-rule pool and n_s represents the number of selected meta-rules. We preserve the trajectory of the decision-making process for subsequent policy updates stage. In each iteration of policy updates, we use proximal policy optimization (PPO) [26] to optimize the policy. We treat a bag of instances sampled in each iterations as a trajectory and calculate the advantage function based on it, and further updates the policy network according to the clipped gradients.

5 Experiments

We conducted a series of experiments to verify the following questions: 1) Whether our meta-rule selection policy can enable AbdGen to utilize data more effectively and reduce training time compared to using all meta-rules and random meta-rules? 2) Whether our method can approach the performance level of handmade optimized meta-rules without human bias? 3) Whether our meta-rule selection policy can generalize to unseen tasks that have patterns similar to those in the training tasks? The neural and logical components of our method are implemented using PyTorch [19] and SWI-Prolog [29], respectively. The experiments were conducted on server clusters equipped with NVIDIA RTX A5000 and 4090 GPUs. Major experimental setups are presented in the following section and more details are provided in the appendix.

5.1 Experimental Setup

Meta Rules Pool. The meta-rules pool used in our experiments is summarized in Table 1. This pool includes 6 classic and commonly used logical meta-rules that the model can select to use in logical programming system. The meta-rules are designed to represent different logical patterns and relationships.

Table 1. Meta-rules pool

Name	Meta-rule
Identity	`metarule([P,Q],[P,A,B],[[Q,A,B]]).`
Inverse	`metarule([P,Q],[P,A,B],[[Q,B,A]]).`
Precon	`metarule([P,Q,R],[P,A,B],[[Q,A],[R,A,B]]).`
Postcon	`metarule([P,Q,R],[P,A,B],[[Q,A,B],[R,B]]).`
Chain	`metarule([P,Q,R],[P,A,B],[[Q,A,C],[R,C,B]]).`
Recursion	`metarule([P,Q],[P,A,B],[[Q,A,C],[P,C,B]]).`

Datasets and Tasks. We conducted our experiments on two datasets: the Mario dataset [17] and the MNIST dataset [14]. Each dataset consists of a variety of tasks, each designed to test the ability of our meta-rule selection policy to find the most suitable meta-rules corresponding to the data patterns of each task. It is important to note that each task in the datasets is independent and does not influence the others. The tasks are summarized in Table 2 and Table 3. The tasks underlined in Table 2 are unseen during the Pre-training phase, but there are tasks with similar patterns in the train tasks.

Comparison Methods. To evaluate the effectiveness of our meta-rule selection policy, we compared it with the following baseline methods:

- Handmade optimized meta-rule: Manually crafted optimal meta-rules tailored for each task.
- Random Meta-rule: Randomly selected two meta-rules from the meta-rule pool for AbdGen training.
- All meta-rule: Utilizing all meta-rules in the meta-rule pool for training.

Performance Metrics. We used several performance metrics to evaluate our meta-rule selection model's effectiveness and efficiency applied to AbdGen:

Table 2. Task description on Mario dataset.

Task	Rule	Meta-Rule	Description	Case Length
Right priority (up, left, down)	f(A, B) :-right(A, C), f(C, B). f(A, B) :-f$_1$(A, B). f$_1$(A, B) :-up(A, C), f$_1$(C, B). f$_1$(A, B) :-terminate(A, B).	Identity Recursion	Mario follows the path to the right and then up to reach the target.	2,3,4,5
Just up (down, left, right)	f(A, B) :-up(A, C), terminate(C, B). f(A, B) :-up(A, C), f$_1$(C, B). f$_1$(A, B) :-up(A, C), terminate(C, B).	Chain	Mario follows the path just to the up to reach the target.	2,3
Right one step (down, left, up)	f(A, B) :-right(A, C), terminate(C, B).	Chain	Mario moves one step to the right to reach the target.	2
Bomb far	f(A, B) :-far(A, B), bomb(B)	Postcon	If target is a bomb, Mario goes further.	2
Flower	f(A, B) :-right(A, C), f(C, B). f(A, B) :-f$_1$(A, B), flower(B). f$_1$(A, B) :-up(A, C), f$_1$(C, B). f$_1$(A, B) :-terminate(A, B), flower(B).	Postcon Chain	If background is flower, Mario follows the path to the right and then up to reach the target.	2,3,4,5
Chess jump	f(A, B) :-terminate(A, B), chess(B). f(A, B) :-jump(A, C), f(C, B).	Postcon Chain	If background is chess, Mario jumps Diagonally to reach the target.	2,3,4,5

Table 3. Task description on MNIST dataset.

Task	Rule	Meta-Rule	Description	Case Length
Add priority (multi)	f(A, tB):-add(A, C), f(C, B). f(A, B):-f$_1$(A, B). f$_1$(A, B):-multi(A, C), f$_1$(C, B). f$_1$(A, B):-eq(A, B).	Identity Recursion	Add first then multi on a list of uncertain length. Result is given last	3,4,5
Cumulative sum (product)	f(A, B):-add(A, C), f(C, B). f(A, B):-eq(A, B).	Identity Recursion	Cumulative sum on a list of uncertain length. Result is given last	3,4,5
Reverse cumulative sum (product)	f(A, B):-f$_1$(B, A). f$_1$(A, B):-add(A, C), f$_1$(C, B). f$_1$(A, B:-f$_2$(B, A). f$_2$(A, B):-eq(A, B).	Inverse Recursion	Cumulative sum on a list of uncertain length. Result is given first.	3,4,5
Increasing sequence	f(A, B):-less(A, C), f(C, B). f(A, B):-less(A, B), zero(B).	Postcon Recursion	If the last number is zero, the previous list is a increasing sequence.	3,4,5
Decreasing sequence	f(A, B):-f$_1$(B, A). f$_1$(A, B):-more(A, C), f$_1$(C, B). f$_1$(A, B):-more(A, B), zero(B).	Inverse Postcon Recursion	If the first number is zero, the following list is a decreasing sequence.	3,4,5

- Symbol grounding accuracy: The symbol grounding accuracy of the model as training iterations progress.
- Training time: The time to reach a certain training iterations.
- Rule learning performance: This metric includes the rate of *success*, *timeout* (proportion of the trials where the system times out, set at a threshold of 30 s), and *other error* (proportion of the trials where the system returns no suitable rule) for rule learning.
- Rule based Generation Quality: The quality of the generated outputs, measured by the adherence of generated images to the specified logical rules and the visual consistency of these images. Due to space limitation, the illustration of generation results are provided in the appendix.

5.2 Results

Pre-Training Phase Findings. Our experiments yielded two significant findings during the pre-training phase:

1) Discovery of fewer meta-rules: Our meta-rule selection model was able to find solutions that required fewer meta-rules than those initially preset. Specifically, for the Mario Just Up and MNIST Reverse Cumulative Sum tasks, we found that fewer meta-rules could explain all cases. Table 4 shows that the discovered rules used fewer meta-rules compared to the preset rules. In the Mario Just Up task, the reduction in meta-rules is attributed to the constraint of the 3×3 Mario grid map, which allows for a simpler explanation. For the MNIST Reverse Cumulative Sum task, the fewer meta-rules are due to the neural networsk's reward-driven approach, which can discover higher-reward explanations that may be outside the linear, sequential thinking typically employed by humans. Namely, the rules generated with fewer meta-rules may require a slight shift in thinking for humans to understand. This indicates that the model can optimize the meta-rule selection process, finding more efficient logical meta-rules to solve the tasks.
2) Generalization to Unseen Tasks: We observed an unexpected but promising behavior where the meta-rule selection probabilities for unseen tasks with patterns similar to the training tasks also adjusted in the correct direction as training progressed. Figure 4 shows the heatmaps of the changing probabilities for different meta-rules being selected for both exemplified training tasks and unseen tasks. These results suggest that our model can generalize well to new pattern-like tasks, effectively transferring knowledge from the training tasks to unseen tasks.

Table 4. Discovery of fewer meta-rules

Task	Preset Rule	Preset Meta-Rule	Discovered Rule	Fewer Meta-Rule
Mario Just up	f(A,B):-up(A,C),f(C,B). f(A,B):-terminate(A,B).	Identity Recursion	f(A,B) :-up(A,C),terminate(C,B). f(A,B) :-up(A,C),f_1(C,B). f_1(A,B) :-up(A,C),terminate(C,B).	Chain
MNIST Reverse cumulative Sum	f(A,B):-f_1(B,A). f_1(A,B):-add(A,B),f_1(C,B). f_1(A,B):-eq(A,B).	Identity Inverse Recursion	f(A,B):-f_1(B,A). f_1(A,B):-add(A,C),f_1(C,B). f_1(A,B):-f_2(B,A). f_2(A,B):-eq(A,B).	Inverse Recursion

Table 5. Performance comparison.

Task	Method	Timeout Rate	Other Error Rate	Success Rate
Mario Right Priority	Handmade optimized meta-rule	0.005±0.001	0.036±0.012	0.959±0.012
	Ours selected meta-rule	0.006±0.002	0.120±0.003	0.874±0.002
	Random meta-rule	0.147±0.007	0.692±0.005	0.161±0.003
	All meta-rule	1.000±0.000	0.000±0.000	0.000±0.000
MNIST Cumulative Product	Handmade optimized meta-rule	0.045±0.011	0.003±0.002	0.952±0.009
	Ours selected meta-rule	0.111±0.009	0.077±0.011	0.812±0.007
	Random meta-rule	0.067±0.002	0.760±0.014	0.173±0.013
	All meta-rule	1.000±0.000	0.000±0.000	0.000±0.000

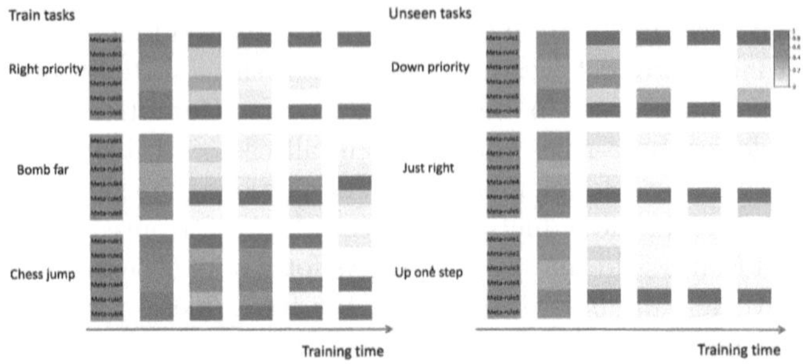

Fig. 4. The changing probabilities of different meta-rules being selected for different tasks during pre-training

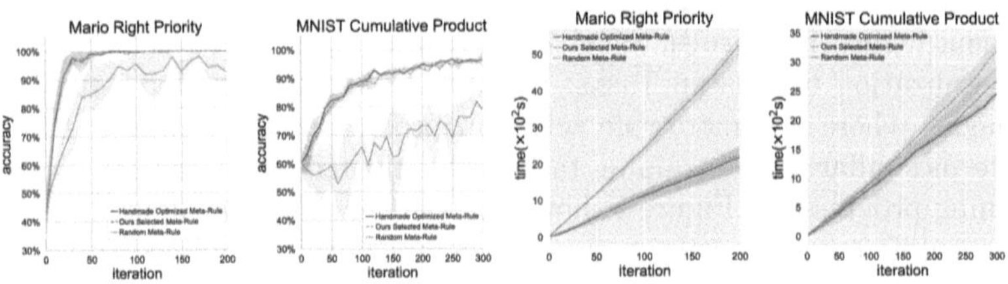

Fig. 5. Performance on train tasks. Comparisons on train tasks Mario *Right priority* and MNIST *Cumulative product* of our meta-rule selection model, hand-made optimized meta-rules and random meta-rules on grounding accuracy (↑) and training time(↑) over AbdGen iterations.

Symbol Grounding accuracy and Training Time over AbdGen iterations. The expriments of application phase are conducted on the Mario *Right priority* and MNIST *Cumulative product* tasks. We compare the performance of our meta-rule selection model with handmade optimized meta-rules and random meta-rules. The objective is to evaluate how effectively our model can select most correct meta-rules and then boost the symbol grounding and the time efficiency over AbdGen training iterations.

Figure 5 presents the results of our symbol grounding experiments. The left two subfigures illustrate the symbol grounding accuracy over iterations for the tasks Mario *Right priority* and MNIST *Cumulative product*. It is evident that our selected meta-rules achieve comparable accuracy to handmade optimized meta-rules and significantly outperform random meta-rules. The right two subfigures depict the training time over iterations for the same tasks. For Mario *Right priority* task, our selected meta-rules demonstrate a significant reduction in training time compared to the use of random meta-rules. The peorformance is close to that of handmade optimized meta-rules, demonstrating the accuracy of our pre-trained model in selecting meta-rules even when there is significant noise in the symbol values. Conversely, for MNIST *Cumulative product* task, the training time for random meta-rules is shorter. This task has fewer predicates prepared (5 predicates: `add`, `multi`, `eq`, `head`, `empty`), resulting in a smaller

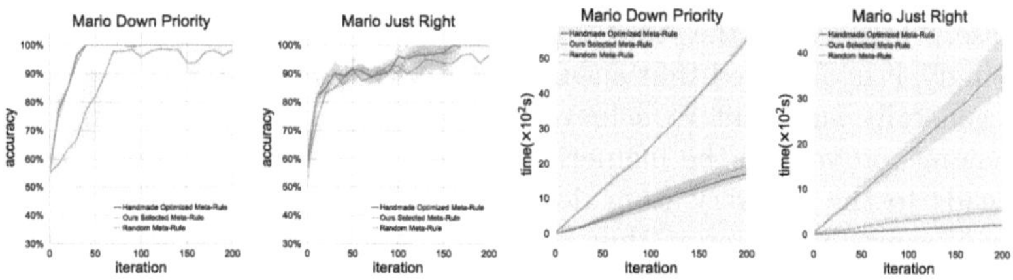

Fig. 6. Performance on unseen tasks. Comparisons on unseen tasks Mario *Down priority* and Mario *Just Right* of our meta-rule selection model, hand-made optimized meta-rules and random meta-rules on grounding accuracy (↑) and training time(↑) over AbdGen iterations.

search space. Many incorrect meta-rule combinations quickly lead to no rule being learned, which results in a rapid output but zero data utilization.

Figure 6 illustrates the performance of our pre-trained meta-rule selection model on unseen tasks with similar patterns to the training tasks, which is a discovery in the pre-training phase. These results demonstrate that our model can effectively generalize to new tasks it has not encountered during pre-training, maintaining a high level of selecting correct meta-rules. For Mario *Just Right* task by randomly selecting meta-rules, as long as selecting *Chain* as one of the meta-rules can derive the rule. Therefore, the difference in the grounding accuracy curve is not as pronounced as in the other tasks. However, the time consumption for random meta-rule selection is significantly higher for redundant or wrong meta-rules. Furthermore, the results of all meta-rules baseline are not shown in Fig. 5 and Fig. 6 because each training iteration results in a timeout.

Table 5 provides a detailed performance comparison across different methods, including the timeout rate, other error rate, and success rate of logical programming system with differently sampled meta-rule inputs. Overall, these results demonstrate that our pre-trained model can select meta-rules without human intervention, achieving a data utilization level close to that of manually chosen meta-rules. For the rates of MNIST *Cumulative product* task by random meta-rule, We can interpret that as only when meta-rule *Inverse* and meta-rule *Recursion* are selected simultaneously does the search fall into a loop, causing a timeout. When the selected meta-rules are *Identity* and *Recursion*, the data can be utilized for sure. Additionally, if the sampled 2 positive cases both have a length of only 3, selecting *Chain* as one of the meta-rules can also explain these cases, which is similar to the concept illustrated in Table 4.

Robustness to Unseen Grounding Errors. An additional interesting observation from the experiments is the robustness of the selection policy to unseen grounding errors. During pre-training phase, the symbol groundings of the data are fully labeled, thus the selection policy can be trained under ground-truth groundings. However, during application phase, especially at the early period of AbdGen training, the pseudo groundings are usually inaccurate and unseen during pre-training. A small set of labeled data is introduced in the application phase, which avoids the AbdGen model to make too large grounding errors. Interestingly, it is observed that ensuring the initial grounding error to be below 50% is generally sufficient to achieve the desirable performance. In our view, this phenomenon verifies the memorization ability of attention mechanism [23], which leads to the recovery from deviations of local minima, and the relative stability of symbolic patterns, thus is worth further researches to investigate.

6 Conclusion

In this paper, we propose the method of pre-training the meta-rule selection policy for boosting the training efficiency of visual generative abductive learning. The method builds upon the embedding mechanism as well as the disentanglement of symbolic and sub-symbolic information of the AbdGen model [20], which can utilize pure symbolic data for pre-training, hence is of low additional time cost. The experimental results show that the proposed approach the policy effectively reduces the time cost of AbdGen training, meanwhile it can also deal with unseen learning tasks and robust to unseen grounding errors.

Acknowledgement. This work was supported by National Key R&D Program of China (2022ZD0114804) and National Natural Science Foundation of China (62206245).

A Detailed Experimental Setups

A.1 Data Configurations

- **Mario Dataset.** For the Mario dataset, we consider a 3×3 grid map with target types divided into coin and bomb. The background types include sea, flower, chessboard. The frame types are categorized as brick1, brick2, brick3, green panel, white panel, glass, and concrete. This results in a total of 3402 images, corresponding to 3402 sets of symbolic data. For each task, an image (symbol) case contains between 2 to 5 images (symbol data sets), as detailed in Table 2 of the main paper.
  - **Pre-training phase.** For the pre-training process, we use the pure symbolic instance of all tasks. Due to the different settings of each task, the number of positive cases that can be generated is limited. For the *Priority* task, 1134 positive cases can be formed. For the *Just* and *Flower* tasks, 378 positive cases each can be formed. The *One Step* task can form 252 positive cases. The *Sea* task can form 126 positive cases, and the *Chess jump* task can form 3640 positive cases. Negative cases, in theory, can be any combination that is not a positive case. However, to ensure that the negative cases are informative for rule learning, we increased the proportion of meaningful negative cases for each task. We uniformly generated 3000 negative cases for each task. In this phase, we do not specify the number of positive and negative cases in each instance. Instead, we set

a maximum allowable number of 20 positive and 50 negative cases per instance that the model can handle, aiming for the application phase to adapt to varying numbers of cases, ensuring flexibility and robustness across different scenarios.

  - **Application phase.** For the application phase, we use the raw image instance. For the *Right (Down) priority* task, there are 1134 positive cases composed of 1218 different images and 3000 negative cases composed of 2552 (2553) different images. For the *Just right task*, there are 378 positive cases composed of 378 different images and 3000 negative cases composed of 2776 different images. Each instance contains 5 positive cases and 20 negative cases. For each task, we initially use 1% of the total number of images, approximately 20–30 images, for few-shot supervised training. This is done to achieve around 50% accuracy which is an acceptable error margin for the meta-rule selection model, to activate the meta-rule selection model.

- **MNIST Dataset.** For the MNIST dataset, we start with approximately 6000 original images for each digit from 0 to 9. The task data for subsequent tasks are sampled from these original images. Each image (symbol) case contains 3 to 5 images (symbol data sets).
  - **Pre-training phase.** For the pre-training process, we use the symbol cases from all tasks, similar to the Mario dataset. For each task, we sample 3000 positive cases and 3000 negative cases. Similarly to the Mario dataset, we apply informative restrictions on the generation of negative cases and set a maximum allowable number of 10 positive and 20 negative cases per instance.
  - **Application phase.** For the application phase, we use raw image instances. For the Cumulative Product task, we re-sample 3000 positive and 3000 negative grounding symbol cases and extract the corresponding raw data to form the raw image instance dataset. The positive cases are composed of 10,887 different images, while the negative cases are composed of 8,892 different images. Each instance contains 2 positive cases and 1 negative cases. We initially use 0.1% of the total number of images, 20 images, for few-shot supervised training. This is done to achieve around 60% accuracy to activate the meta-rule selection model.

A.2 Implementation Details

- **Embedding** The positive and negative cases are directly encoded according to their symbol grounding and then expanded to the maximum supported number of positive and negative examples. The dimension of the meta-rule embedding is set to 16.
- **Attention Mechanisms** The network uses Hopfield attention layers [23] for self-attention and cross-attention with padding mask on and 8 parallel attention heads.

- **Probability Prediction** A one-layer full connect network is used to predicts the probability of selecting each meta-rule with Sigmoid activations and clamped to ensure values are within a valid range.

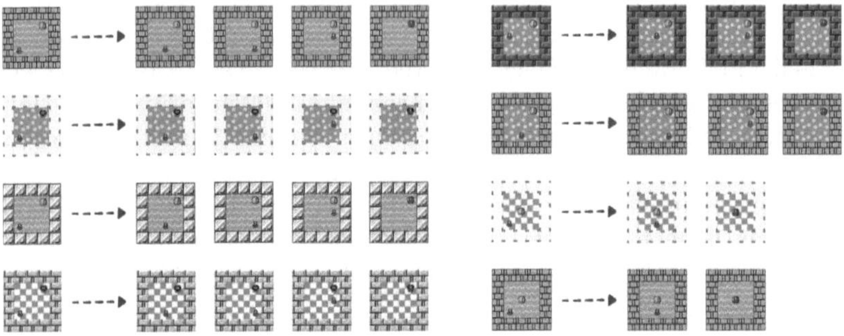

Fig. 7. Rule based generation on Mario. Generation results of AbdGen on Mario *Right priority* task given the input image, AbdGen generates a sequence of images based on the learned correct rules.

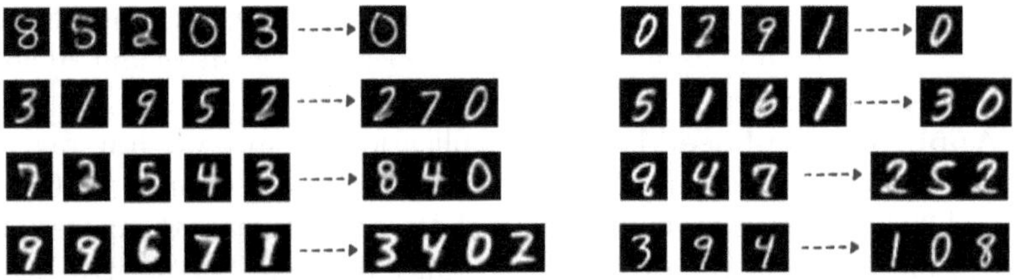

Fig. 8. Rule based generation on MNIST. Generation results of AbdGen on MNIST *Cumulative product* task given the input images, AbdGen generates a sequence of images that represent the answer based on the learned correct rules.

The pre-training process is conducted for 400 iterations for Mario dataset and 200 iterations for MNIST dataset . We utilize Adam optimizer with a learning rate of 0.00001 for both two datasets.

For AbdGen process, the pre-training phase is conducted for 500 iterations, and the application phase is conducted for 30000 iterations. We utilize Adam optimizer [13] with a learning rate of 0.0001 for Mario dataset and with a learning rate of 0.001 for at the first 10000 iterations and 0.0001 at the last 20000 iterations for MNIST dataset. It should be noted that the abduction accuracy converges within 300 iterations. Therefore, Fig. 5 and Fig. 6 in the main paper only display the results for the first 200 or 300 iterations.

B Generation Results

Our generation results are shown in Fig. 7 and Fig. 8, which demonstrate that the AbdGen model with meta-rule selection can successfully learn the correct rules to explain all cases and generates images based on these learned rules with high quality and consistent style.

References

1. Bahdanau, D., Cho, K., Bengio, Y.: Neural machine translation by jointly learning to align and translate. arXiv preprint arXiv:1409.0473 (2014)
2. Cropper, A., Dumančić, S.: Inductive logic programming at 30: a new introduction. J. Artif. Intell. Res. **74**, 765–850 (2022)
3. Cropper, A., Muggleton, S.H.: Logical minimisation of meta-rules within meta-interpretive learning. In: Davis, J., Ramon, J. (eds.) Inductive Logic Programming. LNCS, vol. 9046, pp. 62–75. Springer, Cham (2015). https://doi.org/10.1007/978-3-319-23708-4_5
4. Cropper, A., Muggleton, S.H.: Metagol system. https://github.com/metagol/metagol (2016). https://github.com/metagol/metagol
5. Cropper, A., Tourret, S.: Logical reduction of metarules. Mach. Learn. **109**, 1323–1369 (2020)
6. Dai, W.Z., Muggleton, S.H.: Abductive knowledge induction from raw data. arXiv preprint arXiv:2010.03514 (2020)
7. Dai, W.Z., Xu, Q., Yu, Y., Zhou, Z.H.: Bridging machine learning and logical reasoning by abductive learning. In: Proceedings of the 33rd International Conference on Neural Information Processing Systems (2019)
8. De Raedt, L., Bruynooghe, M.: Interactive concept-learning and constructive induction by analogy. Mach. Learn. **8**, 107–150 (1992)
9. Emde, W., Habel, C., Rollinger, C.R.: The discovery of the equator or concept driven learning. In: IJCAI, pp. 455–458 (1983)
10. Ferilli, S., Esposito, F., Basile, T.M.A., Di Mauro, N.: Automatic induction of first-order logic descriptors type domains from observations. In: Camacho, R., King, R., Srinivasan, A. (eds.) ILP 2004. LNCS (LNAI), vol. 3194, pp. 116–131. Springer, Heidelberg (2004). https://doi.org/10.1007/978-3-540-30109-7_12
11. Hsu, J., Mao, J., Tenenbaum, J., Wu, J.: What's left? Concept grounding with logic-enhanced foundation models. Adv. Neural Inf. Process. Syst. **36** (2024)
12. Kietz, J.U., Wrobel, S.: Controlling the complexity of learning in logic through syntactic and task-oriented models. Inductive Logic Programming (1992)
13. Kingma, D.P., Ba, J.: Adam: a method for stochastic optimization. arXiv preprint arXiv:1412.6980 (2014)
14. LeCun, Y., Cortes, C., Burges, C.: Mnist handwritten digit database. ATT Labs. http://yann.lecun.com/exdb/mnist **2** (2010)
15. Manhaeve, R., Dumančić, S., Kimmig, A., Demeester, T., Raedt, L.D.: Deepproblog: neural probabilistic logic programming (2018)
16. McCreath, E., Sharma, A.: Extraction of meta-knowledge to restrict the hypothesis space for ilp systems. In: AI-CONFERENCE, pp. 75–82. Citeseer (1995)
17. Misino, E., Marra, G., Sansone, E.: Vael: bridging variational autoencoders and probabilistic logic programming (2022)

18. Muggleton, S.H.: Meta-interpretive learning: achievements and challenges (Invited Paper). In: Costantini, S., Franconi, E., Van Woensel, W., Kontchakov, R., Sadri, F., Roman, D. (eds.) RuleML+RR 2017. LNCS, vol. 10364, pp. 1–6. Springer, Cham (2017). https://doi.org/10.1007/978-3-319-61252-2_1
19. Paszke, A., et al.: Pytorch: an imperative style, high-performance deep learning library. Adv. Neural Inf. Process. Syst. **32** (2019)
20. Peng, Y., et al.: Generating by understanding: neural visual generation with logical symbol groundings. arXiv preprint arXiv:2310.17451 (2023)
21. Picado, J., Termehchy, A., Fern, A., Pathak, S.: Towards automatically setting language bias in relational learning. In: Proceedings of the 1st Workshop on Data Management for End-to-End Machine Learning, pp. 1–4 (2017)
22. Ramesh, A., et al.: Zero-shot text-to-image generation. In: International Conference on Machine Learning, pp. 8821–8831. PMLR (2021)
23. Ramsauer, H., et al.: Hopfield networks is all you need. arXiv preprint arXiv:2008.02217 (2020)
24. Rombach, R., Blattmann, A., Lorenz, D., Esser, P., Ommer, B.: High-resolution image synthesis with latent diffusion models. In: Proceedings of the IEEE/CVF Conference on Computer Vision and Pattern Recognition, pp. 10684–10695 (2022)
25. Saharia, C., et al.: Photorealistic text-to-image diffusion models with deep language understanding. Adv. Neural Inf. Process. Syst. **35**, 36479–36494 (2022)
26. Schulman, J., Wolski, F., Dhariwal, P., Radford, A., Klimov, O.: Proximal policy optimization algorithms. arXiv preprint arXiv:1707.06347 (2017)
27. Tourret, S., Cropper, A.: SLD-resolution reduction of second-order horn fragments. In: Calimeri, F., Leone, N., Manna, M. (eds.) JELIA 2019. LNCS (LNAI), vol. 11468, pp. 259–276. Springer, Cham (2019). https://doi.org/10.1007/978-3-030-19570-0_17
28. Van Den Oord, A., Vinyals, O., Kavukcuoglu, K.: Neural discrete representation learning. Adv. Neural Inf. Process. Syst. **30** (2017)
29. Wielemaker, J.: An overview of the swi-prolog programming environment. In: Proceedings of the 13th International Workshop on LP Environments (2003)
30. Yi, K., Wu, J., Gan, C., Torralba, A., Kohli, P., Tenenbaum, J.: Neural-symbolic vqa: disentangling reasoning from vision and language understanding. Adv. Neural Inf. Process. Syst. **31** (2018)
31. Zhou, Z.-H.: Abductive learning: towards bridging machine learning and logical reasoning. SCIENCE CHINA Inf. Sci. **62**(7), 1–3 (2019). https://doi.org/10.1007/s11432-018-9801-4

Leveraging Inductive Logic Programming and Deep Learning for Trustworthy Vision

Zahra Chaghazardi(✉), Saber Fallah, and Alireza Tamaddoni-Nezhad

University of Surrey, Guildford, UK
{z.chaghazardi,s.fallah,a.tamaddoni-nezhad}@surrey.ac.uk

Abstract. Deep learning serves as a crucial component in computer vision, enabling accurate predictions from raw data. However, unlike human cognition, deep learning models are vulnerable to adversarial attacks. This paper introduces a new method for traffic sign recognition that employs Inductive Logic Programming (ILP) to generate logical rules from a limited set of examples. These rules are used to assess the logical consistency of predictions, which is then incorporated into the neural network through the loss function. The study investigates the effect of incorporating logical rules into deep learning models on the robustness of vision tasks in autonomous vehicles (AV). The experimental results show that the proposed method significantly improves the accuracy of traffic sign recognition in the presence of adversarial attacks.

Keywords: Inductive Logic Programming · Autonomous Vehicles · Deep learning

1 Introduction

In recent years, the widespread adoption of deep learning has revolutionised various fields, including vision-based systems, with remarkable performance. However, alongside their achievements, these systems have also revealed susceptibility to adversarial attacks. An adversarial attack is designed to produce adversarial examples to deceive machine learning systems. Despite their subtle alterations from genuine samples, these adversarial examples result in misclassification [13].

The vulnerability of deep learning models to adversarial attacks poses a significant security threat to safety-critical applications. For instance, researchers have shown that stop signs can be manipulated to be misidentified as speed limit signs by autonomous vehicles [8]. Figure 1 illustrates the various stop signs, each subjected to different attack strategies with the intended misclassification target being a speed limit sign, and the results showed that the altered Stop signs were misclassified as speed limit 45 signs by the image classifier.

In contrast to deep learning, which can be easily fooled, humans leverage prior knowledge, extract high-level attributes as factual data, and apply logical constraints on these facts to make robust and reliable decisions, even when confronted with ambiguity or adversarial inputs. For example, recognising the

W.-Z. Dai (Ed.): ILP 2024, LNAI 16059, pp. 181–194, 2026.
https://doi.org/10.1007/978-3-032-09087-4_12

Fig. 1. Different Stop signs manipulated by the RP2 attacks were misclassified as speed limit sign by the image classifier [8]

octagonal shape of a traffic sign combined with the logical fact that only stop signs have this shape assists humans in avoiding mistakenly identifying it as other signs. We hypothesise that incorporating similar mechanisms into deep learning models can enhance their resilience against adversarial attacks. In line with this idea, some studies, such as [5] and [4] have introduced methods that utilised logical programming for traffic sign recognition, which led to enhanced resilience against adversarial inputs.

This paper presents a method, to enhance the trustworthiness of Neural Networks (NNs) based traffic sign recognition. Building on our previous work [6], this approach highlights the importance of incorporating Background Knowledge (BK) to bolster robustness by integrating additional features into the learning process. Our approach involves integrating human knowledge to improve the reliability of traffic sign recognition, mirroring human perception. We automatically extract logical rules by leveraging ILP from positive and negative examples. Subsequently, these rules are mapped into propositional logic, forming a logical constraint matrix. We then evaluate the satisfaction of constraints for each prediction, and the resulting constraint dissatisfaction is integrated into the loss function, ensuring compliance with BK.

2 Proposed Framework

In this section, we introduce the proposed framework aimed at improving the robustness of NNs against adversarial attacks by incorporating human knowledge. This framework utilises human-provided attributes extracted from the input images. For each traffic sign category, these attributes are identical.

Furthermore, the proposed approach leverages ILP to systematically derive rules and logical constraints from human-provided knowledge. Integrating these constraints into the neural network's loss function significantly enhances the model's resilience. The architecture of the Reference model and the proposed neuro-symbolic framework is illustrated in Fig. 2.

The Convolutional Neural Network (CNN) serves as a multilabel classifier in the Reference model. During the training phase, the CNN processes an input image of a traffic sign alongside four corresponding labels: traffic sign class,

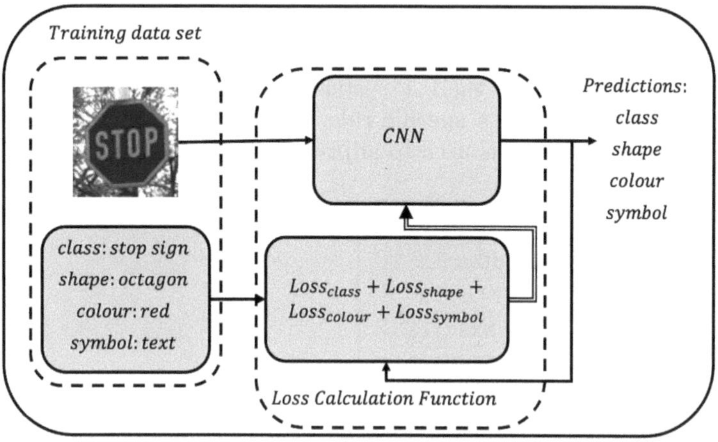

(a) Reference Framework

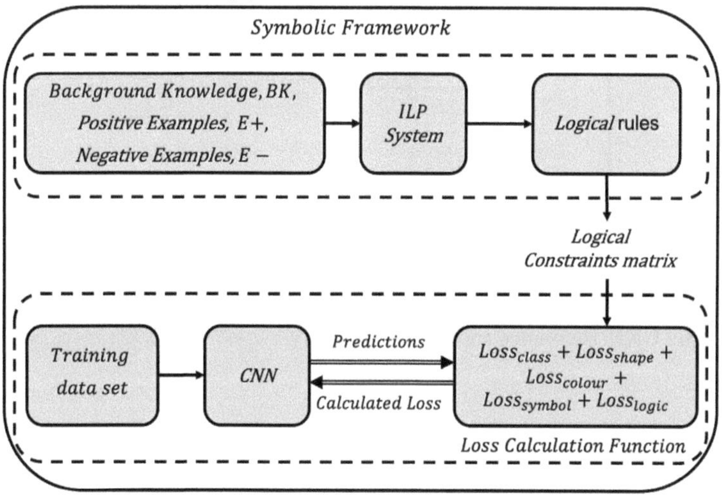

(b) Proposed Framework

Fig. 2. a) Reference framework and b) Proposed framework for the traffic sign classifier incorporating logical constraints

shape, colour, and symbol. Once trained, the model is capable of predicting the class, shape, colour, and symbols of any input traffic sign image.

The proposed model consists of two main components: a symbolic framework and a modified Reference framework with an adjusted loss function. In the symbolic framework, BK is given to the ILP system, which leverages it to induce rules and logical constraints systematically.

These logical constraints are subsequently used to modify the loss function of the Reference framework. During the training process, the CNN model's predictions are input into the loss calculator, which assesses how well the predicted labels align with the derived logical constraints. A regularisation term is then incorporated into the loss function to enforce compliance with these rules.

In this classification task, the ILP system generates one rule per class. Each traffic sign is thus linked to a specific rule, and during training, the rule that best matches the prediction is used to adjust the loss function.

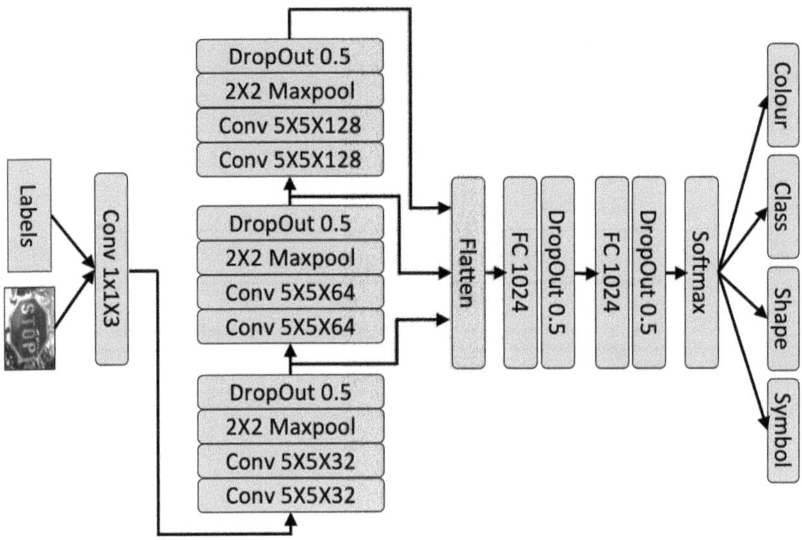

Fig. 3. Architecture of the attributes Convolutional Neural Network (ACNN) model utilised as the CNN Reference model in our study.

2.1 Material

We adapted a CNN architecture implementation [18], originally designed for traffic sign recognition, to create a multilabel classifier. The adopted model is illustrated in Fig. 3 as our Reference model. The training configuration included the Adam optimiser with a learning rate of 0.001, 20 epochs, a batch size of 32, and the Cross-Entropy loss function.

This multilabel classifier was trained on the German Traffic Sign Recognition Benchmark (GTSRB) [17] For our training, we focused on a subset of eleven traffic sign categories, with each category represented by 150 training images. Figure 4 illustrates the traffic signs employed in our study, organised by their specific attributes such as colour, shape, and symbol.

We selected 50 images from each class of the GTSRB dataset to create a normal test dataset. Furthermore, In this study, the proposed classifier undergoes testing across various adversarial attack datasets, including GRATS (Dirty) [2], Dart [16], and Shadow [22] attack datasets. These datasets introduce various challenges, enabling the assessment of the classifier's robustness across different adversarial scenarios.

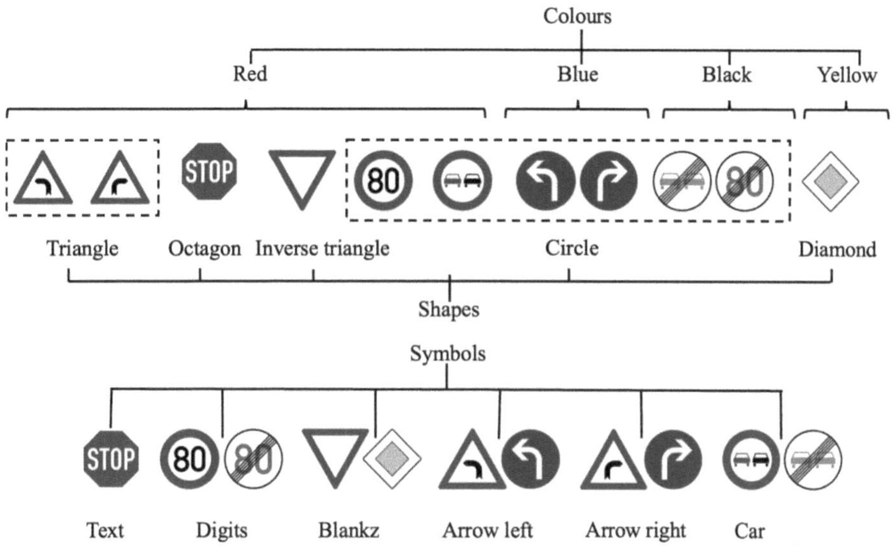

Fig. 4. A set of eleven traffic signs utilised in this study, each associated with corresponding shape, colour and symbol labels.

2.2 Logical Constraint Extraction

We employ an ILP system to extract comprehensive and optimal logical constraints. ILP is an inductive reasoning technique at the intersection of Machine Learning and Logic Programming, specifically designed to derive logical rules from a few sets of examples [15]. For this framework, we have utilised the ILP system Aleph [3].

The Aleph system operates through a procedure that begins with selecting a positive example to generalise. The system then constructs a specific clause, called the bottom clause, based on the selected example and corresponding BK. Next, the system searches for a more general clause than the bottom clause. The best general clause is then added to the hypothesis set, redundant examples are removed and the process returns to the first step. This process continues until no more examples are left. The outcome is a set of induced hypotheses that should cover as many positive and as few negative examples as possible.

After the ILP system induces interpretable logical rules, the next stage involves mapping these rules into a constraint matrix denoted as "C" which is depicted as follows:

$$C = \begin{bmatrix} c_{11} & c_{12} & \cdots & c_{1L} \\ c_{21} & c_{22} & \cdots & c_{2L} \\ \vdots & \vdots & \ddots & \vdots \\ c_{N1} & c_{N2} & \cdots & c_{NL} \end{bmatrix}$$

Here, N represents the number of rules or constraints, where each traffic sign category is associated with a specific rule. L denotes the number of labels, which is four in our case, corresponding to the attributes of colour, shape, symbol, and class.

The element c_{ij} denotes the value of the index related to a specific attribute j that appeared in a specific rule i. Each attribute l includes S_l categories, for instance, the 'shape' attribute includes different geometrical categories such as circles, triangles, and rectangles. This indexing system systematically captures the relationships between rules and attributes.

In this configuration, the matrix will have dimensions of $N \times L$, which is considerably smaller compared to the constraint matrix proposed by [11], whose size is $N \times (S_1 + \ldots + S_L)$. In our case study with 11 rules, 4 colours, 5 shapes, 6 symbols and 11 classes, the constraint dimension for our proposed method is 11×4. This more compact representation is advantageous, particularly for larger problems.

2.3 Logic-Integrated Loss

We introduced a logic-based regularisation term into the multi-label classification loss to enhance robustness. This term quantifies the level of satisfaction of the CNN model's predictions with respect to the applied logical constraints. Equation 1 represents the total loss L_{total}, where the first term consists of a combination of cross-entropy losses for each attribute, and the second term is an additional logical loss, which ensures that the model adheres to logical constraints.

$$\mathrm{L}_{total} = \sum_{l=1}^{L} L_{attribute} + L_{logic} \tag{1}$$

The process of logical loss computation begins by considering each rule (c), represented as a row in the logical constraint matrix (C), which specifies the corresponding indices for each attribute (class, shape, colour, and symbol) for that rule. The predicted values associated with these indices are selected and evaluated according to the chosen type of logic operation, either "product" or "Gödel".

If the logical operation is set to "product", the satisfaction score is computed as the product of these predicted values. Alternatively, if the logical operation follows the Gödel t-norm, the satisfaction is determined by selecting the minimum value from the predicted labels including class, shape, colour and symbol probabilities. The rule with the highest satisfaction score is then selected as the best match, and the loss is computed based on this rule as 1 - satisfaction.

The rule matrix C of size $N \times L$, contains elements c_{nl}, representing the index of the attribute l associated with the respective rule n. For each attribute l, the deep learning model generates a prediction vector P_l, containing n_l predictions. Here n_l represents the number of categories for that attribute.

Given C and P, our objective is to determine the satisfaction level of each constraint for the corresponding prediction. To achieve this, we define a matrix

G of dimensions $N \times L$, each element G_{nl} is determined by the probability from prediction vectors $P_l(c_{nl})$. This relationship is expressed as:

$$G_{nl} = P_l(c_{nl}), \quad \text{for } n = 1, \ldots, N \text{ and } l = 1, \ldots, L \tag{2}$$

The satisfaction level G' is computed using a t-norm (conjunction) operation along the second dimension (attributes) followed by a t-conorm (disjunction) across the first dimension (rules):

$$G' = \text{t-conorm}(\text{t-norm}(G, dim = 2), dim = 1) \tag{3}$$

For evaluating the satisfaction of each rule, we consider the Gödel and Product t-norms. The logical conjunction operator is substituted with the product t-norm ($x \wedge_p y \equiv xy$) or the Gödel t-norm ($x \wedge_g y \equiv \min(x, y)$). Additionally, product t-conorm ($x \vee_p y \equiv 1 - (1 - x)(1 - y)$) or the Gödel t-conorm ($x \vee_g y \equiv \max(x, y)$) is employed as a disjunction.

Equation 3 first applies a t-norm operation to compute the satisfaction level for each rule across the attributes. For example, if we use the Gödel t-norm, the satisfaction score for each rule is obtained by taking the minimum value across all attributes for that rule (t-norm$(G, \text{dim} = 2) = \min(G_{n,1}, \ldots, G_{n,l})$). Once the satisfaction level for each rule is computed, a t-conorm operation is applied to aggregate the satisfaction levels across the rules. In the case of Gödel t-conorm, this involves taking the maximum value among the computed satisfaction scores. This operation helps in selecting the rule with the highest overall satisfaction. The logic loss is then defined as:

$$L_{logic} = 1 - G' \tag{4}$$

The resulting dissatisfaction is then incorporated into the loss function as a regularization term. Let's consider an example with this logical constraint for an input image:

```
Shape: octagon
Color: red
Symbol: text
Class: stop sign
```

The CNN provides output probabilities for various attributes. For example, consider the shape prediction vector:

P_shape : [0.1, 0.2, 0.0, 0.7, 0.0]

This vector indicates that the probability of the shape being an octagon is 0.7. Similarly, from P_colour, P_symbol and P_class, the deep learning model obtains probabilities of 0.9 for the colour being red, 0.6 for the symbol being text and 0.8 for the sign being a stop sign.

In the product t-norm, rule satisfaction is computed by multiplying the probabilities of the conditions, while in the Gödel t-norm, it is determined by selecting the minimum value among them.

$$\text{Product t-norm rule satisfaction} = 0.7 \times 0.9 \times 0.6 \times 0.8 = 0.3 \tag{5}$$

$$\text{Gödel t-norm rule satisfaction} = \min(0.7, 0.9, 0.6, 0.8) = 0.6 \tag{6}$$

This process is repeated for all rules. Once the satisfaction for each rule is computed, a t-conorm operation is used to determine the overall satisfaction across all rules. The complement of this overall satisfaction value is then incorporated into the loss function as a regularization term.

3 Results and Discussion

In this section, we evaluate the robustness of the proposed model by comparing it with the Reference model[1] Each model was independently trained over ten iterations, and the average accuracy was calculated.

Figure 5 illustrates the accuracy of basic and various 4-attribute models including Reference, Non_Logic, Logic_Product, and Logic_Gödel models when tested on targeted stop signs. The evaluation was conducted across several datasets, including Normal, Dart, Dirty, and Shadow. Results show that while the Logic_Gödel closely matches the Reference model's performance on the Normal dataset, it significantly outperforms other models on the attack test datasets, demonstrating the enhanced robustness of the proposed logic-based approach.

Logic_Product also surpasses the Reference and Non_Logic models in all attack methods, though it consistently underperforms when compared to Logic_Gödel, which underscores the latter's superior robustness against adversarial attacks.

To investigate the impact of incorporating additional related attributes on the robustness of logic_based models against adversarial attacks, we compared a 3-attribute model (including shape, colour, and class attributes) with a 4-attribute model (including shape, colour, symbols, and class attributes) across various test datasets. Figure 6 illustrates the accuracy of both the 3-attribute and 4-attribute models for Logic_Product and Logic_Gödel on the Normal, Dart, Dirty, and Shadow datasets. The results indicate that the 4-attribute Logic_based models outperform the 3-attribute Logic_based models, highlighting the significance of incorporating additional background knowledge.

Figure 7 presents the predictions from both the Non_Logic and proposed Logic_G"odel 4-attribute models for targeted stop signs across various attack

[1] The code required to reproduce the experiments detailed in this paper can be accessed at https://github.com/Chaghazardi/Leveraging-Inductive-Logic-Programming-and-Deep-Learning-for-Trustworthy-Vision.

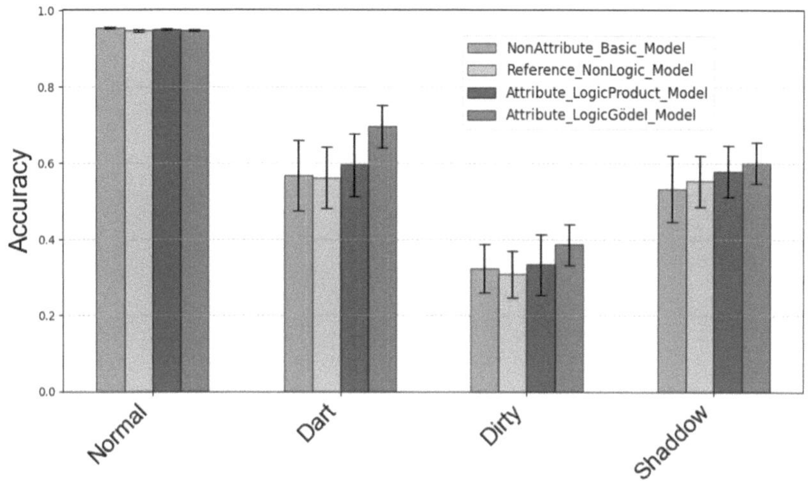

Fig. 5. Comparison of accuracy among Non_Logic (described in Fig. 3), Logic_Product, and Logic_Gödel on normal and targeted stop signs by various attack datasets including Dart, Dirty and Shadow.

scenarios, including Dart, Dirty, and Shadow attacks. The results demonstrate that the Logic_Gödel model produces more robust and confident predictions compared to the Non_Logic model predictions.

4 Related Work

This section overviews current research efforts aimed at integrating prior knowledge into neural networks, either by network architecture adjustment or loss function modification or data transformation. These strategies aim to improve performance, support learning from limited data, and ensure that the model adheres to existing knowledge [12].

In the former category, methods construct a constrained layer on top of a neural network ensuring full constraint satisfaction. For instance, MultiplexNet [14], Coherent-by-Construction Network (CCN) [10] and Semantic Probabilistic Layer (SPL) [1] approaches exemplify this strategy. MultiplexNet augments the prediction layer with transformations that allow the output layer to function like a logical circuit multiplexor. The CCN approach employs a dual methodology, introducing a supplementary top layer that modifies the output to meet specified constraints and integrates these constraints into a collaborative loss function. While SPL integrates a compiled logic circuit layer into the network to enforce constraints directly.

Our approach aligns with the second category, where domain knowledge is integrated through modifications to the loss function, which is optimized during the deep network's training process. In this method, a penalty is introduced into the loss function to reflect the degree to which the model's predictions satisfy the

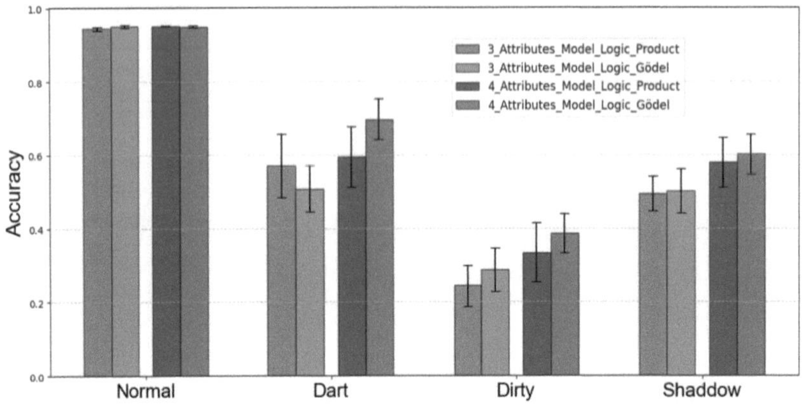

Fig. 6. Accuracy comparison between 3-attribute and 4-attribute logic-based models on the Normal dataset and various adversarial datasets, including Dart, Dirty, and Shadow.

constraints imposed by the domain knowledge. This ensures that the network not only learns from the data but also adheres to the specific requirements dictated by the background knowledge.

Several studies have explored the integration of domain-specific knowledge into neural network training through modifications to the loss function. For example, Xu et al. [21] introduced a syntax-independent semantic loss function that remains effective regardless of how constraints are expressed. Logic Embedding Network with Semantic regularisation (LENSR) [20] integrates logical constraints into the loss function by using a Graph Convolutional Network (GCN) to project logical formulas onto a manifold. The model then learns to minimize the distance to satisfying assignments. DL2 [9] expanded on this by translating constraints into convex sets and adding to the loss function, allowing for additional features such as querying model decisions. Wang and Pan [19] employed a parallel neuro-reasoning engine, generating an output consistent with the neural process and incorporating the disparity between the two outputs into the loss function. This innovative method aims to leverage both neural networks and reasoning engines to enhance model performance and adherence to logical constraints.

Another approach, categorized as the third method, integrates domain knowledge into deep networks by modifying inputs to include symbolic domain-specific attributes. For example, By transforming input data into graph representations, GNNs can effectively incorporate relational domain knowledge into learning.

For a comprehensive review of the integration of logical constraints in deep learning, please refer to [7].

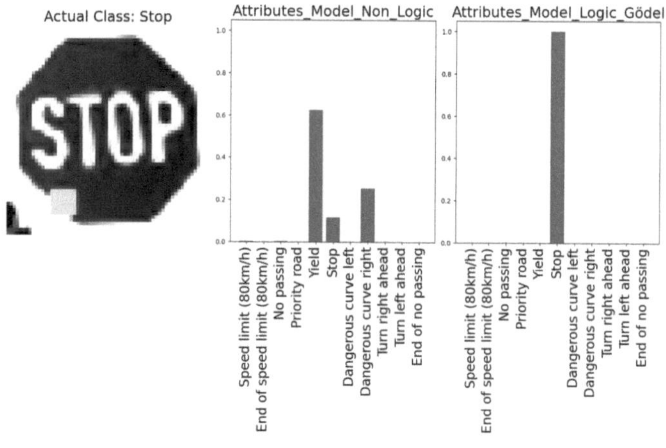

(a) Dart

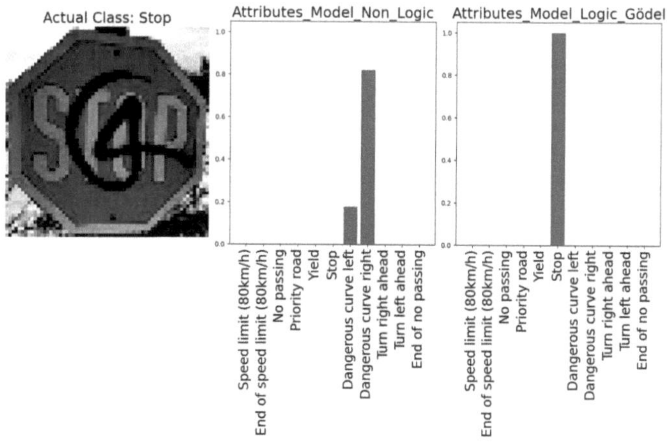

(b) Dirty

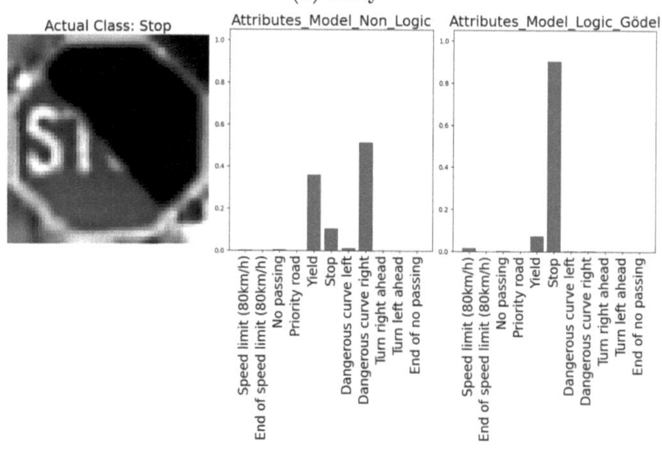

(c) Shadow

Fig. 7. Exemplifying predictions generated by both the Non_Logic and the proposed Logic_Gödel models for targeted stop signs subjected to various attacks.

5 Conclusion

In summary, our experiments highlight significant advancements achieved by the proposed Logic-based model, particularly in accurately detecting adversarial traffic signs. Despite training on a relatively limited dataset of 1650 images, the proposed model exhibits substantial enhancements in accuracy, underscoring its robustness in handling challenging scenarios.

One critical aspect of our approach is the integration of logical rules into the neural network architecture. This fusion of logic into deep learning not only enhances the model's performance but also fortifies its reliability. By incorporating domain-specific knowledge through logical rules, the proposed model can better generalise from limited data and correctly recognise traffic signs with adversarial manipulations that might deceive traditional neural networks.

These findings underscore the potential of the logic-based approach as a valuable strategy for bolstering the trustworthiness of neural networks in real-world applications, particularly in the domain of autonomous vehicles. By combining the strengths of deep learning and symbolic logic, the logic-based model presents a robust framework for enhancing the accuracy and reliability of vision systems in autonomous driving. Future work could explore expanding the dataset and refining the logical rules to further improve the model's performance and applicability to a broader range of scenarios.

Acknowledgments. The first author would like to acknowledge her PhD grant funding from the Breaking Barriers Studentship Award at the University of Surrey. The third author would like to acknowledge the EPSRC Network Plus grant on Human-Like Computing (HLC) and the EPSRC grant on human-machine learning of ambiguities.

References

1. Ahmed, K., Teso, S., Chang, K.W., Van den Broeck, G., Vergari, A.: Semantic probabilistic layers for neuro-symbolic learning. Adv. Neural. Inf. Process. Syst. **35**, 29944–29959 (2022)
2. Apostolidis, K.D., Gkouvrikos, E.V., Vrochidou, E., Papakostas, G.A.: Traffic sign recognition robustness in autonomous vehicles under physical adversarial attacks. In: Daimi, K., Alsadoon, A., Coelho, L. (eds.) Cutting Edge Applications of Computational Intelligence Tools and Techniques. Studies in Computational Intelligence, vol. 1118, pp. 287–304. Springer, Cham (2023). https://doi.org/10.1007/978-3-031-44127-1_13
3. Ashwin Srinivasan: The aleph manual (2001). https://www.cs.ox.ac.uk/activities/programinduction/Aleph/aleph.html
4. Chaghazardi, Z., Fallah, S., Tamaddoni-Nezhad, A.: Explainable and trustworthy traffic sign detection for safe autonomous driving: an inductive logic programming approach. In: Proceedings of the 39th International Conference on Logic Programming. Electronic Proceedings in Theoretical Computer Science, vol. 385, pp. 201–212. Open Publishing Association, Imperial College London, UK (2023). https://doi.org/10.4204/EPTCS.385.21

5. Chaghazardi, Z., Fallah, S., Tamaddoni-Nezhad, A.: A logic-based compositional generalisation approach for robust traffic sign detection. In: International Joint Conference on Artificial Intelligence 2023 Workshop on Knowledge-Based Compositional Generalization (2023). https://openreview.net/forum?id=jfU2Xv84_O
6. Chaghazardi, Z., Fallah, S., Tamaddoni-Nezhad, A.: Trustworthy vision for autonomous vehicles: a robust logic-infused deep learning approach. In: 2024 IEEE 27th International Conference on Intelligent Transportation Systems (ITSC), pp. 2869–2874. IEEE (2024)
7. Dash, T., Chitlangia, S., Ahuja, A., Srinivasan, A.: A review of some techniques for inclusion of domain-knowledge into deep neural networks. Sci. Rep. **12**(1), 1040 (2022)
8. Eykholt, K., et al.: Robust physical-world attacks on deep learning visual classification. In: Proceedings of the IEEE Conference on Computer Vision and Pattern Recognition, pp. 1625–1634 (2018)
9. Fischer, M., Balunovic, M., Drachsler-Cohen, D., Gehr, T., Zhang, C., Vechev, M.: DL2: training and querying neural networks with logic. In: International Conference on Machine Learning, pp. 1931–1941. PMLR (2019)
10. Giunchiglia, E., Lukasiewicz, T.: Multi-label classification neural networks with hard logical constraints. J. Artif. Intell. Res. **72**, 759–818 (2021)
11. Giunchiglia, E., Stoian, M.C., Khan, S., Cuzzolin, F., Lukasiewicz, T.: ROAD-R: the autonomous driving dataset with logical requirements. Mach. Learn. 1–31 (2023)
12. Giunchiglia, E., Stoian, M.C., Lukasiewicz, T.: Deep learning with logical constraints. arXiv preprint arXiv:2205.00523 (2022)
13. Gui, J., Sun, Z., Wen, Y., Tao, D., Ye, J.: A review on generative adversarial networks: algorithms, theory, and applications. IEEE Trans. Knowl. Data Eng. (2021)
14. Hoernle, N., Karampatsis, R.M., Belle, V., Gal, K.: MultiplexNet: towards fully satisfied logical constraints in neural networks. In: Proceedings of the AAAI Conference on Artificial Intelligence, vol. 36, pp. 5700–5709 (2022)
15. Muggleton, S.: Learning from positive data. In: Muggleton, S. (ed.) ILP 1996. LNCS, vol. 1314, pp. 358–376. Springer, Heidelberg (1997). https://doi.org/10.1007/3-540-63494-0_65
16. Sitawarin, C., Bhagoji, A.N., Mosenia, A., Chiang, M., Mittal, P.: DARTS: deceiving autonomous cars with toxic signs. arXiv preprint arXiv:1802.06430 (2018)
17. Stallkamp, J., Schlipsing, M., Salmen, J., Igel, C.: Man vs. computer: benchmarking machine learning algorithms for traffic sign recognition. Neural Netw. **32**, 323–332 (2012)
18. Yadav, V.: German sign classification using deep learning neural networks (2016). https://github.com/vxy10/p2-TrafficSigns
19. Wang, W., Pan, S.J.: Integrating deep learning with logic fusion for information extraction. In: Proceedings of the AAAI Conference on Artificial Intelligence, vol. 34, pp. 9225–9232 (2020)
20. Xie, Y., Xu, Z., Kankanhalli, M.S., Meel, K.S., Soh, H.: Embedding symbolic knowledge into deep networks. Adv. Neural Inf. Process. Syst. **32** (2019)

21. Xu, J., Zhang, Z., Friedman, T., Liang, Y., Broeck, G.: A semantic loss function for deep learning with symbolic knowledge. In: International Conference on Machine Learning, pp. 5502–5511. PMLR (2018)
22. Zhong, Y., Liu, X., Zhai, D., Jiang, J., Ji, X.: Shadows can be dangerous: stealthy and effective physical-world adversarial attack by natural phenomenon. In: Proceedings of the IEEE/CVF Conference on Computer Vision and Pattern Recognition, pp. 15345–15354 (2022)

Measurement and Evaluation of Intelligent Robots

Claude Sammut(✉)

School of Computer Science and Engineering, The University of New South Wales, Sydney, Australia
c.sammut@unsw.edu.au
http://www.cse.unsw.edu.au/~claude

Abstract. As in many other fields, Machine Learning has had a significant impact on Robot-ics. We discuss how Machine Learning has impacted the design and development of software for robots, including areas such as robot vision, locomotion, manipulation and decision making. We also discuss how the performance of these systems can be evaluated objectively. Typically, machine learning algorithms are assessed on standard datasets, but in robotics, it is necessary to have the integrated robot system perform in a replicable environment with clear measurement criteria. This is one of the primary motivations for robotics competitions, such RoboCup, where robots are required to perform tasks all the tasks previously mentioned in arenas defined by a technical committee for the purpose of obtaining measurable performance results.

Keywords: Robotics · Evaluation · Artificial Intelligence and Machine Learning

1 Introduction

At the same time as machine learning research and applications have rapidly increased, so too have developments in robotics. These advances in robotics have been aided by open source software made available through ROS[1] package library and communication system, which has effectively become the standard for intelligent robotics. ROS significantly reduces development time because most of the robot's capabilities do not have to be programmed from scratch, so developers can focus on the unique aspects of an application. Many of these packages have been built by ma-chine learning. For example, off-the-shelf machine vision systems like YOLO[2] are commonly used for object detection, person tracking and gesture recognition. Other packages include programs for navigation, mapping, manipulation, speech and language processing and more.

While ROS enables developers to integrate a variety of capabilities in separate modules, another approach is the use end-to-end reinforcement learning [5],

[1] https://www.ros.org.
[2] https://docs.ultralytics.com.

W.-Z. Dai (Ed.): ILP 2024, LNAI 16059, pp. 195–202, 2026.
https://doi.org/10.1007/978-3-032-09087-4_13

which learns to associate inputs to desired outputs in a single model. End-to-end learning often starts the training in a high-fidelity simulator before translating to the real robot. Learning to associate perception with action can also be done by imitation learning [1,9] or behavioural cloning [4,10]. In any application of machine learning, we want to know the quality of the learned model and to benchmark it against other learning systems. Most often this is done by comparing the accuracy or similar measure on standard datasets. In robotics, however, the want to know how the system, as a whole, performs in an actual task. Thus, the measurement necessary combines the performance of the learned model, control systems, perceptual systems, planners, etc. embedded in the entire robot architecture.

However, making comparisons between robotics systems is problematic because evaluations are often done with different hardware on tasks that may not be well con-trolled. For example, there are many YouTube videos of very impressive performances by robots doing complicated tasks, but we don't know exactly what all the components do; we don't know how it was trained; we don't know how many takes were required to get the desired performance or how the video was edited. Even if the re-search is reported in a reputable journal, the effects of differences in laboratory equip-ment are almost impossible to quantify.

This problem is one of the principal motivations for the creation of robotics com-petitions, such as the DARPA Grand Challenges for autonomous vehicles and for humanoid rescue robots. In these two cases, there was a single primary objective and the competitions were not repeated or only repeated once, so there has been no monitoring of progress. RoboCup, is an international competition that has been run annually since 1997. It consists of four major challenges, rescue robots, industrial robots, domestic robots, and the one for which it is best known, soccer robots. Each league emphasises different aspects of robotics and makes different demands on the software systems the control the robots.

In the remainder of this paper, we describe the structure and objectives of the com-petition. We describe the ways in which AI methods are employed and we describe the evaluation methods used to measure the performance of the robots.

2 The Competition

A technical committee in each league is responsible for setting the rules of the competition. This includes a detailed specification of the arenas, the required capabilities of the robots and the scoring system. The rules are usually revised each year, so that as teams reach a certain level of competence, the tasks are made more difficult, with the aim of challenging teams to keep improving and innovating.

2.1 Robot Soccer

There are several sub-leagues of robot soccer for wheeled and legged robots and for different sizes of robot. Rather than describe each one, we will focus on the

Fig. 1. The standard platform league is played with seven NAO robots a side.

Standard Platform League (see Fig. 1). Here, all teams use the same robot and are competing on the quality of their software. Currently, the standard platform is the NAO humanoid robot from Aldebaran[3].

The are several challenges in this league. Being small and relatively low cost, the robot's mobility is limited as is the onboard computing power. Despite these limitations, a robot must, in real time, execute computer vision algorithms to see the ball, field lines, robots and goals; decide, in cooperation its team members, what action to perform; control its bipedal locomotion; and listen to the referee's whistle to start and stop and in case of penalties.

Machine learning has been used in mostly for robot vision and for improving bi-pedal locomotion. For example, Cruz, *et al.* [2] used a convolutional neural net to recognise balls and field lines, Lu and Sammut [8] used a hybrid neural network to segment the camera images to remove off-field distractors. In both cases, large amounts of training data were required, as expected, and significant effort was required to optimise the models to run on the limited onboard computer. However, it has become clear in terms of wins and losses that machine learning in the vision system gives advantages to the teams.

Machine learning has also contributed to refining bipedal locomotion. For example, Hengst [6] used reinforcement learning to learn the parameters of a bipedal walk-ing motion to keep the robot balanced when perturbed by external forces, such as contact with another robot. The initial learning was done on a simulator of the robot before transferring to the real robot. This method was so successful that it gave a significant advantage to Hengst's team, which won

[3] https://www.aldebaran.com/en/nao.

Fig. 2. The logistics league simulates a factory floor in which robots must perform tasks at different workstations. This is mainly a planning and optimisation problem, as the goal is to complete a set of tasks in minimum time.

consecutive championships. Sub-sequently, most of the other teams in the league adapted and improved on this walk-ing engine. For example, Fiedler and Laue [3] added further neural learning to predict falls and take corrective action to maintain balance. It was possible to do this kind of learning because high-fidelity simulators were available to be able to run many trials.

In related work by Haarnoja *et al.* [5], used end-to-end learning on robots similar to the NAO to learn to walk and kick towards a goal. These robots did not have onboard sensing or computation. While capable of learning this subset of robot soccer, this approach has not yet been scaled to play a full game with multiple players. This would significantly complicate learning.

The Standard Platform League provides (literally) a level playing field on which to compare the overall performance of different methods. The final score is the ultimate comparison, but since all robots are the same, it is possible to separately measure speed, agility, stability, visual accuracy, etc., and attribute differences to the algorithms used.

2.2 Logistics League

The logistics league is an industrial robot competition. Teams of robots are placed in a simulated factory floor that has several different kinds of works stations. The teams must complete an assembly task by collected material from

Fig. 3. "TidyBoy" RoboCup@Home robot preparing breakfast.

one workstation, placing different parts in different workstations to join parts, and deliver the final product to an output station (see Fig. 2).

Again, all the teams use the same robot platform. So direct comparisons can be made on how well the robot team optimises its behaviour.

The most successful teams in this league are the ones with the best planning and multi-agent optimisation algorithms. Little use is made of machine learning because these robots require reasoning and planning. An example of a successful team is de-scribed by Hofmann *et al.* [7]. They mostly use ROS packages for navigation and manipulation, but they optimise their path planning and they have a top-level reactive behaviour layer for fast planning.

2.3 Domestic Robots

The RoboCup@Home league is in some ways, the most "AI complete" league. The robots are intended to perform typical tasks in a home and may act as assistive robots. They must be able to map and navigate around an unstructured domestic environment. They must be capable of complex manipulation to perform tasks like preparing breakfast (see Fig. 3), clearing the table and staking a dishwasher, cleaning a toilet, fetching groceries from shelves. They must also be able to interact with humans by speech, recognise individuals and track

Fig. 4. The rescue robot competition operates in an arena that simulates conditions in a disaster site.

their movements, including recognising gestures. The test arena is set up as a small apartment with a bedroom, kitchen, living room, bathroom and typical furniture. The competition starts with simple tasks such entering and greeting the judges, the tasks them become progressively harder, some focussing on manipulation and others on human-robot interaction including complex natural language understanding and tracking multiple judges as they move around and occlude each other.

All teams use ROS packages to provide most of the basic capabilities and then augment them with their own work. Developing these robots would extremely difficult were it not for pre-built vision systems, like YOLO and speech recognition systems built by machine learning. While these off-the-shelf packages give teams a head start, there are still complications, mainly due to the fact the neural net learning systems do not generalise well. If the test arena has objects that the vision system has not been trained on, then additional training is required, but that means collecting many and varied new training examples and running a time-consuming learning procedure on the fly. The same is true for using speech recognition. The judges can have very different accents. The acoustic environment can be echoey and noisy. Often retraining is not practical, so the advantages of these particular machine learning methods are diminished.

2.4 Rescue Robots

The rescue robot league has the most rigorous evaluation methodology. Since its inception, it has been run for RoboCup by the US National Institute of Standards and Technology (NIST). One of their missions is to define standards for emergency services robots. They devise measures of the capabilities of the robots including mobility over rough terrain, visual acuity, dextrous manipulation and levels of autonomy. Unlike the other leagues, these robots may be tele-operated, fully autonomous or mix teleoperation and autonomous operation.

The rescue arena has elements that simulate conditions in a disaster site, such as a collapsed building after an earthquake (see Fig. 4). There is uneven flooring, staircases with obstacles, sections with different kinds of rubble, etc. There are also simulated victims. In the finals of the competition, the robots must navigate through the arena, searching for simulated victims and map their locations, along with the condition of the victim. But before reaching the finals, the robot must demonstrate individual skills such as reading eye charts at different distances and in locations where it is difficult to place a camera. Manipulation is tested by trying to open valves that may also be placed at odd angles. Opening a door is also challenging. Mobility is tested on different surfaces and the robots must be able to reliable cross narrow pathways or move through sand and gravel pits. Each of these tests is scored and only teams that show consistent performance across the different skills progress to the finals, which then test overall performance. The finals are scored on the quality of the map, the number and accuracy of placement of the victims found and time to completion.

The collaboration with NIST is mutually beneficial. For NIST, the competition is a way for them to test their tests. The test methods are based on the real-life experience of first responders to real emergencies. For example, after the accident at the Fukushima nuclear power station, robots were sent in to assess the state of the reactors, since it was not safe for humans to enter the building. However, the robots were not able to access all parts of the plant due to obstacles they could not traverse, such as staircases with debris fallen from the ceiling. Subsequently, new test methods were devised with obstacles across staircases, and these were first trailed in the rescue com-petition and then rolled out as a standard test method. Now all robots that are market-ed to emergency services can be assessed on these test methods, which have been adopted in many countries.

As might be expected, most of the capabilities of the robots are the result of a lot of hardware development. However, AI plays an important role in mapping and path panning for the mobility platform, trajectory planning if the robot carries an arm for manipulation, which also usually has a camera. Vision systems provide automatic recognition of victims and other objects, such as hazard warnings.

3 Conclusion

Objective comparisons of the capabilities of robots is not as straightforward as in most other areas of AI. A robot is an assembly of many components, both hardware and software. Even if each component performs well individually, if the components are not well integrated, the system, as a whole, may perform poorly. Therefore, objective evaluation requires testing the integrated system, as well as its parts. These tests must also be conducted in the real world. Simulations are excellent tools for initial development, simulations rarely capture all the complexities of a physical environment.

Robot competitions provide a means of objective comparison because the test methods are devised by technical committees that are independent of the research teams. The teams must perform onsite and on time and be assessed by independent judges on tasks executed in realistic environments.

Acknowledgments. The material presented on RoboCup is the result of the hard work of many RoboCup teams too numerous to mention and over many years.

Disclosure of Interests. The authors have no competing interests to declare that are relevant to the content of this article.

References

1. Abbeel, P., Ng, A.Y.: Apprenticeship learning via inverse reinforcement learning. In: International Conference on Machine Learning. ACM, New York (2004)
2. Cruz, N., Lobos-Tsunekawa, K., Ruiz-del-Solar, J.: Using convolutional neural networks in robots with limited computational resources: detecting NAO robots while playing soccer. In: Akiyama, H., Obst, O., Sammut, C., Tonidandel, F. (eds.) RoboCup 2017. LNCS (LNAI), vol. 11175, pp. 19–30. Springer, Cham (2018). https://doi.org/10.1007/978-3-030-00308-1_2
3. Fiedler, J., Laue, T.: Neural network-based joint angle prediction for the NAO robot. In: Buche, C., Rossi, A., Simões, M., Visser, U. (eds.) RoboCup 2023. LNCS, vol. 14140, pp. 66–77. Springer Nature Switzerland, Cham (2024). https://doi.org/10.1007/978-3-031-55015-7_6
4. Florence, P., et al.: Implicit behavioral cloning. In: Faust, A., Hsu, D., Neumann, G. (eds.) Proceedings of the 5th Conference on Robot Learning. Proceedings of Machine Learning Research, vol. 164, pp. 158–168. PMLR (2022)
5. Haarnoja, T., et al.: Learning agile soccer skills for a bipedal robot with deep reinforcement learning. Sci. Robot. **8**(89) (2023)
6. Hengst, B.: Reinforcement learning of bipedal lateral behaviour and stability control with ankle-roll activation, pp. 411–418. World Scientific Press (2013)
7. Hofmann, T., Limpert, N., Mataré, V., Ferrein, A., Lakemeyer, G.: Winning the RoboCup logistics league with fast navigation, precise manipulation, and robust goal reasoning. In: Chalup, S., Niemueller, T., Suthakorn, J., Williams, M.-A. (eds.) RoboCup 2019. LNCS (LNAI), vol. 11531, pp. 504–516. Springer, Cham (2019). https://doi.org/10.1007/978-3-030-35699-6_41
8. Lu, W., Sammut, C.: D-flow: a real time spatial temporal model for target area segmentation. In: IEEE-RAS 21st International Conference on Humanoid Robots (Humanoids), Okinawa, Japan (2022)
9. Pomerleau, D.A.: Neural Network Perception for Mobile Robot Guidance. Kluwer Academic Publishers, Boston (1993)
10. Sammut, C., Hurst, S., Kedzier, D., Michie, D.: Learning to fly. In: Sleeman, D., Edwards, P. (eds.) Proceedings of the Ninth International Conference on Machine Learning, pp. 385–393. Morgan Kaufmann, Aberdeen (1992)

An Inductive Logic Programming Approach for Feature-Range Discovery

Daniel Cyrus(✉), Dany Varghese, and Alireza Tamaddoni-Nezhad

University of Surrey, Guildford GU2 7XH, UK
{d.cyrus,dany.varghese,a.tamaddoni-nezhad}@surrey.ac.uk

Abstract. In this paper, we present NumLog, an Inductive Logic Programming (ILP) system designed for feature range discovery. NumLog generates quantitative rules with clear confidence bounds to discover feature-range values from examples. Our approach focuses on generating rules with minimal complexity from numerical values, ensuring the assessment of methods that could impact accuracy and comprehensibility. Traditional ILP systems, especially those intersecting with computer vision, struggle with numerical data. This convergence presents unique challenges, often hindering the generation of meaningful insights due to the limited capabilities of conventional ILP systems to handle numerical values. NumLog stands out by incorporating an advanced range discovery mechanism that generates low-complexity rules while maintaining high accuracy and comprehensibility. This enhancement significantly improves interpretability, promoting more effective human-machine learning collaboration. We compare NumLog with the state-of-the-art ILP systems such as NumSynth and Aleph and conduct comprehensive experiments on several datasets. We evaluated our approach by measuring accuracy, precision, F1 score, and rule complexity to demonstrate the effectiveness of the methodology.

Keywords: Human-Machine Learning · Inductive Logic Programming · Numerical Reasoning · Explainable AI

1 Introduction

Inductive logic programming (ILP), as introduced by Muggleton [15], represents an explainable machine learning approach capable of deriving comprehensible rules from a set of examples. These rules are expressed as logical statements, symbolic and close to natural language, making them relatable and directly readable, which closely mirrors human reasoning processes. Additionally, ILP can seamlessly incorporate existing domain knowledge into its learning process, enhancing learning efficiency and the clarity of how new knowledge is derived. This integration is particularly useful in scenarios where data is scarce or expensive to collect, such as in domains with privacy concerns, enabling ILP to generalise effectively from smaller datasets [21]. The transparency and clarity of the

W.-Z. Dai (Ed.): ILP 2024, LNAI 16059, pp. 203–217, 2026.
https://doi.org/10.1007/978-3-032-09087-4_14

models generated by ILP not only foster trust among users and stakeholders - crucial in sensitive areas like healthcare, finance, and legal advising - but also support ethical AI practices. Moreover, ILP's capability to discover new patterns and regularities in data allows it to contribute to scientific and academic discovery [20], proposing new hypotheses and logical rules that may not have been previously considered.

In the field of Inductive Logic Programming (ILP), certain challenges arise when the system attempts to learn rules involving numerical values from continuous domains. ILP systems excel at handling discrete data and symbolic information, but often struggle with continuous or numerical data, especially from infinite domains [3,4,22]. This limitation stems from the difficulty in formulating generalisable logical rules that can accurately represent and make predictions based on such data.

To tackle the limitations inherent in existing ILP systems, particularly their struggle with handling numerical values from infinite domains, we introduce a novel approach that enhances their capacity to identify and process numeric value ranges. We implement this appraoch in a ILP system called NumLog[1]. Our methodology extends the conventional range of positive and negative examples in ILP systems, thereby enabling the inclusion of a broader spectrum of values from both positive and negative domains. Central to our strategy is the prioritisation of retaining the highest and lowest numerical values within binned data, a tactic aimed at preserving essential information about the extremities in the dataset. This is complemented by the integration of specialised predicates into the hypothesis space of the ILP system. These predicates are designed to capture intricate relationships and patterns in the data, significantly increasing the expressiveness and flexibility of the model. The enriched hypothesis space allows the system to engage more effectively with diverse numerical data distributions, thereby enhancing decision-making capabilities and ensuring robust performance across a variety of scenarios. Through this integrated approach, our ILP system is better equipped to manage and learn from complex numerical inputs, marking a significant advancement in the field.

1.1 Background

Inductive Logic Programming (ILP) [15] is a branch of artificial intelligence focused on deriving hypothesised predicate definitions. ILP uniquely employs logic programs to represent examples, background knowledge, and hypotheses uniformly. Unlike most other machine learning approaches, ILP stands out due to its use of a highly expressive representation language and its capability to utilise logically encoded background knowledge [16]. Finn et al. [7] presented a case study of Pharmacophore Discovery. Their approach was to generate rules to identify potential pharmacophores. Although the method employs numerical reasoning to generate rules, it lacks the ability to identify the range of numerical values.

[1] NumLog:**Num**erical reasoning using **Log**ic programming.

Range Discovery [5,10,14] is a method used to find the maximum and minimum values for each group of positive examples in relation to the nearest negative examples. Range discovery is mostly used to adjust a threshold between positive and negative examples.

2 Related Work

Quantitative Classification based on Associations (QCBA) [13] is a method that represents rules derived from pattern discovery. Its goal is to recover missing information in quantitative yet sparse data. While the approach includes pruning, the resulting rules can still become complex. Additionally, QCBA discretises continuous values, which can lead to a loss of information. In contrast, NumLog addresses both of these issues effectively. TILDE [2] discretises continuous values during the learning process by splitting numerical data based on an optimal criterion. However, this approach does not always align with the true underlying structure of the data. NumLog addresses this issue by retaining the best thresholds between data points for improved accuracy. Aleph Lazy evaluation procedure [17,18] is a technique on numerical reasoning. Lazy evaluation is a programming technique where an expression is not evaluated until its value is actually needed. In Aleph, every definition used in lazy evaluation operates independently, thereby hindering its ability to infer hypotheses involving multiple literals that necessitate shared variables for lazy evaluation, such as upper and lower bounds for a single variable. NUMSYNTH [12] employs satisfiability modulo theories solvers (SMT) to efficiently learn programs with numerical values. The method can identify numerical values in linear arithmetic fragments, such as real difference logic, and from infinite domains, such as real numbers or integers. NUMSYNTH is a library for Popper [4] that leverages the Popper system and lazy evaluation for numerical reasoning. NUMSYNTH's key distinction from NumLog is that it avoids discretisation, but this can lead to difficulties in generalizing to unseen data.

3 Overview of the Methodology

This section provides an overview of our methodology, highlighting the key techniques and processes used to achieve our research objectives. Our methodology focuses on threshold analysis and generalisation of numerical values.

FOL Language. First-Order logic (FOL) includes predicates, quantifiers, and logical connectives to express complex statements about objects and their relationships. Each predicate is associated a certain number of variables/terms. The number of variables/terms associated with a predicate is called $Arity(n)$. If a predicate $\mathcal{P}$ is associated with two entities, we will represent it as $\mathcal{P}/2$. We define a FOL language as an alphabet consisting of sets of predicate symbols $\mathcal{P} = \{P, Q, R, ...\}$, function symbols $\mathcal{F} = \{f, g, h, ...\}$, constants $\mathcal{C} \subseteq \mathcal{F} = \{a, b, c, ...\}$, variables $\mathcal{V} = \{x, y, z, ...\}$, logical connectors $\neg, \wedge, \vee, \rightarrow, \Leftrightarrow$, quantifiers $\exists, \forall$ and punctuation symbols . , (and).

Numerical Reasoning. [6,19] is an approach that allows individuals to analyse and draw conclusions from numerical data, facilitating informed decision-making. The NumLog system employs a dedicated learning algorithm that exclusively explores numerical values. The rules generated by this process are appended to the background knowledge for subsequent program searches using multi-class search. Algorithm 1 delineates the NumLog learning process and its focus on numerical search.

The final hypothesis produced by NumLog is a set of rules structured as $P \leftarrow Q \wedge R$. These rules are represented as

$$r(A) \leftarrow numerical\_feature(A,B), numerical\_range(B,C),$$

where A is the input argument representing an instance with numerical feature B, and C is a constant that indicates the range of the numerical value B.

3.1 Data Preprocessing

In the context of data preprocessing, our method involves sorting values in sequence and removing redundant entries. The system then collects all numerical values and categorise by feature type from background knowledge across all positive (E^+) and negative (E^-) examples into a universal set, which we refer to as U_i.

$$\begin{aligned} \text{Let } E^+ &= \{p(x_1^+), p(x_2^+), ..., p(x_n^+)\} \\ \text{Let } E^- &= \{p(x_1^-), p(x_2^-), ..., p(x_n^-)\} \\ \forall p(x^+)\exists\{\mathrm{f}_1(x^+, v_1^+), \mathrm{f}_2(x^+, v_2^+), ..., \mathrm{f}_n(x^+, v_n^+)\} \\ \forall p(x^-)\exists\{\mathrm{f}_1(x^-, v_1^-), \mathrm{f}_2(x^-, v_2^-), ..., \mathrm{f}_n(x^-, v_n^-)\} \\ U_i = \{v_i^{1\pm}, v_i^{2\pm}, ..., v_i^{n\pm}\} &\text{ such that } v_i^{1\pm} \leq v_i^{2\pm} \leq ... \leq v_i^{n\pm} \end{aligned} \tag{1}$$

Each example p consists of a value x that is associated with a set of features f, where each feature has a numerical value v. All numerical values in U are defined by binning them across the entire range of negative values, effectively grouping positive feature values according to their proximity to negative feature values, resulting in the set we define as $\bar{U}$.

$$\begin{aligned} \text{Let } \bar{U_i} = \{G_i^1, G_i^2, ..., G_i^n\} &\text{ such that } v^- \nexists G_i \text{ and } G_i^j \subset U_i \\ G_i = \{v_i^{j_1}, v_i^{j_2}, ..., v_i^{j_n}\} &\text{ where } v_i^{j_n} < v_i^{j+1_1} \end{aligned} \tag{2}$$

Informal Expression. The Eq. 1 and 2 are utilised to process all values for each feature type. For instance, one feature type includes the positive set {1,2,3,6,7} and negative set {4,5}. These sets are combined and sorted into a set U, thus, $U = \{1, 2, 3, 4, 5, 6, 7\}$. The system then groups them by removing the negative values, resulting in $\bar{U} = \{\{1, 2, 3\}, \{6, 7\}\}$.

3.2 Threshold Analysis

The system supplements each group of feature values G_i by adding additional values. Discrete data can exhibit extensive distribution, leading to the possibility of encountering positive values during assessment. NumLog has the capacity to learn from data with the inclusion of a tolerance value.

$$\mu_i = \frac{1}{n}\Sigma_{i=1}^{n} G_i$$
$$\sigma_i = \sqrt{\frac{\Sigma(G_i^j - \mu_i)^2}{N_i}} \tag{3}$$
$$pdf_i(G_i) = \frac{1}{\sqrt{2\pi\delta_i^2}} \exp^{(-\frac{(v_i^j - \mu_i)^2}{2\delta_i^2})}$$

The Eq. 3 calculates the average μ, standard deviation σ and probability density function *pdf* for each group G. The initial value r_0 is the estimated threshold value between each group G, determined by calculating the average μ for each pair of groups:

$$r_0 = \frac{\mu_i + \mu_{i+1}}{2} \tag{4}$$

Final threshold value calculates by finding the root value R of pair functions *pdf* and initial value r_0, where $R = \{r \in \mathbb{R} | pdf(r) = 0\}$ and r is the value where two *pdf*s are equal:

$$r_k = r_0 + k\epsilon$$
$$pdf_i(r_k) - pdf_{i+1}(r_k) = 0 \tag{5}$$

In the Eq. 5, the value k represents an incremental value that starts from 1 and continues until the root of the function reaches 0. The system determines the threshold point that separates each group G, see Fig. 1.

Informal Expression. For instance, if a bin of positive data consists of numbers *1.2, 1.4, 1.6*, and negative examples *1.7, 1.8* and *1.95*, the analysis introduces a new value, *1.65*, as a threshold. Consequently, the positive group now includes *1.2, 1.4, 1.6*, and *1.65*. Thus a group of positive example G_1 consists of *{1.2,1.4,1.6,1.65}*. The system then concentrates exclusively on the upper and lower bounds of each bin, incorporating these bounds directly as literals into the new dataset. Thus the first group of positive feature value includes *{1.2,1.65}*,

3.3 Generalisation on Numerical Values

Generalizing numerical values entails identifying broader patterns or principles that apply to a dataset. This process relies on analyzing the dataset's patterns and distribution [1,8]. We combine each group of distributions by assessing the overlap of their normal distributions and the quantity of data in each group [9,11]. Calculating $x_i \sim \mathcal{N}(\mu, \delta^2)$ indicates that the data points x_i follow an approximate normal distribution $\mathcal{N}$ with mean μ and variance δ^2, implying that the data tends to cluster around the mean with a narrow range of values, see Fig. 2. By measuring the overlap of normal distributions and the quantity of data in each group, we can effectively combine groups of distributions. This generalisation process reduces the number of groups by merging similar ones. The resulting consolidated group can then be utilised for ILP approaches, enhancing the efficiency and accuracy of the analysis.

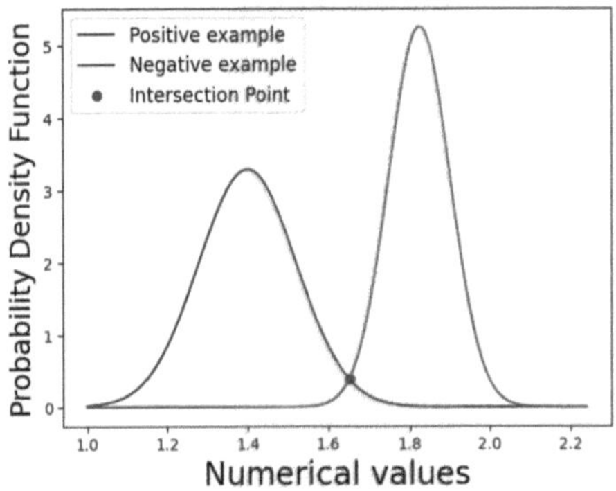

Fig. 1. The Figure illustrates an instance of a threshold separating two sets of positive and negative feature values. Positive values fall within the range of *1.2–1.6*, while negatives are within the range of *1.7–1.95*. The threshold value is *1.65514*

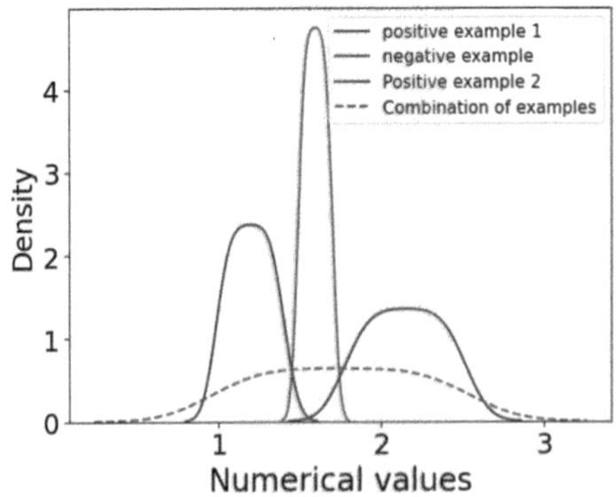

Fig. 2. Combining numerical feature values based on their distributions. The graph illustrates how closely clustered negative distribution can be merged with other positive distributions

$$\mathcal{T} = \frac{(max(U_i) - min(U_i)}{\epsilon}$$
$$C' = \frac{(\frac{Max(G_i^n) - min(G_i^n)}{\epsilon})}{\mathcal{T}} \quad (6)$$
$$l = \frac{|U_i|}{|G_i^n|}$$

where $\mathcal{T}$ denotes the normalised size of all feature values and C' is the normalised feature size for specific group of values. We define the combination value $\mathcal{C}$ to determine if a group of values can be combined by verifying if $\mathcal{C} < C'$ and $\mathcal{C} \geq l$.

4 NumLog Algorithm

NumLog accepts a tuple as its input, $(E^+, E^-, \mathcal{M}, \mathcal{C})$, where E^+ and E^- are positive and negative examples respectively. The value $\mathcal{M}$ defines maximum number of clauses, generated in final hypothesis and $\mathcal{C}$ is the combination value (Refer Sect. 3.3). The epsilon value ϵ is used for three purposes: first, to determine the density of two points in a normal distribution; second, to set the minimum threshold between two groups of examples; and third, to represent the allowable error in the approximation of the root, defined as $|f(x)| < \epsilon$. The ϵ value is adjusted on each learning iteration using minimum gap δ between samples by the equation $\epsilon \leftarrow min(\epsilon, \delta_i)$. The learning process of NumLog is illustrated in Algorithm 1.

4.1 Background Knowledge

In this section, we define the background knowledge and hypothesis space used in NumLog. We utilise specific functions and notations to represent constraints and relationships between input values and constants. Let A denote the input value and B and C denote the constants. We define three primary functions to capture the relationships between parameters (Table 1):

Table 1. Function Definitions

Function	Mathematical definition	Description
leq(A, B)	$A \leq B$	A is less than or equal to B
geq(A, B)	$A \geq B$	A is greater than or equal to B
inRange($A, B \pm$ D)	$B - D \leq A \leq B + D$	A is within the range

Algorithm 1: NumLog (E^+, E^-, $\mathcal{M}$, $\mathcal{C}$)

Data: Positive examples E^+, negative examples E^-, max number of clauses $\mathcal{M}$, and merging value $\mathcal{C}$
Result: Hypothesis ($\mathcal{H}$) to explain numerical ranges
$H \leftarrow \varnothing$;
sorted(E^+), sorted(E^-);
$U \leftarrow append(E^+, E^-)$;
$\epsilon \leftarrow 100$; `// Initial value for epsilon`
for $i = 0$ *to* $n - 1$ **do**
  $\delta_i \leftarrow U[i+1] - U[i]$;
  $\epsilon \leftarrow \min(\epsilon, \delta_i)$;
end
$\bar{U} \leftarrow U - (U \cap E^-)$; `// Group examples by removing negative values`
foreach $G \in \bar{U}$ **do**
  $G_i \leftarrow$ Abduce values using Eq. 5 and ϵ;
end
$\bar{U} \leftarrow$ Generalize values from $\bar{U}$ using Eq. 6 and $\mathcal{C}$;
$\bar{H} \leftarrow [BK, \bar{G}_i]$; `// For each group` $\bar{G}_i$ `in` $\bar{U}$`, generate literal using BK`
Generate all possible rules ($\mathcal{R}$) from $\bar{H}$ using Eq. 7;
foreach $\mathcal{R}$ **do**
  prove($\mathcal{R}_i$);
  if *accuracy($\mathcal{R}_i$) is the best accuracy* **then**
    Add $\mathcal{R}_i$ to h;
  end
end
Find the best hypothesis with respect to $\mathcal{C}$;
Evaluate each $\mathcal{R}_i$ from h;
Select the best hypothesis $\mathcal{H}$ from h;
return $\mathcal{H}$;

4.2 Complexity of Rules

The complexity of a rule can be defined by the user, depending on the specific requirements of the application. The complexity might be influenced by the number of conditions, the types of relationships, and the logical operations used to combine these conditions.

$$\text{Combinations} = \bigcup_{N=0}^{\text{MaxLength}} \text{combinations}(N, \text{List}) \tag{7}$$

$\bigcup$ represents the union of all these sets for N ranging from 0 to MaxLength.

4.3 Hypothesis Space

The hypothesis space is defined by the combination of constraints and conditions that can be applied to the input values. We denote the hypothesis space by $\mathcal{H}$, which is a combination of the constraints defined above. The set of all possible hypotheses can be represented as:

$$\mathcal{H} = \{h \mid h = \text{feature}/2 \wedge \text{leq}/2 \vee \text{geq}/2 \vee \text{inRange}/2\} \tag{8}$$

The specific hypothesis chosen from this space can be tailored by adjusting the parameters as per the requirements of the problem. By defining the hypothesis space in this structured manner, we can systematically explore the possible rules and constraints that apply to our input values, ensuring a comprehensive analysis of the problem domain.

5 Experiments

In our study, we apply our methods to the breast cancer [23] and pharmacophores datasets [12]. The breast cancer dataset is a well-established benchmark for classification tasks. It includes a diverse array of numerical features obtained from real-world medical diagnoses, offering a solid basis for testing algorithms that emphasize numerical reasoning and classification. Moreover, the dataset's balanced distribution of positive and negative cases, combined with its straightforward binary outcome, makes it an excellent platform for assessing the performance of our system in processing medical data and generating interpretable hypotheses.

Pharmacophores are structural features in a molecule that interact with a receptor site, influencing biological activity. A pharmacophore model identifies the spatial arrangement of these critical features, aiding drug discovery by pinpointing compounds with similar structures and potential effects. In 3D, it highlights essential attributes like functional groups and hydrogen bond donors or acceptors, with precise distances between them crucial for effective binding.

Our approach improves Inductive Logic Programming (ILP) systems by enabling more effective processing and learning from numerical data in these interactions. The experiments are structured to assess the effectiveness of our proposed ILP-based method, as outlined in the previous section. To achieve this, we test several null hypotheses, which serve as baseline assumptions, asserting that our ILP-based approach yields no significant effects or improvements. By evaluating these null hypotheses, we aim to rigorously assess the validity and performance of our method, ensuring a thorough evaluation of the proposed approach.

Null Hypothesis 1. NumLog is unable to effectively learn from numerical values using ILP and generalisation approaches.

Null Hypothesis 2. Expanding numerical examples by incorporating new values through threshold analysis does not yield significant improvements in accuracy.

Null Hypothesis 3. The clause inRange/2, alongside leq/2 and geq/2, does not contribute to reducing the complexity of the rule.

In Our first experiment we usilised breast cancer dataset including *569* records. We select *100* random samples for the test set, comprising *50* positive examples and *50* negative examples. Our training set starts with *0* samples, increasing by *20* samples each time up to *100* examples, in addition to a final set with *200* samples, see Fig. 3.
Listing 1.1 presents a generalised sample rule indicating that entity A is classified as having cancer if its worst fractal dimension falls within the range of approximately *0.0904* and its worst area is less than *1032.30447*.

Listing 1.1. Learned rule generated by NumLog from iris breast cancer dataset

```
cancer(A) ← worst_fractal_dimension(A,B),
                inRange(B,0.09048 ± 0.03544),
                worst_area(A,C),leq(C,1032.30447).
```

Table 2. We claimed that our approach generate lowest complexity on rule generating. The table shows the rule complexity for either number of literals and number of disjoint rules

Number of Examples	Average Number of Rules		
	Aleph	NumSynth	NumLog
20	2	1.2	**1**
40	3.2	1.8	**1**
60	4	2.8	**1**
80	6.2	6	**1.6**
100	6.2	5.6	**1.6**
200	10.4	6.4	**1.8**

In our second experiment, we utilised the Pharmacophore dataset from the study by C. Hocquette et al. [12], which is explained and structured according to the work of P. Finn et al. [7]. We enriched the data with additional grounded background knowledge, particularly incorporating distances between each feature. This augmented dataset served as the basis for constructing pharmacophores, which are spatial arrangements of molecular features.

Listing 1.2 displays a generalised rule suggesting that atom A exhibits the trait of a hydrogen bond acceptor, in conjunction with zinc, at a distance of *14.2494* units, with a minimum and maximum range of *0.212* units.

Listing 1.2. Learned rule generated by NumLog from pharma dataset

```
active(A) ← hacc_zincsite_distance(A,B),
              inRange(B, 14.249 ± 0.212).
```

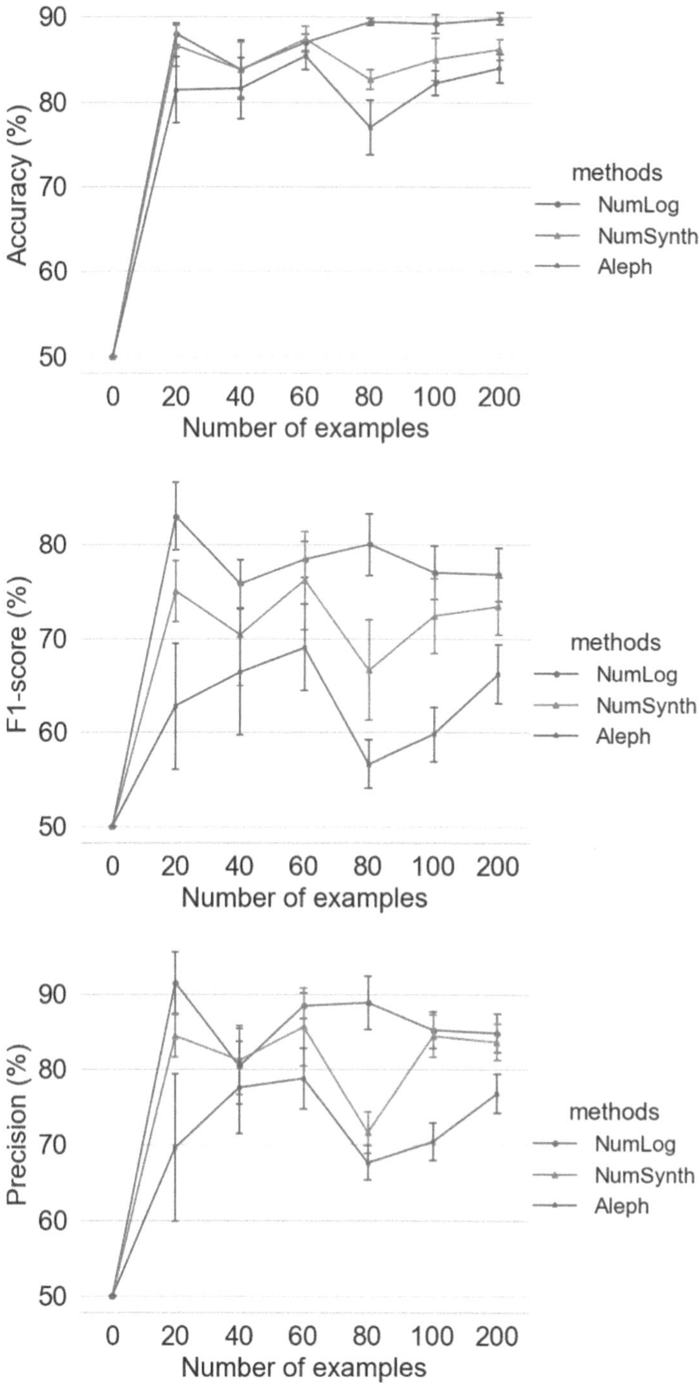

Fig. 3. Comparison of Accuracy, F1 score and Precision metrics across different models

We assess the accuracy of our work using NumSynth and Aleph, following the same training set approach as outlined in [12]. Specifically, we use *60* negative and *60* positive examples. The results are presented in Table 3. As indicated in Listing 1.2 and 1.1, NumLog is capable of learning from numerical values, and the inclusion of a single clause inRange aids in reducing the complexity of the rule. Consequently, Null Hypotheses 1 and 3 are refuted. Furthermore, Table 3 and Fig. 3 illustrates that our system achieves commendable accuracy in learning. Therefore, Null Hypothesis 2 is rejected.

Table 3. Rounded accuracy to integer values with standard error. Aleph and Numsynth accuracy value given from [12]

Tasks	Aleph	NumSynth	NumLog
pharma1	82 ± 1	99 ± 0	99 ± 0
pharma2	83 ± 1	95 ± 1	**99 ± 0**
pharma3	81 ± 1	98 ± 1	**99 ± 0**
pharma4	76 ± 1	92 ± 1	**95 ± 2**

5.1 Results and Discussion

The ultimate goal of NumLog is to reduce the complexity of the rules it generates. This entails choosing the most straightforward set of rules that sufficiently describe the data, avoiding overfitting and unnecessary intricacies. Conversely, NumLog places a high value on making the generated rules easy to interpret and understand, see Table 2. Although NumLog demonstrates proficient learning capabilities with numerical values, even in the presence of noise and sparse data, its effectiveness may be compromised when dealing with datasets characterised by high levels of noise and sparsity. The current iteration of NumLog is specifically tailored for learning within first-order logic using numerical data. To extend its applicability to higher-order logic programming and datasets lacking grounded background knowledge, NumLog may need to be adapted and integrated with other ILP systems. This adaptation would enhance its robustness and effectiveness in a broader range of applications. By organising and abducting values within each group, the system generates all potential hypotheses. However, due to computational constraints, NumLog aims to identify the most accurate rule, which may result in a lack of completeness and consistency.

6 Conclusion

In conclusion, this paper has presented an innovative approach to numerical reasoning through the application of NumLog coupled with threshold analysis and diverse sets of positive and negative examples. By leveraging NumLog's capabilities, we have demonstrated the effectiveness of this methodology in handling numerical data and extracting meaningful insights. Through rigorous experimentation and analysis, we have showcased how the careful selection of thresholds and the incorporation of varied examples enrich the learning process and improve the accuracy of classification tasks. Furthermore, by addressing the challenges of rule complexity and redundant information, we have enhanced the efficiency and practicality of the proposed framework. Overall, this research contributes to the advancement of numerical reasoning techniques and underscores the potential of integrating symbolic and statistical methods for tackling real-world problems in diverse domains.

7 Future Work

In future work, we plan to enhance the NumLog system by incorporating Support Vector Machine Inductive Logic Programming (SVILP). This integration aims to leverage the strengths of SVILP in handling both classification and regression tasks, using declarative background knowledge to provide learning bias. Specifically, we will focus on comparing the performance of NumLog with SVILP against several established approaches. We will evaluate NumLog's performance against the histogram-based binning method introduced by D. Varghese [20,22]. This method organises numerical data into bins or intervals, enabling the identification of patterns, outliers, and overall data distribution. By comparing these techniques, we aim to assess the effectiveness of NumLog in handling continuous numerical data. We will integrate SVILP, as described by Muggleton [16], into NumLog. SVILP combines SVM and ILP, providing a learning bias through declarative background knowledge. We will test NumLog's ability to handle numerical data within this framework and compare its performance to other SVM-based methods. The current version of NumLog generates deterministic rules. In the future, we plan to incorporate a feature that allows the system to learn from features with multiple numerical values, enabling it to produce non-deterministic rules.

Acknowldegement. The first author acknowledges the PhD scholarship from the EPSRC and the University of Surrey. The authors acknowledge the EPSRC grant on human-machine learning of ambiguities. The third author acknowledges the EPSRC Network Plus grant on Human-Like Computing (HLC). We acknowledge Dr. Céline Hocquette for her comments and feedback on this work.

Supplementary Material. We have provided supplementary material on GitHub https://github.com/hmlr-lab/NumericalReasoning to accompany NumLog. Codes are implemented in Prolog, offering a valuable resource for researchers and practitioners interested in exploring and extending our work. This repository contains comprehensive documentation, including detailed explanations of NumLog's functionalities, usage examples, and guidelines for integration into other projects.

References

1. Bishop, C.M.: Pattern recognition and machine learning by Christopher M. Bishop. Springer Science+ Business Media, LLC (2006)
2. Blockeel, H., De Raedt, L.: Lookahead and discretization in ILP. In: Lavrač, N., Džeroski, S. (eds.) ILP 1997. LNCS, vol. 1297, pp. 77–84. Springer, Heidelberg (1997). https://doi.org/10.1007/3540635149_36
3. Corapi, D., Russo, A., Lupu, E.: Inductive logic programming in answer set programming. In: Muggleton, S.H., Tamaddoni-Nezhad, A., Lisi, F.A. (eds.) ILP 2011. LNCS (LNAI), vol. 7207, pp. 91–97. Springer, Heidelberg (2012). https://doi.org/10.1007/978-3-642-31951-8_12
4. Cropper, A., Morel, R.: Learning programs by learning from failures. Mach. Learn. **110**(4), 801–856 (2021). https://doi.org/10.1007/s10994-020-05934-z
5. Danbold, F., Unzueta, M.M.: Drawing the diversity line: numerical thresholds of diversity vary by group status. J. Pers. Soc. Psychol. **118**(2), 283 (2020)
6. Demšar, D., Gams, M.: Implementing numerical reasoning in ILP. IPSI BgD Trans Internet Res. 40 (2006)
7. Finn, P., Muggleton, S., Page, D., Srinivasan, A.: Pharmacophore discovery using the inductive logic programming system progol. Mach. Learn. **30**, 241–270 (1998)
8. Friedman, J.: The elements of statistical learning: Data mining, inference, and prediction. (No Title) (2009)
9. Grice, J.W., Barrett, P.T.: A note on Cohen's overlapping proportions of normal distributions. Psychol. Rep. **115**(3), 741–747 (2014)
10. Hastie, T., Tibshirani, R., Friedman, J.: The Elements of Statistical Learning: Data Mining, Inference, and Prediction. Springer, Cham (2009)
11. Hill, T.P., Miller, J.: How to combine independent data sets for the same quantity. Chaos: Interdisciplinary J Nonlinear Sci **21**(3) (2011)
12. Hocquette, C., Cropper, A.: Relational program synthesis with numerical reasoning. In: Proceedings of the AAAI Conference on Artificial Intelligence, vol. 37, pp. 6425–6433 (2023)
13. Kliegr, T., Izquierdo, E.: QCBA: improving rule classifiers learned from quantitative data by recovering information lost by discretisation. Appl. Intell. **53**(18), 20797–20827 (2023)
14. Morrison, J.A., Shamos, M.H.: Intersection of normal distributions: theory and applications. J. Stat. Theory Appl. **3**(2), 123–145 (2005)
15. Muggleton, S.: Inductive logic programming. New Gener. Comput. **8**, 295–318 (1991)
16. Muggleton, S., Lodhi, H., Amini, A., Sternberg, M.J.E.: Support vector inductive logic programming. In: Hoffmann, A., Motoda, H., Scheffer, T. (eds.) DS 2005. LNCS (LNAI), vol. 3735, pp. 163–175. Springer, Heidelberg (2005). https://doi.org/10.1007/11563983_15
17. Srinivasan, A.: The aleph manual (2001)
18. Srinivasan, A., Camacho, R.: Experiments in numerical reasoning with inductive logic programming. J. Logic Prog. (1997)
19. Srinivasan, A., Camacho, R.: Numerical reasoning with an ILP system capable of lazy evaluation and customised search. J. Logic Prog. **40**(2–3), 185–213 (1999)
20. Varghese, D., Barroso-Bergada, D., Bohan, D.A., Tamaddoni-Nezhad, A.: Efficient abductive learning of microbial interactions using meta inverse entailment. In: International Conference on Inductive Logic Programming, pp. 127–141. Springer, Cham (2022). https://doi.org/10.1007/978-3-031-55630-2_10

21. Varghese, D., Bauer, R., Baxter-Beard, D., Muggleton, S., Tamaddoni-Nezhad, A.: Human-like rule learning from images using one-shot hypothesis derivation. In: International Conference on Inductive Logic Programming, pp. 234–250 (2021)
22. Varghese, D., Bauer, R., Tamaddoni-Nezhad, A.: Few-shot learning of diagnostic rules for neurodegenerative diseases using inductive logic programming. In: International Conference on Inductive Logic Programming, pp. 109–123 (2023)
23. Wolberg, William, M.O.S.N., Street, W.: Breast Cancer Wisconsin (Diagnostic). UCI Machine Learning Repository (1995), https://doi.org/10.24432/C5DW2B

Language-Agnostic Semantics for Implicit Learning as Reasoning: Extended Abstract

Vaishak Belle(✉)

University of Edinburgh, Edinburgh EH8 9AB, UK
vaishak@ed.ac.uk

Abstract. We consider the problem of answering queries about formulas of a logical language, based on background knowledge partially represented explicitly as other formulas, and partially represented as examples. Many approaches to this problem have been considered to date, perhaps the most popular among them is the inductive logic programming (ILP) paradigm based on logic programming. PAC semantics, introduced by Valiant, is one such proposal too, based on examples independently drawn from a fixed probability distribution, possibly unknown. However, with ILP, one has to make careful assumptions about the hypothesis space for it to be learned. And with PAC-semantics, most results are discouraging, mainly owing to the very general assumptions behind the learned knowledge base.

One recent thread, however, in the PAC-semantics approach considers the idea of implicit learning, where an explicit hypothesis is not constructed, but the observations alone are used to answer the queries. In this work, taking inspiration from that approach, we tease apart a simple semantical setup that allows us to discuss the learning of an implicit hypothesis from examples to answer queries. This yields a language-agnostic framework, potentially allowing it to be useful for a variety of formal languages, from propositional logic to first-order logic to possibly even modal logic.

1 Introduction

The tension between deduction and induction is perhaps the most fundamental issue in areas such as philosophy, cognition and artificial intelligence. The deduction camp concerns itself with questions about the expressiveness of formal languages for capturing knowledge about the world, together with proof systems for reasoning from such knowledge bases [12]. The learning camp attempts to generalize from examples about partial descriptions about the world [19]. This leads to the holy-grail problem in logic and learning: that of answering queries about formulas of a logical language, based on background knowledge partially represented explicitly as other formulas, and partially represented as examples.

Many approaches to this problem have been considered to date, perhaps the most popular among them is the inductive logic programming (ILP) paradigm based on logic

The author is grateful to the Royal Society for financial support.

W.-Z. Dai (Ed.): ILP 2024, LNAI 16059, pp. 218–227, 2026.
https://doi.org/10.1007/978-3-032-09087-4_15

programming [16]. In this paradigm, the goal is to learn a hypothesis from given examples that, when combined with background knowledge, logically entails all of the examples. The hypothesis should represent a generalized pattern, often in the form of a quantified formula, from a set of ground atoms. The classical paradigm has enjoyed many extensions, including the use of neural techniques [8], and weakening the requirement for the hypothesis to only capture only a subset of examples defined by, for example, a probability distribution [18].

In an influential paper, Valiant [20] recognized that the challenge of learning should be integrated with deduction. In particular, he proposed a semantics to capture the quality possessed by the output of (probably approximately correct) PAC-learning algorithms when formulated in a logic. Although weaker than classical entailment, it allows for a powerful framework for answering queries. Unfortunately, from the standpoint of learning an expressive logical knowledge base and reasoning with it, most PAC results are discouraging. It turns out that the rigorous definition of PAC semantics, which allows us to model the idea that the data could be drawn from arbitrary unknown distributions, makes learning hard. In fact, it is likely that even learning DNF formulas is hard [5, 11].[1]

Recently, Juba [10] observed that by using examples directly to check the entailment of a query, we can eliminate the need to construct an explicit hypothesis, leading to the notion of "implicit learning". This has now been extended to multiple languages beyond propositional logic, such as universally quantified first-order formulas [2], and quantifier-free linear arithmetic formulas [14]. However, this framework is also defined in terms of distributions on the models in the language, which means that each of these results needs to be carefully extended for a new language. On one hand, it allows for arbitrary distributions that we sample observations from, as well as for these observations to be noisy, but on the other hand, this also means that results can be difficult to prove for other fragments of first-order logics, non-classical logics, or modal logics. They are likely also difficult to implement, as evidenced by [17] – the first implementation of the PAC-semantics implicit learning framework. Moreover, the number of samples needed to guarantee that we have robustly learned may be too high for many real-world settings.

In this paper, our goal is to take a simplified version of these PAC-semantics results and develop a semantics and a framework for introducing the concept of implicit learning in a logic. By focusing on noise-free learning in the first instance, we are able to simplify the spirit of the proposal and look to apply it to a variety of logical languages. This yields a language-agnostic framework, potentially allowing it to be useful for a variety of formal languages, from propositional logic to first-order logic to possibly even modal logic. Owing to space reasons, we will focus only on the propositional fragment here, which provides an overview of how the algorithm is set up. We will briefly discuss what other extensions might look like, and leave it for an extended report.

[1] There are also approaches that are not based on examples being entailed by a hypothesis, but instead look at the probabilistic fit of the hypothesis with respect to the data. For example, there are techniques in statistical relational learning based on likelihood measures [19]. We gloss over these types of techniques in this paper.

What is also worth noting is that we do not characterize the correctness of learnability against arbitrary (unknown) distributions as done with PAC-semantics results [5], but against just the data that is observed, very much in the spirit of ILP. So this proposal sits between the benefits of the two learning paradigms. On the one hand, we are interested a hypothesis that simply characterizes the observations (a la ILP), which makes it simpler to discuss the correctness of learning, but on the other hand, we do not construct an explicit hypothesis at all (a la implicit learning).[2]

We believe that our results are not limited to noise-free settings as we can adapt the idea to account for, say, a ratio-based measure of correctness, similar to, say, probabilistic ILP [7]. In other words, our approach could focus on constructing an implicit hypothesis that does not necessarily capture every observation, but rather entails a significant majority. We plan to explore this direction further in the future.

2 Formal Environment

We define a logical language and a semantics in a general and agnostic way, i.e. not specifying the meaning of sentences but assuming they are interpreted wrt some set of structures. Let $\mathcal{L}$ be a language defined over finite or possibly infinitely many atoms, $\mathcal{A}$, and let $\mathcal{M}$ be the set of models that interpret the atoms $\mathcal{A}$. That is, for every $a \in \mathcal{A}$ and $M \in \mathcal{M}$, $M[a] \in \{0, 1\}$.

We assume that well-defined formulas can be constructed from $\mathcal{A}$ and the Boolean connectives in $\mathcal{L}$, such that we can inductively provide a semantics for every $\varphi \in \mathcal{L}$. In particular, given that $M \in \mathcal{M}$ provides a truth value for every atom $a \in \mathcal{A}$, by extension we assume that for every $\varphi \in \mathcal{L}$, $M[\varphi] \in \{0, 1\}$.

A theory $\mathcal{T}$ is a triple $(\mathcal{L}, \mathcal{M}, \models)$, where $\mathcal{L}$ is a set of sentences called the language of the theory, $\mathcal{M}$ a set called the models of the theory, and $\models$ a subset of $\mathcal{M} \times \mathcal{L}$ called the *satisfiability* relation.

For $\varphi \in \mathcal{L}$ and $M \in \mathcal{M}$, we write $M \models \varphi$ to say that M satisfies φ, that is, $M[\varphi] = 1$. We say a formula φ is *valid* iff φ is satisfied at every model, which is then written as $\models \varphi$. We let $M(\phi)$ denote $\{M \in \mathcal{M} | M \models \phi\}$.

2.1 Explicit Learning

The idea now is that, given some background theory and observations – essentially models – we are expected to induce a hypothesis captured by the models. Then, we are to check whether the background and the hypothesis entail a formula of interest, which we will refer to as a *query*.

Classically, in the explicit learning paradigm as seen in inductive logic programming [16], what we want is to guess a hypothesis from a reasonable hypothesis space such that the following properties are true:

- On the one hand, the background knowledge and the hypothesis entails the examples; and

[2] Note: One can apply PAC-type guarantees to approaches such as inductive logic programming by characterizing the number of examples needed to justify the hypothesis [6]. Such results could carry over to the implicit setting we propose in this work too, with some effort.

- on the other, that every observation is a model of the hypothesis (cf. learning from interpretations in [4]).

We will now provide an account without formulating an explicit hypothesis.

2.2 Partial Observations

The simplest idea of learning from interpretations is to assume that the observations are simply elements of the set of models $\mathcal{M}$.[3] However, in the real world, observations coming from sensors and other sources often provide only a partial view of the world [1]. Especially in first-order settings and other infinitary languages, models may define truth-values for infinitely many atoms. In these cases, we cannot expect observations to be such objects, but only to refer to a finite subset of the truth valuations in them.

Taking inspiration from [13], we define the notion of a *masking process* that basically hides aspects of models. It only reveals the truth-values for a subset, possibly a finite subset, of the atoms.

Notationally, let $\circ$ be a masking process. Recall that $M \in \mathcal{M}$ determines the value of every atom in $\mathcal{L}$. Then we would let M° determine the value of a subset of atoms such that for this subset M° and M agree.

More precisely, given the set of atoms $\mathcal{A}$ of $\mathcal{L}$, we let $\circ \subseteq \mathcal{A}$. Abusing notation, for any $M \in \mathcal{M}$, we define M° as follows:

- for every $a \in \circ$, $M^{\circ}[a] = M[a]$;
- for every $a \notin \circ$, $M^{\circ}[a] = -1$.

So the truth value is undefined for every $a \notin \circ$. Essentially, our knowledge of the world will be obtained from a set of partial models that are the examples. This will then constitute the hypothesis.

We will assume henceforth that when we speak of observations, we mean these to be partial observations – that is, $o_1 = M_1^{\circ}, \ldots, o_n = M_n^{\circ}$ – and the masking function is unknown. Moreover, these observations are assumed to be consistent with the background knowledge B. That is, $B \wedge o_i$ is satisfiable in $\mathcal{L}$, for every i.[4]

3 Learning Framework

Now we are ready to define the learning procedure, and justify the conditions under which it is correct.

[3] We interchangeably refer to examples as observations or as (partial) models.

[4] We will assume that the observations can be written down as formulas. Certainly in a propositional language over a finite vocabulary, partial models can be expressed as a conjunction of the atoms true at the model.

3.1 Algorithm

For input, we are given a query ϕ and a set of observations – that is, partial models – $o_1, \ldots, o_n$, as well as $B \in \mathcal{L}$. Classically, as mentioned above, we would learn a hypothesis that captures the examples. We would then be interested to know whether the hypothesis together with the background theory entails the query. Procedurally, we have:

- **Input:** $B, \phi, o_1, \ldots, o_n$
- **Guess** H such that $B \wedge H \models o_i$ for every i
- **Return** TRUE **if** $B \wedge H \models \phi$ **Else Return** FALSE

The key idea of implicit learning [2, 10] is to avoid constructing the hypothesis H by simply checking whether ϕ is entailed by the observations directly. The justifications for the correctness of those works are different, however, because they are based on distributions on the set of models and the number of samples needed to provably capture the probability space. We will adapt that idea but will require a different flavor of justification for the correctness of the approach. In our approach, given background knowledge $B \in \mathcal{L}$, we determine if $B \wedge o_i \models \phi$ for every i. If it is, then we say that ϕ is entailed by the background knowledge B and the implicitly learned hypothesis.

Concretely, our procedure looks like this:

- **Input:** $B, \phi, o_1, \ldots, o_n$
- **Return** TRUE **if** $B \wedge o_i \models \phi$ for every i; **Else Return** FALSE

We will now argue for the correctness of this algorithm wrt soundness and completeness separately. Note that there are three reasons to iterate over each observation separately in the second line rather than consider the conjunction. Firstly, observations correspond to partial models and a conjunction over these partial models does not have to be satisfiable. For example, suppose we have the formula $p \vee q$, and consider two models of that formula: $M_1 \models p \wedge q$ and $M_2 \models p \wedge \neg q$. It is not the case that $M_1 \wedge M_2$ is satisfiable, although both M_1 and M_2 satisfy $p \vee q$ and p.

Second, when allowing for (probabilistic) noise, observations may be corrupted, in which case the truth values of some atoms may be corrupted [2]. In this case, repeated observations that refer to the same model may not be consistent with each other. In a robotic setting, this often corresponds to getting different measurements of the sonar sensor even though a robot has not moved [1]. (We leave a treatment of probabilistic noise for the future.)

The final reason for iterating over each observation separately is when we induce a hypothesis that "generalizes" across the observations – for example, in a quantified setting such as first-order logic. Here, the hypothesis may introduce quantifiers, and we will want to ensure that when limited to the constants from a particular observation [4], the (ground) hypothesis is entailed by the observation. Otherwise, (atomic) observations would surely not entail the quantified formula over an arbitrary domain of quantification. That is, from $P(a)$ we want to induce $\forall x P(x)$, and if the domain is just the single constant a, then $P(a) \models \forall x P(x)$. We return to this point subsequently.

3.2 Correctness: Soundness

The proof of correctness is as follows. What we want to show is that the formulas entailed by the explicit approach is precisely those captured by the implicit approach. Note that for this proof to work, we have to place some assumptions on the explicit approach, which we will discuss below.

Consistency of Observations. Firstly, by assumption, the observations must also be consistent with the background knowledge. Otherwise, the union of the background knowledge and the hypothesis would be inconsistent. So, $B \wedge o_i$ is satisfiable for every i.

Learning by Entailment. Suppose we were to construct an explicit hypothesis H in the style of, for example, inductive logic programming. Let H be such a hypothesis. When considering the "learning by entailment" paradigm [4], $B \wedge H$ entails every observation. That is, $B \wedge H \models o_i$, for every i.

Stipulations for Soundness. In sum, we have the following stipulation with respect to the background knowledge hypothesis and examples: $B \wedge o_i$ is satisfiable, and $B \wedge H \models o_i, \forall i$.

We are now in a position to claim the soundness of using the implicit learning approach.

Theorem: For any $\phi \in \mathcal{L}$, if $B \wedge o_i \models \phi, \forall i$, **then** $B \wedge H \models \phi$.

That is, if we obtain success using the implicit algorithm, then we will also obtain success with the explicit algorithm.

Proof: Suppose the condition is true, but the consequent is not. That is, $B \wedge H \not\models \phi$. This must mean $B \wedge H \wedge \neg\phi$ is satisfiable. Using the stated stipulations, it must also follow that $B \wedge o_i \wedge \neg\phi$ is satisfiable. This contradicts the assumption that $B \wedge o_i \models \phi$. □

3.3 Correctness: Completeness

For the proof of completeness we have to complement our stipulation above by ensuring that the observations completely capture the hypothesis, and there is no additional knowledge in the hypothesis.

Learning from Interpretations. For the hypothesis H to be captured implicitly, we must also borrow the stipulation from the "learning from interpretations" paradigm [4], and insist that each observation o_i is a model of $H \wedge B$. This ensures that the observations are capturing the knowledge in the assumed hypothesis. Moreover, because we are dealing with partial interpretations in this paper [6], we could consider the notion that given a partial model o_i, there must be extension of o_i to a full interpretation $M_i \in \mathcal{M}$ such that $M_i \models H \wedge B$.[5] In other words, $o_i \wedge H \wedge B$ is satisfiable for every i.

[5] It is interesting to contrast our results with the work in [6]. In that work, various reductions and relationships are established between "learning from interpretations" and "learning from entailment" in the context of explicit learning. Often, these results are under further stipulations on the language. What we propose in this work, in contrast, is a combination of the two paradigms – learning from interpretations vs from entailments –and providing justification for why implicit learning captures learnability.

Nonetheless, the stipulations above are too weak for us to be using the observations in place of the hypothesis. The hypothesis could be much more general than as captured by the observations. Therefore, we provide a slight variant of the condition from [6] in suggesting that the hypothesis logically follows from every observation, relative to the background theory.[6] The idea here is that the hypothesis captures exactly the examples and nothing more.

Stipulations for Completeness. In sum, we have the following two stipulations with respect to the background knowledge hypothesis and examples:

1. $B \wedge H \models o_i$ for every i; and
2. $B \wedge o_i \models H$ for every i.

We are now in a position to claim the completeness of using the implicit learning approach.

Theorem: For any $\phi \in \mathcal{L}$, if $B \wedge H \models \phi$ **then** $B \wedge o_i \models \phi$, $\forall i$.

That is, if we obtain success using the explicit algorithm, then we will also obtain success with the implicit algorithm.

Proof: Suppose the condition is true, but the consequent is not. That is, $B \wedge o_i \not\models \phi$. This must mean $B \wedge o_i \wedge \neg\phi$ is satisfiable. Using stipulation (2), it must also follow that $B \wedge H \wedge \neg\phi$ is satisfiable. This contradicts the condition $B \wedge H \models \phi$. □

We will now discuss the application of this framework (and slight modifications thereof) in a few different settings and show that it works as expected. Let us consider three propositions $\{p, q, t\}$.

Suppose we have an empty background theory, and suppose we have two observations: $o_0 = \{p, q\}$ and $o_1 = \{p, \neg q\}$.

Presumably, the masking process is not revealing anything about the proposition t, but beyond that, the observations correspond to partial models, which means that they have to reveal the truth of every proposition in a model outside of those hidden by the masking process.

It is not hard to see that a reasonable (explicit) hypothesis here would be p, and so the query p as well as the query $p \vee q$ are entailed. Suppose now we receive an additional observation: $o_2 = \{\neg p, q\}$.

It is clear that the explicit hypothesis in this case should be $p \vee q$, and not p. Using the implicit framework, the query $p \vee q$ is entailed, as well as $p \vee q \vee t$, but not p, as desired.

4 Implications and Discussion

It worth reflecting on what exactly this result has achieved and what its implications are. Some readers might wonder if it is not the case that simply conjoining the observations is an obvious exercise. That is, some may argue that it is not really a type of learning.

[6] Such a stronger requirement was stipulated in [9].

Firstly, as can be seen, conjoining the observations would lead to an unsatisfiable formula. So we have to iterate over each observation individually. Moreover, as we show in the proof of correctness, it is indeed a kind of learning, and in fact, at least as far as soundness goes, it very much captures the spirit of learning by entailment. For completeness, we can then also see it as a combination of learning by entailment and learning by interpretations. One way to think about our result is to imagine that we have an appropriate hypothesis space and provided a hypothesis from this space captures the observations in the way we have stipulated, constructing the hypothesis is not really needed because our procedure involving just the observations captures that hypothesis exactly.

Nonetheless, the downside of keeping around the observations and building a procedure with them is that it can be prohibitive when the number of observations are large. In contrast, with a hypothesis, we have an interpretable representation in hand. Thus, we are not suggesting that implicit learning is better than explicit learning – in fact, it is almost surely the case that an explicit hypothesis is better owing to its interpretability. With PAC-semantics results, the argument would be that implicit learning allows us to sidestep the negative results we have with explicit learning even in propositional fragments [10]. In this paper, by treating the idea in a language-agnostic way and without PAC-related constructs, we are showing the formal connection between the explicit and implicit approaches.[7] It is also providing an option with expressive logics where constructing the explicit hypothesis may be challenging. In contrast, all we need for an implicit hypothesis is a satisfiability solver, as seen in the second line of the algorithm.

In an extended report, we will consider a number of variations. For example:

- Although our framework does, in principle, allow us to evaluate the query against partial observations, it is still the case that each of these partial observations have to individually determine the truth value of the set of atoms as to be learned. This is justified because the masking process hides the truth of some set of atoms, and what is revealed are the remaining partial models.
  We might imagine a slightly different setting, where the observations reveal formulas directly that correspond to the real world. These formulas themselves might express uncertainty, for example using disjunctions. Our algorithm would be essentially unmodified from above.
- An equally interesting avenue is generalisation to quantified hypotheses.
  What we want here is that based on the examples – usually conjunctions of atoms – to induce a quantified formula that applies to all of the domain. This means that it is not sufficient to simply consider the conjunction of all the observations, especially if the query involves atoms that have not been observed in the data directly before. This will require a slight modification of how the correctness of the hypothesis is ascertained, because it will involve a quantified sentence whose grounding may

[7] It is curious to note that with neural networks, there is also no explicit hypothesis [21]. The hypothesis is implicit and likely represented by a combination of the weights on the nodes as well as the architecture itself. So there is structural bias, but beyond that, there is no representation of the hypothesis. An interesting question then is whether an implicit learning framework like ours can be used to understand and characterize the hypothesis space learned by a neural network.

invoke constants not seen in the observations. (For example, the father of a father is a grandfather, regardless of the individuals observed.)
- There are a couple of variations we can look into which would allow us to deviate from the exacting stipulations we have needed for soundness and completeness. Indeed, the version of the algorithm above checks for the entailment of the query against the background knowledge and each observation individually. We could allow for a certain level of noise. Rather than requiring that the hypothesis is consistent with all observations, we might say it is consistent with a subset of them.
- Finally, we may tackle the case of implicit learning in multi-agent epistemic logic, by assuming the observations and hypotheses mention modalities. We would be reproducing the setting of [15]. However, the results they show depend on a stipulation for what is believed defined in terms of the nesting of certain operators (cf. representation theorem in [3]). Their framework requires considerable machinery beyond the standard results on PAC-semantics in propositional logic [10], and likely difficult to implement. So our approach could be significantly simpler.

All of these will be discussed in an extended report.

5 Conclusions

In this work, we looked at the problem of learning from observations, particularly in order to answer queries against background knowledge and the induced knowledge. What we show is that there is a very simple account involving observations, their conjunctions, or swapping constants that allows us to characterise which queries are entailed. The hypothesis is implicit.

It lacks the benefit of an explicit hypothesis, which could be useful for explainability. But in many cases, the cost of constructing the hypothesis is expensive – especially in expressive logics – and therefore an implicit result is useful. By carefully considering the type of generalization desired in an explicit framework, it might be possible to construct an implicit model as well.

We can also look at a number of variations that do not need to consider a conjunction over all observations, but only a subset of them. Likewise, extensions to the quantified and modal setting can also be explored, results that we clarify in an extended report.

Of course, one major disadvantage of implicit learning, here and in other works [17], is that it is prohibitive when the number of observations is large. What might then be preferable is to consider a combination of implicit and explicit learning: for the observations collected so far, we might seek to compute an explicit hypothesis when the agent is offline. When online, use the incoming observations in an implicit sense to reason incrementally.

References

1. Bacchus, F., Halpern, J.Y., Levesque, H.J.: Reasoning about noisy sensors and effectors in the situation calculus. Artif. Intell. **111**(1–2), 171–208 (1999)

2. Belle, V., Juba, B.: Implicitly learning to reason in first-order logic. In: Advances in Neural Information Processing Systems, vol. 32 (2019)
3. Belle, V., Lakemeyer, G.: Multiagent only knowing in dynamic systems. J. Artif. Intell. Res. **49** (2014)
4. Cropper, A., Dumančić, S.: Inductive logic programming at 30: a new introduction. J. Artif. Intell. Res. **74**, 765–850 (2022)
5. Daniely, A., Shalev-Shwartz, S.: Complexity theoretic limitations on learning DNF's. In: Conference on Learning Theory, pp. 815–830. PMLR (2016)
6. De Raedt, L.: Logical settings for concept-learning. Artif. Intell. **95**(1), 187–201 (1997)
7. De Raedt, L., Dries, A., Thon, I., Van den Broeck, G., Verbeke, M.: Inducing probabilistic relational rules from probabilistic examples. In: Proceedings of 24th International Joint Conference on Artificial Intelligence (IJCAI), vol. 2015, pp. 1835–1842. IJCAI-INT JOINT CONF ARTIF INTELL (2015)
8. Evans, R., Grefenstette, E.: Learning explanatory rules from noisy data. J. Artif. Intell. Res. **61**, 1–64 (2018)
9. Greiner, R., Grove, A.J., Kogan, A.: Knowing what doesn't matter: exploiting the omission of irrelevant data. Artif. Intell. **97**(1–2), 345–380 (1997)
10. Juba, B.: Implicit learning of common sense for reasoning. In: Twenty-Third International Joint Conference on Artificial Intelligence (2013)
11. Kearns, M.J., Schapire, R.E., Sellie, L.M.: Toward efficient agnostic learning. In: Proceedings of the Fifth Annual Workshop on Computational Learning Theory, pp. 341–352 (1992)
12. Levesque, H.J., Lakemeyer, G.: The Logic of Knowledge Bases. MIT Press, Cambridge (2001)
13. Michael, L.: Learning from partial observations. In: IJCAI, pp. 968–974. Citeseer (2007)
14. Mocanu, I.G., Belle, V., Juba, B.: Polynomial-time implicit learnability in SMT. In: ECAI 2020, pp. 1152–1158. IOS Press (2020)
15. Mocanu, I.G., Belle, V., Juba, B.: Learnability with PAC semantics for multi-agent beliefs. Theory Pract. Logic Program. **23**(4), 730–747 (2023)
16. Muggleton, S., et al.: ILP turns 20. Mach. Learn. **86**(1), 3–23 (2012)
17. Rader, A., Mocanu, I.G., Belle, V., Juba, B.: Learning implicitly with noisy data in linear arithmetic. In: Proceedings of the Thirtieth International Joint Conference on Artificial Intelligence (2021)
18. Raedt, L.D., Kersting, K.: Probabilistic inductive logic programming. In: Probabilistic Inductive Logic Programming, pp. 1–27 (2008)
19. Raedt, L.D., Kersting, K., Natarajan, S., Poole, D.: Statistical relational artificial intelligence: logic, probability, and computation. In: Synthesis Lectures on Artificial Intelligence and Machine Learning, vol. 10, no. 2, pp. 1–189 (2016)
20. Valiant, L.G.: Robust logics. In: Proceedings of the Thirty-First Annual ACM Symposium on Theory of Computing, pp. 642–651 (1999)
21. Zilke, J.R., Loza Mencía, E., Janssen, F.: DeepRED – rule extraction from deep neural networks. In: Calders, T., Ceci, M., Malerba, D. (eds.) DS 2016. LNCS (LNAI), vol. 9956, pp. 457–473. Springer, Cham (2016). https://doi.org/10.1007/978-3-319-46307-0_29

Reasoning About Neural Network Perception in the Situation Calculus

Vaishak Belle and Daxin Liu(✉)

The University of Edinburgh, Edinburgh, Scotland
{vbelle,daxin.liu}@ed.ac.uk

Abstract. The Situation Calculus is perhaps one of the most widely studied formalisms in knowledge representation communities where we consider actions and the changing state of the world resulting from these actions. The formalism is defined in first-order logic with limited features from second-order logic, and standard Tarski semantics suffice to interpret the properties of a domain. The situation calculus has been extended with many powerful features ranging from narrative actions to agent programs, multi-agent programs, epistemic, and hybrid aspects. Although many attempts have been made to connect it to robotic applications, it is still somewhat of an art, rather than science, as to how exactly one can design high-level agent specifications that uniquely connect with perceptual models. In this paper, we are mainly concerned with the following question. Assuming that we have a perception unit whose functionality is provided by a neural network, how exactly are we to interpret the results of the output of the neural network as objects in the situation calculus language? We propose a simple and elegant solution to this problem by using the likelihood of actions in the probabilistic situation calculus. We develop a number of examples to show the ideas.

1 Introduction

The Situation Calculus [14,16] is perhaps one of the most widely studied formalisms in knowledge representation communities where we consider actions and the changing state of the world resulting from these actions. The formalism is defined in first-order logic with limited features from second-order logic, and standard Tarski semantics suffice to interpret the properties from an axiomatization of the domain. Over the years, the situation calculus has been extended with many powerful features that have had limited study in most areas of AI & computer science, ranging from narrative actions to concurrency [7], agent programs [10], multi-agent programs [8], epistemic [17], hybrid aspects, and abstraction, among other features. Although some of these have been studied individually in sub-communities of computer science e.g. concurrency and abstraction, a wide range of results for a single formalism is uncommon. Additionally, several translation results have been established between the situation calculus and ASP, fluent calculus [20], and dynamic epistemic logic [21], making it a powerful formalism to express various aspects of action and changing properties in a dynamic world.

W.-Z. Dai (Ed.): ILP 2024, LNAI 16059, pp. 228–237, 2026.
https://doi.org/10.1007/978-3-032-09087-4_16

Interestingly, despite the deterministic nature of the classical situation calculus, attempts have been made to connect it to robotic applications. Early work by Dieter and Lakemeyer applied the GOLOG programming language of the situation calculus to the museum robot Minerva [6], separating high-level control specified in the situation calculus from low-level sensor-based perceptual aspects, often utilizing probabilistic components but which was abstracted away for the deterministic specification language. Extensions, including the relational decision-theoretic language DT-GOLOG [5], aimed to address decision-theoretic models concerning perceptual components.

Although these approaches presented new opportunities for logic-based formalisms to engage with perceptual components, it is still somewhat of an art, rather than a science, as to how exactly one can design high-level agent specifications that uniquely connect with perceptual models. This is where the work of Bacchus et al. [1] and later extensions by Belle and Levesque [3] and Liu and Lakemeyer [13] are particularly relevant because they provide an opportunity to reason about probabilistic events directly within the language. The extension most relevant to this paper is the work of Bacchus et al. [1], exploring probabilistic models by specifying probabilities over first-order formulas as well as probabilities over actions and sensing results within the formalism. This allows for reasoning about belief states, stochastic actions, and stochastic observations akin to POMDPs.

In this paper, we continue this line of work, and we are mainly concerned with the following question. Assuming that we have a perception unit whose functionality is provided by a neural network—and in this case, we consider any classical neural network potentially dealing with single-label how exactly are we to interpret the results of the output of the neural network as objects in the situation calculus language?

Contribution. Although there have been attempts as discussed to build robots using languages of the situation calculus or fluent calculus with real-world perception units as discussed above, there is no theory that provides a concrete way to connect the dots. What we show in the paper is that there is a surprisingly simple way to understand and interpret the neural network outputs as objects in the first-order language. We show in this paper that one could think of the neural network output as a functional system consisting of the following two possible specifications.

- *accuracy*: the label of the neural network can be directly mapped to objects in reality, in which case we can think in terms of accuracy or lack of accuracy. So for instance, we can say that an object being detected in the image is given a positive label with 98% accuracy or fails with a probability of 2%, which is a less granular way to reason about the output of the network.
- But more concretely, you can also think model's output distribution in terms of the *true positive*, *true negative*, *false positive*, and *false negative* directly as conditions in the probabilistic semantics of these perceptual outputs in the language. This provides a very systematic way to reason and evaluate how exactly the neural network's outputs are used within the language.

By virtue of the specification likelihood of actions, we can connect the ontology of probabilistic situation calculus [1] and neural networks. Somewhat interestingly, as a benefit and as a feature of our construction, it does not really matter if the machine learning system at hand is a neural network. We treat this at an abstract/functional level, which means that any machine learning model whose output distribution can be understood in terms of true positive, true negative, false positive, and false negative can be modeled. We develop a number of examples that show how this works from object detection and character recognition to scene understanding.

2 A Probabilistic Formalism of Beliefs and Actions

The language $\mathcal{L}$ of the situation calculus [16] is a many-sorted first-order language (with some second-order features), with sorts for actions, situations, and objects (for everything else, and includes the set of reals $\mathbb{R}$ as a subsort). A situation represents a world history as a sequence of actions. The initial situations correspond to the initial states the world might be. Successor situations can be constructed by actions using a special function $do(a, s)$. Namely, $do(a, s)$ returns the unique situation resulting from doing action a in situation s. This notion can be extended easily from single action to action sequences, that is, we use $do(\alpha, s)$ where α is the sequence $[a_1, \ldots, a_n]$ to denote the term $do(a_n, do(\ldots, do(a_1, s)\ldots))$. Initial situations are defined as situations without predecessor:

$$Init(s) \doteq \neg\exists a, s'.s = do(a, s').$$

We denote the actual initial situation by S_0 and use the variables ι to range over initial situations only. The languages feature a binary relation $Poss(a, s)$ expressing that action a being executable in situation s; action functions, e.g. $move(x, y)$; a finite set of fluent whose last argument is a situation term e.g. $HeightOf(A, s)$. Here we assume without loss of generality that all fluents are functional.

Basic Action Theories. A formula ψ is uniform in a situation term s if ψ does not mention any other situation terms except s, does not quantify over situation variables, and does not mention $Poss$. The situation calculus uses a set of axioms called basic action theory (BAT) $\mathcal{D}$ to specify the dynamics of a domain that consists of:

1. the initial situation axiom $\mathcal{D}_0$, which is a set of sentences uniform in S_0 describing what is true initially;
2. the action precondition axioms $\mathcal{D}_{ap}$;
3. the successor state axioms $\mathcal{D}_{ss}$ describe how the actions change the fluents, incorporating a solution to the frame problem [16];
4. domain-independent foundational axioms Σ [9], which ensure that situations are well-structured.

The agent reasons about actions by means of the entailments of $\mathcal{D}$, for which standard Tarskian models suffice. We assume henceforth that models also assign the usual interpretations to $=, <, >, 0, 1, +, \times$, etc.

Likelihood and Degree of Belief. The BHL model of belief builds on the formalism of knowledge by Scherl and Levesque [18]. We adopt a simplified version that only includes two binary special fluent l and p.

The term $l(a, s)$ is intended to denote the likelihood of action a in situation s. For example, suppose $sonar(z)$ is the action of reading the value z from a sensor that measures the distance to the wall, h. We might assume that this action is characterized by the following error model:

$$l(sonar(z), s) = u \equiv (z = h(s) \wedge u = 0.8) \vee (1 = |h(s) - z| \wedge u = 0.1) \tag{1}$$

That is, with 0.8 likelihood, the read value equals the actual distance, while with 0.1 likelihood, the read value differs 1 unit from the actual distance. In general, the action theory $\mathcal{D}$ is assumed to include a set of additional action likelihood axioms, one for each action type A, of the form $l(A(\mathbf{x}), s) = u \equiv \phi_A(\mathbf{x}, u, s)$, where ϕ_A specifies the conditions under which action $A(\boldsymbol{x})$ has likelihood u in s.

Next, the p fluent is a weighted version of the usual accessibility relation among situations, namely, the term $p(s', s)$ denotes the relative weight accorded to situation s' when the agent is in situation s. The BAT $\mathcal{D}$ now includes an additional axiom on p to ensure that the weights are non-negatives:

$$\forall \iota, s.p(s, \iota) \geq 0 \wedge (p(s, \iota) > 0 \supset Init(s)). \tag{2}$$

This ensures that all initial situations ι have non-negative weight. To ensure p is non-negative for all possible situations, BHL proposes to use a successor state axiom on p in the following form:

$$\begin{aligned} p(s', do(a, s)) = u \equiv \exists s''[s' = do(a, s'') \wedge Poss(a, s'') \wedge u = p(s'', s) \times l(a.s'')] \\ \vee \neg\exists s''[s' = do(a, s'') \wedge Poss(a, s'') \wedge u = 0] \end{aligned} \tag{3}$$

Namely, the weight of situations s' relative to $do(a, s)$ is the weight of their predecessors s'' times the likelihood of a contingent on the successful execution of a at s''. Under such construction, one can assure that $p(s', s) > 0$ holds if and only if s and s' share the same history of actions.

With the above specification of fluents l and p, the degree of beliefs in BHL can be defined as the total weight of all accessible situations. Let ϕ be a formula with a single free variable s of sort situation[1]. Then the degree of belief in ϕ in situation s is defined as an abbreviation by

$$Bel(\phi, s) \doteq \frac{1}{\gamma} \sum_{\{s' : \phi[s']\}} p(s', s)$$

where γ, the normalization factor, is understood as the same expression as the numerator but with ϕ replaced by TRUE.

[1] The ϕ is usually written either with the situation variable suppressed or with a distinguished variable *now*. In any case, $\phi[t]$ is used to denote the formula with that variable replaced by t.

The appealing point of the BHL's formalism of degree of belief is that we can partially specify the agent's initial degree of belief with whatever information we have, along with a BAT that specifies the dynamics of a domain, the agent's beliefs after actions simply emerge as logical consequences that are entailed by the initial degree of belief. For example, if we assume the initial degree of belief is specified as[2]

$$p(\iota, S_0) = \begin{cases} \frac{1}{3} & h(\iota) \in \{1,2,3\} \\ 0 & o.w. \end{cases} \tag{4}$$

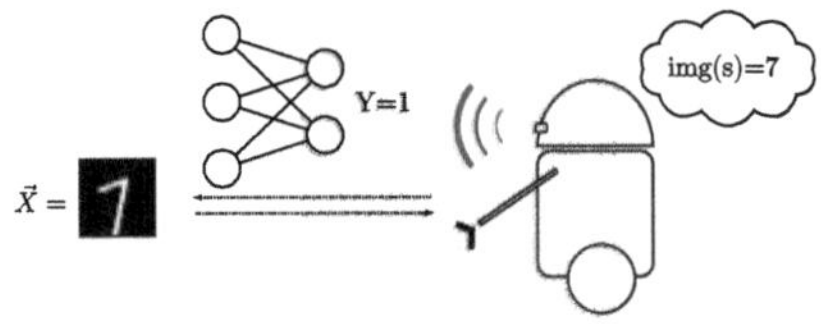

Fig. 1. A robot recognizing characters in an image.

i.e. the agent believes the distance to the wall is uniformly distributed among $\{1, 2, 3\}$, then the basic action theory $\mathcal{D}$ which consists of Eq. (1) (2) (3) (4) entails the following:

- $Bel(h = 4, S_0) = 0$.
  The agent has no belief that the distance to the wall is 4.
- $Bel(h = 2, do(sonar(2), S_0) = 0.8$.
  The agent's belief of being 2 units distant from the wall is enhanced by receiving a sonar read value of 2.
- $Bel(h = 1, do(sonar(2), S_0) = 0.1$ and
  $Bel(h = 3, do(sonar(2), S_0) = 0.1$.
  The agent's belief of being 1 or 3 units distant from the wall is decreased by receiving a sonar read value of 2.

3 Interpreting Neural Output

We view a neural network model as a function $f : \mathbf{X} \mapsto Y$ from some input features $\mathbf{X}$ to the output label Y. For simplicity, we only consider a single label. This means that we are not confining to specific types of neural networks, but instead considering any functional systems including other classical machine learning models. The objective of the neural network is to learn the underlying mapping $f_{real} : \mathbf{X} \mapsto Y$ between the features and labels. Hence, the neural network model f is just an approximation of f_{real} where one can define *accuracy*, *true positive*,

[2] The initial degree of belief does not have to be a complete distribution, instead, it can be well-formed formulas.

true negative, *false positive*, and *false negative* [15] etc. In what follows, we use Y_{real} to denote the real label and Y the label predicated by a neural network.

The question of interest is how can we interpret the output Y of a neural network as objects in the situation calculus. This is an important question if one wishes to harness the power of learning of a neural system and the power of reasoning of a logical one, especially, in a partially observable stochastic setting. The solution we propose is to exploit the likelihood axioms in BHL to interpret the output Y. To see this more concretely, let us turn to the following character recognition example. Suppose that we have a single digital reader embedded with some neural network to predict the digit of an image (See Fig. 1). Supposing further the digital numbers of images in use are only in $\{1, 7\}$ and the real label Y_{real} of the image at hand is modeled in the situation calculus by the function fluents $img(s)$, namely, in situation s which is the current situation, the agent finds itself that the image that it actually sees is given by the function img. To interpret the network's output $Y \in \{1, 7\}$, we simply assume a noisy sensing action $sdr(y)$, where $y = Y$. Additionally, we could have the error models of the sensing:

$$l(sdr(y), s) = \begin{cases} 0.8 & y = img(s) \\ 0.2 & o.w. \end{cases}$$

It turns out that under such an interpretation, the likelihood of 0.8 corresponds to precisely the *accuracy* of the neural network. This idea can be refined to cover more complex examples. Suppose that the neural network's task is to predict if a scene contains a human, i.e. $Y = \{0, 1\}$, and the actual label Y_{real} is modeled by a fluent predicate $Human(s)$. To interpret the output Y, we can assume a sensing action $scenehuman(y)$ where $y \in \{0, 1\}$ and a likelihood axiom as follows:

$$l(scenehuman(y), s) = \begin{cases} 0.88 & Human(s) \wedge y = 1 \\ 0.12 & Human(s) \wedge y = 0 \\ 0.8 & \neg Human(s) \wedge y = 1 \\ 0.2 & \neg Human(s) \wedge y = 0 \end{cases}$$

Under such construction, the likelihood of $scenehuman(y)$ corresponds exactly to the measures of the neural network. More concretely, the number 0.88 (likewise for 0.12, 0.8, and 0.2) is just the *true positive rate* (respectively *false negative rate*, *false positive rate*, *true negative rate*) of the network.

Of course, this idea does not confine itself to binary classification tasks. For the handwritten digits recognition tasks where the input of the neural network are images of digital numbers, i.e. $\boxed{0}, \boxed{1}, \ldots \boxed{9}$. The network classifies each image to output labels $Y \in \{0, 1, \ldots 9\}$. Supposing again the real label Y_{real} is modeled by a function fluent $img(s)$. To interpret the output Y, we could use a noisy sensing action $nread(y)$ with a certain error model such as:

$$l(nread(y), s) = \begin{cases} M(y, img(s)) & img(s), y \in \{0, \ldots 9\} \\ 0 & o.w. \end{cases}$$

where $M(y, img(s))$ are entries of the *normalized confusion matrix* [15] of the neural network with indexes y and $img(s)$.

We want to emphasize that the merits of this method to interpret neural network outputs are multi-fold. First, it is simple and elegant. By utilizing the likelihood axioms in the BHL formalism, we bridge a direct connection between concepts and objects in the situation calculus and the neural network. Second, by virtue of this connection, one could use the reasoning mechanisms in the situation calculus, such as progression and regression, [4,11] to draw conclusions about beliefs after actions that are essentially determined by the nature of the neural network in one hand, and also exploit techniques in machine learning to optimize the errors models of sensors so that reasoning about high-level beliefs could be less uncertain. See also below for an extended example to appreciate this.

Suppose that a robot tries to open a safe with a three-digital numerical key. We denote the constants for the possible combinations of digits as triples in the situation calculus,[3] e.g. $\langle 1,7,1\rangle$ represents the input of three digits $1,7,1$ in sequence. The robot captures three images with digits that someone opened the safe (like the images of digits in Fig. 1), and the robot tries to use the same neural network to recognize all these images. In the high-level modeling, the actual key of the safe is modeled by a fluent $key(s)$, and initially, the robot's belief of the key is uniformly distributed, namely,

$$p(\iota, S_0) = \begin{cases} 0.001 & key(\iota) \in C_{key} \\ 0 & o.w. \end{cases} \tag{5}$$

where $C_{key} = \{\langle 0,0,0\rangle, \langle 0,0,1\rangle, \ldots, \langle 9,9,9\rangle\}$ denotes the set of all possible key constants. In such a scenario, to interpret the output of the neural network, we could use a noisy sensing $read(y_1, y_2, y_3)$ where y_i corresponds to the predicted labels of the i-th image, thereafter, a possible modeling of the likelihood of sensing could be:

$$l(read(y_1.y_2, y_3), s) = \begin{cases} M(y_1,x_1)M(y_2,x_2)M(y_3,x_3) & \exists x_1, x_2, x_3.\phi(x_1,x_2,x_3) \\ 0 & o.w. \end{cases} \tag{6}$$

where $\phi(x_1, x_2, x_3)$ denotes the formula $key(s) = \langle x_1, x_2, x_3\rangle \wedge \langle x_1, x_2, x_3\rangle \in C_{key} \wedge \langle y_1, y_2, y_3\rangle \in C_{key}$ and $M(y_i, x_i)$ are the entries of the confusion matrix of the underlying neural network with index y_i, x_i. If we suppose further that the normalized confusion matrix of the network M is given as:

$$M = \begin{bmatrix} 1 & 0 & \ldots & 0 & 0 & 0 \\ 0 & 0.8 & \ldots & 0.2 & 0 & 0 \\ & & \ddots & & & \\ 0 & 0.2 & \ldots & 0.8 & 0 & 0 \\ 0 & 0 & \ldots & 0 & 1 & 0 \\ 0 & 0 & \ldots & 0 & 0 & 1 \end{bmatrix} \tag{7}$$

namely, the neural network can perfectly recognize digits other than $\{1,7\}$, and it has 20% chance to classify to its opposite when it comes to 1 and 7,

[3] In fact, one can assume a rigid function $encode(x_1, x_2, x_3, s)$ with three parameters to encode such triples into constants, i.e. $\langle 1,7,1\rangle$ refers to the constant denoted by $encode(1, 7, 1, s)$.

then the basic action theory $\mathcal{D}$ which consists of Eq. (2) (3) (5) (6) entails the following:

- $Bel(key = \langle 0, 7, 0\rangle, do(read(0, 1, 0), S_0) = 0.2$
  The agent believes the key is $\langle 0, 7, 0\rangle$ with degree 0.2 when the neural network output 0, 1, 0 in sequence;
- $Bel(key = \langle 0, 7, 1\rangle, do(read(0, 7, 1), S_0) = 0.64$
  The agent believes the key could be $\langle 0, 7, 1\rangle$ with degree 0.64 when the neural network output 0, 7, 1 in sequence;
- $Bel(key = \langle 0, 7, 7\rangle, do(read(0, 7, 1), S_0) = 0.16$,
  $Bel(key = \langle 0, 1, 1\rangle, do(read(0, 7, 1), S_0) = 0.16$,
  and $Bel(key = \langle 0, 1, 7\rangle, do(read(0, 7, 1), S_0) = 0.04$.

4 Tracking Beliefs with an Implemented Classifier

Previously, we handcrafted a normalized confusion matrix M for the BAT of the safe-key domain and discussed the agent's beliefs after sensing in terms of logical entailment. In this section, we will use an implemented classifier, a CNN classifier, from [19] and discuss how beliefs change after numbers of sensing in the same setting of BAT. The purpose here is to demonstrate the feasibility of our approach in a neuro-symbolic system.

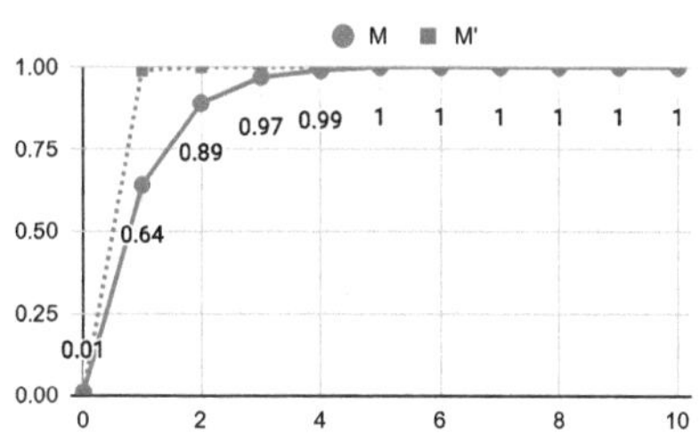

Fig. 2. Belief changes after sensing with different neural error profiles.

The normalized confusion matrix of the classifier is given as $M' =$

$$\begin{bmatrix} 0.995 & 0 & 0.003 & 0 & 0 & 0 & 0.002 & 0 & 0 & 0 \\ 0 & 1 & 0 & 0 & 0 & 0 & 0 & 0 & 0 & 0 \\ 0 & 0 & 0.998 & 0 & 0 & 0 & 0 & 0.002 & 0 & 0 \\ 0 & 0 & 0 & 1 & 0 & 0 & 0 & 0 & 0 & 0 \\ 0 & 0 & 0 & 0 & 0.988 & 0 & 0 & 0.005 & 0 & 0.007 \\ 0 & 0 & 0 & 0.003 & 0 & 0.987 & 0.003 & 0 & 0.002 & 0.005 \\ 0.002 & 0 & 0 & 0 & 0 & 0 & 0.998 & 0 & 0 & 0 \\ 0 & 0 & 0 & 0.002 & 0 & 0 & 0 & 0.988 & 0 & 0.01 \\ 0 & 0.002 & 0 & 0 & 0 & 0 & 0 & 0.003 & 0.995 & 0 \\ 0 & 0 & 0 & 0 & 0.002 & 0 & 0 & 0 & 0.003 & 0.995 \end{bmatrix}$$

It is not hard to see that, compared with our conceived network in Eq.(7), the CNN classifier performs better in recognizing digits 1 and 7 and worse in other digits. We are interested in the agent's degrees of belief of the key under different error models of sensors with identical output. Namely, the $Bel(key = \langle 0, 7, 1\rangle, s)$ where s are set to the situations of $1 \leq i \leq 10$ number of $read(0, 7, 1)$ in sequel.

The overall result is shown in Fig. 2. As one can see, with the increase of the number of $read(0, 7, 1)$, the agent's belief of the key to be $\langle 0, 7, 1\rangle$ converges to 1. Yet, the belief converges faster for neural networks with higher accuracy, i.e. M'. We hope that through this example, we demonstrated how the measures of the low-level neural network affect the high-level robot belief in our approach to connect the neural network and the situation calculus.

5 Conclusion

In this paper, we study the problem of interpreting and reasoning the output of a neural network in a probabilistic variant of the situation calculus. Our proposal of using the likelihood axioms of sensing to encode the measures, such as accuracy, of a neural network provides a simple and elegant solution to interpret the neural output as objects in the situation calculus. This approach is promising if one wishes to harness the power of learning of a neural system and the power of reasoning of a logical one, especially, in a partially observable stochastic setting. For future work, we plan to incorporate our approach in Allegro [2], an interpreter of belief programs [12] which are probabilistic variants of GOLOG program, and evaluate in a systematic way.

References

1. Bacchus, F., Halpern, J.Y., Levesque, H.J.: Reasoning about noisy sensors and effectors in the situation calculus. Artif. Intell. **111**(1–2), 171–208 (1999)
2. Belle, V., Levesque, H.: Allegro: belief-based programming in stochastic dynamical domains. In: IJCAI (2015)
3. Belle, V., Levesque, H.J.: Reasoning about discrete and continuous noisy sensors and effectors in dynamical systems. Artif. Intell. **262**, 189–221 (2018)
4. Belle, V., Levesque, H.J.: Regression and progression in stochastic domains. Artif. Intell. **281**, 103247 (2020)
5. Boutilier, C., Reiter, R., Soutchanski, M., Thrun, S., et al.: Decision-theoretic, high-level agent programming in the situation calculus. In: AAAI/IAAI, vol. 2000, pp. 355–362 (2000)
6. Burgard, W., et al.: Experiences with an interactive museum tour-guide robot. Artif. Intell. **114**(1–2), 3–55 (1999)
7. De Giacomo, G., Lespérance, Y., Levesque, H.J.: Congolog, a concurrent programming language based on the situation calculus. Artif. Intell. **121**(1–2), 109–169 (2000)
8. Finzi, A., Lukasiewicz, T.: Game-theoretic agent programming in golog. In: Proceedings of the 16th European Conference on Artificial Intelligence, pp. 18–22 (2004)
9. Levesque, H., Pirri, F., Reiter, R.: Foundations for the situation calculus. Comput. Inf. Sci. **3**(18) (1998)

10. Levesque, H.J., Reiter, R., Lespérance, Y., Lin, F., Scherl, R.B.: Golog: a logic programming language for dynamic domains. J. Logic Program. **31**(1–3), 59–83 (1997)
11. Liu, D., Feng, Q.: On the progression of belief. Artif. Intell. **322**, 103947 (2023)
12. Liu, D., Huang, Q., Belle, V., Lakemeyer, G.: Verifying belief-based programs via symbolic dynamic programming. In: ECAI 2023, pp. 1497–1504. IOS Press (2023)
13. Liu, D., Lakemeyer, G.: Reasoning about beliefs and meta-beliefs by regression in an expressive probabilistic action logic. In: IJCAI, pp. 1951–1958 (2021)
14. McCarthy, J.: Situations, actions, and causal laws. Stanford Univ CA Dept of Computer Science, Technical report (1963)
15. Murphy, K.P.: Probabilistic Machine Learning: An Introduction. MIT press, Cambridge (2022)
16. Reiter, R.: Knowledge in Action: Logical Foundations for Specifying and Implementing Dynamical Systems. MIT press, Cambridge (2001)
17. Sardina, S., De Giacomo, G., Lespérance, Y., Levesque, H.J.: On the semantics of deliberation in indigolog—from theory to implementation. Ann. Math. Artif. Intell. **41**(2), 259–299 (2004)
18. Scherl, R.B., Levesque, H.J.: Knowledge, action, and the frame problem. Artif. Intell. **144**(1–2), 1–39 (2003)
19. Shamsuddin, M.R., Abdul-Rahman, S., Mohamed, A.: Exploratory analysis of MNIST handwritten digit for machine learning modelling. In: Yap, B.W., Mohamed, A.H., Berry, M.W. (eds.) SCDS 2018. CCIS, vol. 937, pp. 134–145. Springer, Singapore (2019). https://doi.org/10.1007/978-981-13-3441-2_11
20. Thielscher, M.: From situation calculus to fluent calculus: state update axioms as a solution to the inferential frame problem. Artif. Intell. **111**(1–2), 277–299 (1999)
21. Van Ditmarsch, H., van Der Hoek, W., Kooi, B.: Dynamic Epistemic Logic, vol. 337. Springer, Cham (2007)

Benchmarking in Neuro-Symbolic AI

Robin Manhaeve[1(✉)], Francesco Giannini[2], Mehdi Ali[3,4], Damiano Azzolini[5], Alice Bizzarri[5], Andrea Borghesi[6], Samuele Bortolotti[7], Luc De Raedt[1], Devendra Dhami[8], Michelangelo Diligenti[9], Sebastijan Dumančić[10], Boi Faltings[11], Elisabetta Gentili[5], Alfonso Gerevini[12], Marco Gori[9], Tias Guns[1], Martin Homola[13], Kristian Kersting[14], Jens Lehmann[15], Michele Lombardi[6], Luca Lorello[16,17], Emanuele Marconato[7], Stefano Melacci[9], Andrea Passerini[7], Debjit Paul[11], Fabrizio Riguzzi[5], Stefano Teso[7], Neil Yorke-Smith[10], and Marco Lippi[16]

[1] Department of Computer Science, KU Leuven, Leuven, Belgium
robin.manhaeve@kuleuven.be
[2] Scuola Normale Superiore, Pisa, Italy
[3] Fraunhofer IAIS, Sankt Augustin, Germany
[4] Lamarr Institute, Dortmund, Germany
[5] University of Ferrara, Ferrara, Italy
[6] University of Bologna, Bologna, Italy
[7] University of Trento, Trento, Italy
[8] Eindhoven University of Technology, Eindhoven, The Netherlands
[9] Università di Siena, Siena, Italy
[10] TU Delft, Delft, The Netherlands
[11] EPFL, Lausanne, Switzerland
[12] Università degli Studi di Bresci, Brescia, Italy
[13] Comenius University in Bratislava, Bratislava, Slovakia
[14] Technical University of Darmstadt, Darmstadt, Germany
[15] Amazon, Seattle, USA
[16] DISMI, University of Modena, Modena, Italy
[17] Reggio Emilia, Italy

Abstract. Neural-symbolic (NeSy) AI has gained a lot of popularity by enhancing learning models with explicit reasoning capabilities. Both new systems and new benchmarks are constantly introduced and used to evaluate learning and reasoning skills. The large variety of systems and benchmarks, however, makes it difficult to establish a fair comparison among the various frameworks, let alone a unifying set of benchmarking criteria. This paper analyzes the state-of-the-art in benchmarking NeSy systems, studies its limitations, and proposes ways to overcome them. We categorize popular neural-symbolic frameworks into three groups: model-theoretic, proof-theoretic fuzzy, and proof-theoretic probabilistic systems. We show how these three categories have distinct strengths and weaknesses, and how this is reflected in the type of tasks and benchmarks to which they are applied.

Keywords: Neural-Symbolic AI · Benchmarks · Evaluation of learning and reasoning

W.-Z. Dai (Ed.): ILP 2024, LNAI 16059, pp. 238–249, 2026.
https://doi.org/10.1007/978-3-032-09087-4_17

1 Introduction

Building systems that integrate learning, reasoning and optimization has long been a dream for artificial intelligence (AI). One of the major challenges within this context is evaluating novel ideas and frameworks on appropriate benchmarks. Too often, the tasks and the datasets that are considered and proposed for experimental evaluation are tailored to specific algorithms or methodologies and limited to ad-hoc scenarios and application domains. More generally, the neuro-symbolic (NeSy) community lacks a generally accepted perspective to test the existing approaches across a variety of different tasks and under different conditions, making deep experimental comparisons hard to obtain [44]. In addition, when a new system is proposed, it is often tested either on appositely introduced benchmarks, to emphasize the advantages of the novel approach (which is understandable and legitimate), or on well-known "old-fashioned" datasets and tasks. While a comparison on such classic benchmarks is useful to get an idea of the performance of an approach for some reference points, new challenges are necessary to drive the development of NeSy systems forward. For example, several well-known datasets in image classification such as MNIST or CIFAR have been used to design a variety of artificial tasks, each time with a specific goal: to propose a setting for continual learning or few-shot learning, to introduce explicit knowledge for reasoning, or to integrate rules and constraints for collective classification [4,24,25]. These datasets have become real benchmarking frameworks, but their environments are too limited for evaluating the development of systems integrating different paradigms.

To enable better benchmarking in NeSy AI we make the following contributions: (i) analyzing the current state of the art for what concerns the existing datasets and benchmarks at the intersection of learning, reasoning and optimization; (ii) studying their limitations; (iii) analyzing the existing systems that have been applied to such data; (iv) providing a list of the desiderata that new benchmarks should include; (v) proposing novel ideas for the evaluation and comparison of different approaches. This is all intended to provide insight into the abilities and limitations of current and future learning and reasoning systems.

2 A Categorization of Neural-Symbolic Benchmarking

Let us start off by taking a look at current benchmarking in NeSy AI. To do this, we use a categorization of the different types of neural-symbolic tasks due to Vermeulen et al. [44].

Distant Supervision. In this setting, we have a set of i.i.d. supervised examples, but supervision is not available at the level of the classifier that needs to be trained. Rather, it is available on the logic that is defined over the classifiers. A classic example is that of the MNIST Addition task [24], where the training examples are tuples of handwritten images, labelled with their sum. The learning task however is to learn to recognize individual digits.

Structured Prediction. In this setting, the system needs to classify entities connected by a logical structure (e.g., a graph). Often, a subset of the entities is labelled, while the label of the majority of entities needs to be inferred by taking into account entity-specific attributes, as well as the relational structure connecting them. This is typically done through logic knowledge. An example is the Citeseer [17] dataset. Here, individual entities are scientific papers, represented as a bag of the words present in the paper. The goal is to predict the domain to which the paper belongs. The citation graph is also provided, which includes an edge if one paper cites another. The background knowledge is that if one paper cites another, it likely belongs to the same domain.

Knowledge Base Completion. In this classic setting, we have a knowledge base with missing links between the entities that need to be completed. Although this is generally not a neural-symbolic setting, the idea is that the entities might have sub-symbolic attributes, or that a deep learning-based system might learn embedding representations and patterns that are not easily learned by a symbolic system. As a result, enhancing a symbolic data collection with a neural model may produce a significant improvement in solving the task, as shown, e.g., on the Countries [23,26] datasets

Learning to Optimize. In this setting, the goal is to generate solutions to computationally intractable tasks. The model is trained to approximate the optimal solution. The logic is used to make it more likely that a consistent solution is generated.

Overview of Popular Neural-Symbolic Benchmarks

Below is an overview of popular neural-symbolic benchmarks for each these category.

- Distant supervision (50): Add 2x2, Apply 2x2, BDD-OIA, CelebA, Chess, CLE4EVR, CLEVR, CLEVR-Hans, CLEVR-Math, Context-sensitive grammars, Crop yield prediction, CUB, DBA, DOT, Follow Suit Winner, Handwritten formulas, Hanoi, Indoor scene classification, Kandinsky patterns, Math, Member, MIMIC-II, MNIST Addition, MNIST AddMul, MNIST Even-Odd, MNIST Following Pairs, MNIST Half, MNIST Pairs, MNIST Sequential, MonumAI, Mutagenicity, Operator 2x2, Path, Predictive toxicology, RAVEN, ROAD-R, RPS, Shapeworld, Shortest path, Sudoku grid validity, Tic tac toe, Tic tac toe - next move, Trigonometry, vDEM, Visual Sudoku, V-LOL, VQAR, Well-formed parantheses, Word-algebra problems, XOR
- Structured prediction (5): AbstRCT, Arnetminer, CiteSeer, Cora, IPC
- Knowledge base completion (16): Countries, CQ2SPARQLOWL, EMBER/PE Malware Ontology, FB15k-237, Kinship, MedHop, MMKB, Nations, PharmKG, Pizza ontology, PubMed, Randomly generated KBs, UMLS, WebKB, WikiHop, WN18RR
- Learn to optimize (2): Hardware/Algorithm Dimensioning, Transprecision computing

3 A Comparison of Neural-Symbolic Systems

To discuss the state-of-the-art of neural-symbolic systems, we follow the categorization introduced in Marra et al. [27]. Here, NeSy systems were categorized along 6 dimensions. We exploit some of these dimensions below to provide a rough categorization of neural-symbolic systems. This is followed by an analysis of their capabilities. An up-to-date version of the tables are available at https://sites.google.com/view/benchmarking-in-nesy-ai.

3.1 Dimensions of Neural-Symbolic Systems

Proof- vs Model-Theoretic. The first dimension we select is the proof-theoretic vs model-theoretic dimension, as this property has a profound impact on the type of inference that is carried out by the systems. Proof-theoretic systems work by finding proofs for a query by chaining together several steps of logical inference using either backwards or forward reasoning. This type of inference thus has a defined direction and is strongly connected to (logic) programming. On the other hand, the model-theoretic approach considers the satisfying models for a given logical theory, which is related to SAT-solving. *Logical semantics.* Marra et al. [27] distinguish between three different levels of semantics: minimal, stable, and classical semantics. If the logical theory is limited to definite clauses, its semantics is generally defined in terms of the least Herbrand model. It is the unique *minimal* set of atoms that can be derived from the clauses. When relaxing this constraint allowing any type of clause, this minimal set might not be unique. Instead, the semantics is defined by all *stable* models. Finally, the semantics of arbitrary logical theories is defined by the *classic* semantic definition of First-Order Logic. These semantics can be extended by defining a probability distribution over models.

Structure vs Parameter Learning. For most machine learning models in a learning setting, the structure is fixed, but the parameters inside the structure have to be learned. For many logic-based methods, however, the structure itself defines the model as there are no other parameters. For neural-symbolic methods, this dichotomy becomes even more important, and whether structure learning is supported becomes a defining aspect of the system. In this paper, all systems support parameter learning, so we only indicate whether they support structure learning.

3.2 Overview

In Table 1, we give an overview of all neural-symbolic systems discussed in this paper. A lot of entries are reused from Marra et al. [27] with permission.

3.3 Categorization

Analyzing Table 1 from [27] only according to the dimensions mentioned above, we now identify three distinct groups of systems. In Table 2 we give a per-category overview of these properties with respect to the number of NeSy systems having them.

Group 1: Model-Theoretic Systems. The systems that only use a model-theoretic approach are quite uniform. They all use classical logical semantics, and almost none of them supports structure learning. The group is further divided into systems that use a fuzzy or a probabilistic interpretation on top of the classical semantics, with some systems offering (a mix of) both.

Group 2: Proof-theoretic fuzzy systems. Within the proof-theoretic dimension, we have a clear splitting between fuzzy and probabilistic systems. Most fuzzy systems use minimal semantics, and almost all of them support parameter learning.

Group 3: Proof-theoretic probabilistic systems. The probabilistic proof-theoretic systems are divided between minimal and stable model semantics. Furthermore, very few of them have support for structure learning. This is potentially due

Table 1. All neuro-symbolic systems considered in this survey.

System	Inference	Semantics	Learning	Benchmark type
	(P)roof (M)odel	(C)lassical (M)inimal (S)table (P)robability (F)uzzy	(P)arameters (S)tructure	(D)istant supervision (S)tructured prediction (K)B completion
αILP [35]	P+M	S+P	P+S	D
Concept Embedding Models (CEM) [12]	M	C+P+F	P	D
Deep Concept Reasoner (DCR) [4]	P	F	P+S	D
Deep Logic Models (DLM) [28]	M	C+P+F	P	D+K
DeepProbLog [24]	P+M	M+P	P+S	D+S
DeepStochLog [46]	P	M+P	P	D+S
Feed-Forward Neural-Symbolic Learner (FFNSL) [9]	P	S+F	P+S	D
Greedy Neural Theorem Provers (GNTP) [30]	P	M+F	P+S	K
Lifted Relational Neural Networks (LRNN) [37]	P	M+F	P+S	D+K
Logic Explained Networks (LEN) [7]	P+M	C+F	P+S	D
Logic Tensor Networks (LTN) [3]	M	C+F	P	D+K
NeurASP [49]	P+M	S+P	P	D
NeuralLP [47]	P	M+F	P	K
Neural Markov Logic Networks (NMLN) [29]	M	C+P	P+S	K
Neural Probabilistic Soft Logic (NeuPSL) [32]	M	C+F	P	D+S
NLog [42]	P	M+P	P	D
NLProlog [45]	P	M+P	P+S	K
Neural Theorem Prover (NTP) [33]	P	M+F	P+S	K
Reason-able Embeddings [1]	M	C+F	P	K
Relational-Concept Based Models (R-CBM) [5]	P+M	P+F	P+S	D+S+K
Relational Neural Machines (RNM) [26]	M	C+P	P	D+S
Relational Reasoning Networks (R2N) [26]	P+M	C+F	P	S+K
Semantic Based Regularization (SBR) [11]	M	C+F	P	S+K
Scallop [21]	P	M+P	P	D
SLASH [36]	P+M	S+P	P	D
TensorLog [8]	P	M+P	P	S+K

to the more expressive nature of probabilistic inference, making search over the space of rules expensive.

3.4 Capabilities

The category of a NeSy system has a large impact on what type of tasks it can be applied to. This is made clear by the benchmarks each system is generally evaluated on. In this section, we exemplify this by indicating which tasks the different categories of systems are evaluated on. The resulting signature is indicative of the capabilities of a system. We count these signatures for each system in the categories listed above ((D) Distant supervision, (S) Structured prediction, (K) Knowledge base completion). We then count how often each task type appears in these signatures. Here, we omitted the optimization-based tasks as they were not used in the systems used in this comparison.

The results of the categorization are shown in Table 3. From subtables (a)-(c) we can see that distant supervision tasks are common among all systems. Also, both model-theoretic and proof-theoretic systems are quite versatile. Proof-theoretic probabilistic systems seem to be mostly focused on distant supervision. This is probably due to the more expensive probabilistic inference that prevents them from being successfully applied to structured prediction and knowledge-base tasks.

Table 2. An overview of the properties of the systems in the different categories along the 3 dimensions.

Category	Proof- vs model-	Semantics	Fuzzy vs probability	Structure learning	#systems
	(P) Proof (M)odel	(C) Classical (M) Minimal (S) Stable	(P) Probability (F) Fuzzy	(✓) yes (X) no	
model	M	C	P + F	X	2
	M	C	F	✓	1
	M	C	F	X	4
	M	C	P	✓	1
	M	C	P	X	1
fuzzy	P	C	F	✓	1
	P	C	F	X	1
	P	M	F	✓	3
	P	M	F	X	1
	P	S	F	✓	2
probabibilistic	P	M	P	X	1
	P	S	P	✓	1
	P	S	P	X	2
	P	M	P	✓	1
	P	M	P	X	4

Table 3. Capabilities of each system category. We report the count of systems evaluated on a combination of (D)istant supervision, (S)tructured prediction, and (K)nowledge base completion tasks.

(a) Model-theoretic

	D	S	K	# Systems
	X	X		2
	X		X	2
	X			2
		X	X	1
			X	2
# Systems	6	3	5	

(b) Proof-theoretic fuzzy

	D	S	K	# Systems
	X	X	X	1
	X		X	1
	X			2
		X	X	1
			X	3
# Systems	4	2	6	

(c) Proof-theoretic probabilistic

	D	S	K	# Systems
	X	X		2
	X			5
		X	X	1
			X	1
# Systems	7	3	2	

4 Limitations of the State of the Art

We now discuss some limitations identified in the existing benchmarks, which have led to the recent introduction of novel benchmarks for the NeSy community.

Concerning Data. Combining data from different sources, and integrating low-level perceptual stimuli (images, videos, text, signals) with knowledge of any kind remains a cornerstone of most existing NeSy benchmarks. A large part of such benchmarks utilizes images as input, whereas text remains largely under-explored by the NeSy community [19]. The rise of Large Language Models (LLMs) has also rapidly changed the landscape, representing an additional element to account for. The integration of LLMs within NeSy approaches, to address reasoning and optimization tasks, seems a very promising though challenging research direction for the future. Images, instead, are the most frequently used category of input data, since they can be easily manipulated to create synthetic datasets with desired properties and characteristics. Moreover, they can be employed across a wide variety of applications like, e.g., game playing, as in Tic-Tac-Toe, constraint solving in Visual Sudoku, visual question answering as in CLEVR-Hans [39], plain classification as in Kandinsky Patterns [31]. Knowledge is usually implicit when dealing with certain input data categories, such as knowledge graphs, whereas the definition of specific tasks often requires the use of explicit knowledge, typically in the form of (soft or hard) logic rules: this is the case, for example, for the many benchmarks created, with different goals, from the MNIST dataset, or from CLEVR-based settings, such as CLE4EVR [25]. To mitigate the lack of explicit logic knowledge, several approaches have started co-learning a set of logic rules on knowledge graphs, or preprocess the graph with an external rule miner such as AMIE [14] or DRUM [34], and then use them for knowledge graph reasoning [10,18]. However, the extracted rules are often very different, and therefore it is difficult to build a comprehensive view of the capabilities enabled by exploiting this knowledge, even if evaluated on the same datasets.

Concerning Paradigms and Tasks. Besides traditional paradigms and tasks, such as classification and reasoning, interesting and novel research directions have emerged, leading to the identification as well as the design, of novel benchmarks. This is the case, for example, for benchmarks inspired by an incremental or continuous learning process, such as MNIST Sequential, CLE4EVR, or KANDY. Yet, we believe that this direction is still largely under-explored, and it actually represents a true element of novelty that should be further considered by future benchmarks, and by systems as well. Moreover, existing benchmarks are often too specific and do not properly model complex and real-world interactions. In this regard, some interesting advances toward a more general perspective have been considered on the crossword application [50], where knowledge and constraints can be used to solve or generate thematic world puzzles. The possibility of having a human-in-the-loop is also a crucial ingredient to enhance explainability and trustworthiness in AI systems. Benchmarking the capability of a system to extract the correct explanation is quite challenging, some recent attempts, however, have been made on specific topics, such as universal algebra [16] and electrical power grids [43]. A novel task that has been recently addressed within the NeSy community is that of reasoning shortcuts (e.g., BDD-OIA on autonomous driving predictions, and MNIST Half or Sequential). Although some of the existing benchmarks allow for the definition of tasks in small-data regimes (i.e., few-shot learning), semi-supervised learning, or even unsupervised learning, we also consider this aspect as an open challenge for the design of NeSy benchmarks.

Concerning Performance. Measuring the performance of NeSy systems with metrics that can capture properties beyond plain accuracy in classification or pattern recognition still remains an open issue, and it is a highly relevant problem within the NeSy community [22]. Among the novel benchmarks proposed within the TAILOR project, there have been some attempts to include performance metrics that take into account properties like interpretability and trustworthiness. This is the case, for example, for the works that have been studying concept learning, as well as reasoning shortcuts [25]. In this case, beyond the accuracy of the classification task, the idea is to analyze to what extent the learned representations are aligned with a set of pre-defined concepts. Energy efficiency to reduce the carbon footprint is another dimension that is gaining relevance. In this context, some recently proposed benchmarks, related to hardware dimensioning and transprecision computing, are exploiting energy-related metrics [13,38].

Concerning Implementation. From a more practical perspective, we remark that the comparison of the same system across different benchmarks, or of different systems on the same benchmark, is made difficult by the heterogeneity of the formalisms used to represent data and to model background knowledge. A standardization of frameworks would represent a crucial step to improve such comparisons and to advance the state-of-the-art: this could be enabled by providing APIs to the systems, by providing knowledge in different formats, or by including benchmarks within existing platforms such as OpenML. Ongoing work is looking into creating a knowledge representation language for NeSy that could be used to unambiguously and uniformly represent the knowledge in tasks and benchmarks [20].

Concerning Domains. Analysis of existing datasets may be very useful in highlighting how some domains are under-represented in the panorama of benchmarks usually considered by the NeSy community. Planning is an example of an under-represented domain, as it can easily provide both symbolic data, such as activity traces or maps, and numeric data, coming from perception. Novel benchmarks have been proposed within TAILOR for goal recognition and classic planning [6]. The medical and legal domains also represent two scenarios where background knowledge provided by experts could be a crucial element to boost the performance of purely data-driven systems: such knowledge could be provided in various formats, including knowledge graphs, ontologies, or even plain natural language. Biomedical data have been proposed as benchmarks for knowledge graph completion (e.g., the PharmKG benchmarks [10,51]), whereas legal documents (e.g., online terms of service) have been proposed for tasks related to distant supervision. Yet, more opportunities will likely emerge in these fields in the coming years. Regarding textual documents, computational argumentation and argument mining could be an additional research field where symbolic knowledge might be employed, for example, to encode argument models. Some preliminary works using NeSy systems for this kind of task have been proposed [15]. Finally, safety-critical applications have also been identified as a domain, where it is common to have hard and soft constraints that intelligent agents have to satisfy when interacting with the environment: even if some work in, e.g., autonomous driving [40], reinforcement learning [48] or malware detection [2,41], has been done in this context, a more extensive and systematic application of NeSy systems in this setting could also be an interesting research direction for the future.

5 Conclusions

In this paper, by borrowing relevant criteria from other work, we have given a categorization and overview of popular systems and benchmarks within neural-symbolic AI. We have categorized popular neural-symbolic frameworks into three categories: model-theoretic, proof-theoretic fuzzy, and proof-theoretic probabilistic systems. Our analysis shows that these three systems have distinct strengths and weaknesses, and this is reflected in the type of tasks to which they are applied. Going forward, we will further deepen our analysis of both systems and benchmarks with a more fine-grained analysis of the state-of-the-art.

References

1. Adamski, D.M., Potoniec, J.: Reasonable embeddings: learning concept embeddings with a transferable neural reasoner. Semantic Web (Preprint), 1–33 (2023)
2. Anthony, P., et al.: Explainable malware detection with tailored logic explained networks. arXiv preprint arXiv:2405.03009 (2024)

3. Badreddine, S., Garcez, A.d., Serafini, L., Spranger, M.: Logic tensor networks. Artif. Intell. **303**, 103649 (2022)
4. Barbiero, P., et al.: Interpretable neural-symbolic concept reasoning. In: International Conference on Machine Learning, pp. 1801–1825. PMLR (2023)
5. Barbiero, P., Giannini, F., Ciravegna, G., Diligenti, M., Marra, G.: Relational concept based models. arXiv preprint arXiv:2308.11991 (2023)
6. Chiari, M., Gerevini, A.E., Percassi, F., Putelli, L., Serina, I., Olivato, M.: Goal recognition as a deep learning task: the grnet approach. In: Proceedings of the International Conference on Automated Planning and Scheduling, vol. 33, pp. 560–568 (2023)
7. Ciravegna, G.: Logic explained networks. Artif. Intell. **314**, 103822 (2023)
8. Cohen, W.W., Yang, F., Mazaitis, K.: Tensorlog: a probabilistic database implemented using deep-learning infrastructure. J. Artif. Intell. Res. **67**, 285–325 (2020)
9. Cunnington, D., Law, M., Lobo, J., Russo, A.: FFNSL: feed-forward neural-symbolic learner. Mach. Learn. **112**(2), 515–569 (2023)
10. Diligenti, M., Giannini, F., Fioravanti, S., Graziani, C., Falaschi, M., Marra, G.: Enhancing embedding representations of biomedical data using logic knowledge. In: 2023 International Joint Conference on Neural Networks (IJCNN), pp. 1–8. IEEE (2023)
11. Diligenti, M., Gori, M., Sacca, C.: Semantic-based regularization for learning and inference. Artif. Intell. **244**, 143–165 (2017)
12. Espinosa Zarlenga, M., et al.: Concept embedding models: beyond the accuracy-explainability trade-off. Adv. Neural. Inf. Process. Syst. **35**, 21400–21413 (2022)
13. Francobaldi, M., et al.: Tinderai: support system for matching AI algorithms and embedded devices. In: The International FLAIRS Conference Proceedings, vol. 36 (2023)
14. Galárraga, L.A., Teflioudi, C., Hose, K., Suchanek, F.: Amie: association rule mining under incomplete evidence in ontological knowledge bases. In: Proceedings of the 22nd International Conference on World Wide Web, pp. 413–422 (2013)
15. Galassi, A., Lippi, M., Torroni, P.: Investigating logic tensor networks for neural-symbolic argument mining. In: Proceedings of 1st International Joint Conference on Learning, Reasoning, pp. 1–7 (2021)
16. Giannini, F., et al.: Interpretable graph networks formulate universal algebra conjectures. Adv. Neural Inf. Process. Syst. **36** (2024)
17. Giles, C.L., Bollacker, K.D., Lawrence, S.: Citeseer: an automatic citation indexing system. In: Proceedings of the Third ACM Conference on Digital Libraries, pp. 89–98 (1998)
18. Guo, S., Wang, Q., Wang, L., Wang, B., Guo, L.: Knowledge graph embedding with iterative guidance from soft rules. In: Proceedings of the AAAI Conference on Artificial Intelligence, vol. 32 (2018)
19. Hamilton, K., Nayak, A., Božić, B., Longo, L.: Is neuro-symbolic AI meeting its promises in natural language processing? A structured review. Semantic Web (Preprint), 1–42 (2022)
20. van Krieken, E., Badreddine, S., Manhaeve, R., Giunchiglia, E.: Uller: a unified language for learning and reasoning. arXiv preprint arXiv:2405.00532 (2024)
21. Li, Z., Huang, J., Naik, M.: Scallop: a language for neurosymbolic programming. Proc. ACM Program. Lang. **7**(PLDI), 1463–1487 (2023)
22. Lorello, L.S., Lippi, M.: The challenge of learning symbolic representations. In: d'Avila Garcez, A.S., Besold, T.R., Gori, M., Jiménez-Ruiz, E. (eds.) Proceedings of the 17th International Workshop on Neural-Symbolic Learning and Reasoning, La

Certosa di Pontignano, Siena, Italy, 3–5 July 2023. CEUR Workshop Proceedings, vol. 3432, pp. 44–61. CEUR-WS.org (2023). https://ceur-ws.org/Vol-3432/paper4.pdf
23. Maene, J., De Raedt, L.: Soft-unification in deep probabilistic logic. Adv. Neural Inf. Process. Syst. **36** (2024)
24. Manhaeve, R., Dumancic, S., Kimmig, A., Demeester, T., De Raedt, L.: Deepproblog: neural probabilistic logic programming. Adv. Neural Inf. Process. Syst. **31** (2018)
25. Marconato, E., Bontempo, G., Ficarra, E., Calderara, S., Passerini, A., Teso, S.: Neuro-symbolic continual learning: knowledge, reasoning shortcuts and concept rehearsal. In: Proceedings of the 40th International Conference on Machine Learning, pp. 23915–23936 (2023)
26. Marra, G., Diligenti, M., Giannini, F.: Relational reasoning networks. arXiv preprint arXiv:2106.00393 (2021)
27. Marra, G., Dumancic, S., Manhaeve, R., De Raedt, L.: From statistical relational to neurosymbolic artificial intelligence: a survey. Artif. Intell. **328**, 104062 (2024). https://doi.org/10.1016/J.ARTINT.2023.104062
28. Marra, G., Giannini, F., Diligenti, M., Gori, M.: Integrating learning and reasoning with deep logic models. In: Brefeld, U., Fromont, E., Hotho, A., Knobbe, A., Maathuis, M., Robardet, C. (eds.) ECML PKDD 2019. LNCS (LNAI), vol. 11907, pp. 517–532. Springer, Cham (2020). https://doi.org/10.1007/978-3-030-46147-8_31
29. Marra, G., Kuželka, O.: Neural markov logic networks. In: Uncertainty in Artificial Intelligence, pp. 908–917. PMLR (2021)
30. Minervini, P., Bosnjak, M., Rocktäschel, T., Riedel, S., Grefenstette, E.: Differentiable reasoning on large knowledge bases and natural language. In: AAAI, pp. 5182–5190. AAAI Press (2020)
31. Müller, H., Holzinger, A.: Kandinsky patterns. Artif. Intell. **300**, 103546 (2021)
32. Pryor, C., Dickens, C., Augustine, E., Albalak, A., Wang, W.Y., Getoor, L.: Neupsl: neural probabilistic soft logic. In: IJCAI, pp. 4145–4153. ijcai.org (2023)
33. Rocktäschel, T., Riedel, S.: End-to-end differentiable proving. Adv. Neural Inf. Process. Syst. **30** (2017)
34. Sadeghian, A., Armandpour, M., Ding, P., Wang, D.Z.: Drum: end-to-end differentiable rule mining on knowledge graphs. Adv. Neural Inf. Process. Syst. **32** (2019)
35. Shindo, H., Pfanschilling, V., Dhami, D.S., Kersting, K.: αilp: thinking visual scenes as differentiable logic programs. Mach. Learn. **112**(5), 1465–1497 (2023)
36. Skryagin, A., Stammer, W., Ochs, D., Dhami, D.S., Kersting, K.: Neural-probabilistic answer set programming. In: KR (2022)
37. Sourek, G., Aschenbrenner, V., Zelezny, F., Schockaert, S., Kuzelka, O.: Lifted relational neural networks: efficient learning of latent relational structures. J. Artif. Intell. Res. **62**, 69–100 (2018)
38. Spillo, G., De Filippo, A., Musto, C., Milano, M., Semeraro, G.: Towards sustainability-aware recommender systems: analyzing the trade-off between algorithms performance and carbon footprint. In: Proceedings of the 17th ACM Conference on Recommender Systems, pp. 856–862 (2023)
39. Stammer, W., Schramowski, P., Kersting, K.: Right for the right concept: revising neuro-symbolic concepts by interacting with their explanations. In: Proceedings of the IEEE/CVF Conference on Computer Vision and Pattern Recognition, pp. 3619–3629 (2021)
40. Stoian, M.C., Giunchiglia, E., Lukasiewicz, T.: Exploiting t-norms for deep learning in autonomous driving. arXiv preprint arXiv:2402.11362 (2024)

41. Švec, P., Balogh, Š., Homola, M., Kl'uka, J., Bisták, T.: Semantic data representation for explainable windows malware detection models. arXiv preprint arXiv:2403.11669 (2024)
42. Tsamoura, E., Hospedales, T.M., Michael, L.: Neural-symbolic integration: a compositional perspective. In: 35th Conference on Artificial Intelligence, AAAI 2021, Virtual Event, 2–9 February 2021, pp. 5051–5060. AAAI Press (2021). https://doi.org/10.1609/aaai.v35i6.16639
43. Varbella, A., Amara, K., Gjorgiev, B., Sansavini, G.: Powergraph: a power grid benchmark dataset for graph neural networks. In: NeurIPS 2023 Workshop: New Frontiers in Graph Learning (2023)
44. Vermeulen, A., Manhaeve, R., Marra, G.: An experimental overview of neural-symbolic systems. In: International Conference on Inductive Logic Programming, pp. 124–138. Springer, Heidelberg (2023). https://doi.org/10.1007/978-3-031-49299-0_9
45. Weber, L., Minervini, P., Münchmeyer, J., Leser, U., Rocktäschel, T.: Nlprolog: reasoning with weak unification for question answering in natural language. In: ACL (1), pp. 6151–6161. Association for Computational Linguistics (2019)
46. Winters, T., Marra, G., Manhaeve, R., De Raedt, L.: Deepstochlog: neural stochastic logic programming. In: Proceedings of the AAAI Conference on Artificial Intelligence, vol. 36, pp. 10090–10100 (2022)
47. Yang, F., Yang, Z., Cohen, W.W.: Differentiable learning of logical rules for knowledge base reasoning. Adv. Neural Inf. Process. Syst. **30** (2017)
48. Yang, W.C., Marra, G., Rens, G., De Raedt, L.: Safe reinforcement learning via probabilistic logic shields. In: Proceedings IJCAI (2023)
49. Yang, Z., Ishay, A., Lee, J.: Neurasp: embracing neural networks into answer set programming. In: IJCAI, pp. 1755–1762. ijcai.org (2020)
50. Zeinalipour, K., Iaquinta, T., Angelini, G., Rigutini, L., Maggini, M., Gori, M.: Building bridges of knowledge: innovating education with automated crossword generation. In: 2023 International Conference on Machine Learning and Applications (ICMLA), pp. 1228–1236. IEEE (2023)
51. Zheng, S., et al.: Pharmkg: a dedicated knowledge graph benchmark for biomedical data mining. Brief. Bioinf. **22**(4), bbaa344 (2021)

Formal Reasoning with Large Language Models

MisCC: Misinformation Detection on Counterfactual Claims

Xue Li, Vaishak Belle, and Björn Ross(✉)

University of Edinburgh, Edinburgh, UK
{xue.shirley.li,vbelle,b.ross}@ed.ac.uk
https://sweb.inf.ed.ac.uk/bross3/

Abstract. Counterfactual claims (CCs) play an important role in everyday conversations, but they are difficult to fact-check automatically and understudied in fact-checking research. We investigated the nuances of misinformation in CCs, considering various potential truth values for antecedents and consequents, as well as causality. Through logic-based analysis, we present a logical theory comprising an algorithm for detecting misinformation in CCs and an approach for ensuring that the result is free of inconsistencies when needed. Finally, we propose a pipeline that integrates large language models (LLMs) with our theory for fact-checking CCs. In this approach, LLMs assist in interpreting natural language and making initial predictions based on their knowledge. Subsequently, our theory verifies the consistency of LLMs' initial predictions as well as computes CCs' truth values. We also created and released a comprehensive dataset of CCs, which supports multiple CC-related tasks, including classifying 1) CCs, 2) the verifiability of a statement 3) the truth value of a statement and 4) the truth values of CCs. Then GPT4 and Llama3 with zero-shot were applied as the baseline. Our approach improves their F1 scores for classifying CC's false class, the misinformation, from 0.55 to 0.64 and 0.46 to 0.61, respectively. Notably, the inconsistency checker only benefits the prediction of true classes. The large portion of false CCs in our dataset represents the portion of misinformation in CCs on social media and the poor performance of GPT4 and Llama3 in classifying the false class highlights the need for more research on fact-checking CCs.

Keywords: Counterfactuals · Fact-checking · LLMs · Neuro-symbolic AI

1 Introduction

With the popularity of social media, false claims spreading online have been harmful and significantly impact people's opinions, democracy and even mental health [28]. Since internet data is widely used for training large language models (LLMs), e.g., GPT4 [1], false claims also damage the development of LLMs. Automated fact-checking systems attempt to debunk false claims by classifying the truth value of a claim into true, false or unknown.

W.-Z. Dai (Ed.): ILP 2024, LNAI 16059, pp. 253–267, 2026.
https://doi.org/10.1007/978-3-032-09087-4_18

Although there is a lot of research into fact-checking, much of it still focuses on relatively simple factual statements, e.g., *'Mount Donaldson is east of the Osicki Glacier'*, and on claims known to be check-worthy, i.e. commonly known and debunked misinformative tropes [13]. One particular form of claims that remains understudied in the field of automatic fact-checking is counterfactual claims (CCs). These claims typically take the form below [26].

$$\text{If A were true then B would be true.} \tag{1}$$

CCs allow us to reason about possible alternative worlds and have been used in defining causation [7], explaining machine learning predictions [29] and supporting decision-making for future actions [23], but surprisingly there has been very little research on fact-checking counterfactual claims that people make.

This lack of research is problematic because counterfactual claims can misinform. Take for example the claim *'if she had not taken the COVID vaccine, she would not be having fertility problems'*, a common trope in COVID misinformation. The claim asserts that (1) the subject of the sentence has taken the COVID vaccine, (2) has fertility problems and (3) there is a causal link between vaccination and fertility. Clearly, this claim is much harder to check than the earlier example of a simple factual statement, because it requires checking the veracity of each of the sub-claims and the link between them. These challenges mean that fact-checking CCs is a fantastic testbed for advances in AI and for the integration of neural (e.g. LLMs) and symbolic AI (e.g. logic programming). In this work, we focus on climate misinformation in particular, because it is widespread and has severe consequences.

LLMs are powerful tools for debunking misinformation from previously unknown claims, as they have been pre-trained to capture a wide range of contextual semantics despite potential inconsistencies in accuracy [21]. However, approaches that rely only on LLMs are unreliable as they rely on LLMs' own interpretations of a CC and their understanding (if any) of what makes a CC false. Therefore, our hypothesis on a neuro-symbolic approach is:

> *by integrating logical theory about CCs with LLMs, the performance in predicting misinformation can be improved.*

Accordingly, our contributions[1] are:

- a logical theory for guiding LLMs in fact-checking CCs and checking whether LLMs' predictions are consistent;
- the fact-checking pipeline for CCs based on the proposed theory;
- a comprehensive dataset of CCs, called MisCC, which supports classifying CCs, the verifiability and truth value of a CC's sub-claim and misinformation in CCs (misinformation in CCs);
- a baseline of MisCC as the evaluation of the neuro-symbolic pipeline with GPT-4 and Llama3.

[1] Our code and dataset are available at https://github.com/smash-edin/MisCC.

A comprehensive dataset is crucial for investigating CC-related tasks in AI. To the best of our knowledge, MisCC is the only dataset of CCs with truth value labels for both sub-claims and the causality between sub-claims. The designed pipeline will be applicable to assist human experts in debunking misinformation on social media by directly predicting the truth value of a CC.

2 Related Work

Fact-checking systems aim to debunk disinformation and misinformation, where the former is intended to mislead people while the latter does not consider whether the false claim is created on purpose [2], it can also be interpreted where the speaker did not know the claim is false [25]. Fake news is also targeted by fact-checking systems, which mimic mainstream news and are sometimes seen as a part of disinformation, as in [25]. In this paper, we do not consider whether the false claims were created on purpose, i.e., we focus on the truth value of a claim and refer to misinformation detection as it is usually unsure whether the speaker knew a CC was false.

Pretrained LLMs, such as BERT [8], are commonly used tools for verifying claims and their logical relationships without additional evidence, relying on the information LLMs learned during training. In the validity and novelty prediction shared task in 2022, GPT3 secured first place [14], with [22] coming in second by combining BART with information extracted from knowledge graphs. While LLMs were previously limited in their ability to generate explanations, generative LLMs like GPT4 can now provide some explanations, as demonstrated in the multistate essay examination test by [17]. However, consistency check is essential to LLMs' applications [32]. We will propose an approach for checking the consistency of LLMs' responses in fact-checking CCs in §3.2.

Counterfactuals are valuable in different fields, e.g., explaining fact-checking models' predictions using validity classifier [6] and debiasing for claim verification [30]. However, no research has investigated the truth value of CCs that are expressed in natural language except for [3], which computes the probability of a CC being true based on prior probabilities of causal dependencies. In addition, [26] introduces the logic of counterfactuals that relies on possible worlds with minimal changes (or most similar p-worlds). However, similar to causal graphic models [20] and single world interventional graphs [4], these are valuable but purely conceptual papers, which require the prior probabilities or the network of causal dependencies. As the required information is unavailable for a previously unseen CC from online posts, they are currently inapplicable for detecting misinformation in real-life CCs, as encountered, for example, on social media.

A natural language processing task that has received some attention is the task of *recognising* counterfactual claims in text, an example is SemEval-2020 Task 5 whose organisers published a dataset for counterfactual recognition [31]. However, it does not contain labels on truth values. In addition, they only contain the start and end positions of sub-claims in a CC rather than extracting accurate sub-claims as discussed at the beginning of the next section.

Another related NLP task is *recognising textual entailment* (RTE). A claim A is said to (textually) entail another claim B if typically, a human reading A would infer that B is most likely true [5]. For the counterfactual claim "if A were true, then B would be true", there is some similarity between fact-checking the causal relationship between A and B and the textual entailment between A and B. What is more, the problem of fact-checking individual claims such as A and B can be seen as a variant of RTE: given a body of evidence (E), we can confirm whether E supports or refutes A or there is not enough evidence by treating it as a textual entailment problem. This is also known as the claim verification task in fact-checking research [13]. FEVER is the largest fact verification dataset, consisting of 185,445 claims [27], and a variant of it, CLIMATE-FEVER contains 7,675 evidence-claim pairs generated from 1,535 real-world claims about climate change.

3 Misinformation in CCs: Theory and Pipeline

Formally, the counterfactual claim contains two sub-claims, the antecedent (ANT) and the consequent (CON), written in the subjunctive conditional structure [26]. When extracting a sub-claim, these linguistic conventions should be considered, as shown in the following example where key changes are highlighted in red.

C 1 *If climate change was true, Edinburgh would be underwater now.*

C1's ANT: *climate change* is *true.*
C1's CON: *Edinburgh* is *underwater now.*

By taking sub-claims into account, we will define the misinformation and the corresponding truth value of a CC, followed by a pipeline with a consistency checker in this section.

3.1 Misinformation in CCs and Related Truth Values

Linguistic implicature refers to the content that is implicitly indicated rather than explicitly expressed [12]. The (pragmatic) implication in CCs is that ANTs and CONs should be counterfactual, i.e., false in reality. Despite current research only focusing on the causality of a CC, like in [26], we argue that it is important also to consider the truth value of CCs' sub-claims. For example, from C2 given below, we can infer that Tom has not graduated from university and is not a climate scientist.

C 2 *If Tom had graduated from University, he would be a climate scientist now.*

Accordingly, we define the convention of CCs regarding the truth value of sub-claims as the *Denial Implicature*[2].

[2] Thanks to Dr. Imogen Morris, who named the term to describe this linguistic phenomenon.

Definition 1 (Denial Implicature). *Based on linguistic convention, a CC implicitly suggests its ANT and CON are false, i.e., they are the subjects of the denial implicature.*

Denial Implicatures in C2 include: *Tom has not graduated from university* and *Tom is not a climate scientist.*

Theorem 1 (Misinformation on Denial Implicature (MDI)). *When the subject of the denial implicature, i.e., ANT or CON, is true, the CC contains MDI.*

We call *MDI subject to antecedent* when the antecedent is true, and *MDI subject to consequent* when the consequent is true.

Assuming Tom in C2 has actually graduated from university, this deceptive CC contains MDI that misleads others into believing Tom has not.

There are claims whose truth values are unknown. One reason for the unknown is that, although the claim has a truth value, the individual/agent does not know it due to the limit of their knowledge. Alternatively, the claim does not have a truth value because it is not verifiable [9,13], as defined in Definition 2.

Definition 2 (Verifiability). *A claim is verifiable if its truth value can be derived or tested to be true or false based on specified knowledge.*

Claims given by examples C3 and C4 are unverifiable because the former is a subjective statement about personal opinions, and the latter is not testable, respectively. Accordingly, we consider the truth value of unverifiable claims to be 'Unknown' for simplicity. Another special case is comparison to reality, which states a situation different from reality. A claim with such a comparison is always false, even if it is about personal opinions that are usually unverifiable, e.g. the sub-claims of C5.

C 3 *This summer is too hot to have a holiday.*

C 4 *I believe climate change is happening.*

C 5 *If the last summer was hotter, I would stay inside more.*

Under Definition 1, a non-verifiable sub-claim cannot be the subject of MDI. This definition can be seen as a practice of innocent until proven guilty in misinformation detection, which fits our main targeted application: debunking misinformation on social media.

As studied in the majority of the literature, an obvious reason for misinformation is that a CC's ANT does not cause the CON, i.e., a CC is invalid [24]. For example, the causality in C2 depends on whether Tom graduating from university causes him to become a climate scientist. Whether or not this is true depends on related factors, e.g., whether he studied climate science.

Definition 3 (Misinformation on Causality (MoC)). *A CC spreads misinformation on the causality if its ANT does not cause its CON.*

A CC is seen as true only if it is known to not contain any misinformation. Therefore, we define a CC's truth value based on whether it contains MDI or MoC.

Definition 4 (A CC's Truth Value)). *A CC is false if it contains MDI or MoC. A CC is true if it is known to contain neither MDI nor MoC. Otherwise, its truth value is unknown.*

Firstly, we define an unary function $\mathcal{T}$ to return the truth value of its argument: $\top$ for true, $\bot$ for false and ω for unknown. Thus, $\neg\bot = \top$ and $\neg\omega = \omega$. Then, the truth value of a counterfactual claim C can be calculated by the following equation, where C_a is its antecedent, C_c is its consequent, and C_{caus} is its causality.

$$\mathcal{T}(C) = \begin{cases} \top, & (\neg\mathcal{T}(C_a)) \wedge (\neg\mathcal{T}(C_c)) \wedge \mathcal{T}(C_{caus}) \\ \bot, & \mathcal{T}(C_a) \vee \mathcal{T}(C_c) \vee (\neg\mathcal{T}(C_{caus})) \\ \omega, & \text{otherwise} \end{cases} \tag{E2}$$

The first and second conditions in c cannot be satisfied at the same time. When the first condition is true, then $\mathcal{T}(C_a) = \mathcal{T}(C_c) = \neg\mathcal{T}(C_c) = \bot$. In this case, the second condition is false, and vice versa.

C6 and C7 depict false CCs, where the first contains MoC and the latter is a mix of MDI and MoC. Given C7, for people who do not know the truth values of all sub-claims but that Mount Donaldson is NOT underwater, if they trust all causalities, they will draw a completely incorrect conclusion about glaciers and climate change: *glaciers are NOT melting and climate change is NOT real.*

C 6 *If all electricity was from wind, summer would be as cool as* $-60°$ *C.*
C 7 *If climate change was real, the glaciers would be melting, and if the glaciers were melting, Mount Donaldson would be underwater.*

3.2 Inconsistency Check

According to Definitions 1 and 3, we have the following theorem, which can be used as an inconsistency checker.

Theorem 2. *If a CC contains MDI subject to its antecedent without MoC, then it must have MDI subject to its consequent.*

The proof is straightforward: if ANT and CC are true then CON should be true rather than false. In contrast, if a CC contains neither MDI w.r.t. ANT nor MoC, it is unknown whether it has MDI on its consequent because the CON may not happen or may be caused by factors other than the ANT.

Another straightforward inconsistency check is for a sub-claim that has been classified as unverifiable and then been classified as true or false, which violates Definition 2.

3.3 Pipeline

Based on the above discussion, a neuro-symbolic pipeline is depicted in Fig. 1. The input claim is classified as containing misinformation when the output is false. The inconsistency checker provides extra information w.r.t. the reliability of the output.

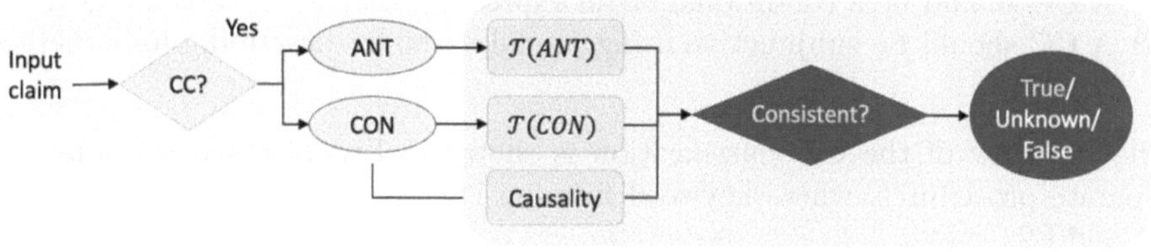

Fig. 1. A neuro-symbolic pipeline for fact-checking in CCs: *all blue notes are tasks done by LLMs with the purple node and the whole flow structure based on logical reasoning.* (Color figure online)

LLMs can be used to filter CCs and extract a CC's antecedent and consequent. Then LLMs will continue to predict sub-claims verifiabilities, truth values and causalities, based on which the truth value of the input CC will be calculated using (E2). The consistency of predicted truth values will be checked: if the answers of LLMs regarding the truth values of sub-claims and causalities are inconsistent, the system can and will choose an appropriate solution, e.g., giving these CCs to human experts.

This combination guarantees the classification of CCs following our logical theory on fact-checking CCs with given truth values of sub-claims and causalities from LLMs. Without applying our theory or this pipeline, pure LLMs dependant approaches are unreliable as they rely on LLMs' own interpretations of a CC and their understanding of what makes a CC false. Breaking down such a task into sub-tasks bears some resemblance to *chain-of-thought (CoT)* prompting, which is widely reported to improve LLMs' performance at reasoning tasks [10].

This pipeline allows training or fine-tuning separate models for individual sub-tasks which may also result in better performance than directly training or fine-tuning models on the task of predicting the truth value of the CC as a whole given the text of the full claim (a highly complex task).

4 MisCC Dataset

We create a dataset of counterfactual claims, MisCC. Candidate claims were collected from subreddits about climate change using Reddit's public API. Subreddits are *'climateskeptics'*, *'climatechange'*, *'ClimateOffensive'*, *'climate_science'*, *'RenewableEnergy'*, *'climatedisalarm'*, *'conspiracy'* and the posts date from between 2017 and 2022. All CCs in MisCC have been manually checked to ensure that they do not contain any personal information or any private identifiers. The dataset creation process was approved by our institution's ethics committee.

4.1 CCs Collection and Annotation

CCs have two important features, given below. Although it is possible that a CC may omit either ANT or CON for simplicity in dialogue, only CCs with both ANT and CON were collected in MisCC to make sure that the dataset can be used to study causality in CCs.

F1 A CC should be a conditional claim expressing that ANT causes CON.
F2 A CC should be subjunctive using modal verbs for describing hypothetical scenarios.

The workflow of the CC classification is shown in Fig. 2, which contains two separate procedures, where keyword filtering is chosen based on CC's features F1 and F2.

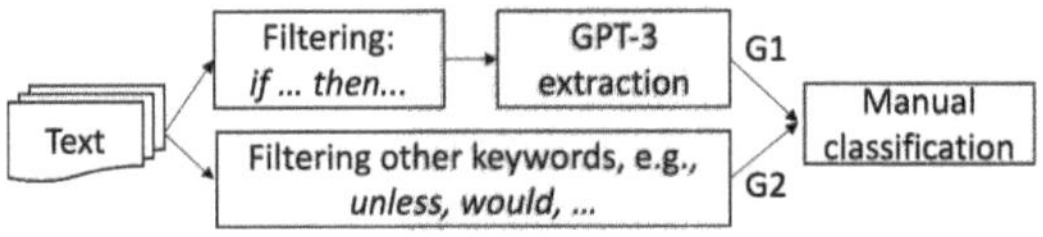

Fig. 2. CCs classification in MisCC: *G1 and G2 were manually classified separately.*

From original posts, sentences were extracted from each collected post using *sent_tokenize* from the NLTK toolkit [19]. Firstly, 2937 sentences with the presence of keywords "if ... then" were selected, among which 2500 sentences (G1) were classified as "CC" by the GPT-3 model, named $gpt - text - davinci - 002$ [15] using few-shot learning. Then the group of candidate CCs containing 1327 claims, G1 in Fig. 2, were randomly selected and manually annotated, among which 1234 CCs were found. However, only 224 did not need manually reforming to be subjunctive. Secondly, the group of 350 candidates, G2 in Fig. 2, were collected by considering other keywords flagging F1 or F2 such as "unless" and "would", among which 122 CCs were found. In G2, only 29 CCs did not need manual reforming into proper CCs.

After cleaning up, there were 2768 sentences containing 1346 CCs with their ANTs and CONs extracted manually. Among classified CCs, 1147 were further annotated with truth values by six native English speakers, who are PhD students. Each CC was annotated by three or four annotators and the majority vote among labels of "Yes", "No" and "Others" was taken as the final label. We define the majority vote as the only label given by most annotators or the one with the highest confidence level among labels given by most annotators. According to (E2), a CC's truth value can be calculated when $\mathcal{T}(C_a)$, $\mathcal{T}(C_c)$ and $\mathcal{T}(C_c)$ are given. Thus, the task of labelling a CC's truth value was decomposed into these three sub-tasks in our annotation, where the verifiability of a sub-claim was labelled prior to its truth value.

Altogether, the careful process adopted to obtain annotations ensures their quality, with the trade-off being the reasonable size of the resulting dataset.

4.2 Statistics and Analysis on the Dataset

Krippendorff's α is commonly used to evaluate the reliability of data annotation [18]. For sub-claims, the values for the verifiability and truth value are $\alpha = 0.38$ and $\alpha = 0.3$, respectively. Although they are not high, at least two annotators out of three chose the same label in 86.9% of CCs. As they needed to apply implicit arguments to interpret a given CC based on their commonsense and personal knowledge, it is reasonable that their interpretations of the same CC vary even if they understand the annotation task very well. For causality, $\alpha = 0.17$, which is in the range of the corresponding agreements in a similar task of entailment in CLIMATE-FEVER, i.e. 0.106 and 0.316 [9]. The annotation in most entailment datasets is easier because they are usually direct entitlement, e.g., 34% in FEVER in a sample of 50 claims, where a claim is partially contained semantically by the other to some extent [16]. For example, "London is the capital city of the UK" directly entails "London is a British city". Causality is usually non-direct entailment, e.g., "London is a city of the UK" vs "Among British cities, London has a high population density". It can be seen that background knowledge and inference are essential in understanding and analysing causality.

In addition, the claims of the aforementioned other datasets are well-written mainly from online encyclopedia resources, i.e. Wikipedia and Debatepedia, which are not representative of claims from social media where users typically use oral language [11]. Therefore, our dataset MisCC is particularly valuable because it is constituted of real-world CCs from social media and their truth values.

Table 1. Statistics of all classes in MisCC.

	Is it a CC?	*Is it MisInfo?*	*Verifiable*		*Truth Value*		*Causality*
			ANT	*CON*	*ANT*	*CON*	
Yes	1346	528	449	329	32	21	383
No	1422	360	560	732	73	69	499
Others	– –	259	138	86	344	239	265
Total	2768	1147	1147	1147	449	329	1147

The label distribution of the 1147 CCs' truth values is given by Table 1. In this dataset, the majority of CCs are false. As our dataset was originally from social media without specific selection w.r.t. factors that obviously affect truth values, this distribution indicates that misinformation is likely to be common in CCs, highlighting the importance of misinformation detection on CCs.

5 Evaluation: a Baseline

This evaluation aims to 1) assess whether incorporating our logical theory improves LLMs' performance in detecting misinformation on CCs and 2) provide a benchmark for the zero-shot prompting method with the state-of-the-art LLMs, GPT4 and Llama3-8B, whose names are *gpt-4* and *Meta-Llama-3-8B*, respectively. Llama3-8B was applied in our experiments due to the feasibility of deployment and we will call it Llama3 for succinctness in this paper. The temperature of both models was set as 0 so that these models select the answer with the highest probability and then all other parameters were the default values provided by the APIs of OpenAI and Ollama, respectively.

5.1 CC Classification

Llama3 with the same prompt template was applied to classifying CCs on the whole MisCC dataset, a subset of MisCC and SemEval 2020 Task 5 [31], respectively. Figure 3 (a) shows the performance on the true class. To study whether the recognition of a subjunctive claim is a bottleneck in CCs' classification, we pruned 1094 CCs that were manually reformed from conditional but not subjunctive non-CCs in MisCC. For example, both C8 and C9 are from MisCC and the subset of MisCC contains C8 but not C9. The performance on this subset of MisCC is denoted by *MisCC-subset* in the figure, where the precision dropped dramatically while recall remained similar. This evidence supports that Llama3 is able to recognise subjunctive claims in CC classification. Furthermore, the performance in the MisCC-subset is similar to the related *SemEval* task, which evidences that the difficulty in CC classification of the subset of MisCC is similar to that of the SemEval dataset for Llama3.

C 8 (Non-CC) *If there are not infinite realities, then there are not infinite realities that are exactly like this one down to the particle.*

C 9 (Reformed CC) *If there were not infinite realities, then there would not be infinite realities that are exactly like this one down to the particle.*

5.2 CCs' Truth Values

To investigate the hypothesis: whether our logical theory improves the performance in detecting misinformation in CCs, we assessed GPT4 and Llama3-8B on classifying CCs' truth values with approaches P1 - P3, listed below[3]. Here <> was replaced with the corresponding text from our dataset. P2 and P3 test the application of our theory as CoT prompting and the proposed neuro-symbolic pipeline, respectively. The prediction results are denoted by Fig. 3 (b).

P1 Direct prompt: "*Given the counterfactual claim: <>. Is that claim true?*".
P2 Our equation as CoT prompting (E2): "*A CC is false if its ANT is true or its CON is true or its CON does not follow the ANT. In addition, a CC is true if neither its ANT nor its CON is true and its ANT causes the CON. Otherwise, it is unknown whether a CC is true. Given the CC: <> The ANT is: <> The CON is: <> Is the CC true?*"

[3] To be succinct, we continue to use acronyms of CC, ANT and CON in the demonstration and omit the end of our promptings about how the model should respond, e.g., in JSON format and answers should be Yes, no or others.

P3 Combine LLMs with our equation: only query for sub-tasks about ANT and CON's truth values and causality. Then compute a CC's truth value with sub-tasks results based on (E2).

Interestingly, the informative CoT prompting in P2 resulted in the highest F1 score of Llama3 but the lowest of GPT4. The improvement is intuitive as the prompting tells the model how to decide the truth value. The reason for GPT4's counterintuitive decrement may be due to the complexity of prompting challenged the model w.r.t. understanding logics or conducting logic-based computation.

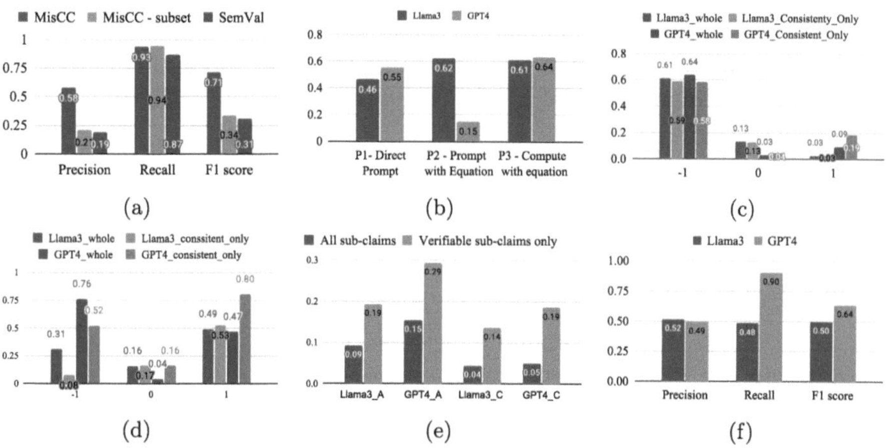

Fig. 3. Classification tasks on (a) a given claim being CCs (b) a CC being false, i.e., misinformation, (c) the truth value of CCs' with consistency check, (d) the verifiability of sub-claims, (e) the true class of sub-claims, where the suffix A and C represent sub-claims of ANTs and CONs, respectively, (f) the false class of causality between a CC's ANT and CON; *F1 scores are given in (b–e).*

As shown by P2 in Fig. 3 (b), directly describing the theory as CoT prompting was the most helpful approach for Llama3 but considerably harmful for GPT4. On the other hand, the application of our equation in a neuro-symbolic approach, P3, improved GPT4 and Llama3's performance to 0.64 and 0.61, respectively. Thus, our hypothesis is supported: integrating logical theory as a neuro-symbolic pipeline improved both tested models' performance. Notably, the pipeline has the potential for further improvement as it allows users to develop "expert models" targeting each sub-task.

Figure 3 (c) depicts how consistency check affects models' performance among different truth value classes of CCs'. The comparison was between the whole dataset and the subset containing only CCs of which the model's responses about sub-tasks were consistent. The F1 scores dropped slightly for both models on the false class and remained similar on the unknown class. Meanwhile, Llama3 and GPT4's F1 scores on the true class of CCs increased by 0.002 and 0.093, respectively. Although these changes are not significant, it is interesting to see that the consistency checker helped both models recognise the true CCs. This indicates that when LLMs' responses are consistent, they are more likely to make the correct decision on recognising the truth. As a result, one can be more confident about a CC classified as true actually being true when the LLM's responses about that CC passed the consistency checker.

Sub-tasks in the Pipeline. In our best-performed baseline P3, The performance of sub-tasks directly affects the final result. Statistics of GPT4 and Llama3's performance on these sub-tasks are discussed in this section.

The following are the promptings for detecting MID (sub-claims' truth value) and MoC (causality), defined in Definition 1 and 3. Some promptings were chosen based on the instructions of LLMs' producers.

Prompting for MID: Claim1, below, is either the ANT or CON of a CC.
Verifiability *A claim is verifiable if its truth value can be derived or tested to be true or false based on specified knowledge. Is Claim1 verifiable? Claim1 is originally from the CC in an online conversion. Claim1: "<>" CC: "<>"*
truth value : *Is Claim1 true? Claim1 is originally from the CC in an online conversion. Claim1: "<>". CC: "<>"*
Prompting for MoC: *Antecedent: <> Consequent: <> Does the consequent follow the antecedent? Does the antecedent cause the consequent?*

Both models have similar performance in classifying the verifiable sub-claims w.r.t. F1 score, shown by Fig. 3 (d). The best performance was achieved by GPT4 aided by the inconsistency checker. Here inconsistency checker has the same effect as shown in Fig. 3 (c): it damaged both models' performance on predicting the false class but was helpful on the true class.

The true class of sub-claims is crucial in misinformation detection in CCs because it directly results in MDI. Figure 3 (e) depicts F1 scores on the true class of sub-claims. The comparison was between all sub-claims and verifiable sub-claims only. Both models' performances were similarly poor with better results on verifiable sub-claims only. This result shows that these models tend to assign true or false as the truth value of a non-verifiable statement. Meanwhile, it is interesting to see that ANTs are generally easier than CONs for both models. A possible reason is that CONs are more likely to be unseen claims than ANTs, e.g., not existing in LLMs training data. Figure 3 (f) shows the performance of the two models in predicting that an ANT does not cause a CON. It can be seen that GPT4 is better at detecting the false class than Llama3 on the MisCC dataset.

In conclusion, our neuro-symbolic pipeline improves both model's performance in classifying the false class of CCs and enabled GPT4 to achieve the highest F1 score of 0.64. On the other hand, Llama3's own best F1 score is 0.62

with our logical theory as CoT prompting. Meanwhile, the consistency checker is helpful in predicting the true class in nearly all tested tasks. Despite GPT4 and Llama3 being powerful, these initial results demonstrate that fact-checking CCs is a challenging task given the complexity and flexibility of claims in daily conversations.

6 Conclusion

We argue that more research is needed on fact-checking counterfactual claims in natural language. We argue that such claims can misinform, by incorrectly implying that the antecedent or the consequent of the claim is untrue when it is in fact true, or by incorrectly implying that there is a causal link between antecedent and consequent. We detail the circumstances under which such claims can be said to misinform.

More research is needed, but ultimately we believe this will be helpful in understanding and countering the spread of misinformation on topics such as the climate. Existing research on online misinformation and fact-checking has often focused on verifying individual facts while devoting little attention to more complex topics such as conditionals and causality. We argue that to check these more complex claims, neural models (such as LLMs) alone are not sufficient but that a neuro-symbolic AI approach is needed that draws on both the powerful abilities of LLMs and the rich tradition of symbolic logic.

We define relevant terms and propose a first pipeline here, along with an algorithm for detecting misinformation in counterfactual claims. We construct the MisCC dataset from social media posts in climate change-related subreddits. The dataset can be used for training and evaluation in multiple natural language processing tasks related to counterfactual claims, such as classifying CCs, determining the verifiability (or not) of a claim, and determining the truth values of a counterfactual claim's sub-claims and of the counterfactual claim itself. Our dataset contains many untrue counterfactual claims, which likely reflects the real-life distribution of false counterfactual claims. This further underlines the importance of research into checking such complex claims.

Our results on two powerful LLMs, GPT4 and Llama3, show that our neuro-symbolic approaches outperform the approach of prompting the LLM directly to return the truth value of the counterfactual claim. Notably, our pipeline improved the performance of both models allowing GPT4 to achieve the highest F1 score of 0.64, while describing the logical theory as CoT prompting negatively impacted GPT4's performance but was beneficial for Llama3, enabling it to achieve its own best F1 score of 0.62. Although our study focuses on counterfactual claims, the experiments evidenced that different LLMs may benefit from different approaches with neuro-symbolic AI as a promising direction for enhancing LLMs. In the future, our approach can be further extended by drawing, for example, on causal knowledge graphs and automated reasoning.

Acknowledgments. This work was supported by the ELIAI (Edinburgh Laboratory for Integrated Artificial Intelligence) EPSRC (grant no EP/W002876/1); the UKRI (grant EP/S022481/1) and the School of Informatics, University of Edinburgh. We would like to thank Dr. Edmund Morris, Dr. Imogen Morris, Sandrine Chausson, Eddie Ungless, Agostina Calabrese, Dr. Ibrahim Abu Farha, Pavel Stepachev and all data annotators for their support and valuable discussions.

References

1. Achiam, J., et al.: Gpt-4 technical report. arXiv preprint arXiv:2303.08774 (2023)
2. Aïmeur, E., Amri, S., Brassard, G.: Fake news, disinformation and misinformation in social media: a review. Soc. Netw. Anal. Min. **13**(1), 30 (2023)
3. Balke, A., Pearl, J.: Counterfactual probabilities: computational methods, bounds and applications. In: Uncertainty in Artificial Intelligence, pp. 46–54. Elsevier (1994)
4. Beazley, D.M.: Automated scientific software scripting with swig. Futur. Gener. Comput. Syst. **19**(5), 599–609 (2003)
5. Dagan, I., Glickman, O., Magnini, B.: The PASCAL recognising textual entailment challenge. In: Quiñonero-Candela, J., Dagan, I., Magnini, B., d'Alché-Buc, F. (eds.) MLCW 2005. LNCS (LNAI), vol. 3944, pp. 177–190. Springer, Heidelberg (2006). https://doi.org/10.1007/11736790_9
6. Dai, S.C., Hsu, Y.L., Xiong, A., Ku, L.W.: Ask to know more: generating counterfactual explanations for fake claims. In: Proceedings of the 28th ACM SIGKDD Conference on Knowledge Discovery and Data Mining, pp. 2800–2810 (2022)
7. David, H., et al.: Enquiry Concerning Human Understanding. Charles River Editors (2018)
8. Devlin, J., Chang, M.W., Lee, K., Toutanova, K.: Bert: pre-training of deep bidirectional transformers for language understanding. arXiv preprint arXiv:1810.04805 (2018)
9. Diggelmann, T., Boyd-Graber, J., Bulian, J., Ciaramita, M., Leippold, M.: Climate-fever: a dataset for verification of real-world climate claims. arXiv preprint arXiv:2012.00614 (2020)
10. Fu, Y., Peng, H., Sabharwal, A., Clark, P., Khot, T.: Complexity-based prompting for multi-step reasoning. In: The Eleventh International Conference on Learning Representations (2022)
11. Gee, J.P., Hayes, E.R.: Language and Learning in the Digital Age. Routledge, Abingdon (2011)
12. Grice, H.P.: Logic and conversation. In: Speech Acts, pp. 41–58. Brill (1975)
13. Guo, Z., Schlichtkrull, M., Vlachos, A.: A survey on automated fact-checking. Trans. Assoc. Comput. Linguist. **10**, 178–206 (2022)
14. Heinisch, P., Frank, A., Opitz, J., Plenz, M., Cimiano, P.: Overview of the 2022 validity and novelty prediction shared task. In: Proceedings of the 9th Workshop on Argument Mining, pp. 84–94 (2022)
15. Kalyan, K.S.: A survey of GPT-3 family large language models including chatgpt and gpt-4. Nat. Lang. Process. J. 100048 (2023)
16. Kamoi, R., Goyal, T., Rodriguez, J.D., Durrett, G.: Wice: real-world entailment for claims in wikipedia. arXiv preprint arXiv:2303.01432 (2023)
17. Katz, D.M., Bommarito, M.J., Gao, S., Arredondo, P.: Gpt-4 passes the bar exam. Phil. Trans. R. Soc. A **382**(2270), 20230254 (2024)

18. Krippendorff, K.: Agreement and information in the reliability of coding. Commun. Methods Meas. **5**(2), 93–112 (2011)
19. Loper, E., Bird, S.: Nltk: the natural language toolkit. arXiv preprint cs/0205028 (2002)
20. Pearl, J.: Causal diagrams for empirical research. Biometrika **82**(4), 669–688 (1995)
21. Quelle, D., Bovet, A.: The perils and promises of fact-checking with large language models. Front. Artif. Intell. **7**, 1341697 (2024)
22. Saadat-Yazdi, A., et al.: Kevin: a knowledge enhanced validity and novelty classifier for arguments. In: Proceedings of the 9th Workshop on Argument Mining, pp. 104–110 (2022)
23. Schulam, P., Saria, S.: Reliable decision support using counterfactual models. Adv. Neural Inf. Process. Syst. **30** (2017)
24. Shramko, Y., Wansing, H.: Truth values. In: Zalta, E.N. (ed.) The Stanford Encyclopedia of Philosophy. Metaphysics Research Lab, Stanford University, Winter 2021 edn. (2021)
25. Shu, K., Wang, S., Lee, D., Liu, H.: Mining disinformation and fake news: concepts, methods, and recent advancements. In: Disinformation, Misinformation, and Fake News in Social Media: Emerging Research Challenges and Opportunities, pp. 1–19 (2020)
26. Starr, W.: Counterfactuals. In: Zalta, E.N., Nodelman, U. (eds.) The Stanford Encyclopedia of Philosophy. Metaphysics Research Lab, Stanford University, Winter 2022 edn. (2022)
27. Thorne, J., Vlachos, A., Christodoulopoulos, C., Mittal, A.: Fever: a large-scale dataset for fact extraction and verification. arXiv preprint arXiv:1803.05355 (2018)
28. Verma, G., Bhardwaj, A., Aledavood, T., De Choudhury, M., Kumar, S.: Examining the impact of sharing covid-19 misinformation online on mental health. Sci. Rep. **12**(1), 8045 (2022)
29. Verma, S., Dickerson, J., Hines, K.: Counterfactual explanations for machine learning: a review, **2**. arXiv preprint arXiv:2010.10596 (2020)
30. Xu, W., Liu, Q., Wu, S., Wang, L.: Counterfactual debiasing for fact verification. In: Proceedings of the 61st Annual Meeting of the Association for Computational Linguistics, vol. 1: Long Papers, pp. 6777–6789 (2023)
31. Yang, X., Obadinma, S., Zhao, H., Zhang, Q., Matwin, S., Zhu, X.: Semeval-2020 task 5: counterfactual recognition. arXiv preprint arXiv:2008.00563 (2020)
32. Zhao, F., Jin, G., Huang, J., Zhao, R., Tan, F.: Consistency matters: explore llms consistency from a black-box perspective. arXiv preprint arXiv:2402.17411 (2024)

Towards Enhancing LLMs with Logic-Based Reasoning: A Meta Inverse Entailment Approach

Dany Varghese(✉), Ghazal Afroozi Milani, and Alireza Tamaddoni-Nezhad

Department of Computer Science, University of Surrey, Guildford, UK
{dany.varghese,g.afroozimilani,atn}@surrey.ac.uk

Abstract. Large Language Models (LLMs) have achieved remarkable success in various natural language processing tasks. However, their ability to perform tasks requiring formal representation and reasoning remains limited. This paper explores the integration of Meta Inverse Entailment (MIE) with LLMs to enhance their reasoning capabilities. In our experiments, we examine a hybrid GPT-MIE model on a simplified natural language grammar. The results suggest that the accuracy of GPT is significantly improved when it incorporates the grammar learned using MIE. This hybrid approach demonstrates the potential of combining LLMs' linguistic proficiency with MIE's rigorous formalism, leading to better performance in tasks demanding logical representation and reasoning.

Keywords: Meta Inverse Entailment · Large Language Models · Logical Reasoning · PyGol

1 Introduction

Large Language Models (LLMs) have revolutionised the field of Natural Language Processing (NLP), achieving unprecedented success across a broad spectrum of tasks such as machine translation, text summarisation, question answering, and more [8,29]. These models, exemplified by OpenAI's GPT-3 [3] and Google's BERT [8], leverage vast amounts of data and sophisticated neural network architectures to produce human-like text and understand the context with remarkable accuracy. Their ability to generate coherent and contextually relevant text has found applications in diverse areas, from customer service automation to creative writing and beyond.

Despite their impressive achievements, LLMs face significant challenges when it comes to tasks requiring formal reasoning and representation. While they excel in tasks involving pattern recognition and language generation, their performance drops when dealing with problems that necessitate logical inference and generalisation from a limited number of examples [13]. One critical area where this limitation is evident is in grammar learning from examples, where

W.-Z. Dai (Ed.): ILP 2024, LNAI 16059, pp. 268–282, 2026.
https://doi.org/10.1007/978-3-032-09087-4_19

the ability to abstract rules and apply them to new contexts is essential. LLMs, although powerful, often struggle to deduce and generalise grammatical rules from a few instances, highlighting a gap in their reasoning capabilities.

The importance of integrating 'ultra-strong' machine learning into LLMs becomes apparent in this context. Michie [14] proposed criteria to evaluate machine learning based on predictive performance and the comprehensibility of the learned knowledge. The weak criterion involves the machine learner's ability to enhance predictive accuracy as data increases. The strong criterion not only requires improved performance but also demands that the system presents its hypotheses in a symbolic form. The ultra-strong criterion further extends this by requiring the system to teach the hypothesis to a human, thereby improving the human's performance beyond what they could achieve by studying the training data alone. In the era of explainable AI (XAI), where transparency and interpretability are as crucial as performance, the ability to understand and replicate the reasoning behind model predictions is paramount [1]. 'Ultra-strong' learning embodies these principles, aiming to create models that are both powerful and understandable.

Incorporating 'ultra-strong' learning into LLMs can address their current limitations by enhancing their ability to reason and generalise. This is particularly relevant in tasks such as grammar induction, where understanding and applying rules across different contexts is necessary. A promising approach to achieve this integration is through Meta Inverse Entailment (MIE), a form of Inductive Logic Programming (ILP) that combines logic-based learning with meta-level reasoning [25–27]. MIE allows models to learn compact, human-readable representations of knowledge, which can then be used to reason about new instances effectively.

Inductive Logic Programming (ILP) has long been recognised for its potential to perform reasoning tasks efficiently by inducing hypotheses from observations [16]. ILP systems, such as Progol [17] and Aleph [22], have demonstrated the ability to learn relational theories and generate explanations in a way that is both interpretable and generalisable. MIE extends this capability by employing a meta-level framework that enables the learning of higher-order programs, thus enhancing the expressiveness and applicability of the induced knowledge.

Our research explores the integration of MIE with LLMs to bridge the gap between linguistic proficiency and formal reasoning. We use a novel ILP framework called Meta Inverse Entailment to enhance the reasoning capabilities of LLMs. MIE employs a *compact language model* implemented using PyGol [28], a Python-based ILP system. In our experiments, we utilise simplified natural languages and MIE to learn the underlying grammar rules, which are then incorporated into the GPT model. This hybrid approach leverages the strengths of both LLMs and MIE: the linguistic proficiency of LLMs and the rigorous formalism of MIE.

The results of our experiments indicate a significant improvement in the accuracy of GPT when it incorporates the learned grammar from MIE. This suggests that the hybrid model can better generalise and reason about new instances, aligning with the 'ultra-strong' learning principles. Our findings demonstrate the potential of combining LLMs with MIE to develop AI systems that understand and generate language and are sophisticated in problem-solving and decision-making.

2 Formal Language Notation

The following definitions are taken from Muggleton et al. [18].

Let Σ be a finite alphabet. Σ^* is the infinite set of strings made up of zero or more letters from Σ. λ is the empty string. uv is the concatenation of strings u and v. $\mid u \mid$ is the length of string u. A language L is any subset of Σ^*. Let ν be a set of non-terminal symbols disjoint from Σ. A production rule $r = LHS \rightarrow RHS$ is well-formed in the case that $LHS \in (\nu \cup \Sigma)^*$, $RHS \in (\nu \cup \Sigma \cup \lambda)^*$, and when applied replaces LHS by RHS in a given string. A grammar G is a pair $\langle s, R \rangle$ consisting of a start symbol $s \in \nu$ and a finite set of production rules R.

A grammar is regular Chomsky-normal in the case that it contains only production rules of the form $S \rightarrow \lambda$ or $S \rightarrow aB$ where $S, B \in \nu$ and $a \in \Sigma$. A grammar is linear context-free if it contains only regular Chomsky-normal production rules or rules of the form $S \rightarrow Ab$ where S, $\mathrm{A} \in \nu$ and $b \in \Sigma$. A grammar is context-free if it contains only linear context-free Chomsky-normal production rules or rules of form $S \rightarrow AB$ where $S, A, B \in \nu$. A context-free grammar is said to be deterministic in the case that it does not contain two regular Chomsky-normal production rules $S \rightarrow aB$ and $S \rightarrow aC$ where $B \neq C$.

A sentence $\sigma \in \Sigma^*$ is in $L(G)$ iff given a start symbol $S \in \nu$ there exists a sequence of production rule applications where $R_i \in G$. A language L is regular, linear context-free or context-free in case there exists a grammar G for which $L = L(G)$ where G is regular, linear context-free, or context-free, respectively. According to the context-free pumping lemma [10], if a language L is context-free, then there exists some integer $p \geq 1$ such that any string s in L with $\mid s \mid \geq p$ (where p is a constant) can be written as $s = uvxyz$ with substrings u, v, x, y and z, such that $\mid vxy \mid \leq p$, $\mid vy \mid \geq 1$ and uv^nxy^nz is in L for every integer $n \geq 0$.

3 Meta Inverse Entailment

Traditional Inductive Logic Programming (ILP) approaches commonly employ declarative language bias to reduce the size of the hypothesis space and guide the search during the learning phase. For instance, the state-of-the-art ILP system Aleph [22] utilizes mode declarations as a form of language bias, while the Meta-Interpretive Learning (MIL) approach, Metagol [4], employs metarules to achieve the same goal. These biases help constrain the hypothesis space, making the learning process more efficient and focused on plausible solutions aligned with the given background knowledge. A primary concern is the reliance on these declarative biases within machine learning, which, while crucial for directing the hypothesis search, often requires significant human input and expertise in specific domains. To address the issues associated with declarative language bias, this study employs a novel ILP approach called Meta Inverse Entailment (MIE) [25–27].

The MIE methodology employs the Bottom Clause of Relevant Literals (BCRL) and Meta Theory (MT) to generate individual hypothesis clauses. BCRL is an efficient tool for collecting all literals related to an example derived from background knowledge, thus delineating a boundary to search for a hypothesis during the learning process. Conversely, meta theory encapsulates a higher-order language bias autonomously extracted from background knowledge. The complete explanation of MIE is out of the scope of this paper, so we explain only the main concepts.

Definition 1 ***(Relevant literals*** $(\overrightarrow{\mathcal{R}_e})$***).*** *Let B be the background knowledge, $\overrightarrow{\mathcal{B}}$ be the ordered clause of ground literals of B, and e be an example. Then the relevant literals of e is defined as $\overrightarrow{\mathcal{R}_e} = e \leftarrow L_1, L_2, \cdots, L_n$ if and only if $L_i \in \overrightarrow{\mathcal{B}}$ and L_i be related literal (See Definition 3 in [26]) of either L_j or e such that $1 \leq j < i$.*

Definition 2 ***(Bottom clause of relevant literals*** $(\bot_{e,B})$*. Let B be the background knowledge, e be a definite clause representing an example, $\mathcal{K}$ be a set of constant terms and $\overrightarrow{\mathcal{R}_e}$ be the relevant literals of example e as defined in the Definition 1. Then bottom clause of relevant literals of e, denoted as $\bot_{e,B}$ is $\overrightarrow{\mathcal{R}_e}$ where each unique occurrence of term $t_i \notin \mathcal{K}$ replaced with a new variable.*

The bottom clause of relevant literals introduced in MIE can resemble the bottom clause concept in Progol [17], but it does not use language bias such as mode declaration.

Definition 3 ***(Meta theory of relevant literals*** $(\mathcal{M}_e)$***).*** *Let e be an example, $\overrightarrow{\mathcal{R}_e}$ be the relevant literals of e. Then, a clause $\overrightarrow{C} \in \mathcal{M}_e$ if and only if;*

1. *$\exists \Theta$ such that $\overrightarrow{C}\Theta \succeq_s \overrightarrow{\mathcal{R}_e}$ (Refer Definition 19 in [23]) and*
2. *$\overrightarrow{C}$ is head_connected (Refer Definition 3 in [20]).*

The significant difference between a meta clause and a metarule is that a metarule specifies a relationship between the variables in the body of a rule. In meta theory, however, we avoid the tightly coupled nature of metarules to reduce computational complexity, deriving directly from background knowledge.

In MIE, we introduce a novel concept called the double-bounded hypothesis set. This set is defined as a sequential subsumption of meta theory, relative to the bottom clause of related literals. In this new framework, the hypothesis set of an example is constrained within specific boundaries: the bottom clause of relevant literals at the lower boundary and the encompassing meta theory at the upper boundary.

Definition 4 ***(Double-bounded hypothesis set*** *($HS(\bot_{e,B}, \mathcal{M}_e)$)). Let e be an example, $\bot_{e,B}$ be a bottom clause of relevant literals of e as defined in Definition 2, $\mathcal{M}_e$ be a meta theory as defined in Definition 3. Then*

$$HS(\bot_{e,B}, \mathcal{M}_e) = \{h| \text{ s.t: (1)}h \in \overrightarrow{\mathcal{L}_\bot}, \text{and(2)}h \in \overrightarrow{\mathcal{L}_\mathcal{M}}\}$$

Now, consider the problem specification of ILP. Suppose we are given a Horn program for a background knowledge B and a single Horn clause as an example E, then the hypothesis H should follow;

$$B \wedge H \models E \tag{1}$$

$$B \wedge H \textit{ is consistent} \tag{2}$$

Equations 1 & 2 are equivalent to

$$B \wedge \neg E \models \neg H \tag{3}$$

$$B \not\models \neg H \tag{4}$$

Like inverse entailment, MIE generates some theories that are not derived from B alone but from $B \wedge \neg E$. Instead of the bottom clause, we consider a bridge formula CT. So Eq. 3 can be written as

$$B \wedge \neg E \models CT \tag{5}$$

$$CT \models \neg H \tag{6}$$

Finally, Eq. 6 can also written as

$$H \models \neg CT \tag{7}$$

Also by Eqs. 4 and 6, we have

$$B \not\models CT \tag{8}$$

By Eq. 5, the set of clausal theories, CT, can be obtained by generating the double-bounded hypothesis set. Then

$$HS(\bot_{e,B}, \mathcal{M}_e) \models \neg CT \tag{9}$$

The candidate hypothesis (H) will be a subset of $HS(\bot_{e,B}, \mathcal{M}_e)$.

$$H = \{h|h \in HS(\bot_{e,B}, \mathcal{M}_e) \text{ and } h \models \neg CT\} \tag{10}$$

In Eq. 5, we introduce a bridge formula, a set of clausal theories as CT, which replaces the concept of the bottom clause and characteristic clauses introduced in [11].

Table 1. Grammar, Language and BCRL for a regular language

Example Grammar	L	BCRL
S → 0A		string(S):- move(S, 0, A), move(A, 1, B),
A → 1B	$(01)0^*$	move(B, 0, B),
B → 0B		accept(B)
B → λ		

3.1 MIE Framework Applied to Grammar Learning

The Chomsky language types are organised in a hierarchy of inclusion, wherein regular languages are a subset of context-free languages (regular $\subseteq$ context-free). Within the realm of grammatical inference [6], methods for learning regular languages have been the subject of substantial research. A significant number of these methods start with a prefix tree acceptor and then proceed to merge states in a more gradual manner.

Table 1 demonstrates how the MIE approach can be used to learn a regular language.

Upon a closer examination of the BCRL for the regular grammar in Table 3, it is evident that it shares similar properties with prefix trees.

Proposition 1 (Unique $\bot_R$ for regular languages). *Prefix trees act as a compact bottom theory in the MIE setting for regular languages.*

Proof. Refer to Proposition 6 from [18] for the proof.

Proposition 2 (Unique $\bot$ for context-free languages). *Any $\bot_C$ for a context-free language contains a set of atoms representing a regular prefix tree.*

Proof. Refer to Proposition 7 from [18] for the proof.

Using, Eq. 10, MIE grammar learning generates all the possible sets of hypotheses for regular grammar as follows;

$$H_R = \{h|h \in HS(\bot_R, \mathcal{M}_e) \text{ and } h \models \neg CT\} \tag{11}$$

Equation 11 can also be applied to Context-Free Grammars (CFGs) as follows:

$$H_R = \{h|h \in HS(\bot, \mathcal{M}_e) \text{ and } h \models \neg CT\} \tag{12}$$

Also, it has to be noted that the resulting hypothesis (grammar) is then tested to ensure it does not cover any of the negative examples.

4 Experiments

The following section provides a detailed overview of experiments conducted to evaluate the ability of machine learning models to learn grammars of varying complexities, including regular, context-free, and simplified natural language structures.

We investigate the following Null Hypothesis throughout the experiments.

Null Hypothesis $\mathbf{H_1}$ PyGol cannot learn randomly generated regular/context-free languages.

Null Hypothesis $\mathbf{H_2}$ PyGol cannot outperform GPT in learning randomly generated regular/context-free languages.

Null Hypothesis $\mathbf{H_3}$ PyGol cannot learn simplified natural language grammar.

Null Hypothesis $\mathbf{H_4}$ PyGol cannot outperform GPT in learning a simplified natural language grammar.

Null Hypothesis $\mathbf{H_5}$ GPT's reasoning efficiency in learning simplified natural grammar cannot be significantly improved by including production rules from MIE.

```
f"""
Hey ChatGPT,
The language 'L' accepts strings in positive examples
and rejects them in the negative examples of Training Data.
Training Data:
    Positive examples: {training_positive}
    Negative examples: {training_negative}
Testing Data:
    Positive examples: {testing_positive}
    Negative examples: {testing_negative}
Instructions:
1. For each test string in the Testing Data, determine
if it belongs to the language 'L'.
2. ans = 1 if sentences in the  Testing data that
belong to language 'L'.
3. ans = 0 if sentences in  Testing data that do
not belong to language 'L'.
4. Make a list of 'ans' as in the same order
as in Testing data.

Return the array of 'ans'.
"""
```

Fig. 1. GPT API query for experiment 1

All datasets and learning systems used in these experiments are available at https://github.com/hmlr-lab/Compact-Language-Model.

4.1 Learning Regular and Context-Free Languages

In this experiment, we investigate the capability of PyGol and the GPT model to learn both regular and context-free languages. These experiments assess the performance of PyGol [26,28], compared to the GPT model (gpt-3.5-turbo-0125), highlighting their respective capabilities in grammar learning tasks. The query used in GPT API is shown in Fig. 1.

Materials and Methods. We utilised the grammar generated by Muggleton et al. [18] using a stochastic logic program[1]. This grammar was subsequently refined using Plotkin's reduction algorithm.

Table 2. Average and maximum string lengths for datasets RG_1, RG_2, CFG_1 and CFG_2.

	RG_1	RG_2	CFG_1	CFG_2
Average ± STD	7.67 ± 5.57	30.9 ± 46.04	6.58 ± 4.55	48.76 ± 65.1
Maximum	15	286	15	311

For regular grammar, we utilised two datasets, RG_1 and RG_2, derived from different distributions. Dataset RG_1 comprised examples randomly selected from Σ^* with $\Sigma = \{a, b\}$, while dataset RG_2 included sequences from $\Sigma = \{a, b, c\}$, and featured longer sequence lengths, as detailed in Table 2.

For context-free grammars, we excluded those associated with finite languages or those identifiable through the pumping lemma for context-free grammars. However, not all regular grammar can be filtered using this method, as determining whether context-free grammar is regular is undecidable. Specifically, grammars that cannot be pumped are regular, but pumpable grammars are not necessarily non-regular. To perform our analysis, we used two different datasets, categorised based on the length of the examples in each grammar (CFG_1 and CFG_2), as shown in Table 2.

All four datasets contain 100 randomly selected grammars. The test set size was fixed at 500 examples, with a baseline accuracy of 50%. The training set size varied between 2 and 50 examples for each dataset, allowing us to evaluate the performance across different training conditions.

Results and Discussions. The results of the experiments are shown in Fig. 2, clearly demonstrating that PyGol consistently outperforms the GPT model in learning both regular grammar and context-free grammar. In the case of regular grammars, PyGol achieved near-perfect accuracy across datasets RG_1 and RG_2, while the GPT model struggled, especially when learning from shorter examples in RG_1. This suggests that the GPT model requires more information

[1] The complete dataset is available at http://ilp.doc.ic.ac.uk/metagol/.

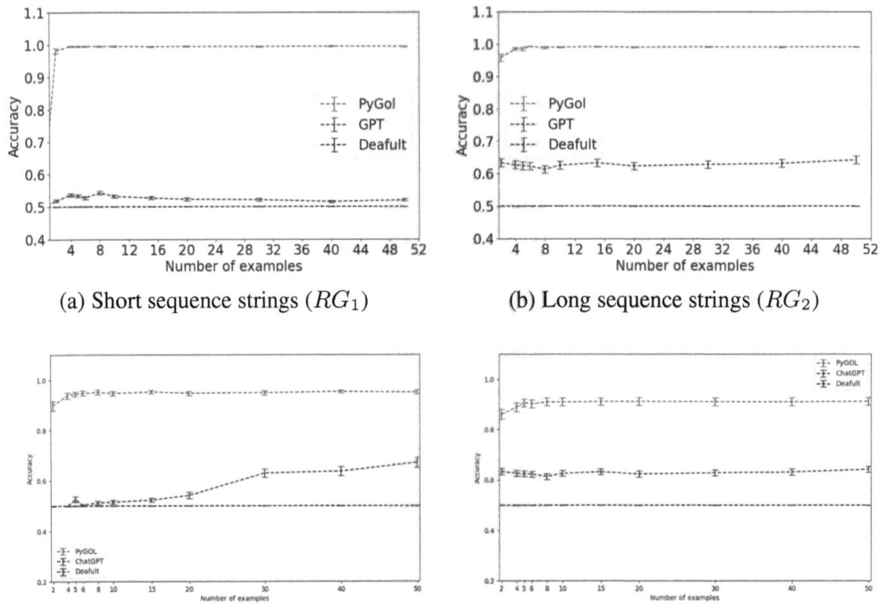

(a) Short sequence strings (RG_1)

(b) Long sequence strings (RG_2)

(c) Short sequence strings (CFG_1)

(d) Long sequence strings (CFG_2)

Fig. 2. Average predictive accuracies for regular & context-free languages

to capture the underlying rules. A similar trend was observed with context-free grammars, where PyGol again outperformed the GPT model, achieving predictive accuracies close to 95% across both datasets CFG_1 and CFG_2. The GPT model, although performing better than the baseline method, faced difficulties in learning from shorter sequences in CFG_1, similar to the challenges observed with RG_1. These findings led to the rejection of Null Hypotheses H1 and H2, further supporting the superior performance of PyGol in both regular and context-free grammar tasks, especially when dealing with limited data.

4.2 Evaluating GPT's Reasoning Efficiency with MIE Production Rules

In this experiment, we evaluate the Null Hypotheses H3, H4 and H5.

Materials and Methods. Our approach to generating and evaluating grammar is based on training examples from the same domain described by Muggleton et al. [19]. The dataset includes 50 sentences from a simplified natural language grammar (SNG), such as "*a ball hits the small dog*" with an equal distribution of positive and negative examples, leading to a baseline accuracy of 50%. We used the training data to generate the grammar and evaluated it against a separate test dataset. For each leave-out size, we sampled ten times, and for each sample, predictive accuracies were computed using 10-fold cross-validation. In the API (Refer Fig. 3) used to evaluate the GPT model with production rules, we have clearly mentioned that grammar learned from GPT is ‘partial grammar’ for the language.

```
f"""
Hey ChatGPT,
The language 'L' accepts sentences in  positive examples and
rejects in the negative examples of Training Data.
The possible production rules of  partial  grammar for 'L' is
given, in which "vp" means verb phrase, "np" means noun
phrase,  "det" means determiner, "adj" means  adjective
and "prep"  means peposition.

production rules: {H}
Training Data:
    Positive examples: {training_positive}
    Negative examples: {training_negative}
Test Data:
    Positive examples: {testing_positive}
    Negative examples: {testing_negative}
Instructions:
1. For each test sentence in the Test Data, determine if it
                                belongs to the language 'L'.
2. ans = 1 if sentences in the  Testing data belong to the
                                language 'L'.
3. ans = 0 if sentences in Testing data do not belong to the
                                language 'L'.
4. Make a list of 'ans' as in the same order as in Testing data.
Return just the array of 'ans'."""
```

Fig. 3. GPT API query for experiment 2

Results and Discussion. The results from the experiment are illustrated in Fig. 4. It is evident that adding production rules from PyGol increases the learning efficiency of GPT, resulting in an average accuracy improvement of 8 ± 6 ($max = 18$). This evidence allows us to refute Null Hypothesis H3. Furthermore, Fig. 4 shows that combining ChatGPT with production rules from PyGol significantly enhances performance compared to using ChatGPT alone, highlighting the value of integrating structured knowledge, so hypotheses H4 and H5 also can be rejected. However, as the number of examples increases, the combined model might start overfitting to specific patterns in the training data, which do not generalise well to the test data. Overfitting occurs when a model becomes too tailored to the nuances of the training set, causing it to lose effectiveness on unseen data. This phenomenon likely explains why the combined model's accuracy drops after incorporating more than 10 examples with respect to PyGol.

Additionally, the results of the experiment show that the True Negative (TN) value is much better than the True Positive (TP) value. This indicates that the model is more effective at correctly identifying negative examples (i.e., correctly rejecting instances that do not belong to the target class) than it is at correctly identifying positive examples (i.e., correctly accepting instances that do belong to the target class). This disparity suggests that the model might be more conservative in its predictions, leaning towards correctly identifying non-target examples but potentially missing some target examples.

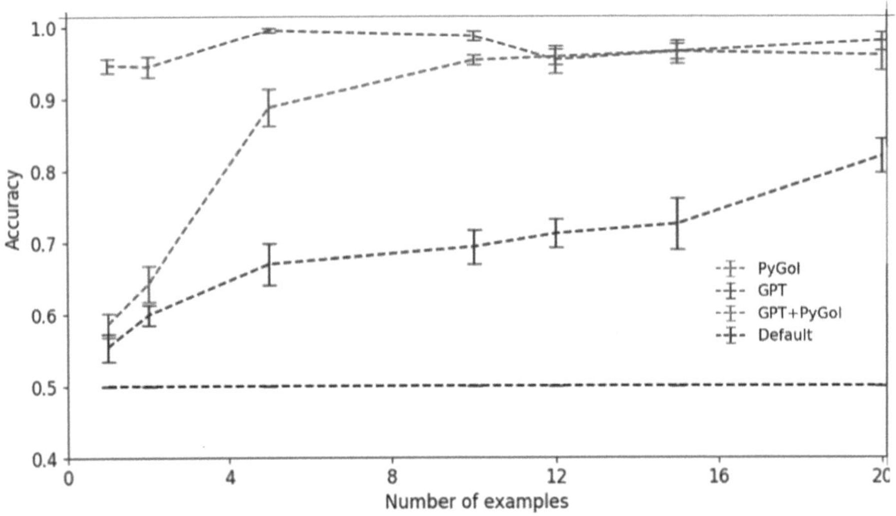

Fig. 4. Average predictive accuracies of GPT enhanced with production rules

5 Related Work

Grammatical inference, or grammatical induction, is learning grammar from examples, closely linked to machine learning and formal language theory. It has significant real-world applications, including speech recognition [30], computational linguistics [9], and computational biology [12]. The problem of learning regular languages, represented by deterministic finite state automata, has been well-studied, with efficient algorithms existing since the 1950s [15]. Learning context-free languages is widely considered intractable, with the current state of the art largely comprising negative results [6]. Some positive PAC (Probably Approximately Correct) learning results exist for regular languages [7], but these have not been extended to context-free grammar.

ILP has been applied to grammatical inference along with other machine-learning approaches. The first seminal work for grammatical inference in ILP involved the system MERLIN 2.0 [2], a successor to an earlier system where predicate invention is guided by sequences of input clauses in SLD-refutations of positive and negative examples relative to an overly general theory. Unlike its predecessor, which searches for the minimal finite-state automaton to generate all positive and no negative sequences, MERLIN 2.0 induces Hidden Markov Models from positive sequences only. ILP systems typically require predicate invention even for learning regular languages, a problem recognised since the early days of ILP. Although Cussens and Pulman [5] applied ALEPH to learning natural language grammar, their approach avoids predicate invention by assuming all predicates, like noun phrases (np), are known in the background knowledge. The first seminal work to learn context-free grammar using ILP was developed by Muggleton et al. [18] using Meta Interpretive Learning. The MIL framework implements predicate invention and recursive generalisations through abduction with respect to a meta-interpreter. This approach is based on a previously unexplored case of Inverse Entailment for grammatical inference of regular languages, marking a significant advancement in the field.

Large language models (LLMs) [24], such as GPT (Generative Pre-trained Transformer) [31], have revolutionised the field of natural language processing (NLP). These models leverage the Transformer architecture, introduced by Vaswani et al. [29], which is based on self-attention mechanisms to efficiently capture long-range dependencies and contextual relationships within text data. LLMs are typically pre-trained on extensive and diverse corpora, allowing them to learn rich linguistic patterns, syntactic structures, and semantic nuances. This pre-training phase equips LLMs with a broad understanding of language, enabling them to perform a wide array of NLP tasks with remarkable proficiency [21]. Technically, LLMs consist of multiple layers of Transformer encoders and decoders, which process input text through a series of attention heads and feed-forward neural networks. Each layer refines the representation of the input by focusing on different aspects of the context, effectively enabling the model to attend to relevant parts of the text. The pre-training phase involves unsupervised learning, where the model predicts the next word in a sentence, thereby learning from the sequential structure of the language. Following pre-training, LLMs undergo fine-tuning on task-specific datasets, enhancing their performance on particular applications such as machine translation, text summarisation, and question answering. The scalability and adaptability of LLMs make them a cornerstone of modern NLP research, driving advancements in the development of more sophisticated and human-like language processing systems.

6 Conclusion

This paper explores the implementation of the MIE approach for a variety of languages/grammars ranging from regular to natural grammar. The MIE framework offers several advantages over the standard Inductive Logic Programming (ILP) framework, particularly in incorporating predicate invention and mutual recursion. Our experiments utilised an ILP framework called MIE, implemented using PyGol. A key advantage of MIE is its ability to avoid the use of declarative language bias, such as meta-rules, making MIE more user-friendly and reliable. Additionally, MIE's hybrid learning approach, with its double-bounded hypothesis space, enables efficient hypothesis learning, predicate invention, and recursion. The results suggest that the generalisation power of MIE is both efficient and accurate, closely matching the MIL approach introduced by Muggleton et al. [18].

The first set of experiments demonstrates the limitations of the GPT model in learning both regular and context-free grammars, particularly when examples are short or limited in number. PyGol, on the other hand, consistently achieves high predictive accuracy across both types of grammar, demonstrating its ability to efficiently learn recursive and structural rules. These results underscore PyGol's effectiveness in grammatical learning tasks, highlighting its advantage over models like GPT when dealing with finite datasets and complex recursive patterns.

Learning natural language grammar from a small number of examples presents significant challenges for models like ChatGPT. The primary issues include insufficient data coverage, leading to poor generalisation and a tendency to overfit specific examples. Although GPT models possess extensive background knowledge of natural language, they lack the structured information necessary for formal grammar and are not inherently designed for explicit rule learning, which is crucial for understanding and applying the strict grammatical rules of natural languages.

To address these limitations, we proposed a hybrid model that combines production rules learned from Meta-Interpretive Learning and GPT models. This amalgamation represents a form of 'ultra-strong' machine learning, which traditionally emphasises the explainability of machine models using symbolic tools. However, in our approach, symbolic rules are used to enhance the learnability of Large Language Models (LLMs), a popular domain in AI. This integration aims to improve the reasoning capabilities of language models, addressing a fundamental issue in LLMs.

The results of our study indicate that integrating production rules from PyGol with ChatGPT leads to a significant improvement in performance, demonstrating that structured knowledge enhances GPT's learning efficiency. However, as the number of examples increased, the combined model's accuracy declined after incorporating more than 10 examples. This decline suggests overfitting, where the model becomes too tailored to the specific patterns in the training set, leading to reduced generalisation to unseen data.

These findings underscore both the potential and challenges of integrating structured knowledge with machine learning models. While the combination of production rules with GPT enhances performance, the standalone PyGol approach remains superior for simplified natural grammar tasks. Future research could explore more sophisticated integration strategies or hybrid models that leverage the strengths of both PyGol and GPT-based approaches. By doing so, we can aim to create more robust models that effectively balance structured rule learning with the extensive background knowledge inherent in GPT models.

Acknowledgement. The first and third authors acknowledge the EPSRC grant on Human-machine learning of ambiguities to support safe, effective, and legal decision-making (EP/X030156/1). Ghazal Afroozi Milani would like to acknowledge EIT-Digital and Goalshaper Ltd for supporting her PhD. Alireza Tamaddoni-Nezhad also acknowledges the EPSRC Network Plus grant on Human-Like Computing (HLC).

References

1. Adadi, A., Berrada, M.: Peeking inside the black-box: a survey on explainable artificial intelligence (XAI). IEEE Access **6**, 52138–52160 (2018)
2. Boström, H.: Predicate invention and learning from positive examples only. In: Nédellec, C., Rouveirol, C. (eds.) ECML 1998. LNCS, vol. 1398, pp. 226–237. Springer, Heidelberg (1998). https://doi.org/10.1007/BFb0026693
3. Brown, T., Mann, B., Ryder, N., et al.: Language models are few-shot learners. Adv. Neural. Inf. Process. Syst. **33**, 1877–1901 (2020)
4. Cropper, A.: Efficiently learning efficient programs. Ph.D. thesis, Imperial College London (2017)
5. Cussens, J., Pulman, S.: Experiments in inductive chart parsing. In: Cussens, J., Džeroski, S. (eds) LLL 1999. LNCS, vol. 1925, pp. 143–156. Springer, Heidelberg (2001). https://doi.org/10.1007/3-540-40030-3_9
6. De La Higuera, C.: A bibliographical study of grammatical inference. Pattern Recogn. **38**(9), 1332–1348 (2005)
7. Denis, F.: Learning regular languages from simple positive examples. Mach. Learn. **44**, 37–66 (2001)
8. Devlin, J., Chang, M.W., Lee, K., Toutanova, K.: BERT: pre-training of deep bidirectional transformers for language understanding. In: Proceedings of the 2019 Conference of the North American Chapter of the Association for Computational Linguistics: Human Language Technologies, Volume 1 (Long and Short Papers), pp. 4171–4186 (2019)
9. Heinz, J., De la Higuera, C., Van Zaanen, M.: Grammatical Inference for Computational Linguistics. Springer, Cham (2022)
10. Hopcroft, J.E., Motwani, R., Ullman, J.D.: Introduction to automata theory, languages, and computation, 2nd edition. SIGACT News **32**(1), 60 65 (2001). https://doi.org/10.1145/568438.568455
11. Inoue, K.: Induction as consequence finding. Mach. Learn. **55**, 109–135 (2004). https://doi.org/10.1023/B:MACH.0000023149.72125.e2
12. López, V.F., Aguilar, R., Alonso, L., Moreno, M.N., Corchado, J.M.: Grammatical inference with bioinformatics criteria. Neurocomputing **75**(1), 88–97 (2012)
13. Marcus, G., Davis, E.: Rebooting AI: Building Artificial Intelligence We Can Trust. Vintage (2020)
14. Michie, D.: Machine learning in the next five years. In: Proceedings of the 3rd European Conference on European Working Session on Learning, EWSL 1988, pp. 107–122. Pitman Publishing, Inc., USA (1988). https://doi.org/10.5555/3108771.3108781

15. Moore, E.F., et al.: Gedanken-experiments on sequential machines. Autom. Stud. **34**, 129–153 (1956)
16. Muggleton, S.: Inductive logic programming. New Gener. Comput. **8**, 295–318 (1991). https://doi.org/10.1007/BF03037089
17. Muggleton, S.: Inverse entailment and progol. New Gener. Comput. **13**, 245–286 (1995). https://doi.org/10.1007/BF03037227
18. Muggleton, S., Lin, D., Pahlavi, N., Tamaddoni-Nezhad, A.: Meta-interpretive learning: application to grammatical inference. Mach. Learn. **94**(1), 25 – 49 (2014). https://github.com/metagol/metagol
19. Muggleton, S., Lin, D., Tamaddoni-Nezhad, A.: MC-TopLog: complete multi-clause learning guided by a top theory, pp. 238–254 (2011)
20. Muggleton, S., Tamaddoni-Nezhad, A.: QG/GA: a stochastic search for progol. In: Muggleton, S., Otero, R., Tamaddoni-Nezhad, A. (eds.) ILP 2006. LNCS (LNAI), vol. 4455, pp. 37–39. Springer, Heidelberg (2007). https://doi.org/10.1007/978-3-540-73847-3_9
21. Radford, A., Narasimhan, K., Salimans, T., Sutskever, I., et al.: Improving language understanding by generative pre-training (2018)
22. Srinivasan, A.: Aleph: a learning engine for proposing hypotheses. Mach. Learn. **38**, 95–133 (2001)
23. Tamaddoni-Nezhad, A., Muggleton, S.: The lattice structure and refinement operators for the hypothesis space bounded by a bottom clause. Mach. Learn. **76**, 37–72 (2009)
24. Thirunavukarasu, A.J., Ting, D.S.J., Elangovan, K., Gutierrez, L., Tan, T.F., Ting, D.S.W.: Large language models in medicine. Nat. Med. **29**(8), 1930–1940 (2023)
25. Varghese, D.: Explainable and efficient machine learning using meta inverse entailment. Ph.D. thesis, University of Surrey (2024). https://doi.org/10.15126/thesis.901077
26. Varghese, D., Barroso-Bergada, D., Bohan, D.A., Tamaddoni-Nezhad, A.: Efficient abductive learning of microbial interactions using meta inverse entailment. In: Proceedings of the 31st International Conference on ILP (2022). (in press)
27. Varghese, D., Patel, U., Krause, P., Tamaddoni-Nezhad, A.: Few-shot learning for plant disease classification using ILP. In: Garg, D., Narayana, V.A., Suganthan, P.N., Anguera, J., Koppula, V.K., Gupta, S.K. (eds.) IACC 2022. CCIS, vol. 1781, pp. 321–336. Springer, Cham (2023). https://doi.org/10.1007/978-3-031-35641-4_26
28. Varghese, D., Tamaddoni-Nezhad, A.: PyGol (2022). https://github.com/PyGol/
29. Vaswani, A., et al.: Attention is all you need. In: Advances in Neural Information Processing Systems, vol. **30** (2017)
30. Vidal, E., Casacuberta, F., García, P.: Grammatical inference and automatic speech recognition. In: Ayuso, A.J.R., Soler, J.M.L. (eds.) Speech Recognition and Coding. NATO ASI Series, vol. 147, pp. 174–191. Springer, Heidelberg (1995). https://doi.org/10.1007/978-3-642-57745-1_27
31. Zhu, Q., Luo, J.: Generative pre-trained transformer for design concept generation: an exploration. Proc. Design Soc. **2**, 1825–1834 (2022)

Harnessing the Power of Semi-structured Knowledge and LLMs with Triplet-Based Prefiltering for Question Answering

Derian Boer(✉), Fabian Koch, and Stefan Kramer(✉)

Institute of Computer Science, Johannes Gutenberg University Mainz, Staudingerweg 9, 55131 Mainz, Germany
{boer,kramerst}@uni-mainz.de

Abstract. Large Language Models (LLMs) frequently lack domain-specific knowledge and even fine-tuned models tend to hallucinate. Hence, more reliable models that can include external knowledge are needed. We present a pipeline, 4StepFocus, and specifically a preprocessing step, that can substantially improve the answers of LLMs. This is achieved by providing guided access to external knowledge making use of the model's ability to capture relational context and conduct rudimentary reasoning by themselves. The method narrows down potentially correct answers by triplets-based searches in a semi-structured knowledge base in a direct, traceable fashion, before switching to latent representations for ranking those candidates based on unstructured data. This distinguishes it from related methods that are purely based on latent representations. 4StepFocus consists of the steps: 1) Triplet generation for extraction of relational data by an LLM, 2) substitution of variables in those triplets to narrow down answer candidates employing a knowledge graph, 3) sorting remaining candidates with a vector similarity search involving associated non-structured data, 4) reranking the best candidates by the LLM with background data provided. Experiments on a medical, a product recommendation, and an academic paper search test set demonstrate that this approach is indeed a powerful augmentation. It not only adds relevant traceable background information from information retrieval, but also improves performance considerably in comparison to state-of-the-art methods. This paper presents a novel, largely unexplored direction and therefore provides a wide range of future work opportunities. Used source code is available at https://github.com/kramerlab/4StepFocus.

Keywords: Large Language Models · Knowledge Graphs · Question Answering · Triplets · Semi-Structured Knowledge Bases

1 Introduction

Due to their increased capability to perform even complex tasks in recent years, LLMs are now being deployed extensively in day-to-day work, as well as in scientific and research contexts. To ensure accurate and reliable results, it is crucial to

W.-Z. Dai (Ed.): ILP 2024, LNAI 16059, pp. 283–292, 2026.
https://doi.org/10.1007/978-3-032-09087-4_20

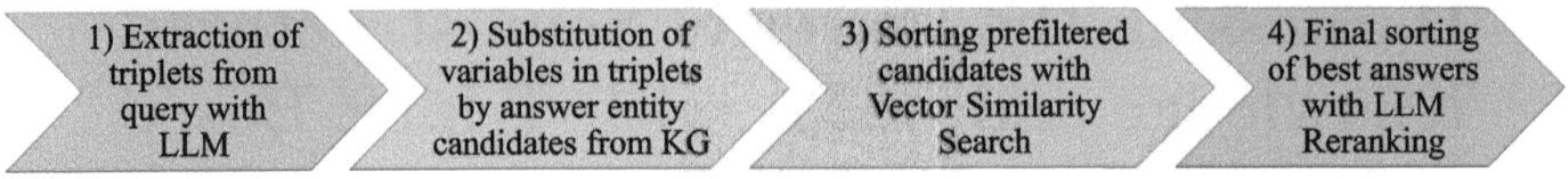

Fig. 1. Pipeline of 4StepFocus that enhances VSS + LLM Reranker by triplet-based prefiltering steps.

understand their abilities and limitations. LLM can sometimes provide incorrect answers, be unaware of gaps in their knowledge, or return biased information [2]. Furthermore, they tend to "hallucinate" [4] in some cases, which can be challenging to detect. There is ongoing debate about their suitability for performing reasoning tasks [7].

General LLMs may be used as *foundation models*, that are customized for improved performance on specific tasks, languages, and contents. Methods such as transfer learning, dedicated prompt engineering, and enhancement with external data and knowledge are commonly employed. Wu *et al.* [18] point out that external sources usually either include structured data, such as knowledge graphs (KGs), or unstructured documents. The authors recently assembled semi-structured knowledge bases (SKBs) and corresponding question-answer (QA) train and test data of three real-world domains in natural language, that require the combination of the included data. The six methods, which are evaluated on this benchmark datasets, are all based on word and graph embeddings. They can be categorized into derivatives of vector similarity searches and graph neural network-based methods: both the dominating approaches in the LLM enhancement literature. In contrast, we explore a novel and straightforward approach, 4StepFocus, to achieve more precise LLM responses whose selection increases traceability. Figure 1 visualizes the pipeline of our framework in short. It can be seen as a preprocessing step for approaches with vector similarity search, but involves having the LLM independently formalize the user input and search a KG for potential answers beforehand. We refer to a KG whose vertices are linked to documents with unstructured data, like user reviews, abstracts, or medical properties, as a semi-structured knowledge base (SKB) in this paper.

Although further development and optimization are needed for better generalization and higher reliability, our experiments already demonstrate superiority over state-of-the-art methods. Importantly, in our method external information used in the decision process is more transparent and interpretable in a human-readable format. This ability to refer to quotable, semi-structured knowledge that is used in the reasoning process counters the current issue of LLMs being black boxes and makes their output more comprehensible for the user.

The rest of this paper is structured as follows: Sect. 2 reviews related work on LLM enhancement for question answering. Section 3 presents a detailed description of our approach. Section 4 describes the evaluation conducted on three QA testsets and compares our results to those of state-of-the-art methods. Section 5 summarizes our findings and outlines several options for future work.

2 Related Work

Our work builds on and extends the existing literature on integrating LLMs with KGs for question answering, which is related to various other applications such as fact-checking and hallucination mitigation. This section discusses several key contributions to these areas and situates our approach within this context. Due to the rapidity of new developments, we include not only peer-reviewed work but also preprints.

Wu *et al.* [18] assembled three SKBs and created corresponding benchmark datasets for evaluating question answering. Their work includes a comparison of six methods:

- *Vector Similarity Search (VSS)* embeds both the query and the concatenated textual and relational information of each candidate entity. Subsequently, it computes the cosine similarity between the query and candidate embeddings.
- *Multi-Vector Similarity Search (Multi-VSS)* represents candidate entities with multiple vectors each to capture detailed features. In our case, textual and relational information of each candidate entity are embedded separately.
- *Dense Retriever* finetunes a query encoder and a document encoder separately using QA pairs from a training dataset.
- *QA-GNN* [19] constructs a subgraph where nodes represent entities found in the question or answer choices, incorporating their neighboring nodes. It integrates semantic embeddings from an LLM, jointly modeling both relational and semantic information.
- *VSS + LLM Reranker* [3,20] reranks the top-v results from VSS using LLMs. The LLM is given background information from the SKB about each of the top v results and prompted to return a score between 0 and 1, quantifying how much each of them fits as an answer to the question. Wu *et al.* employed it with two different LLMs: GPT-4-turbo (gpt-4-1106-preview) and Claude3 (claude-3-opus).

We compare our results against this benchmark study to highlight the efficacy of our approach in Sect. 4.

Much more related work has been done. We only mention a few, related ideas in the following: Guan *et al.* [6] presented a method to mitigate LLM hallucinations via autonomous graph-based retrofitting. It is related to our approach, because it involves triplet generation as well, but still differs in some components, e.g., not involving VSS and not letting the LLM determine the triplets a priori. Wang *et al.* [17] employ embeddings to answer questions spanning multiple documents. FACE-KEG by Vedula and Parthasarathy [16] uses a KG transformer network for explainable veracity prediction. Kundu and Nguyen [8] generate embeddings from a KG containing true claims and another with false claims, which are considered in the LLM's answer. The Knowledge Solver by Feng *et al.* [5] uses an LLM itself for pathfinding between identified and multiple-choice questions. Shakeel *et al.* [15] describe a comprehensive pipeline using graph embeddings and various NLP techniques for fact-checking. Mountantonakis and Tzitzikas [11] provide a semi-automatic web application that assists users in comparing facts generated by ChatGPT with those in KGs by using multiple RDF KGs for enriching ChatGPT responses. Pal *et al.* [12] introduce the Med-HALT dataset and benchmark, focusing on testing LLMs in the medical domain through multiple-choice questions, confidence measures, and link generation. Liu *et al.* [10] train LLMs to generate SPARQL queries with annotated question-SPARQL pairs, facilitating more accurate KG-based question answering. Li *et al.* [9] present a workflow that includes the identification of main entities from queries, like our method, and augments the entities with further directly linked information from a KG. Unlike in our approach, unstructured data are not considered.

Recent surveys [1,14] provide comprehensive overviews of the integration of KGs with LLMs, discussing current challenges and future directions. Another study on the opportunities and challenges at the intersection of LLMs and KGs [13] further explores the potential and obstacles in this interdisciplinary field. Our work advances these lines of research by proposing a novel triplet-based prefiltering method for VSS and LLM Reranking that leverages SKBs, offering deeper contextual "understanding" and improved retrieval accuracy in question-answering.

3 4StepFocus

We introduce a pipeline to enhance an LLM by an SKB in a novel, traceable fashion. A semi-structured knowledge base consists of a knowledge graph $G = (V, E)$ and associated text documents $D = \bigcup_{v \in V} D_v$ [18], where V is a set of graph nodes and $E \subseteq V \times V$ a set of their connecting edges, which may be directed or undirected, and weighted or unweighted.

While Fig. 1 visualizes the pipeline of our framework in short, Algorithm 1 in combination with Algorithms 2 and 3 describe it in more detail.

We define the following helper functions for the algorithms:

- $type(v)$ returns the node type of any node $v \in V$. $V.types = \bigcup_{v \in V} type(v)$ denotes the set of all existing node types in SKB.
- $type(x)$ returns the node type $v \in V.types$ of any variable x.

Algorithm 1. 4StepFocus

Input:
a semi-structured knowledge base $SKB = (V, E)$, a query q in natural language, candidates for query answers $C \subseteq V$, maximum number of candidates to rerank k_{max}

Output: A list of most likely answers to q in descending order

1: $T, x_{target} \leftarrow$ ASK_LLM_FOR_TRIPLETS($q, V.types, E.types$) ▷ extracts triplets T ▷ from q and marks the variable that denotes the final answer to q as x_{target}.
2: $C_{filtered} \leftarrow$ SUBSTITUTE(T, x_{target}, SKB)
3: $C_{filtered}, C_{additional} \leftarrow$ VSS($q, C_{filtered}$)
4: **return** LLM_RERANKER($q, C_{filtered}, C_{additional}, k_{max}$)

- $type(e)$ returns the edge type of any edge $e \in E$. $E.types = \bigcup_{e \in E} type(e)$ denotes the set of all existing edge types in SKB.
- $neigbors(v, e', +)$ denotes a set of all nodes $n \in V$ that are connected to v via an edge of type $e' \in E.types$ pointing from n to v.
- $neigbors(v, e', -)$ denotes a set of all nodes $n \in V$ that are connected to v via an edge of type $e' \in E.types$ pointing from v to n.

Algorithm 1 implements the four steps listed in Fig. 1: In line 1, function ASK_LLM_FOR_TIPLETS($q, V.types, E.types$) prompts the LLM to return a sequence of triplets T which formalizes q. Each triplet consists of a head entity h_i, a tail entity t_i, and a connecting edge type $e_i \in E.types$: $T = ((h_1, e_1, t_1), (h_2, e_2, t_2), ..., (h_{|T|}, e_{|T|}, t_{|T|}))$. Each h_i and t_i needs to be either a constant, i.e., a specific semantic entity, or a variable, i.e., representing an unknown semantic entity of the type $v \in V.types$. Additionally, the LLM returns a reference to the target variable x_{target}. Line 2 calls Algorithm 2, in which the variables in T are substituted by filtered answer candidates $C_{filtered}$ that satisfy the valid triplets. (Line 1 in Algorithm 2 in turn calls Algorithm 3, which checks the validity of triplets and searches constants in T in

Algorithm 2. SUBSTITUTE

Input:
a set of raw triplets T, a target variable x_{target}, a semi-structured knowledge base SKB

Output: A set $C_{filtered}$ of candidate nodes for x_{target}, satisfying all triplets in T

1: $T' \leftarrow$ PREPARE_TRIPLETS_FOR_SUBSTITUTION(T)
2: **for all** $\tau_i = (h_i, e_i, t_i) \in T'$ **do**
3:   **if** h_i is a constant and t_i is a variable **then**
4:     $substitute[t_i] \leftarrow substitute[t_i] \cap neigbors(h_i, e_i, -)$
5:   **end if**
6:   **if** h_i is a variable and t_i is a constant **then**
7:     $substitute[h_i] \leftarrow substitute[h_i] \cap neigbors(t_i, e_i, +)$
8:   **end if**
9:   **if** h_i is a variable and t_i is a different variable **then**
10:     $N_i \leftarrow \emptyset$.
11:     **for all** $h_i^{(j)} \in substitute[h_i]$ **do**
12:       $N_i \leftarrow N_i \cup neigbors(h_i^{(j)}, e_i, -)$
13:     **end for**
14:     $substitute[h_i] \leftarrow substitute[h_i] \cap N_i$
15:     $N_i \leftarrow \emptyset$.
16:     **for all** $t_i^{(j)} \in substitute[t_i]$ **do**
17:       $N_i \leftarrow N_i \cup neigbors(t_i^{(j)}, e_i, +)$
18:     **end for**
19:     $substitute[t_i] \leftarrow substitute[t_i] \cap N_i$
20:   **end if**
21: **end for**
22: Repeat lines 2-21 until no changes occur anymore.
23: **return** $substitute[x_{target}]$

the SKB.) Finally, lines 3 und 4 of the main algorithm call the vector similarity search (VSS) and then LLM_RERANKER, which computes the final rainking of $C_{filtered}$. Both VSS and LLM_RERANKER [18] have been briefly described in the Related Work section. k_{max} denotes the number of those elements, pre-sorted by VSS, that LLM_RERANKER finally ranks. If $|C_{filtered}| < k_{max}$, $k_{max} - |C_{filtered}| = |C_{additional}|$ elements are added to the solutions in our approach, although (V, E) do not support their relevance to q. Hence, candidates in $C_{filtered}$ remain ranked higher.

4 Evaluation

We evaluate our method on the three STaRK benchmark datasets [18] and associated SKBs *AMAZON*, *MAG*, and *PRIME*. While the medical SKB *PRIME* with 10 entity types and 18 relation types has the highest proportion of relational data, STaRK-AMAZON has only 4 node types but a high proportion of unstructured data (i.e., user reviews). Each dataset comes with a subset of manually designed QA pairs and a set of QA pairs that have been automatically created with LLMs included in the mining procedure. The SKBs contain several million nodes and relations. In *PRIME*, all nodes are marked as potential answer candidates, in the other cases it is only a high proportion. In most cases, there is more than one correct answer. We refer to Wu *et al.* [18] for a detailed analysis of the data's properties. We use GPT4-o (*gpt-4o-2024-05-13*)

Algorithm 3. PREPARE_TRIPLETS_FOR_SUBSTITUTION

Input:
a set of raw triplets T
Output: a set of valid, prepared triplets T'
for all variables x present in T **do**
  $substitute[x] \leftarrow \bigcup_{type(c)=type(x)} c \forall c \in C$ ▷ This step is not directly executed in the code implementation to save resources.
end for
$T' \leftarrow \emptyset$ ▷ Initialize a set for all valid triplets.
for all $\tau_i = (h_i, e_i, t_i) \in T$: **do**
  if h_i is a constant and t_i is a constant **then** skip τ_i.
  else if h_i is a constant and t_i is a variable **then**
    if h_i (almost) matches any alias of any $v \in C$ **then**
      $T' \leftarrow T' \cup \tau$ with h_i replaced by the matching actual node v.
    end if
  else if h_i is a variable and t_i is a constant **then**
    if t_i (almost) matches any alias of any $v \in C$ **then**
      $T' \leftarrow T' \cup \tau$ with t_i replaced by the matching actual node v.
    end if
  else if h_i is a variable and t_i is a different variable **then**
    $T' \leftarrow T' \cup \tau$
  end if
end for

as the LLM for 4StepFocus and the embedding model *text-embedding-ada-002* for VSS. We set k_{max} of LLM_Reranker to 20 in order to limit the amount of LLM requests. In the helper function $neigbors(v, e', -)$, we ignore the edge type while finding neighbors, because restricting it turned out to be error-prone in our experiments. We refer to Sect. 2 and Wu *et al.* [18] for details about all other benchmark methods and their configurations.

The following evaluation metrics were used and averaged over all queries. *Hit@k:* 1 if a correct item is among the top-k results from the model, 0 otherwise. *Recall@k:* Proportion of relevant items in the top-k results or the maximum number of correct answers. *Mean Reciprocal Rank (MRR):* Reciprocal of the rank at which the first relevant item appears.

Table 1. Test results on STaRK benchmark datasets. The upper three datasets are synthetically generated, the three datasets below are built by humans directly. For methods that use proprietary LLMs, only 10% of synthetic test sets are used.

STaRK Testset	Metric	Dense Retriever	QA-GNN	VSS	Multi-VSS	VSS & Claude3 Rer.	VSS & GPT4 Rer.	4Step Focus
AMAZON	Hit@1	0.153	0.266	0.392	0.401	0.455	0.448	**0.476**
	Hit@5	0.479	0.500	0.627	0.650	0.711	**0.712**	0.676
	Recall@20	0.445	0.520	0.533	0.551	0.538	0.554	**0.562**
	MRR	0.302	0.378	0.504	0.516	0.559	0.557	**0.565**
MAG	Hit@1	0.105	0.129	0.290	0.259	0.365	0.409	**0.538**
	Hit@5	0.352	0.390	0.496	0.504	0.532	0.582	**0.692**
	Recall@20	0.421	0.470	0.483	0.508	0.484	0.486	**0.658**
	MRR	0.213	0.291	0.386	0.369	0.442	0.490	**0.614**
PRIME	Hit@1	0.045	0.089	0.126	0.151	0.178	0.183	**0.393**
	Hit@5	0.219	0.214	0.315	0.336	0.369	0.373	**0.532**
	Recall@20	0.301	0.296	0.360	0.381	0.356	0.341	**0.559**
	MRR	0.124	0.147	0.214	0.235	0.263	0.266	**0.458**
AMAZON	Hit@1			0.395	0.469	0.560	0.543	**0.605**
	Hit@5	–	–	0.642	**0.728**	**0.728**	**0.728**	0.679
	MRR			0.527	0.587	**0.644**	0.627	0.643
MAG	Hit@1			0.286	0.238	0.381	0.369	**0.476**
	Hit@5	–	–	0.417	0.417	0.464	0.452	**0.512**
	MRR			0.358	0.314	0.424	0.403	**0.492**
PRIME	Hit@1			0.212	0.257	0.284	0.284	**0.505**
	Hit@5	–	–	0.404	0.404	0.477	0.486	**0.655**
	MRR			0.298	0.338	0.362	0.362	**0.579**

Table 1 shows the results of our experiments in the benchmark environment. 4StepFocus strongly improves the results of all previous methods on all measured metrics on the medical, more relational PRIME dataset. The same applies to the MAG dataset, which quite evenly balances relational elements and those that require interpretation of unstructured data in its queries. On the AMAZON dataset, the hit rate of the first given answer of 4StepFocus still outperforms the other approaches, but pure VSS + Reranker and Multi-VSS achieve higher HIT@5 scores on both the human-built and the syntatically generated test sets. One explanation is that some triplets can be misleading. E.g., a triplet filtering "green" products might ignore all "light green" products, since only one out of 1,700 color nodes is chosen. This suggests the integration of VSS during the triplet substitution step as well in the future.

5 Conclusion and Future Work

In this paper, we presented 4StepFocus, a pipeline that substantially improves answers of both LLMs but also other enhancing state-of-the art methods. Additionally, it includes external knowledge in a more traceable and reliable way. Our framework consists of multiple steps: identifying central entities and their relations in a user's query with an LLM, querying a domain-specific SKB for those information, using VSS among possible answers to take unstructured data into account in further prefiltering, and letting an LLM rerank the final results with background information given. Through experiments on a medical, a product recommendation, and an academic paper evaluation QA set, we demonstrated that our approach in contrast to graph embedding-based methods not only adds traceability, but also improves the overall precision of LLMs and makes them more reliable. While the addition to LLMs does not require pretraining, the need of embedded candidates is still a limitation to generalizability, which our approach does not solve yet. However, narrowing potential answers, with prefiltering consequently, can make holding embeddings of all general answer candidates obsolete.

There are several areas that can be explored to enhance our framework. For instance, the search of entities in a SKB could include vector similarity for a higher precision in the future. Further options are considering adjectives and predicates to capture more nuanced information, replacing pronouns with referenced objects/subjects for clarity, applying external reasoning taking quantifiers and negations into account, and combining multiple knowledge bases. By pursuing these avenues of future work, we can continue to enhance the capabilities of LLMs in accessing external knowledge and conducting autonomous reasoning for more evidence-based question answering.

Acknowledgments. This work was part of the cluster for atherothrombosis and individualized medicine (curATime), funded by the German Federal Ministry of Education and Research (03ZU1202NA).

Disclosure of Interests. The authors have no competing interests to declare that are relevant to the content of this article.

References

1. Agrawal, G., Kumarage, T., Alghamdi, Z., Liu, H.: Can knowledge graphs reduce hallucinations in LLMs?: a survey. In: Proceedings of the 2024 Conference of the North American Chapter of the Association for Computational Linguistics: Human Language Technologies, pp. 3947–3960 (2024). https://doi.org/10.18653/V1/2024.NAACL-LONG.219

2. Bender, E.M., Gebru, T., McMillan-Major, A., Shmitchell, S.: On the dangers of stochastic parrots: can language models be too big? In: Proceedings of FaccT 2021, p. 610–623 (2021). https://doi.org/10.1145/3442188.3445922
3. Chia, Y.K., Hong, P., Bing, L., Poria, S.: InstructEval: towards holistic evaluation of instruction-tuned large language models. In: Proceedings of the First edition of the Workshop on the Scaling Behavior of Large Language Models (SCALE-LLM 2024), pp. 35–64 (2024). https://aclanthology.org/2024.scalellm-1.4/
4. Feldman, P., Foulds, J.R., Pan, S.: Trapping LLM hallucinations using tagged context prompts. arXiv preprint (2023). https://doi.org/10.48550/arXiv.2306.06085
5. Feng, C., Zhang, X., Fei, Z.: Knowledge solver: teaching LLMs to search for domain knowledge from knowledge graphs. arXiv preprint (2023). https://doi.org/10.48550/arXiv.2309.03118
6. Guan, X., et al.: Mitigating large language model hallucinations via autonomous knowledge graph-based retrofitting. In: Proceedings of AAAI 2024, pp. 18126–18134 (2024). https://doi.org/10.1609/AAAI.V38I16.29770
7. Kambhampati, S.: Can large language models reason and plan? Ann. N. Y. Acad. Sci. **1534**(1), 15–18 (2024). https://doi.org/10.1111/nyas.15125
8. Kundu, A., Nguyen, U.T.: Automated fact checking using a knowledge graph-based model. In: Proceedings of ICAIIC 2024, pp. 709–716 (2024). https://doi.org/10.1109/ICAIIC60209.2024.10463196
9. Li, Y., Zhang, R., Liu, J.: An enhanced prompt-based LLM reasoning scheme via knowledge graph-integrated collaboration. In: Wand, M., Malinovská, K., Schmidhuber, J., Tetko, I.V. (eds.) ICANN 2024. LNCS, vol. 15020, pp. 251–265. Springer, Cham (2024). https://doi.org/10.1007/978-3-031-72344-5_17
10. Liu, Y., et al.: An in-context schema understanding method for knowledge base question answering. In: Cao, C., Chen, H., Zhao, L., Arshad, J., Asyhari, T., Wang, Y. (eds.) KSEM 2024. LNCS, vol. 14884, pp. 419–434. Springer, Singapore (2024). https://doi.org/10.1007/978-981-97-5492-2_32
11. Mountantonakis, M., Tzitzikas, Y.: Using multiple RDF knowledge graphs for enriching ChatGPT responses. In: De Francisci Morales, G., Perlich, C., Ruchansky, N., Kourtellis, N., Baralis, E., Bonchi, F. (eds.) ECML PKDD 2023. LNCS, vol. 14175, pp. 324–329. Springer, Cham (2023). https://doi.org/10.1007/978-3-031-43430-3_24
12. Pal, A., Umapathi, L.K., Sankarasubbu, M.: Med-HALT: medical domain hallucination test for large language models. In: Proceedings of the 27th CoNLL, pp. 314–334 (2023https://doi.org/10.18653/v1/2023.conll-1.21
13. Pan, J.Z., et al.: Large language models and knowledge graphs: opportunities and challenges. TGDK **1**(1), 2:1–2:38 (2023). https://doi.org/10.4230/TGDK.1.1.2
14. Pan, S., Luo, L., Wang, Y., Chen, C., Wang, J., Wu, X.: Unifying large language models and knowledge graphs: a roadmap. IEEE Trans. Knowl. Data Eng. **36**(7), 3580–3599 (2024). https://doi.org/10.1109/TKDE.2024.3352100
15. Shakeel, D., Jain, N.: Fake news detection and fact verification using knowledge graphs and machine learning. ResearchGate Preprint **10** (2021). https://doi.org/10.13140/RG.2.2.18349.41448
16. Vedula, N., Parthasarathy, S.: FACE-KEG: fact checking explained using knowledge graphs. In: Proceedings of ACM WSDM 2021, pp. 526–534. ACM (2021). https://doi.org/10.1145/3437963.3441828
17. Wang, Y., Lipka, N., Rossi, R.A., Siu, A., Zhang, R., Derr, T.: Knowledge graph prompting for multi-document question answering. In: Proceedings of AAAI 2024, no. 17, pp. 19206–19214 (2024). https://doi.org/10.1609/aaai.v38i17.29889

18. Wu, S., et al.: Stark: benchmarking LLM retrieval on textual and relational knowledge bases. In: NeurIPS 2024, pp. 127129–127153 (2024)
19. Yasunaga, M., Ren, H., Bosselut, A., Liang, P., Leskovec, J.: QA-GNN: reasoning with language models and knowledge graphs for question answering. In: Proceedings of the NAACL 2021, pp. 535–546 (2021). https://doi.org/10.18653/V1/2021.NAACL-MAIN.45
20. Zhuang, H., et al.: Beyond yes and no: improving zero-shot LLM rankers via scoring fine-grained relevance labels. In: Proceedings of the NAACL 2024, pp. 358–370 (2024). https://doi.org/10.18653/V1/2024.NAACL-SHORT.31

Author Index

W.-Z. Dai (Ed.): ILP 2024, LNAI 16059, pp. 293–294, 2026.
https://doi.org/10.1007/978-3-032-09087-4

MIX
Papier aus verantwortungsvollen Quellen
Paper from responsible sources
FSC® C105338

If you have any concerns about our products,
you can contact us on
ProductSafety@springernature.com

In case Publisher is established outside the EU,
the EU authorized representative is:
Springer Nature Customer Service Center GmbH
Europaplatz 3, 69115 Heidelberg, Germany

Printed by Libri Plureos GmbH
in Hamburg, Germany